THE WORLD THE TRAINS MADE

James D. Dilts

THE WORLD

THE TRAINS MADE

A Century of Great Railroad Architecture in the United States and Canada

ForeEdge

ForeEdge

An imprint of University Press of New England

www.upne.com

© 2018 James D. Dilts

Manufactured in China

Designed by Eric M. Brooks

Typeset in Dante by Passumpsic Publishing

For permission to reproduce any of the material in this
book, contact Permissions, University Press of New England,
One Court Street, Suite 250, Lebanon NH 03766; or visit
www.upne.com

Earlier versions of the entries on Grand Central Terminal,
New York City, and on Graver's Lane Station, Philadelphia,
Pennsylvania, appeared under "Architecture" in William D.
Middleton, George M. Smerk, and Roberta L. Diehl, eds.,
Encyclopedia of North American Railroads (Bloomington:
Indiana University Press, 2007).

Earlier versions of the entries on Pennsylvania Station
(Amtrak), Wilmington, Delaware, and King Street Station,
Seattle, Washington, appeared in "Three Amtrak Stations
Take Different Roads to Rehabilitation," *Railroad History*,
fall–winter, 2010, 46–50.

They are used here with the permission of the publishers.

Unless otherwise credited, all photos are by the author.

Library of Congress Cataloging-in-Publication Data
available upon request

Hardcover ISBN: 978-1-61168-802-3

5 4 3 2 1

To the masters of the genre,

JOHN H. WHITE JR.,

the late WILLIAM D. MIDDLETON,

and HERBERT H. HARWOOD JR.;

and to the late TONY JUDT,

who wrote so magnificently

about everything from

modern European history

to railroads.

CONTENTS

PREFACE & ACKNOWLEDGMENTS

This book is about a special kind of architecture. Broadly speaking, railroad architecture encompasses all of the structures the railroads built to conduct their far-flung operations, from great urban terminals to small rural stations, and including train sheds, freight depots, warehouses, grain elevators, office buildings, and grand hotels. Planned suburbs and towns, company owners' mansions, workers' housing, and railroad YMCAs and hospitals also fall in this category. Then there is the basic infrastructure: shops, roundhouses, power stations, towers—such as signal (or interlocking), coal, and water towers—bridges, tunnels, and the trains themselves. Finally, to commemorate their exploits and achievements, the railroads constructed monuments.

The railroads erected some of our finest buildings—the first to express, as an industrial type, the shape and tempo of the modern age. This disparate array of structures represents our greatest architectural legacy from a single industry. Much of it has been ravaged over the years, but a substantial amount remains intact due to its inherent architectural quality and solid construction. (Some 9,000 station buildings and over 86,000 railroad bridges still stand in the United States and Canada.) Like the Romans, the railroads built for the ages.

Civilization literally followed the wave of railroad construction across North America. Spreading westward from the old East Coast ports, new towns and cities and even national parks aligned themselves along the transcontinental armature that the railroad companies laid down. Some cities, such as Las Vegas, Nevada, owe their very existence to the railroad; others—from Miami, Florida, to Vancouver, British Columbia—were jump-started by the locomotives' arrival.

In addition, the railroads were what gave form to urban areas in the nineteenth century, preceding and inspiring the concentrated growth of cities. They served as de facto city planners and suburban developers and, more recently, as land bankers for new urban development. The vast Hudson Yards project on Manhattan's West Side and Millennial Park in Chicago were both constructed on former rail yards.

Railroad buildings and structures are prime candidates for adaptive reuse, which is the subtext of this book. One of the first railroad stations to take on

> We continue to live in
> the world the trains made.
> TONY JUDT,
> "Bring Back the Rails!"

a creative new life was Mount Royal Station, built in Baltimore, Maryland, in the late nineteenth century. It was acquired by the neighboring Maryland Institute College of Art in 1964, and after several subsequent renovations, it continues to serve its alternative purpose in a new century.

Since then there have been many other successful conversions. For example, progressive business and political leaders working with a major artist in Tacoma, Washington, remade an empty train station into a federal courthouse and sparked the redevelopment of the entire downtown. America's oldest roundhouse, in Aurora, Illinois, became a multipurpose bar and restaurant with a bakery and brewery. A bridge in Poughkeepsie, New York, that had not seen a train in years is now a popular state park offering grand views of the Hudson River. Presenting railroad architecture as a coherent subject, this book is intended to serve as a prescriptive guide to renovation and renewal as railroads in the United States and Canada enter a post-renaissance era.

The book is organized by building type. It presents over a hundred of the best examples of railroad architecture, arranged in fourteen categories. The dates of construction range from 1835 to 1995, so the "century" in the title refers not so much to years as to the number of buildings and structures in the book. It highlights the people who designed and built them.

Each chapter is devoted to one of the fourteen building types and begins with a brief introduction and a discussion of an outstanding representative of that type. I have visited all but a few of the featured buildings and other structures. My hope is that the reader will do the same, because the best way to experience and appreciate great works of architecture and engineering is in situ and in context. For that reason, directions are added to the entries in more remote locations, but all structures are easily reached by train or automobile, with perhaps a short walk.

Given the thousands of possible candidates, I had to make some painful choices. The contribution of a great architect or engineer, the existence of a fine photograph, or an especially significant conversion to a new use dictated some of the decisions. Geographical distribution was also a factor, as was a good backstory in a few cases. Another criterion was ready accessibility. The selections are of course arbitrary; many others could justifiably be added. With only a few exceptions, the photographs are recent, as is the information concerning the current use of the structure.

Besides their major function as purveyors of transportation, the railroads were the practical schools for generations of architects and engineers. James Renwick (architect of the Smithsonian Institution, in Washington, D.C., and St. Patrick's Cathedral, in New York City) began his career as a structural engineer on the Erie Railroad. Famous architects such as Frank Furness and Henry Hobson Richardson did important work for the railroads, as did many excellent designers who await their biographers (I have included minibiographies of the latter in the text).

Civil engineers, whose professional code of ethics adjures them to serve the public interest and shun publicity, are as a rule less well known than architects. Even some of the most prominent civil engineers—builders of great bridges, railroads, and canals—lack full biographies. I have therefore included biographical information for virtually all of the civil engineers whose works are discussed.

======

I have been fortunate to work with talented railroad photographers. Scott Lothes, president of the Center for Railroad Photography and Art, in Madison, Wisconsin, whom I met in the early stages of this project, supplied many fine photographs. David Honan, of Seattle, Washington, went the extra mile to produce the excellent pictures of the Seattle and Tacoma station buildings. I thank the many other photographers who supplied photos for the book.

Frank Stroker, archivist at the Pittsburgh History and Landmarks Foundation, provided photographs and information on the Pittsburgh, Pennsylvania, train stations. Miranda Rectenwald, of the University Archives and Special Collections, Washington University Libraries, in St. Louis, Missouri, furnished the illustration of the Eads Bridge, "General Plan of Erecting."

Carla Hall Friedman, of New York City, first alerted me to the railroad building background of her ancestor, William A. Clark. Miriam Kelly, an architect at Beyer, Blinder, Belle, aided me in my research on Grand Central Terminal.

I am grateful to the Lexington Group in Transportation History for providing a Richard C. Overton Research Fellowship in 2008 that enabled me to do research in the Library and Archives Canada, in Ottawa, Ontario. Andrew Rodger, an archivist there, and Joan M. Schwartz, a professor of art history at Queens University, Kingston, Ontario, helped me to negotiate the archive's voluminous collections of railroad photographs.

Railroad experts Mark Reutter and John Hankey read sections of the book and enabled me to make improvements in the text. Justin Simpson got me to see and finally understand the difference between elliptical and parabolic arches. Jeremy Kargon—an architect and associate professor at Morgan State University School of Architecture and Planning, in Baltimore—gave me some needed documentation at an appropriate time.

More friends served as hosts during the past ten years while I was researching the book, offering me welcome food, shelter, and transportation: Wendy Levinson and Jim Shaw in Toronto, Ontario; Eddie and Ruth Lemansky in Brooklyn, New York; and Tom Moffett and Solveig Nielsen in Chicago (and beyond to Wisconsin and Minnesota).

I was fortunate in finding knowledgeable guides to various properties on my site visits to most of the states and provinces. Maxime Aubin—coordinator of sales, marketing, and public relations for the Fairmont Château

Frontenac in Quebec City, Quebec, gave my wife and me a behind-the-scenes tour of the hotel. In Ottawa, David L. Jeanes showed me the Government Center and introduced me to the active Ottawa Railway History Circle.

Jim Tevebaugh—of Tevebaugh Associates, architects, in Wilmington, Delaware, who is president of the Friends of Furness Railroad District—gave me a tour of the Wilmington station buildings and much information on local developments over the years. Allen Hale—president of the Claudius Crozet Blue Ridge Tunnel Foundation and East District Supervisor, in Nelson County, Virginia—guided me to the Blue Ridge Tunnel outside Waynesboro, Virginia. Stewart Dohrman, a civil engineer and historic preservationist, showed me around the many buildings of the Georgia State Railroad Museum in Savannah.

In Albuquerque, New Mexico, Eric DeLony—former chief of the Historic American Engineering Record and a bridge expert—arranged a tour of the Santa Fe Railway shops. Leba Freed—president of the Wheels Museum, which occupies one of the shop buildings—told me about the lengthy effort to restore them and put me in touch with photographers who had captured the buildings over the years.

Elizabeth Morrison, in the office of the president, was more than accommodating during my impromptu visit to United World College, Montezuma (Las Vegas Hot Springs), New Mexico (the former Montezuma Hotel). Erin Sigl—co-owner of the Copper King Mansion, in Butte, Montana—related to me some of the family history of William Clark and his daughter Huguette. And Richard Gibson, secretary-treasurer of the Butte Labor History Center, opened the center and my eyes to the epic and bloody battles between the owners' representatives and the miners over the wealth produced by what has often been called the richest hill on earth.

Sharon Alix, administrator of the Rancho Santa Fe Historical Society, went out of her way to welcome me to Rancho Santa Fe, California, and introduced me to Vonn Marie May, who wrote a book about the community. In Sacramento, California, Phil Sexton, an interpreter with the California State Parks, showed me around the extensive former Southern Pacific Railway shops and came up with photographs of the Leland Stanford Mansion. Brian Henry, an associate transportation planner with the Seattle Department of Transportation, took me through King Street Station while it was undergoing renovation.

I met some indelible characters along the way. One of my favorites was Diane Irwin, a white-haired woodworker who runs a children's art program, the Workshop Wizards, out of half of the former Grand Trunk Railway (now VIA Rail) station built in 1856 in Napanee, Ontario, and takes periodic breaks with the kids to play field hockey on the station platform.

She explained that the door to the waiting room, which I wanted to photograph, opens automatically, but only at train time. "I used to have the key, but that's all changed," she said. "It could be like Port Hope, where they have a more enlightened outlook. But don't get me started."

She suggested I come back at train time, so I did and took my pictures of the waiting room. "Two of the trains don't stop here any more, and I told them to change the timer," she said. "They did for one train, but not for the other. So the door still opens. I also asked them not to cut down my pumpkin vines that we planted outside, and they cut 'em down anyway. Some people are illiterate. But let's not go down that road."

I realized after I left that instead of the barren waiting room, I should have been photographing Diane Irwin and her charges playing trackside field hockey, so I asked her to send me a picture of that. The one she sent showed them happily dousing each other with water guns. Underused train stations need more arts programs—and more Diane Irwins.

At the Starrucca House in Susquehanna, Pennsylvania (not far from the Starrucca Viaduct), the owner Andreas Plonka, originally from Silesia, told a long and involved tale about his struggles with the building. A previous owner had restored the station-hotel–dining hall—built in Gothic Revival style by the Erie Railroad in 1865—and opened a restaurant, but it failed. Plonka acquired the property and moved in with his family. This resulted in court cases because the area was zoned industrial, and residential uses were not allowed. Nevertheless, Plonka (a roofer) remained and started repairing the roof.

There were further problems concerning a container he brought over from Europe filled with railroad artifacts. Customs officials seized it and examined the contents, which Plonka claimed they damaged when they repacked the container, badly, to return to him: another court case resulted. Some of the materials from the container—switch levers and signals, old clocks and telephones—are stored in the two-story, arched-ceiling dining room. As Plonka took me through the building with a flashlight, I could see that more (much more) filled other spaces on the ground floor. A short, stocky man who wears tiny rectangular glasses, Plonka said he wanted to turn Starrucca House into "a world railroad museum."

And who could forget Mr. Jordan, the one-man "unwelcome committee" of Maudlow, Montana? Maudlow was a town on the Milwaukee Road and reportedly contained some railroad workers' housing. A nine-mile drive down a gravel road brought me to the abandoned railroad right-of-way, where I found a few buildings, some of which were relatively new and obviously occupied, and several "No Trespassing" and "Keep Out" signs.

After had I parked my rental car and looked around a little, Mr. Jordan arrived in a black pickup truck. About sixty years old, wearing a battered cowboy hat, and with a long, droopy, salt-and-pepper mustache, he might have been sent over by central casting. He asked what I was doing there. I told him I was a railroad buff out exploring. My inquisitor said that the land was privately owned and implied that I was trespassing: "People think that when they see the city limits sign in their rearview mirror they can come and do whatever they want. Folks around here get a little testy. Wouldn't you?"

I said that I was surprised that people found their way to Maudlow, since it was so far from the highway. "We're inundated on the weekends," said Mr. Jordan. Then he relented and said I might drive up the road to look at the old schoolhouse, but he fired a parting shot: "The guy who owns that will be out this afternoon—and he's not as polite as I am."

Fortunately, most stewards of railroad properties were tolerant of my unannounced arrivals and more often than not willing to provide information about the property and to invite me in to take photographs.

After the proposal for this book made its initial rounds and aroused no interest in limited circles, my friend and sometime collaborator Bill Riggs told me about the University Press of New England, where he and some colleagues had had a book published (*Dartmouth Veterans: Vietnam Perspectives*). I sent my book proposal to Michael P. Burton, the press's director, who liked it well enough to give me a contract for publication. I am very grateful to Bill Riggs and to Mike Burton.

Finally, I would like to thank my personal agent of inspiration, my wife, Penny Williamson.

JAMES D. DILTS
Baltimore, Maryland
May 2017

THE WORLD THE TRAINS MADE

A RAILROAD SUITE OF BUILDINGS
(Terminal Complexes)

Terminal complexes concentrate many different types of railroad structures in a relatively small area. Such complexes were rare to begin with because as the railroads grew with their host cities, their functions quickly became dispersed: the station was in one location near the city center, the office building in another, and the shops and warehouses were scattered on the outskirts. It is surprising that any terminal complexes have survived, for they occupied several acres of valuable downtown real estate, and in the mid-twentieth century—with airlines and highways ascendant and the declining railroads no longer welcome in the city—the land became ripe for redevelopment. Rail passenger service may have been maintained, but the stations were sometimes banished to the hinterlands.

SAVANNAH, GEORGIA

Savannah is a good illustration of this process. Frank Milburn's twin-towered Union Station, a mix of the neoclassical revival and Spanish Renaissance styles, opened in 1902 on the edge of the downtown and was demolished fifty years later to make way for an interstate highway entrance. The 1962 replacement station, built by the Atlantic Coast Line Railroad and now served by Amtrak, is in a remote location.

However, Savannah managed to retain its nearby abandoned set of railroad structures—the oldest and most intact example of an integrated terminal complex in the United States—and turn it into a major tourist attraction. Enlightened city administrators, a visionary college, and a community of dedicated preservationists collaborated to accomplish this feat.

The Central of Georgia Railroad terminal complex dates to 1855. It was an active railroad center for roughly a hundred years, handling passengers, freight, and repairs. The shops were closed in 1963. Just a few years after that, many of the structures stood empty, some were on the verge of collapse, and demolition had begun. Then three things happened to change the course of events: the City of Savannah acquired the thirty-three-acre property in 1972, the Coastal Heritage Society was founded in 1975, and the Savannah College of Art and Design (SCAD) opened its doors in 1979.

The founders of SCAD were attracted to Savannah because of its outstanding architecture and ambiance. They created a campus not by constructing new buildings, but by reusing neglected historic structures, including several in the terminal complex. The Coastal Heritage Society, which began as a group of maritime history enthusiasts, took over the operation of the terminal complex in 1989. In the ensuing years, through the auspices of the society and SCAD, about a dozen railroad structures have been restored and have found new uses.

The Georgia Central, one of the nation's early railroads (it was chartered in 1833), was a cotton road. It was established to counter the effort of Charleston, Savannah's rival port, to capture the cotton trade with its South Carolina Railroad, which began operating in 1833 from Charleston to Hamburg, across the river from Augusta, Georgia. When the Georgia Central started running trains ten years later, most of its revenue came from freight, and most of the freight was cotton being shipped from the interior plantations to Savannah for export.

The terminal complex was built on the site of the Revolutionary War Battle of Savannah in 1779, commemorated by the adjacent Battlefield Memorial Park. The complex faces east and the downtown, and the tracks head west. The overall plan was the work of William L. Wadley, superintendent (and later president) of the Georgia Central. Most of the buildings were designed by Martin P. Muller and Augustus Schwaab, German-born architects and engineers who found their way to Savannah and then formed a partnership in 1870. The former station and office building act as bookends to the terminal, which has a ceremonial entrance (the cotton yard gates) between them.

Figures 1.1 & 1.2
Savannah Visitor Center, Savannah, Georgia

SAVANNAH VISITOR CENTER
(formerly Central of Georgia Railroad station)
1860–65, Muller and Schwaab, Architects, Engineers
301 Martin Luther King, Jr. Blvd. (formerly Broad St.)

The construction of the two-story, red brick, Renaissance revival train station was interrupted by the Civil War, which made unavailable materials such as glass that were needed to complete the station. A long train shed with a series of round-arched openings extends west of the station, paralleling Louisville Road. Helping support this structure is an unusual iron truss system, whose circular connectors are suspended from the roof beams. After the city acquired the property in the 1970s, the interior of the station was cleared and the building converted to a visitors' center with a theater, gift shop, and snack bar. The

Savannah History Museum, operated by the Coastal Heritage Society, has its exhibits in the train shed. Both the head house and the shed received new roofs and were repointed as part of the restoration.

KIAH HALL
(formerly Central of Georgia Railroad office building)
1856, Muller and Schwaab, Architects, Engineers
227 Martin Luther King, Jr. Blvd.

The oldest railroad office building in the United States is a striking Greek revival structure of two stories whose portico is supported by six giant Doric columns. It was known initially as the Gray Building because it was built of Savannah gray brick, but it was renamed Kiah Hall in honor of Virginia Jackson Kiah, an African American artist who settled in Savannah. The building has a metal roof (the present one is a replacement). Some of the original interior features remain, such as a marble mantelpiece, walnut stair railings, and a decorative ceiling medallion. SCAD acquired the building in 1992 and ten years later, after restoring it, made it the SCAD Museum of Art, which houses a collection of contemporary art. A

new gallery building has replaced the train shed that extended to the rear.

COTTON YARD GATES
1867, Muller and Schwaab, Architects, Engineers
Martin Luther King, Jr. Blvd.

To secure the cotton yard following the Civil War, a wall with a central opening was erected between the railroad station and the office building. The brick Tudor Gothic gateway with four-centered arches and crenellation is all that remains; the gatekeeper's house has disappeared. The cotton yard is now used as a parking lot for tour buses and the cars of people coming to the visitors' center.

EICHBERG HALL
(formerly Central of Georgia Railroad office building)
1887, Fay and Eichberg
229 Martin Luther King, Jr. Blvd.

When the railroad needed more office space, it chose the Savannah architectural partnership of Calvin Fay and Alfred S. Eichberg. The result, in a vaguely Italianate style, was a two-story, red brick building on a

Figure 1.3
Kiah Hall, Savannah, Georgia

Figure 1.4
Cotton yard gates and Eichberg Hall, Savannah, Georgia

granite base with a central rooftop pavilion (it was called the Red Building). The handsome main entrance, flanked by stylized composite columns and under compound arches (archivolts), is reminiscent of the doorway of a medieval cathedral. The terracotta decoration incorporates the year of construction. A rear section was added in 1910. The former produce warehouse behind Eichberg Hall dates from 1859 and has a series of segmentally arched freight door openings with fire doors. SCAD acquired the office building and warehouse to house its architecture and interior design programs, and the freight door openings now frame students' studios.

GEORGIA STATE RAILROAD MUSEUM
1855 and later, Muller and Schwab,
    Architects, Engineers
655 Louisville Rd.

The Central of Georgia Railroad shops occupied thirteen acres in the southwest quadrant of the site, separated from the passenger and freight depot and administrative functions by Louisville Road. Here could be produced almost everything the railroad needed for its operations, from locomotives and cars to bridge components.

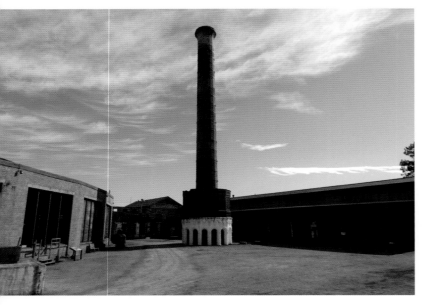

Figure 1.5
Georgia State Railroad Museum, Savannah, Georgia

At the center of the complex was the 123-foot tall polygonal smokestack constructed in 1855 of Savannah gray brick, which vented the smoke from the furnaces and forges in the surrounding shop buildings via underground flues. Around its base, composed of cast-iron panels produced by a local foundry, was a 40,000-gallon, 14-foot tall water tank that supplied the locomotive tenders in the nearby roundhouse. The workmen used the series of arched compartments below the corbel table as privies. In 1967, alert Savannah citizens saw scavengers demolishing the smokestack to salvage the bricks and obtained a court order to stop them. This marked the beginning of the process to preserve the entire terminal complex. The smokestack was restored in 1993.

The compact, two-story powerhouse, built in 1855, was also decorated with a corbel table as well as crenellation. It housed the stationary steam engine that powered most of the machinery and equipment in the shop complex through a system of line shafts and belting. The front wall has been reconstructed.

The restored tender frame shop and blacksmith shop, also dating to 1855, are now used for museum displays and other purposes. The original 1855 iron-roofed roundhouse was rebuilt in the 1920s; other shop buildings also date from that decade. The roofless carpenter's shop, built in 1853, is home to the outdoor Savannah Children's Museum, which hopes to move into the adjoining coach shop when it is restored.

One of the first structures erected at the terminal complex was the 1853 brick viaduct that carried the Georgia Central main line over the Savannah and Ogeechee Canal and Boundary Street near Louisville Road on four elliptical arches. Owned by the City of Savannah, it is being preserved for possible future use by the railroad museum. A short distance to the north is another brick viaduct, also of four arches (segmental) that was built for a yard track. It is now a SCAD walkway. Both bridges were designed by Muller and Schwaab. Nearby, an industrial ruin, a small park, and a new SCAD residence hall are the current features of the northwest corner of the terminal complex. The total restoration cost is estimated to be $24 million.

Figure 1.6
Yard track viaduct, Savannah, Georgia

CHARLESTON, SOUTH CAROLINA

Charleston merchants built the South Carolina Railroad because they were concerned about losing trade to Savannah, Charleston's major competitor as a commercial port. However, even after the railroad to Hamburg, South Carolina, began operations in 1833, Charleston continued to be at a disadvantage. Savannah benefited from having a river, and it was cheaper to ship cotton and rice from Augusta by water than by rail. And Charleston lacked direct connections to either Augusta or its own port: the railroad ended across the river from Augusta, and it was prohibited from entering Charleston. Not until 1853 did Charleston complete these connections—and in the meantime, Savannah businessmen had built their own railroad.

Charleston's terminal complex, second only to Savannah's, has also been restored as a tourist attraction. It is less complete than Savannah's—the shops were located several blocks to the north, on Line Street —but in the area bounded by John, King, Mary and Meeting Streets are several notable structures that have been reused creatively. And Charleston has an outstanding house museum that once served as the railroad's offices.

WILLIAM AIKEN HOUSE
1811, 1831 addition
456 King St.

The house is best seen from the landscaped garden and the interior, which has been restored and furnished with period antiques, paintings, and textiles. The building was expanded several times in the nineteenth century. William Aiken, the first president of the South Carolina Railroad, acquired the three-story, brick Adam style house in 1811. After he died in 1831,

Figure 1.7
William Aiken House, Charleston, South Carolina

Figure 1.8
William Aiken House, ballroom, Charleston,
South Carolina

his widow added an octagonal ballroom wing, two-story verandas, and a Gothic style carriage house. The servants' wing was built in the 1880s.

In 1863, William Aiken Jr., then governor of the state, sold the house to the South Carolina Railroad, which used the building as its offices until the 1920s. Its successor, the Southern Railway, deeded the property to the National Trust for Historic Preservation in 1977. The railroad had neglected the interior, but the stairways, mantelpieces, and ornate plaster ceiling medallions have been refurbished, and the building now functions as a venue for events.

CAMDEN DEPOT
ca. 1850, Edward Brickell White
23 Ann St.

The most prominent remains of the Camden Depot are the two-story brick and stucco towers with battlements that flanked the railroad's right-of-way into the terminal complex. They have been restored. Edward Brickell White was a West Point–trained civil engineer who became a railroad surveyor before settling in Charleston to practice architecture. He designed Charleston's well-known Market Hall and numerous churches in the city. Inside the gates are the

railroad's former engine house and newer buildings that house a children's museum and the Best Friend Train Museum.

SOUTH CAROLINA RAILROAD WAREHOUSE
1857
32 Ann St.

The single-story brick warehouse in the Italianate style extends the full block back to Mary Street. Its

Figure 1.9
Camden Depot, Charleston, South Carolina

Figure 1.10
Warehouse, Charleston, South Carolina

façade, with five bays, features a wheel window over the main entrance, whose keystone is inscribed "SCRR 1857." Howe trusses support the barrel-vaulted roof. The restored warehouse is currently the Music Farm, a concert space. The former railroad right-of-way has become a transit mall for buses.

CHARLESTON VISITOR CENTER
(formerly Deans Warehouse)
1856
375 Meeting St.

Another single-story, block-long, brick warehouse with a series of round-arched openings and a pitched roof was transformed in 1991 into a visitors' center that offers a full range of services in a restored interior with exposed roof trusses.

Figure 1.11
Charleston Visitor Center, Charleston, South Carolina

Figure 1.12
Tower Depot, Charleston, South Carolina

TOWER DEPOT
1850, Edward C. Jones
23 John St.

Edward Jones, a Charleston architect, designed the railroad's first passenger station in the Gothic revival style, with battlements, turrets, flat buttresses, and pointed arches. The two-story brick building (the original three-story tower was a victim of the 1886 Charleston earthquake) proved inefficient—trains had to back into the station—and it was made a freight depot after just two years. Following the Civil War, it served as a bag factory until the Depression, and then it stood empty for sixty years. In 1995, new owners converted the head house into a performance space; it is now the Charleston Music Hall.

The nearby Hampton Inn, at 345 Meeting Street, occupies a former railroad warehouse that was built in 1860 and later renovated.

LINE STREET CAR AND CARPENTER SHOPS
ca. 1857
44 Line St.

Separated from the rest of the complex by several blocks of new construction that occupy the former railroad right-of-way are the Line Street shops. These consist of a two-story brick building facing the street and, backing it, an extended single-story brick shed with arched openings and a polygonal smokestack, very similar to Savannah's. The former car repair shops were damaged in a fire in 1981, and the surviving building is now used as a storage facility.

ROANOKE, VIRGINIA

Roanoke, now the largest city in southwest Virginia and the region's commercial center, was a small agricultural settlement called Big Lick (because of the salt deposits in the area) when the Norfolk and Western (N&W) Railroad arrived in 1882 and made the town its headquarters. The company quickly built a station, hotel, office building, freight depot, and locomotive and car shops, as well as houses for its officers and workers. Two years later, when the town was chartered as the City of Roanoke (named for the river that runs through it), the population had grown to 5,000.

In 1900, there were 22,000 people in Roanoke, and the city continued to prosper with the railroad and the industries it attracted: iron, canned goods, cotton, and tobacco. Two-thirds of the local factory workers were employed in the N&W Railroad shops. A second office building was added to the complex in 1931.

The N&W was built to exploit the rich Pocahontas bituminous coalfields of Virginia and West Virginia and move the coal to the tidewater region at Norfolk, Virginia. In the twentieth century, as the coal flowed west as well as east, the company extended its lines to Cincinnati, Chicago, St. Louis, and Kansas City. The railroad itself was a prime consumer, firing the locomotives it built and serviced in its renowned Roanoke shops with Pocahontas coal. In fact, in 1960 the N&W became the last major railroad to convert to diesel power, a situation exploited by the photographer O. Winston Link, who famously documented the final years of steam operations on the railroad.

In 1982, the N&W Railroad merged with the Southern Railway System, the corporate headquarters was subsequently moved to Norfolk, and a century of railroad growth and prosperity began winding down in Roanoke. The process of decline and abandonment had actually begun twenty years earlier, when the N&W shops—which had 6,000 employees at their high point in the 1930s—lost thousands of jobs with the change from steam to diesel locomotives. (The Norfolk Southern Railroad's Roanoke shops still repair and maintain diesel engines, but the number of workers is down to 100–150.)

Later in the decade, the railroad shuttered the hotel and donated it to a private foundation. Amtrak ended passenger service to Roanoke, and after briefly serving as office space, the station stood empty. The two office buildings and the freight depot were likewise vacated. In finding appropriate new uses for these buildings and the money to restore them, the Norfolk Southern Railroad, the City of Roanoke, and preservation-minded developers and organizations capitalized on the city's railroad heritage and cultivated a fresh audience to experience it. The structures in Roanoke today are an engaging example of the evolution of railroad architectural design.

ROANOKE VALLEY VISITOR CENTER
(formerly N&W Railroad station)
1905
1949, Raymond Loewy, renovation architect
101 Shenandoah Ave.

Clarence H. Clark, a Philadelphia banker who owned the Shenandoah Railroad, bought a bankrupt Virginia east-west line in 1881 and renamed it the Norfolk and Western Railroad. The Shenandoah Railroad was then being built through the Great Valley of Virginia under the direction of Frederick J. Kimball, a civil engineer and partner in Clark's firm. The line extended from Hagerstown, Maryland, at the valley's northern end, to Roanoke, Virginia, its southern extremity—which Kimball selected as the junction of the two railroads. (The grateful voters wanted to name the town after him, but he suggested that they name it for the river instead.)

Kimball was likely responsible for hiring George T. Pearson (1847–1920), a Philadelphia architect, to design the railroad's initial suite of buildings: the station, hotel, and offices, all in the Queen Anne–Tudor

Figure 1.13

Roanoke Valley Visitor Center, Roanoke, Virginia

revival style that Pearson had employed in designing Kimball's Germantown mansion, Red Gate. Pearson, originally from Trenton, New Jersey, had worked as a draftsman for Addison Hutton and other architects in Philadelphia before forming his own firm in 1880. He was a consummate eclectic Victorian designer, combining a variety of historical sources in his buildings—most often successfully. He later did the drawings for several other stations and hotels for the N&W Railroad.

Pearson's Roanoke buildings featured the major elements of the Queen Anne–Tudor revival style: steep roofs with gables; tall, modeled chimneys; towers; and especially half-timbered effects. The union station was built between the tracks of the two railroads (they were later combined), with the hotel and office building on one side and the center of town on the other, an arrangement that still exists in Roanoke. The station was a longitudinal structure whose lengthy pitched-roof track canopies were interrupted in the middle by a two-story main section with half-timbered gables and high, shaped chimneys.

Pearson's station was replaced in 1905, and the new station was on the hotel side, probably to eliminate the awkward situation of passengers having to cross two sets of tracks to reach it. The replacement was a building of brick with stone trim in the neoclassical revival style. The round-arched central section had a hip roof and a temple front; it was flanked by lower, flat-roofed wings with rectangular windows. In the rear, a concourse and covered stairways led to the tracks, again covered by extensive platform canopies.

In 1949, Raymond Loewy redesigned the station. He kept the basic building but removed the temple front and round-arched windows, substituting a severe rectilinear concrete portico and a window wall of metal and glass. On the track side, Loewy created a similar effect with a concrete frame that enclosed ranks of broad horizontal windows meant to suggest a railroad passenger coach. A domed ceiling, long ticket counter, and terrazzo tile floor featuring the N&W logo and a compass rose were the major interior changes.

The new façade has been described as an example of Streamline Moderne, but that style was becoming passé in 1949. The unadorned smooth concrete portico particularly anticipates the new formalism of Edward Durrell Stone. Loewy's timeless designs always looked like the future rather than the past.

Raymond Loewy (1893–1986) was the Frank Lloyd Wright of industrial design, a field that he pioneered. Like the architect, he was supremely gifted in his line of work and equally adept at promoting it (and himself). Loewy was more than just a packager: he designed or was part of the design team for some of the products he wrapped—and what wrappings! The streamlined locomotives for the Pennsylvania Railroad, the Studebaker Avanti, the Greyhound Scenicruiser, and the Air Force One livery, as well as an assortment of consumer products, household appliances, and corporate logos all bore the mark of Loewy's talented hand.

As a teenager, the Paris-born Loewy showed an aptitude for invention and design. He graduated from the University of Paris; served in the French Army in World War I, receiving the Croix de Guerre; and left for America in 1919. His first job in New York was designing department store window displays. Creating costumes for the theatrical productions of Florenz Ziegfeld and a budding career as a fashion illustrator followed. Loewy's breakthrough occurred in 1929, when the Gestetner Company asked him to improve the look of its duplicating machine, which then resembled a fugitive from an early science fiction film. Three days and $2,000 later, Loewy had put an attractive shell around the inner workings and set the result on a handsome cabinet. The design remained basically unchanged until 1949, the year he formed the Raymond Loewy Corporation.

Meanwhile, in the 1930s, the railroads had begun streamlining their steam locomotives. The Pennsylvania Railroad's first such engine, the S-1, was designed by Loewy. (In his 1937 book, *The Locomotive*, Loewy said he spent so much time down at the depot admiring locomotives that it affected his social life.) The running gear, except for the wheels, was encased in a sleek, bullet-shape, aerodynamic metal jacket that was extensively tested in wind tunnels to solve problems of smoke deflection. Practicality was an important consideration for the designer, whose motto was beauty through function and simplification. Loewy is best known in this regard for his work on the GG1 (1936), the Pennsy's double-headed electric workhorse that sped passenger trains between New York and Washington, D.C., for fifty years. Loewy didn't design the engine, but he added the welded (rather than riveted) metal shell and the famous pinstripes to produce a true icon of smart railroad travel. His work for the Pennsylvania Railroad inspired the N&W Railroad officers to invite him to Roanoke.

Loewy's modernized station undoubtedly improved the train traveler's experience, but neither the designer nor the railroad could have foreseen the extent to which rail passenger service would plummet in the decades following the wartime boom years. In 1991, after the passenger trains stopped running to Roanoke, the trackside concourse, stairways, and platform canopies were removed to accommodate double-stack freight trains. The vacant station building was in danger of being demolished. The City of Roanoke, Norfolk Southern Railroad, the Historical Society of Western Virginia, and others came up with a plan to make it a visitors' center. Spectrum Design, a local architecture firm, oversaw the conversion, which included a new stairway, exhibit galleries, and lecture hall or theater at a cost of $3.3 million.

Figure 1.14

Hotel Roanoke and Conference Center, Roanoke, Virginia

In 2004, the historical society opened the O. Winston Link Museum on the lower level, dedicated to the works of the legendary railroad photographer. On the upper level two years later, the Raymond Loewy Gallery was added: the gallery exhibit traces the highpoints of the industrial designer's storied career.

THE HOTEL ROANOKE AND CONFERENCE CENTER

1882, George T. Pearson
1938, west wing, George B. Post and Sons
1995, hotel renovation and conference center,
    Clark, Tribble, Harris, and Li Architects
110 Shenandoah Ave., NW

From the beginning, the hotel was the social center of Roanoke, the place to go for business, personal, and political meetings or to attend cultural events, banquets, dances, and family gatherings. For over a century, natives and out-of-towners alike remained enamored of its southern charm and cuisine. But in 1989 the Norfolk Southern Railroad decided it no longer

wanted to be in in the hotel business, closed the building, and donated it to the Virginia Tech Foundation. The hope was that the building could be renovated and reopened; however, financing had to be obtained in four years or the building would likely be demolished. There followed an extraordinary effort by the foundation (the steward of resources donated to the university), the city, the railroad, local businesses, and the people of Roanoke, who demonstrated their deep affection for the hotel by contributing to a last-minute campaign that raised $5 million. The result was a rehabilitated hotel and a new conference center that opened in 1995, at a cost of $42 million.

Pearson's original thirty-four-room hotel was a long, rambling Tudor revival structure that featured several wooden porches and projecting half-timbered gables. A square tower with a pyramidal roof housed the main entrance. In the 1890s, a wing was added at a right angle to one corner of the building, and the surroundings were landscaped as formal gardens. Additional wings were built in the early twentieth century. Finally, in 1938, Knut W. Lind, a hotel specialist

Figure 1.15
Hotel Roanoke, lobby, Roanoke Virginia

with George B. Post and Sons, created the present hotel (nothing remains of Pearson's 1882 structure).

The hotel now consists of the Y-shape west wing, which has a broad center section where the main entrance is located, under an arcaded portico adjacent to a (new) square tower with a pyramidal roof. The steel-frame, reinforced-concrete building is faced with limestone on the lower stories and brick, stucco, and wood above. It has a slate roof. Again, more wings grew out of the structure in the following decades.

Three original chandeliers hang in the main lobby, whose casual atmosphere and comfortable furniture radiate hotel hospitality. A frieze of paintings depicting Virginia's colonial history decorates the adjacent registration area, and both rooms are paneled in walnut. Up a set of steps in one direction is the more formal Regency Dining Room; at the opposite end is the Oval Room (formerly the Palm Court), a circulation space leading to the bar and meeting rooms. In 2007, the 330 guest rooms were thoroughly renovated at a cost of $6.5 million. The hotel now operates as part of the Hilton chain.

**EIGHT JEFFERSON PLACE,
ROANOKE HIGHER EDUCATION CENTER
(formerly N&W Railroad office buildings)
1896, George T. Pearson
1931, Paul Hayes
8, 108 N. Jefferson St.**

The pair of office buildings, connected by an enclosed skywalk, that are across the street from the hotel present an interesting contrast in styles. Pearson's umber-colored 1896 structure is a skillful blend of second Renaissance revival style elements (quoins, rustication, and a classical entrance bearing the "Norfolk and Western" insignia) with the Commercial style (the ranks of paired windows rising in bays). Its surface is enlivened by patterned brickwork, including the rustication, which is indicated by changes of color rather than plane, and the crowning checkerboard motif. A rear wing was added in 1903, creating an enclosed courtyard.

The six-story building, faced with yellow and brown brick, sits on a granite base; the entrances are framed in stone. Cast-iron and timber columns and beams support the structure, which has concrete floors. The slate hip roof boasts a number of shed dormers.

Figure 1.16
Eight Jefferson Place (*left*), Roanoke, Virginia

Its 1931 neighbor employs the same multicolored brick, but the style, in keeping with the time, is art deco. The eight-story, steel-frame structure was designed by Paul Hayes, an N&W draftsman who later became an architect. It was his first and, he thought, best building. Chevrons, vertical stripes, and other art deco emblems decorate the precast stone and brick exterior. The window grilles on either side of the main entrance, again under the engraved message "Norfolk and Western Ry.," incorporate the railroad's logo. The building encloses a rear courtyard. The handsome lobby offers varicolored marble floors and wainscoting, black marble elevator surrounds, and aluminum wall sconces in the art deco style.

In 1997, the Norfolk Southern Railway donated the vacant office buildings to the Roanoke Foundation for Downtown, which found new uses for them. The older structure was converted to loft apartments, while the newer one now houses several education and health programs.

VIRGINIA MUSEUM OF TRANSPORTATION
(formerly the N&W Railroad freight station)
1918
303 Norfolk Ave., SW

The steel-frame, brick-walled freight station was handsomely restored as a transportation museum in 1986, again with the assistance of the City of Roanoke and Norfolk Southern Railroad. A walkway connects the visitors' center with the museum. The steel Howe trusses that support the gable roof are visible in the interior, which contains exhibits on automobiles and buses, circuses, and African American

Figure 1.17

Virginia Museum of Transportation, Roanoke, Virginia

railroad workers. In the rear, a roofed outdoor exhibit area added in 1996 houses the museum's rolling stock collection, including (when it is not pulling excursion trains) the N&W Railroad's Class J Engine No. 611, a streamlined passenger steam locomotive restored in 2015 (see chapter 13).

At Jefferson Street and Williamson Road is the former Virginian Railway station, built in 1909, consisting of two stories with a cross gable and an open passageway between the ticket office and waiting room and the freight and baggage rooms. The materials were pebble-grain brick on a concrete base, with stone trim and a tile roof. Following a 2001 fire that destroyed the roof, the building has been beautifully restored at a cost of $2.3 million. It is owned by the Roanoke chapter of the National Railway Historical Society, which plans to have its offices there and to open a museum dedicated to the history of the Virginian Railway.

2

TERMINUS

Tell me why train stations are so high. Look at the Gare de Lyons and at Grand Central — they don't really need all that height. At the beginning of the century, a railroad station was a mythical place celebrating the adventure of travel.

RENZO PIANO[1]

Much of our civic pride and identity, even our soul, is invested in our great metropolitan railroad termini (meaning the ends of lines or final destinations). Whether serving their original purpose or converted to other uses, they remain architectural landmarks, beacons of prosperity, grand gateways, and engines of economic development. By necessity located downtown, the station buildings are centers of urban activity extending well beyond the usual comings and goings of daily transport. Hotels, restaurants, stores, and markets draw people to and through these cathedrals of transportation. The most outstanding among them is New York's Grand Central Terminal.

GRAND CENTRAL TERMINAL
1913, Reed and Stem, and Warren and Wetmore, architects;
William J. Wilgus, engineer
89 East 42nd St., New York, NY

"The Grand Central Terminal is not only a station, it is a monument, a civic center or, if you will, a city," said a railroad historian a century ago.[2] Grand Central is America's greatest railroad station, not so much because of its size — although the track area and double level of tracks make it the largest railroad terminal in the world — as because of its very successful combination of engineering, architecture, and urban planning. Innovations such as the use of electricity and air rights were also critical to its success. Grand Central Terminal was the largest electric traction installation to date, developed by Wilgus in collaboration with the electric streetcar pioneer Frank Sprague: together they came up with the third-rail system that enabled safe and efficient operation. And Grand Central pioneered the concept of air rights development. Finally, the station's rescue and restoration (in 1983–98) marked a watershed in the preservation movement in the United States.

The new Grand Central Terminal (there had been two previous stations on the site) was conceived by Wilgus, chief engineer of the New York Central and Hudson River Railroad, in response to a substantial increase in trains and traffic (the number of passengers at Grand Central doubled from 1890 to 1910). As a way to enlarge the station's capacity but not expand the site—which covered some twenty-five city blocks, including the head house, train shed, ancillary facilities, and trackage—Wilgus devised a terminal with stacked track levels and a loop track to turn the trains. This arrangement was possible only with the elimination of steam locomotives, whose smoke and gases had been responsible for major problems in the approaches to the station.

In 1902 low visibility due to smoke and steam caused an engineer to run a signal, resulting in a collision that killed fifteen commuters. When the New York legislature prohibited steam locomotives from using the approaches to Grand Central in 1903, the railroad had already decided to employ electric traction, a relatively new technology. That same year Wilgus presented his plan for a new all-electric, 57-track, bilevel terminal to replace the previous station. A key concept in financing the improvements was the sale of air rights over the area occupied by the train shed and open approaches north of the head house that would now be covered. "Thus from the air would be taken wealth with which to finance obligatory vast changes," said Wilgus.[3] Four architectural firms were asked to submit designs: McKim, Mead and White; Daniel H. Burnham; Samuel Huckel Jr.; and Reed and Stem.

Stanford White's spectacular scheme called for a fourteen-story head house and a sixty-story office tower, from whose peak would rise a 300-foot steam jet illuminated by red floodlights. Reed and Stem's more modest design for a low, wide head house was based on Charles B. Atwood's influential terminal for the Chicago World's Fair of 1893. The major characteristics of Atwood's terminal—large arched portals centrally located and a prominent gabled pavilion expressing on the exterior the vaulted waiting room and concourse within—were later replicated in union stations in other major American cities, including Detroit and Kansas City.

Reed and Stem's proposal, which incorporated a smaller office tower, was chosen. Charles A. Reed

(1858–1911) was born near Scarsdale, New York, and earned a degree in architecture from the Massachusetts Institute of Technology. He then found employment as an architect for several railroads. In 1891 he formed an architectural partnership in St. Paul, Minnesota, with Allen H. Stem (1856–1931). Stem had attended the Indianapolis Art School and then gone to work as a draftsman for his architect father in the same city, later becoming a partner. The same year that Reed and Stem became partners, Wilgus married Reed's sister.

Wilgus made significant contributions to the plan, which included some of the most successful features of the new terminal: the sunken, high-ceilinged open main concourse; a system of ramps rather than stairways to facilitate a gravity-like flow of passengers into and through the station; the upper and lower concourses for long-distance trains and suburban trains respectively; and the elevated passage of Park Avenue around the terminal. Immediately north of the building was the three-block Court of Honor, set aside for the first air rights development.

In 1904 the New York architectural firm of Warren and Wetmore was added to the design team. Whitney Warren (1864–1943), born in New York City, had trained at the École des Beaux-Arts in Paris and begun his career with McKim, Mead, and White. He remained the essential classicist throughout his architectural career. Charles D. Wetmore (1866–1941) was a lawyer. Their extensive social connections gained them many commissions. Warren was a cousin and friend of William K. Vanderbilt, chairman of the New York Central Railroad.

While retaining the major features of the Reed-Wilgus plan, Warren redesigned the head house in true beaux arts fashion, with coupled columns and a clock and large statuary group over the main 42nd Street façade (the office tower was eliminated from the plan).

Construction took ten years. The demolition of some two hundred buildings and the use of 500 tons of dynamite to blast loose the underlying Manhattan schist were required before the terminal complex was completed. The task of removing the train shed,

Figure 2.1

Grand Central Terminal, New York, New York (courtesy of James Rudnick)

which contained 1,700 tons of cast and wrought iron, while maintaining railroad service below, was especially difficult.

Meanwhile, Wilgus resigned in 1907 over a dispute with the New York Central Railroad. After Reed died in 1911, Warren and Wetmore immediately signed a new contract with the railroad, making them sole architects. When Grand Central Terminal was finished, Warren and Wetmore generally received credit as its designers (they still do, according to some press accounts of the restoration). Allen Stem, the surviving partner, later sued to collect his firm's design fees and won his case; Warren was expelled from the American Institute of Architects.

Warren and Wetmore went on to design several nearby air rights structures, including the Biltmore Hotel (since demolished) and the New York Central office building, now the Helmsley Building. They also designed several other railroad stations elsewhere, as

did Reed and Stem. In fact, credit for Grand Central Terminal should be divided equally among Wilgus, author of the basic concept and engineering plan; Reed, who contributed innovative functional features; and Warren, who was largely responsible for the station building design.

Grand Central Terminal is a steel-frame structure faced with Connecticut granite and Indiana limestone. The sculpture group depicting Mercury, the Roman god of commerce, flanked by Minerva and Hercules, is by Jules Coutan, a professor at the École des Beaux-Arts. The main concourse, 120 by 275 feet, with an information booth in the center and ticket windows lining one wall, is paved with Tennessee marble; the walls of imitation Caen stone are trimmed with marble from Botticino, Italy. On the barrel-vaulted ceiling, 125 feet overhead, is a painting of the constellations of the zodiac (in reverse order) by the French artist Paul Helleu, which is composed of 2,500 gold-leaf stars on a blue background. In addition to the huge arched windows, large bronze electric chandeliers light the concourse, balconies, and the waiting room facing 42nd Street. The famous Oyster Bar and Restaurant, between the upper and lower concourses, is vaulted with Guastavino tile.[4] Overhead is the Campbell Apartment, formerly the private office of stockbroker John W. Campbell, which was decorated in the manner of a Venetian palace. It was restored and reopened as an upscale cocktail bar in 1999; in 2017 a new lessee modestly redesigned "The Campbell" and reopened it for a more casual crowd. Originally for suburban train passengers, the lower concourse largely replicates the upper one, which was originally for long-distance passengers—including the central information booth, connected by an internal stairway to the one above (the lower-concourse information booth is inactive).

There were few precedents for a building of the scale and complexity of Grand Central Terminal. Accommodating two levels of moving trains, air rights development on top of them, and the myriad entrances and exits connecting the station to streets, subways, and outside buildings required a structure that was both intricate and strong. All of the steel columns are based on solid rock. Three-foot-deep plate girders support the concrete floors in the head house, and the long-span girders are from seven to ten feet deep. Pratt and Warren trusses hold up the roof and ceiling.

To heat the terminal and provide electricity for its operation, the railroad erected its own power plant (which had four corner towers and resembled a Romanesque church) and substation. To guide the trains in and out, one of the largest and most advanced signal and interlocking systems of the time (including five interlocking towers) was installed. The total cost for the land and terminal was $80 million, nearly double the original estimate.

In 1914, 470 trains and 75,000 passengers used Grand Central Terminal every day; in 1946, it handled 550 trains and 204,000 passengers daily. Besides transportation, "Grand Central City" offered stores, bars, restaurants, a post office, a movie theater, a gymnasium, tennis courts (still active), and an emergency hospital. On either side were the Biltmore and Commodore hotels, both owned by the railroad. The planned Court of Honor north of the head house never materialized, but air rights development proceeded. One of the most important new buildings was the 1931 Waldorf-Astoria Hotel on Park Avenue, between 49th and 50th Streets.

Figure 2.2
Grand Central Terminal, main concourse, New York, New York

By mid-century Grand Central Terminal was in decline, as were the fortunes of its owner, the New York Central Railroad—which recommended the terminal's demolition in 1954. The 1963 construction of the fifty-nine-story Pan Am (now Met Life) Building blocked the view of the station along Park Avenue from the north. That same year Pennsylvania Station was demolished, resulting in the establishment two years later of the New York City Landmark Preservation Commission.

One of the first buildings that the commission designated as a landmark was Grand Central Terminal (in 1967). That designation and the plans of the Penn Central Transportation Company, formed in 1968, to build a fifty-five-story tower atop the station building ignited a public controversy. The railroad and developers filed a court suit challenging the commission's decision and claiming an unconstitutional taking of their property without just compensation.

In 1975, Jacqueline Kennedy Onassis and the architect Philip Johnson formed the Committee to Save Grand Central Station. They were aided in their efforts by the Municipal Art Society and many other organizations and individuals. "The idea," said the architecture critic Ada Louise Huxtable, "is to combine restoration of the terminal's architectural features with strengthening of its mass transit functions and the use of its physical resources—shops, subways, arcades, mezzanines—for a lively commercial and pedestrian center fanning out to other blocks and buildings."[5] In 1978 the US Supreme Court ruled in favor of the preservationists, upholding the constitutionality of the city's landmarks law and the right of local governments to protect their historic architecture. Then began the task of raising the money to restore the building, which had continued to deteriorate. The portions of the majestic interior unobscured by advertising were coated with grime, and the waiting room was occupied mainly by homeless people.

The Metropolitan Transit Authority leased the terminal from Penn Central in 1978 and five years later formed the Metro North Commuter Railroad to operate the suburban train service (long-distance trains had been transferred to Penn Station). Metro North began to make repairs and then—under its first president, Peter E. Stangl—undertook a $200-million, fifteen-year restoration program supervised by the architects Beyer Blinder Belle. After exhaustive research in the archives and the building itself, a new roof was put on; and the sky ceiling, walls, and floors were cleaned of decades of accumulated smoke and dirt and restored—as were the decorative metal-, stone-, and plasterwork, including oak leaves and acorns (symbols of the Vanderbilt family). An eastern stairway and balcony, which were part of the original plans but had not previously been built, were added to the main concourse. New restaurants filled other balcony areas: there are thirty-five restaurants and sixty-eight shops altogether. The chandeliers were repaired and relit in the massive waiting room, which was renamed Vanderbilt Hall—an event space, half of which is now the Great Northern Food Hall. Floors added in the 1920s to expand the ticket offices had turned the ramps leading down to the Oyster Bar into tunnels; the added floors were removed, exposing the soaring overhead space. The lower concourse is now a food court. New heating, ventilating, air-conditioning, electrical, and fire suppression systems were installed.

The restoration of Grand Central Terminal has inspired new development both above and below ground in midtown Manhattan. Now underway with a 2022 completion date is a massive $10-billion construction project to bring the trains of the Long Island Railroad, which now terminate at Penn Station, into Grand Central via new tunnels under the East River.

Over 620 trains carrying some 217,500 passengers pass through the station every day. It is one of the busiest stops on the New York City subway system. Standing in the main concourse is like being in an animated Piranesi print where the ruin has miraculously sprung to life. The Jacqueline Kennedy Onassis foyer, established in 2014 inside the main 42nd Street entrance, neatly summarizes the saga of Grand Central Terminal. Over the inner doors to the waiting room and main concourse is the original message: "To all those who with head, heart and hand toiled

Figure 2.3
Union Station, Chicago, Illinois

in the construction of this monument to the public service this is inscribed." The plaque honoring Onassis ends with a portion of her 1975 letter to Abraham Beame, then mayor of New York: "Is it not cruel to let our city die by degrees, stripped of all her proud monuments until there will be nothing left to inspire our children? If they are not inspired by the past of our city, where will they find the strength to fight for her future?"

Frank Lloyd Wright—perhaps America's greatest architect, but one who disliked cities in general and New York in particular—visited Grand Central Terminal in the 1950s with Andy Rooney (the CBS studios were then in the building). Wright was also known for his acerbic comments about the work of other architects. The two men observed the intricate ballet of the main concourse, lit by shafts of sunlight from above. "It is a grand building, isn't it?" said Wright[6] (see chapter 7 for a discussion of the Helmsley Building).

UNION STATION
1915–25 Graham, Anderson, Probst and White
210 S. Canal St., Chicago, IL

Chicago, the railroad capital of the United States, once had six train stations and a dedicated cab company, Parmelee, to shuttle passengers between them. None of the buildings remain as built, although Union Station is the most intact and functional. Today it is

the city's major station, handling both long-distance Amtrak trains and the busy Metra commuter service.

In fact, four of the six original station buildings have been demolished: Grand Central, Northwestern, LaSalle Street, and Central. However, the rail functions of the last three are now housed in new facilities. Empty lots mark the site of Solon S. Beman's 1890 Romanesque revival Grand Central Station, with its signature tower—regarded as the finest, architecturally, of the group. The idiosyncratic Dearborn Street Station, built in 1885 and designed by Cyrus L. W. Eidlitz, still stands, converted to commercial use, but bereft of the architect's whimsical Swiss clock bell tower and high pitched roofs and dormers, which were victims of a 1922 fire. The former track area is now Dearborn Park.

Daniel Burnham's famous 1909 plan for Chicago proposed a new passenger rail terminal west of the Chicago River that would consolidate the services of the six existing train stations and eliminate the attendant problems of ticketing and transfers. Burnham died in 1912, and the concept of a single rail terminal for the city died with him. However, a few years later construction began on a new Union Station. It was built by three railroads—the Pennsylvania; the Chicago, Burlington and Quincy; and the Chicago, Milwaukee, St. Paul and Pacific (known as the Milwaukee Road)—and designed by Graham, Anderson, Probst and White, the architectural firm that succeeded Burnham's.

Figure 2.4
Union Station, waiting room,
Chicago, Illinois

Chicago's Union Station was closely modeled on New York's neoclassical revival Pennsylvania Station (which was opened in 1910 and in demolished 1963). However, in the Chicago station, the standard waiting room and concourse functions were placed in two separate structures—the head house and the concourse building that stood across Canal Street from it —that were connected by a broad passageway below street level. (The track layout was also unusual: the two sets of tracks approaching from the north and south end on either side of the concourse and do not pass through it.)

The concourse building was the more impressive of the two structures, a gabled pavilion whose spacious interior was lit by skylights carried on steel arches. It was demolished in 1969 and replaced by a pair of office buildings. This resulted in a low-ceilinged and confined concourse level, again much like the current Penn Station in New York—whose airy, expansive interior, inspired by ancient Roman baths, was sacrificed for Madison Square Garden.

The remaining structure—Union Station's head house, an eight-story, steel-frame building faced with limestone from Bedford, Indiana—is a standard hollow office block. The first two stories make up the station, and the upper six stories house offices. The

only noteworthy exterior features are the lengthy colonnades on the east and west (Canal and Clinton Street) façades.

The interior was another matter. Overlooked by balconies, marble stairways (one of which was featured in the film *The Untouchables*) led down to the magnificent waiting room that extended the full width of the station and was lined with Corinthian columns of Travertine. The second story was marked by a series of wide, segmentally arched openings for major entrances from the four surrounding streets or high vaulted passageways leading to other parts of the station. The archway that led to the ticket lobby and concourse was flanked by statues of figures holding a rooster and an owl, referring to the twenty-four-hour nature of railroad transportation. High overhead, 112 feet above the Tennessee marble floor, was a barrel-vaulted skylight that ran nearly the length of the room.

Benches filled the waiting room, in the center of which was an information booth. Two of the notable spaces on the western side were the dining room and the women's waiting room—the latter a columned room with French murals on the walls and a highly ornate decorative plaster ceiling, whose coffers were outlined with ornamental moldings and filled with rosettes. A lunchroom and a barbershop were also available.

The waiting room is now known as the Great Hall. Amtrak assumed ownership of Union Station in 1984 and attempted to alleviate the cramped situation in the concourse. The project was completed in 1991 at a cost of $32 million. Separating the long-distance riders from the commuters by providing different routes for them made the passenger flow through the station more efficient, but moving the ticketing services and other travel facilities to the concourse so the Great Hall could function more as an event space proved counterproductive. Amtrak adopted airline-style gate procedures, so instead of waiting in the Great Hall until it was time to board their trains, people were herded into crowded boarding lounges in the concourse, which one disgruntled passenger likened to a fluorescent dungeon. Behind all these changes was a plan to redevelop the station by converting the Great Hall to other uses and adding several more office floors above it (the foundations were constructed to support twenty-two floors, but only eight were built). Three successive developers tried and failed to do this.

Amtrak currently is concentrating on improving the station for the benefit of the passengers. In 2012 it moved its regional offices into the building and finished a $25-million infrastructure improvement program that included air-conditioning the waiting room. An additional $14-million renovation is now under way. Passengers are again occupying the benches in the Great Hall while waiting for their trains, and in the middle of the room is an Amtrak ticketing kiosk. The skylight is being restored (the paint that covered it during World War II was removed during the 1991 renovations). The former dining room is now the Legacy Club, which offers comfortable chairs and other amenities for a modest admission fee; the adjacent barbershop has become a meeting room. The handsome French murals, columns, and ceiling in the former women's waiting room are being restored, and it will be an event space named the Burlington Room. The new Metropolitan Lounge for business-class and sleeping-car passengers is off the concourse passageway.

Some 300 trains and 130,000 passengers a day use Union Station. These numbers are expected to increase, and with Amtrak, Metra, and the City of Chicago committed to further enhancing the traveler's experience in the building and redeveloping the surrounding properties, Union Station seems to be back on track.

UNION STATION
1894, Theodore C. Link; train shed,
    George H. Pegram, engineer
1985, Hellmuth, Obata and Kassabaum,
    renovation architects
Market St. between 18th and 20th Streets,
    St. Louis, MO

It is almost impossible to enter the grand hall of Union Station without emitting an involuntary gasp, especially since it is now a hotel lobby with carpets and comfortable furniture, a long bar, and an overhead light show. Perhaps this is what it was always meant to be.

The Terminal Railroad Association of St. Louis, which built the station, selected Theodore Link as the result of a design competition that he entered with Edward Cameron, then his partner. The German-born Link trained in engineering at the University of Heidelberg and L'Ecole Centrale in Paris, emigrated to America in 1870, and soon found work with the railroads. He arrived in St. Louis in 1874 as an employee of the Atlantic and Pacific Railroad, but he moved

Figure 2.5
Union Station, St. Louis, Missouri

Figure 2.6
Union Station, Grand Hall, St. Louis, Missouri

on to become the city's Superintendent of Parks and, briefly, a publisher of German-language newspapers in Pittsburgh before returning to St. Louis and opening a civil engineering office. In 1886, he advertised himself as an architect. Link designed over a hundred buildings, from seminaries to state capitols, in a variety of styles, but his strong suit was the Norman revival style, and Union Station was his most important work.

The Norman influence is seen especially in the towers. Link incorporated elements of the French Renaissance (the high pitched roofs and decorated dormers) and the Richardsonian Romanesque (the strong masonry arches at ground level). The building is brick faced with limestone from Bedford, Indiana, and has a red tile roof. Its two-block-long façade makes it difficult to grasp from a single vantage point,

but there are five distinct components. They recede and advance, giving an illusion of depth to a structure that is some 780 feet wide but only 100 feet deep.

The station faces north. The projecting pavilion, under a hip roof and flanked by round stair towers with conical roofs, marks the main entrance and the major interior spaces. The square element to the east, defined by the 230-foot clock tower, housed waiting rooms, with offices on the upper floors. (The tower with the smaller diameter aided the original ventilating system by creating a thermosiphon effect: warm air in the building rose through the stack and drew in cooler air via lower door and window openings, like an attic fan.) The towers, being heavier, have a separate foundation from the station building to prevent unequal settling, which could crack the masonry and produce other deleterious effects. Five shields

—showing a fleur-de-lis, lion, lyre, eagle, and star, respectively—top the engaged columns that separate the upper set of windows, and the copper downspouts are gripped by rings of stone.

To the west is a connecting section featuring three semicircular arches and four dormers ornamented with finials and stone carvings. This link between the entrance pavilion and the hotel block housed a kitchen and dining room, with hotel rooms above. A massive semicircular arch identifies the hotel entrance. A late 1920s addition to the hotel constitutes the fifth and westernmost wing of the building.

The primary station entrance passes beneath a whispering arch (it works) and an art glass window, which shows an allegory of travel with three female figures representing New York, St. Louis (in the middle), and San Francisco. Link provided the design; Davis and Chambers, a local firm, produced the window.

A double stairway ascends to the barrel-vaulted Grand Hall, a space 75 by 125 feet whose ceiling rises to 65 feet over the floor. This was the main waiting room; to the west was a kitchen and the Fred Harvey restaurant (see chapter 8). The vault ribs, the seven arches lining the side walls at the second and third levels, and especially the tympana at either end —featuring seven bas-relief female figures whose outstretched arms hold illuminated torches—offer much to enjoy visually. Mosaics (by Davis and Chambers), scrollwork, gilding, stenciling, elaborate plasterwork, and art glass windows all compete with the ongoing light show.

The room is largely the creation of Louis J. Millet, who worked with Link on its design—which was inspired by the Arts and Crafts movement. Millet taught decorative design at the Art Institute of Chicago, founded the Chicago School of Architecture, and was in charge of mural and decorative painting for the 1893 Chicago World's Fair. He is chiefly known for collaborating with Louis Sullivan on several of that architect's important buildings. The ticketing lobby, on the level below the Grand Hall, was flanked by waiting rooms and another restaurant.

Separating the station from the rear train shed was a concourse, called the Midway, that stretched the breadth of the building. George Pegram's steel train shed—at 606 feet wide, 630 feet long, and 140 feet high, the largest ever built—covered ten acres and thirty tracks. Pegram, primarily a bridge designer and railroad engineer, invented a truss type that he used here. The Pegram trusses were arranged in five longitudinal bays, the center one of which spanned 141 feet.

In its peak periods around the beginning of the twentieth century and during World War II, Union Station served twenty-two railroads, and hundreds of long-distance trains and thousands of passengers passed through it daily. But by the 1970s, there were just six trains per day calling at the station. In 1978, Amtrak left Union Station for smaller quarters.

In 1985, Union Station reopened as a hotel, retail, and restaurant complex developed by the Rouse Company at a cost of $150 million; it was the largest adaptive reuse project in the country. The renovation included the restoration of the station building, a 538-room hotel (there are 65 rooms in the original hotel section and 473 rooms in new infill structures in the concourse and under the train shed), a boat lake (natural springs are beneath the site, which was once a millpond and brewery), a bilevel shopping mall with stores and restaurants, and space for events and parking. The architects removed alternating sections of the wooden train shed roof to bring in natural light. The mall was popular for a few years, but then business fell off.

In 2012, Lodging Hospitality Management bought Union Station for $20 million and began a $30-million renovation program that included all the rooms of the hotel, now a Hilton DoubleTree, the creation of meeting space in the Midway, and a new bar in the Grand Hall. The owners plan to convert the largely vacant retail mall to hotel rooms (bringing the total to 587) and event space, and to build a Ferris wheel at a cost of $60 million. The original station and train shed cost $6.5 million (see the discussion of Drury Inn in chapter 11).

UNION STATION
1939, Parkinson and Parkinson;
Edward Warren Hoak
800 N. Alameda St., Los Angeles, CA

The last of the big city railroad terminals to be built, Union Station in Los Angeles is also the most distinctive and civilized in terms of its architectural style and urban amenities. Its restoration and the addition of rail transit and bus facilities, plus new development on the site, have made Union Station once again the transportation center for southern California, and it is a striking symbol of the railroads' comeback from their dark ages in America during the latter half of the twentieth century.

The high-ceilinged waiting room with its signature upholstered Craftsman-style armchairs is a welcome sight to arriving train passengers emerging from the lower-level concourse that runs beneath the tracks. This is especially true at a time when the waiting rooms in some of our greatest stations (such as New York's Grand Central Terminal) have largely become event venues. On either side of the waiting room lie beautiful landscaped patios that invite people to linger with a cool drink or dine al fresco (Traxx Restaurant has outdoor seating).

Figure 2.7

Union Station, Los Angeles, California

The information desk in the entrance lobby, manned by the Los Angeles Tourism and Convention Board, does a brisk business directing visitors to the sights in the city, most of which are accessible by the Metro Rail (subway), Metrolink (commuter) trains, and regional buses—all of which use Union Station.

Union Station's late construction, compared to those of other big city terminals, was due to the fact that the three railroads in Los Angeles—the Southern Pacific; the Atchison, Topeka and Santa Fe; and the San Pedro, Los Angeles, and Salt Lake (later Union Pacific)—acknowledged that a union station was needed but could not agree on a site. Each had its own rail routes into the city, shop facilities, and stations, the most recent being the Southern Pacific's Central Station, built in 1914 and designed in the prevailing neoclassical revival style by Parkinson and Bergstrom, the predecessor firm to the one that designed Union Station. The many grade crossings on city streets that resulted from these separate facilities created havoc. A 1915 collision between a Santa Fe locomotive and a streetcar that killed five people added urgency to the discussion, but the railroads' dispute over the station site and other matters continued until 1933, ending only after the Supreme Court brought a close to their protracted legal battle among themselves.

The site finally chosen was across from the Los Angeles Plaza, the city's birthplace. Chinatown was located there, but its buildings were razed to make way for the new station. The next question was what the station's style would be—neo-classical revival like the union stations in Washington, D.C. (1907), Kansas City (1914), and Chicago (1925), or something else? At last, the railroads could agree: they wanted the style of the new station to reflect California, and the specific model they had in mind was the Mediterranean-style Santa Barbara Courthouse (1929).

The Mediterranean style is a mélange of the Spanish colonial revival and mission revival styles, with some Moorish and Gothic influences. Tile roofs, towers, shaped parapets, arcades, wrought-iron grillwork, and adobe are its major hallmarks. It is sometimes simply called the California style. William Randolph Hearst's California hilltop castle, San Simeon,

Figure 2.8
Union Station, waiting room, Los Angeles, California
(courtesy of John Kiffe, Getty Research Institute)

designed by Julia Morgan, is a particularly flamboyant example of it.

What emerged from successive studies of Union Station by John and Donald Parkinson (father and son)—refined and simplified by their chief designer, Edward Hoak—was a structure that was both Californian and monumental. It had the required tile roofs, tower, and arcades and, thanks to Hoak, minimal decoration. The abstracted, severe mission revival style, combined with an art deco rectilinearity, might seem to be an unlikely mixture, but in this case it produced an extraordinarily handsome building (the art deco elements include the station signs and the patio lighting pylons).

The L-shape main block houses the ticket concourse, paralleling Alameda Street, and the waiting room, at right angles to it. High arched windows mark the ticket concourse (currently empty) and the prominent main entrance, flanked by the 125-foot plain, square clock tower, topped by a tile-decorated belvedere. An arcade leads to the Mary Colter–designed Harvey House restaurant (also now empty), which has a floor of Spanish tile.

The patios, planted with trees and shrubs native to California, were the creation of Tommy Tomson, a self-taught landscape architect who created residential landscape designs for several Hollywood stars. The lower-level concourse leads to the tracks, accessed by stairways and protected by butterfly canopies.

Union Station is built of reinforced concrete; steel beams, disguised as timber, support the ticket concourse ceiling. Rectangular windows and bronze chandeliers light the waiting room, whose marble and Travertine floor and subdued tile wainscoting and plaster décor help give it an unhurried atmosphere

Figure 2.9
Union Station, patio,
Los Angeles, California
(courtesy of John Kiffe,
Getty Research Institute)

unusual for a train station, despite the 100,000 passengers accommodated here daily.

The closing of the Harvey House restaurant in the 1970s symbolized the station's decline. However, in the following decade, a Metro rail stop was under construction, part of the plan to make the station a transportation center. In 1990, the Catellus Development Corporation bought Union Station and began at $2.5-million restoration (completed in 1992) that included the interior architectural details, the exterior, and patio landscaping.

Over the next twenty years, Catellus oversaw the construction of Gateway Center, a $300-million intermodal transportation complex on the east side of the fifty-acre Union Station property. The East Portal, designed by Ehrankrantz, Eckstut and Kuhn, is a sweeping limestone arch enclosed in a rectangular frame and backed by a structure covered with a half-dome. The lobby, with its faceted ninety-foot steel and etched glass dome, doubles as an arts and performance space. It is decorated by Richard Wyatt's colorful, large-scale mural depicting historical and current residents of the city, and May Sun's inlaid bronze floor images of the local flora and fauna referring to the nearby Los Angeles River. The artistic collaboration, which incorporates an aquarium, is titled "City of Dreams/River of History." The entrance

to the lower-level concourse and Union Station is beneath Wyatt's mural.

Gateway Center also includes a Metro Rail entrance; a landscaped bus plaza; a four-level, 3,300-car subterranean parking garage (whose construction necessitated the removal of thirty feet of contaminated groundwater, which took two years); and a twenty-six-story headquarters building for the Los Angeles County Metropolitan Transportation Authority (MTA).

The architects of the MTA Building, completed in 1995, were McLarand, Vasquez and Partners. The postmodern $300-million steel-frame building is faced with Minnesota limestone, Italian granite, and English brick. In 2011, Metro acquired the Union Station complex from Catellus for $75 million.

WINDSOR STATION
**1889, Bruce Price; 1906, western extension and
entry arcade, Edward Maxwell; 1914, southern
extension and concourse, Walter S. Painter
Rue Peel and Rue de la Gauchetiere, Montreal, QC**

The posters that hung on the building when it opened read "Beats All Creation — The New CPR Station," (reportedly William C. Van Horne's own words). Windsor Station, which included the headquarters of the Canadian Pacific Railway (CPR) Company, was the easternmost physical manifestation, in what was then Canada's largest city, of the 1885 completion of its first transcontinental line, the CPR—stretching from Montreal to Vancouver. Van Horne (1843–1915), the railroad's general manager, had overseen the driving of the last spike, at Craigellachie, British Columbia, in 1885, and finishing the 2,900-mile-long railway across the granite shield north of Lake Superior and through the Canadian Rockies was his signal achievement.

Van Horne had been hired by James J. Hill, a member of the CPR board who recognized in the former superintendent of the Milwaukee Road a measure of his own aggressive energy and hard-driving temperament. Hill and Van Horne did not like to sit in offices: they preferred to be out on the line in all kinds of weather and terrain, reconnoitering and supervising the work. While Hill was focused strictly on business, Van Horne was a violinist, an artist who was knowledgeable about architecture, and an amateur geologist (several fossils are named after him). Allies for a time, they became adversaries after Hill left the CPR to concentrate on completing his own American transcontinental line, the Great Northern Railway. Eventually, Hill and Van Horne emerged as the two premier nineteenth-century railroad builders of North America.

But it was Van Horne's hiring in turn of the architect Bruce Price (1845–1903) that changed Canadian architecture. Born in Cumberland, Maryland, Price attended Princeton University for a time and then became a draftsman and apprentice in a Baltimore architectural firm, before opening a practice of his own with a partner. He married a wealthy socialite (their daughter was Emily Post, the etiquette expert). After spending a few years in Wilkes-Barre, Pennsylvania, Price moved to New York City, where he was soon designing summer cottages to be located in Bar Harbor, Maine; Babylon, New York; and Newport, Rhode Island, for the socially prominent.

In 1885, Pierre Lorillard IV, an heir to a tobacco fortune who owned property north of New York City, hired Price to design Tuxedo Park, an exclusive hunting resort accessible by rail, for the New York gentry. Price drew up the plans for several buildings, including a dozen or so houses and cottages in the shingle style whose axial plans and bold and unusual combination of elements influenced the early architecture of Frank Lloyd Wright. Price also designed the train station in Tuxedo, today a gated residential community (see chapter 4).

Once described as "an elegant gentleman and erratic genius,"[7] Price was architecturally adept in the Richardsonian Romanesque, neoclassical revival, shingle, and château styles. It is thought that he came to the attention of Van Horne because of his work at Tuxedo Park and his design of a bay-window parlor car for the Pennsylvania Railroad. The sides of the car were not straight but moved in and out in a series of glazed bays that reportedly expanded the passengers' views of the passing scene. Price also designed the interior of the car, which was carpeted and finished in white oak and brass. It was built in the railroad's Altoona shops.

Shortly after Price started work on Windsor Station in 1886, he was commissioned to design the CPR's hotel at Banff Springs, Alberta. The result was curiously muted in style for Price, but his next exercise in the genre was anything but. Van Horne had become president of the company in 1888, the same year the Banff Springs Hotel opened, and he was soon involved in another hotel project in Quebec City that Price also designed.

The Château Frontenac, on a spectacular site overlooking the St. Lawrence River, opened five years later. In line with the French origins of the city, Price had chosen the château style, based on sixteenth-century French châteaus. Buildings in the style were of masonry with high, steep hip roofs and large, decorated wall dormers. They were surrounded by turrets that had tall, conical roofs. Asymmetrical plans and picturesque silhouettes were other hallmarks of the style. ("Scottish baronial" is another term sometimes used to describe buildings with these characteristics.) Van Horne, who was very much involved in the design of the hotel, believed that it would be "the most talked-about hotel on this continent."[8]

Figure 2.10
Windsor Station, Montreal, Quebec

Figure 2.11
Windsor Station, main entrance, Montreal, Quebec

It was certainly the most influential, at least in Canada. With later additions, the Château Frontenac established the stylistic model not only for future CPR hotels and those of rival railroads, but also for the federal government, which in the early twentieth century recommended using the château style for official buildings in Ottawa. In fact, several federal buildings in the style were built in the capital. Van Horne and Price helped to make the château style the national style of Canada in much the same way that John Russell Pope established the neoclassical revival as the official government style of Washington, D.C.

Price submitted four designs for Windsor Station in Montreal, and Van Horne chose the fourth. It was in the Richardsonian Romanesque style, but with some château style elements: the decorated wall dormers and the corner turrets. The five-story building, built of local gray limestone, had iron floor beams. The main entrance was on Rue de la Gauchetiere, but the longer elevation, anchored by a ten-story square medieval tower, was on Rue Peel. In the arches rising through three stories and the row of smaller arches at the top, there were echoes of Henry Hobson Richardson's Marshall Field Wholesale Store in Chicago (1885, later demolished). The interior, finished in Vancouver cedar, offered passengers a granite vaulted

waiting room. The tracks, extending westward, were perpendicular to the building.

Edward Maxwell had worked for Shepley, Rutan and Coolidge, the successor firm to Richardson's. His steel-frame expansion of Windsor Station, faced with stone, extended westward along Rue de la Gauchetiere. It duplicated Price's façade as a bookend and in between added a three-story section fronted by a five-bay porte cochere. Walter Painter's addition—in the same style and also with a steel frame—ran southward along Rue Peel to Rue Saint-Antoine and turned the corner, where there was a second entrance. Facing Rue Peel, a fifteen-story tower with a high steep roof gave the station a fresh visual presence on the city's skyline. It was now a U-shape structure that enclosed the tracks and canopies. Inside was a new skylit concourse. (Both Maxwell and Painter enjoyed long careers with the CPR and also made major additions to the Château Frontenac.)

In 1970, the CPR's passenger service was in decline, the railroad announced a plan to demolish Windsor Station and build a high-rise office building on the site. Michael Fish, a Montreal architect, formed the Friends of Windsor Station to save it. The redevelopment scheme did not proceed. After VIA Rail was established in 1978 to operate the nation's passenger trains, Montreal's long-distance trains were consolidated at the Canadian National Railways' nearby, and newer, Central Station. The CPR's renovation of Windsor Station, completed in 1984, included putting on new slate and copper roofs, restoring the façade, and installing new elevators and a heating, ventilating, and air-conditioning system. The construction of the Molson Center (now the Bell Center) on the track area to the west severed Windsor Station from the rail line. Completed in 1996, the center is the home of the Montreal Canadiens. That same year, the CPR moved its corporate headquarters to Calgary, Alberta.

In 2009, the railroad sold Windsor Station to the developer Cadillac Fairview for $86 million, and a plan was announced to turn the station into an intermodal center (involving more than one type of transit). However, the plan was never implemented. Five years later, Cadillac Fairview said that it would restore the station as part of a mixed-use development for the area, composed mainly of high-rise residential and office towers.

Today, shorn of its reason for being, the station is a shadow of its former self. Except for a single remnant, the track canopies are gone, replaced by a public square with a reflecting pool. The concourse—watched over by Coeur de Lion MacCarthy's bronze statue *Winged Victory*, which commemorates the 1,100 CPR employees who died in World War I—is mostly empty (other versions of the statue stood in CPR stations in Winnipeg, Alberta, and Vancouver). Now an event space, the concourse hosts an annual beer festival. However, rail connections are still made at Windsor Station, which functions largely as a subterranean conduit to the Montreal Metro, Agence Métropolitaine de Transport (AMT) commuter trains, and the Bell Center.

Price also designed the Place Viger Station-Hotel (at 700 Rue St. Antoine), which opened in 1898 in Old Montreal, near the river. Built in the château style and fronted by landscaped gardens and a broad arcade, the brick and stone building rose to a dramatic, central round tower encircled by turrets and dormers. It replaced the nearby Dalhousie Station. The hotel closed in 1935 and the train station in 1951, after which the City of Montreal acquired the building, removed the interior and converted it to office space. The gardens were sacrificed to an expressway in the 1970s. The station-hotel building, occupied by Lightspeed and other firms, is under renovation as part of a multimillion-dollar redevelopment plan for Old Montreal.

Dalhousie Station at Notre Dame and Berri Streets, designed by Thomas C. Sorby and opened in 1884, was the CPR's first station in Montreal. It was used for freight storage from 1898 to 1984, when the City of Montreal bought it. The station, the surrounding square, and the Notre Dame Street Viaduct have been restored. The building houses Cirque Eloize. Only the ground story, whose stone walls are cut with large, semicircular arches, is original (see chapter 6, Silo No. 5, and chapter 7, Grand Trunk Railway Building).

UNION STATION
1914–27, Ross and MacDonald, Hugh G. Jones, John M. Lyle
65 Front St., Toronto, ON

The Canadian author Pierre Berton wrote: "It is no accident that the great station resembles a temple, for there was a time when we worshipped railways as ardently as the ancients worshipped Zeus or Apollo."[9]

It took thirteen years to build Union Station and thirteen minutes for the Prince of Wales to open it officially. And it may take eight years, until 2018, to finish the ongoing $800-million revitalization program. The station, whose construction was delayed by World War I, was actually completed in 1921. However, a dispute between the railroads that built it, the Canadian Pacific and the Grand Trunk, over grade separations and approaches delayed its opening until 1927. And it took three more years before trains could reach the building, which meant that passengers had to hike a quarter-mile from the previous Union Station. Finally, in 1930, the access viaduct and train sheds were completed.

The train sheds were almost twice as long (1,200 feet) as the station itself and covered ten tracks.

Figure 2.12
Union Station, Toronto, Ontario

Designed by the station company's bridge engineer A. R. Ketterson, they were a variation of the Bush shed, spanning two tracks rather than one (as at Hoboken, New Jersey, for example). Supported on steel trusses, the sheds had timber roofs and linear concrete smoke ducts over the tracks.

The monumental station building, the largest in Canada, is in the neoclassical revival style. The Montreal firm of Ross and MacDonald had experience in train station design. Its predecessor firm, Ross and MacFarlane, of which MacDonald was a member, was the architect for Ottawa's Union Station and Château Laurier Hotel, built in 1912 (see chapter 3). Born in Montreal, George Allen Ross had attended the Massachusetts Institute of Technology and the École

des Beaux-Arts in Paris, and later worked for the architects Parker and Thomas in Boston and Carrere and Hastings in New York. Robert Henry MacDonald was born in Australia, became an architectural draftsman in Montreal, and worked for George B. Post and Sons in New York before forming the partnership with Ross. Hugh Jones was a CPR architect, and John Lyle, who also attended the École des Beaux-Arts, practiced architecture in Toronto.

The façade and form of Union Station bear more than a passing resemblance to New York's former Pennsylvania Station. The steel-frame structure—faced with Bedford, Indiana, limestone—is made up of a center block with entrances on either side fronted by a Doric colonnade; the twenty-two limestone columns are each 40 feet high and weigh twenty tons. Flanking this block are wings ending in pavilions. The entire Front Street façade stretches 750 feet, or about two and a half city blocks.

Behind the entrance block rises a central pavilion, marking the station's major interior space. Union Station's vast Great Hall (originally called the ticket lobby) resembles a Roman basilica, except that the ceiling is a coffered segmental barrel vault of Guastavino tile, instead of being flat. Clerestory windows line the long side walls, and more light enters from the four-story windows located in the vaulted vestibules at either end of the room. The long list of stations, from Halifax to Vancouver, served by the railroads that used the station circles the room below the crown molding. The walls are Zumbro stone from Minnesota, and the floor is Tennessee marble.

Ticket windows occupied one wall, an information booth stood in the center of the room, and opposite the Front Street entrance, under pairs of Corinthian columns and pilasters, a ramp led down to the waiting room–concourse. From there, stairways gave access to the train platforms above: the tracks, which ran parallel to the station, were raised on a viaduct. The ramp crossed a lower passageway that connected with the baggage and post office level below the waiting room–concourse. The ramp system was similar to the one connecting the waiting room with the upper and lower concourses in New York's Grand Central Terminal.

Ross and MacDonald, with the Toronto architects Sproatt and Rolph, also designed the Royal York Hotel. Built by the CPR and opened in 1929, the hotel is across Front Street from the station (and connected to it by tunnel). The thousand-room hotel was then the largest in Canada. Resembling a New York skyscraper with setbacks, the twenty-eight-story steel-frame building is faced with Bedford, Indiana, limestone. There are hints of the Gothic in the second story windows (Sproatt was a Gothicist) and of the château style in the steeply sloped copper-covered roof.

The handsome two-story lobby is ringed by marble columns and a balcony under a beamed ceiling.

At its center is a four-faced clock and a stairway descending to the retail level's shops and services. The Imperial Room off the lobby, where Marlene Dietrich sang and Duke Ellington's orchestra played, and the wood-paneled library with a fireplace on the mezzanine level are now respectively an event space and a meeting room. The hotel also boasted a concert hall and a roof garden. It gained several hundred rooms in a 1959 addition. A five-year, $100-million program to refurbish the guest rooms and add amenities was completed in 1993. The lobby and mezzanine level and the Library Bar were restored for $15 million in the early 2000s. Today the Fairmont Royal York has 1,363 rooms.

Subway lines (Toronto Transit Commission, or TTC) and commuter trains (GO Transit) were added to Union Station in the 1950s and 1960s. During the same period—the dark ages for railroads in North America—various redevelopment schemes were proposed to demolish the station and replace it with the

Figure 2.13

Union Station, Great Hall, Toronto, Ontario

Figure 2.14
Union Station, train shed, Toronto, Ontario

customary mixed-use, high-rise towers. Fortunately, these plans did not move forward.

The City of Toronto acquired Union Station in 2000. Ten years later the ongoing $800-million renovation and restoration project began. Union Station is the biggest and busiest railroad station in Canada, with more than 200,000 daily passengers—a figure that is expected to double by 2030. A main feature of the renovation is the erection of a flat glass canopy over the central portion of the train sheds, directly behind the station's Great Hall. Designed by Zeidler Partnership Architects, it re-creates the airy expansiveness of the old balloon train sheds that were made obsolete by the Bush sheds. The latter, though more efficient, could be dark and claustrophobic in a large installation such as Toronto's. The rest of Union Station's Bush sheds will be restored; just the steel trusses will remain for the portion under the canopy.

The renovation is under the general supervision of NORR Architects and Engineers. New commuter rail and subway concourses are under construction, and a lower-level retail concourse is being added below them. This requires the replacement of some 450 concrete columns that support the train tracks. New entrances, stairways, escalators, and elevators are being built to provide access to all levels of the station, and a restaurant will be part of the restored Great Hall.

3

CITY GATEWAYS

The train station in a metropolitan area was considered the ceremonial entrance to the city. For local politicians and businessmen, as well as the average citizen, it conferred status, signaled progress, and promised future economic growth. Architecturally, the train station ranked among the most important buildings in the downtown; it could even be the centerpiece of the city's urban plan. Gala parades and marching bands and florid speeches accompanied its opening.

Some major city train stations, still standing but bereft of their traditional use and lacking a new one and therefore a reason for being, have fared poorly. The abandoned Union Terminal in Buffalo, New York, is one example. Another is Detroit's Michigan Central Station, which has become the poster child for urban decay.

Cleveland's Terminal Tower was designed to be the city's landmark building and still is, after almost ninety years. Its traditional uses—transit center, shops, restaurants, and offices—are very much in evidence today, although they have assumed new forms.

TOWER CITY CENTER
(formerly Terminal Tower)
1930, Graham, Anderson, Probst and White
Public Square, Cleveland, OH

Terminal Tower was built by the Van Sweringen brothers, Oris Paxton (1879–1936) and Mantis James (1881–1935), popularly referred to as "O. P." and "M. J." or collectively as "the Vans." Shy and secretive, the Van Sweringens' reclusiveness probably accounts for their relative obscurity compared to the Morgans, Vanderbilts, and Goulds, but at the height of their power (the year Terminal Tower opened) the brothers controlled seven railroads—the Chesapeake and Ohio (C&O), Nickel Plate, Erie, Pere Marquette, Wheeling and Lake Erie, Missouri Pacific, and Chicago and Eastern Illinois—and had interests in several more. Altogether the lines covered more than 29,000 miles, a tenth of the US railroad mileage and "the largest single segment of the country's transportation system."[10]

Civic pride demands a fitting gateway and it is in the best interest of the railroad to do its share.

JOHN A. DROEGE,
Passenger Terminals and Trains

The brothers never married, and throughout their lives they worked closely together and kept their own counsel. A business magazine referred to them as the bachelors of railroading. Through an interlocking network of syndicates and holding companies, they also invested in trucking, rapid transit, coal mining, and Cleveland real estate.

The Van Sweringen brothers arrived in Cleveland at a young age. Their mother had died, and their father had turned into an alcoholic (he had been severely wounded at Gettysburg during the Civil War and seemingly could not find long-term employment afterward). They left school after eighth grade and found their way into real estate, after working for others and starting their own—mostly unsuccessful —businesses. In 1905, in their early twenties and determined to succeed, the brothers acquired 1,400 acres in what is now Shaker Heights, east of Cleveland. Their idea was to create a planned community for well-to-do businessmen who desired a suburban retreat. One of their models was Roland Park, in Baltimore, Maryland, an early planned commuter suburb.

To get the new residents back and forth quickly, the brothers decided to build the Shaker Heights Rapid Transit line. In 1916, they bought their first railroad, the Nickel Plate, in part to acquire needed right-of-way. The next requirement was a downtown terminus. They picked Public Square, Cleveland's traditional civic center, and began to buy property there. For the needed capital, they sought out investors in Cleveland and beyond, and they proved to be adept coalition builders and negotiators.

Now that they were in the real estate and the transportation business, the Van Sweringens expanded their ideas about the transit line's downtown terminal to include the railroads that passed through Cleveland several blocks away, on the south shore of Lake Erie. However, this put them in conflict with the 1903 "Group Plan" for Cleveland, which had been developed by an architects' commission headed by Daniel Burnham. Inspired by the 1893 Chicago World's Fair and the growing City Beautiful movement, the plan called for a new civic center consisting of major public buildings to be located between Public Square and

the lakefront, terminating in a new lakeside train station. (This plan was later executed, minus the train station, locating City Hall, the courthouse, the library, and other buildings in a park setting now known as the Cleveland Mall.)

The Van Sweringens matured their scheme for a terminal at Public Square during World War I. The railroads (with the exception of the Pennsylvania Railroad) were gradually brought to accept the idea, even though the downtown terminal would be operationally inefficient and would require them to build stub end tracks and elevated approaches to Public Square from the main rail lines near the lake and to switch to electric engines, since steam locomotives were prohibited from operating in the city.

Public Square, while still a transit hub, had gone through some hard times as Cleveland's commercial development migrated further west along Euclid Avenue. Four- and five-story buildings full of down-and-out tenants stood on the brothers' property. The first physical evidence of their attempt to return the square to its earlier prominence was the Hotel Cleveland. Designed by Graham, Anderson, Probst and White, the successor firm to D. H. Burnham and Company, the twelve-story hotel opened in 1918. The Van Sweringens formed the Cleveland Union Terminal Company the same year and hired the same architects to design it.

The new terminal would combine railroads, public transit, stores, and offices and would involve electrified rail operations and air rights development. Many of these ideas, down to the use of ramps instead of stairways, were adopted from New York's Grand Central Terminal (H. D. Jouett, Grand Central's engineer, was later brought in as construction engineer in Cleveland). The main terminal building, to be built next to the hotel, was a Y-shape high-rise structure whose wings spread out from a short clock tower.

Because it ran counter to the earlier plan for a new lakeside rail station and favored the Van Sweringens because of their previous investments in Public Square, the Terminal Tower idea proved politically controversial. But the brothers' bold proposal survived a local public referendum in 1919 and subsequent challenges

Figure 3.1
Terminal Tower, Cleveland, Ohio

at the federal level. In the same year, the Van Sweringens announced that the abbreviated tower shown in the earlier drawings would be replaced by a much higher one, making up 75 percent of the now fifty-two-story building. And the tower was to be set back behind an entrance lobby. Angled wings connected the central tower to the hotel building on one side and a symmetrical structure on the other, balancing the composition.

The brothers were influenced by two important buildings that had appeared during the previous decade in New York City. They were Cass Gilbert's sixty-story Woolworth Building of 1913, and McKim, Mead and White's Municipal Building, forty stories high, that opened the following year. The latter had angled wings and a tower culminating in a structure that resembled a Greek temple, which became a model

for Cleveland's tower. The main entrance off Public Square was marked by seven soaring arches separated by Ionic columns that looked more like the grand entrance to a train station than the former version's single arched opening.

Following the clearance of over a thousand buildings, excavation began in 1922 for the steel and concrete piers to support the office building and tower at street level and the concourse and track levels below it. Using the Chicago or open caisson method, eighty-seven caissons several feet in diameter were sunk to bedrock 250 feet below the surface. By 1926, ironworkers were assembling the steel frame.

Terminal Tower was completed in 1930. Gray limestone covered the steel frame; the floors were of reinforced concrete. Inside the main doors was a two-story entrance lobby with a coffered, barrel-vaulted ceiling and walls of Botticino marble. It was lit by high arched windows and chandeliers. The floor was of pink Tennessee marble, and murals by Jules Guerin, an architectural illustrator who did perspective drawings for Daniel Burnham's famous 1909 plan of Chicago, decorated the tympana of the arches.

There were numerous entrances from the surrounding streets. Four ramps led down to the concourse, waiting room, and ticket office. The concourse was lined with restaurants and shops—including a drugstore and newsstands—operated by the Fred Harvey organization (see chapter 8). Decorative metalwork in brass and bronze brightened the marble walls. From the concourse, stairways descended to twenty-four railroad tracks and ten rapid transit tracks located behind the tower complex. The tracks were overlaid with highways.

Floors twelve to fourteen in the tower, next to the hotel, housed the brothers' private apartment, including a two-story library–living room, dining rooms, and bedrooms; they used it for business meetings. Years later, when the C&O Railroad had its headquarters in the building, it was named the Greenbrier Suite (the railroad owned the Greenbrier Hotel, in White Sulphur Springs, Virginia) and hosted visiting railroad officials and dignitaries. Subsequently restored as a private law office, it is not open to the public except on special occasions.

Terminal Tower alone took up about half of the thirty-five-acre site. Three eighteen-story buildings—Medical Arts, Builders Exchange, and Midland Bank—stood nearby, built on air rights (they are currently known as the Landmark Office Towers). A twelve-story structure, a counterpart to the Hotel Cleveland, was under construction for the Higbee Department Store that had earlier moved out of Public Square and that the Van Sweringens had acquired. A post office was also being built.

Terminal Tower stood where home plate would have been on Public Square, facing the 1894 Soldiers and Sailors Monument (at first base) and the Mall and lakefront (at third base). For several decades the tower was the tallest building in North America outside of New York City. It was illuminated at

Figure 3.2
Terminal Tower, lobby, Cleveland, Ohio

night with floodlights, and the rotating light on its top proved powerful enough to serve as a beacon for incoming ships and airplanes. From the observation floor at the top, viewers could see evidence of an expanding metropolitan area, knit together by rapid transit. According to a contemporary promotional publication, "the Public Square, heart of the city and hub of urban transportation, becomes the gateway of convenient travel."[11]

The Van Sweringens' real estate and transportation empire collapsed in the wake of the Depression. Their new downtown office space stood empty, and some of their railroads went bankrupt. The brothers died within a year of each other in the mid-1930s, before the economic recovery had begun.

Cleveland's rapid transit system was expanded in the 1950s, and in the following decade the city became the first in the United States to offer a direct transit link to its airport. After the private railroads ended intercity rail service to Terminal Tower in the 1970s, Amtrak decided not to use the station, instead constructing the current Lakefront Station. Shortly thereafter, the private rapid transit services, centering on Terminal Tower, were merged into the Greater Cleveland Regional Transit Authority (RTA).

Forest City Enterprises bought Terminal Tower in 1990 and initiated a $400-million redevelopment, producing a three-level shopping mall designed by RTKL Associates. Renamed Tower City Center, the building contains seventy-five specialty shops, six restaurants, and a movie theater. The track area became a parking garage. The rapid transit facilities were rebuilt, and two new office towers were added. In 2010, the Forest City group spent $40 million to restore the tower's façade and upgrade the windows and lighting. The hotel is now the Renaissance Cleveland Hotel, and the former Higbee's Department Store is home to the Jack Cleveland Casino. The group sold Terminal Tower in the fall of 2016 for $38.5 million; its new owners plan to convert twelve of its lower floors to apartments.

In the 1950s Shaker Heights began to do away with its restrictive covenants designed to exclude blacks and other residents considered to be undesirable and initiated a policy of integration and inclusion, which has continued. It remains an attractive community and a desirable place to live. The Cleveland RTA Green Line still connects Terminal Tower with Shaker Heights, heading out of the city in the median strip along the tree-lined Shaker Boulevard; stopping at Shaker Square, the shopping center the brothers envisioned; and passing Tudor revival homes set back on ample lawns.

No park, building, or university bears the Van Sweringen name, but the citizens of Cleveland recognize that the enigmatic urban visionaries who conceived and executed their own master plan for the city and erected its signature building created the enduring symbol of Cleveland.

STATION SQUARE
(formerly the Pittsburgh and Lake Erie [P&LE] Railroad complex)
1901, William George Burns
Smithfield and West Carson Sts., Pittsburgh, PA

Across the Monongahela River from the Golden Triangle, at the end of Gustav Lindenthal's rare lenticular-trussed Smithfield Street Bridge (1883, expanded in 1891) sits the P&LE Railroad complex. Besides the station building, it encompasses a freight depot, office annex, and warehouse. Its significance lies in its transformation into Station Square, with new offices, restaurants, and shops, plus other attractions. A top tourist site in Pittsburgh, it draws three million visitors a year, including many city residents.

Station Square was the creation of the Pittsburgh History and Landmarks Foundation, cofounded in 1964 by Arthur Ziegler (who still serves as its president), and the Allegheny Foundation, headed by the late Richard Mellon Scaife. At that time, passenger rail was in free fall, and the isolated industrial site was becoming a commercial wasteland. The forty-acre railroad complex was slated for clearance to make way for a $400-million redevelopment project that included residential and office space, a hospital, hotel, and convention center.

This scheme was never carried out, and in 1976 the foundation, with Allegheny Foundation financing, leased the property from the railroad. Its intention was to show that historic preservation was not incompatible with large-scale commercial redevelopment and could succeed economically, without any government subsidy. During the following fifteen years, $45 million (nearly $100 million in 2016 dollars) in private funds was invested to convert five railroad buildings to new uses. Additional structures —a hotel, parking garage, and other amenities such as the Riverwalk—were built later. Featuring shopping and entertainment, Station Square today is one of the largest and most successful examples of adaptive reuse in the United States.

The centerpiece is William Burns's station building, whose staid exterior gives no indication of what

Figure 3.3
Station Square, waiting room, Pittsburgh, Pennsylvania
(courtesy of Jim Judkis)

lies within: a magnificent two-story, barrel-vaulted, skylit waiting room that critics have called one of the finest Edwardian interiors in the city. It was finished by Crossman and Sturdy, a Chicago firm of interior decorators and furnishers. The grand marble staircase at one end leads to a two-story arcaded court and the main entrance from Smithfield Street. The fanlight over the track entrance at the other end is filled with painted glass, the same material used in the skylight. Faux marble Corinthian columns separate the central space from narrower areas on either side, like the nave and side aisles of a cathedral. The waiting room is surrounded on the second level by Palladian windows, also filled with painted glass. The mosaic floor and mahogany woodwork are original.

A key to the early success of Station Square was finding the right tenant for the space. That turned out to be C. A. Muer of Detroit, Michigan, who had a chain of seafood restaurants. In 1978, following a $2.7-million restoration that included removing the roofing material that covered the skylight, Muer opened his Grand Concourse Restaurant, with a bar on one side. It immediately became popular and remains in operation. Other than the new ceiling chandeliers and restaurant furniture, the waiting room looks as it must have when it first welcomed passengers.

The P&LE Railroad began operating in 1879 and ten years later came under the control of the New York Central, which wanted access to Pittsburgh and the steel industry to compete with the Pennsylvania Railroad. The P&LE hauled mainly the ingredients for steel—coal, coke, iron ore, and limestone —as well as the finished product, and it became so prosperous in doing so, in proportion to its relatively short mileage, that it was known as the Little Giant. It also had a passenger service, and its lavish

Figure 3.4
Station Square, Pittsburgh, Pennsylvania (courtesy of
Pittsburgh History & Landmarks Foundation)

accommodations in Pittsburgh, the railroad's headquarters, matched its reputation.

Burns was born in Toronto and began his career as a carpenter. He worked as an apprentice and draftsman in architects' offices there and gained more experience in New York City. He later moved to Pittsburgh, where he was appointed staff architect for the P&LE Railroad. In 1899 he was given the job of designing its new headquarters (he later worked for Pittsburgh architectural firms and then returned to Toronto and opened his own firm).

Burns's seven-story, steel-frame, Commercial style building is faced with stone, brick, and terra-cotta. A cast-iron portico marks the main entrance on Smithfield Street. At the top of the building is a pedimented gable that displays important dates for the railroad and a steam locomotive. Below the wide cornice appears some beaux arts decoration: swags and cartouches. The structure is U-shape, and the open court at the rear provides light for the waiting room. The station building was restored at a cost of $6.8 million and reopened as office space in 1985. The entrance is now at street level, through the restaurant. The Pittsburgh History and Landmarks Foundation has offices on the fourth floor.

Adjacent to the station building is the 1897 freight depot, with four adjoining two-story, steel-frame, brick-faced sections—each with a central monitor and exposed interior trusses. The freight depot was restored for $9 million and reopened in 1979 as the Shops at Station Square.

The next building to be done over was the seven-story central warehouse, a steel and concrete structure faced with brick that had been built in 1917. The building, with an inner section removed to create a central atrium, was converted to office space in 1982 for $24 million and renamed Commerce Court. The six-story, brick-faced Annex office building, constructed in 1916 at Smithfield and West Carson Streets, was renovated for office space in 1984 for $2.2 million and is now called the Gatehouse.

A Sheraton Hotel at Station Square opened in 1981. The site has expended over the years to cover fifty-two acres. The Pittsburgh History and Landmarks

Foundation, which acquired ownership of the station building and other property in 1987, sold its interest to Forest City Enterprises in 1994.

THE PENNSYLVANIAN
(formerly the Pennsylvania Railroad Station)
1902, D. H. Burnham and Company
1100 Liberty Ave., Pittsburgh, PA

Not to be outdone, for its new station in Pittsburgh, the Pennsylvania Railroad brought in Daniel H. Burnham, the man largely responsible for the classical architecture of the 1893 Chicago World's Fair. He did not disappoint.

Prominently located at the northern apex of the Golden Triangle and at the head of Liberty Avenue, one of Pittsburgh's major streets, the present building is the fourth station on the site (the second one was burned during the riots that accompanied the Great Railroad Strike of 1877). Burnham took advantage of the street layout and the rise in topography to create the rotunda, his frontispiece for the station–office building. This grand gateway to the city is "unique among monuments of the Railroad Age,"

Figure 3.5

The Pennsylvanian, Pittsburgh, Pennsylvania (courtesy of Pittsburgh History & Landmarks Foundation)

according to James D. Van Trump (an architectural historian and cofounder, with Arthur Ziegler, of the Pittsburgh History and Landmarks Foundation).[12]

The curved approach road slopes up to the rotunda, built in the beaux arts style with terra-cotta tile over a steel frame. Four large corner pavilions with semicircular arches anchor the structure. It consists of four broad elliptical arches supporting a coffered pendentive dome under a lantern and skylight. In the spandrels between the arches, smiling female heads crowned with acanthus leaves beam down over the names of the four major cities served by the railroad: New York, Philadelphia, Pittsburgh, and Chicago. More female heads and urns appear on the corner pavilions. The beaux arts decorative motif is carried over to the twelve-story office building behind the structure, in the form of broken pediments and cartouches interspersed with lions' heads.

The rotunda, a porch for vehicles (or a glorified cab stand), formed the entrance to the station's waiting room. Like its counterpart in the P&LE Railroad Station across the Monongahela River, this is a large (70 by 160 feet), two-story open space lit by a skylight, but unlike the waiting room in the P&LE station, this one is flat rather than vaulted. Columns supporting round arches surround the room, and the coved ceiling curves inward to meet the skylight. Lounges for men and women, a restaurant, and ticket and baggage offices were located around the perimeter. The waiting room has a tile floor and is colorfully decorated with glazed terra-cotta tiles fronting the columns, more human faces and cartouches, and stenciling and decorative plasterwork overhead.

The Pennsylvania Railroad Station's recent history bears a striking resemblance to that of the P&LE station. Penn Station was also set to be demolished, as part of an enormous, 148-acre renewal plan announced by the railroad in 1966. Again, the plan was never implemented—due in part to the bankruptcy of the merged Penn Central Railroad in 1970 and the formation of Amtrak a year later.

Other ideas were floated over the next two decades —a federal office building, a new city hall, and housing for the elderly. But in 1986, Historic Landmarks

Figure 3.6

The Pennsylvanian, rotunda, Pittsburgh, Pennsylvania (courtesy of Pittsburgh History & Landmarks Foundation)

Figure 3.7

The Pennsylvanian, waiting room, Pittsburgh, Pennsylvania

for Living, a Philadelphia developer, acquired the property and began a $20-million restoration. Burnham's hollow-core structure, with its steel frame and brick and terra-cotta facing, was converted from railroad offices to residential apartments. The paint was removed from the skylight so that it once again admitted natural light. Offices (one of them occupied by an international architectural firm) remain on the ground floor and the two floors above. The former waiting room, renamed the Grand Concourse, is reserved for special events; it is not open to the public. Burnham's majestic rotunda can still be viewed and, absent the vehicles, is very photogenic—even though the entrance road leading to it has become a parking lot.

Meanwhile, train passengers have been relegated to a mingy Amtrak station constructed below grade in the former baggage-handling area and loading dock. No longer a gateway, it is more like the back entrance into Pittsburgh. *Sic transit gloria mundi.*

The station platform canopies in the rear date from the mid-twentieth century. Nearby are the David L. Lawrence Convention Center, built on the site of the Pennsylvania Railroad's former freight depot and redesigned by Rafael Vinoly in 2003; and the railroad's very heavily constructed, double-decked Fort Wayne Bridge that crosses the Allegheny River with a single Pennsylvania truss span (built in 1903 and raised in 1918). It is now owned by the Norfolk Southern Railroad.

PENNSYLVANIA STATION
(Amtrak) 1908, Frank Furness
100 S. French St., Wilmington, DE

Wilmington contains the greatest collection of Frank Furness's remaining railroad architecture. Much of his finest railroad work, such as Philadelphia's Baltimore and Ohio (B&O) Railroad Station—a fantastic Flemish Gothic combination of iron, masonry, and glass—has disappeared. Wilmington's Pennsylvania Railroad Station, rather plain by comparison; the adjacent office building; and the nearby B&O Railroad Station, more typical of Furness, have all been restored, and the last two have new uses.

In 1905 the Pennsylvania Railroad completed a three-mile-long grade-separation project through Wilmington, with a huge granite and steel viaduct wide enough to accommodate four tracks spanning French Street at the station. The new Pennsylvania

Figure 3.8

Pennsylvania Station (Amtrak), Wilmington, Delaware

Station, opened in 1908, replaced a Victorian street-level station. Furness literally wrapped his building around the viaduct and slung the concourse beneath it. In a subdued (for the architect) Italian Renaissance style, the steel-frame station sits on a granite base and is faced with brick and terra-cotta; its hip roof is covered with tile.

A three-story clock tower that once housed the station agent's office marks the narrower Front Street section, which had a small waiting room at track level for southbound trains. Opposite it, in the much wider portion of the station, were two-story, classically styled waiting rooms for men and women, lit by large arched windows. The concourse was below them.

The architect arranged his station with two entrances from French Street, which runs perpendicular to the tracks. The entrance from Front Street, which parallels them, leads to the station's major axis. It proceeds past stairways up to the track platforms and terminates at Furness's wonderful metal staircase (reminiscent of the one he designed for the B&O's Philadelphia station) that ascends to the waiting rooms. The concourse ceiling was the station's armature, with the tremendous riveted steel beams and brick jack arches that supported the tracks (and

Figure 3.9
Pennsylvania Station (Amtrak), stairway,
Wilmington, Delaware

the trains) all exposed. The concourse presents Furness at his finest: a rational plan married to powerful architectonic—and idiosyncratic—expression.

"The essence of Furness's work was industrial realism, to show the materials and systems out of which modern buildings were made, not to hide them behind veneers," according to Michael J. Lewis an architectural historian and biographer of Furness. "He first perfected this language of modern metal and masonry construction in his 1886 B&O station in Philadelphia, which was demolished in the 1960s. Since then, the Wilmington station has been the last important survivor of his urban railroad work."[13]

Amtrak's plan to restore the station proved controversial in some quarters, since the agency intended to apply what it calls contemporary finishes to Furness's industrial strength concourse—with one of the models being New York's current Penn Station, hardly a paragon of good design. However, the two-year, $38-million restoration by Wilmington's Bernardon, Haber, Holloway Architects was completed in 2011 with generally laudable results.

The exterior was restored and waterproofed (the track structure over the concourse had leaked), and

a high-level platform for Amtrak's Acela trains was added. The men's and women's waiting rooms, with their high beamed ceilings (closed in a 1984 Amtrak renovation that made the concourse into the waiting room), have been refurbished as event spaces. The restored grand staircase leading to them has regained its former prominence. A new access ramp from the street for people with disabilities and new elevators and escalators have been installed, along with a new heating, ventilating, and air-conditioning (HVAC) system. In the concourse–waiting room, the ceramic tile and wooden benches that surrounded the support columns have been replaced by tubular steel enclosures and long rows of metal seating. A new ticket office and train information display panels have been added. While partly obscuring Furness's metal and masonry ceiling, the new light-emitting diode (LED) lighting system makes the space more legible. The station has been renamed the Joseph R. Biden Railroad Station in honor of the former US vice president and senator from Delaware, a long-time train rider between Wilmington and Washington, D.C.

PENNSYLVANIA RAILROAD OFFICE BUILDING
1905, Frank Furness
112 S. French St., Wilmington, DE

The similarly restrained five-story railroad office building adjacent to the train station (once connected

Figure 3.10
Pennsylvania Railroad Office Building,
Wilmington, Delaware

Figure 3.11
B&O Railroad Station,
Wilmington, Delaware

to it by a second-story enclosed walkway) likewise has a tile hip roof and a matching set of dormers. It is also a steel-frame structure, faced with brick and terra-cotta. Pilasters divide the bays of square-headed windows.

The Penn-Central Company sold the building in 1968, and it stood empty for a time while various redevelopment schemes were proposed. Very little remains of the original interior. The central double-loaded corridors were converted to an open floor plan during a 2003 renovation, when new mechanical and electrical systems were installed. In 2007, ING Direct Bank, headquartered in Wilmington, occupied the building and spent $8 million renovating it for offices. New owners acquired ING Direct Bank in 2011, and the building is currently for rent.

B&O RAILROAD STATION
1888, Frank Furness
S. Market and Water Sts., Wilmington, DE

More representative of Furness's unique designs is Wilmington's small former B&O Railroad Station. It and a station in Aberdeen, Maryland, are the only survivors of the two dozen or more stations the architect crafted for the B&O's Philadelphia line. The fractured roofline, which dominates the building and presents a wide range of dormers, window treatments, and shaped chimneys, steps down in stages from a high hip roof to one-story pavilions at either end. The ground story of the building is brick; the upper story is wood covered with slate. The entrance through a two-story vestibule under a pyramidal roof led to men's and women's waiting rooms with fireplaces, a ticket office, a baggage room, and other areas. The second floor was devoted to offices.

The building later became a freight station and was abandoned for several years. It survived a fire but was in a state of near-collapse in 2000 when ING Direct Bank bought it and spent $1.3 million to restore it for use as a conference center. The restoration was completed the following year. Timber cribbing and a steel platform allowed contractors to raise the building two feet and place it on a new foundation. Little remains of the original interior except the fireplaces and stairway.

Wilmington's Tevebaugh Associates was the architect for the B&O Railroad Station conversion, as well as the simpatico two-story parking structure of brick, cast stone, and terra-cotta located between the station and the Pennsylvania Railroad Office Building. In 2007, James Tevebaugh and others formed the Friends of Furness Railroad District to celebrate and promote Furness's three railroad buildings in

Wilmington. The Railroad District is an important part of the multimillion-dollar redevelopment of the riverfront by the city and state. Since the formation of the Riverfront Development Corporation in 1996, the blocks surrounding the train stations, once the home of industries such as shipbuilding, have been transformed from a derelict area consisting mostly of parking lots to a successful commercial district with a market, restaurants, hotels, banks, apartment buildings, businesses, and arts organizations.

MAIN STREET STATION
1901, Wilson, Harris and Richards
1500 E. Main St., Richmond, VA

Suddenly encountering the floodlit façade of Main Street Station at night is a little like being in Venice or Paris and coming unexpectedly on the illuminated front of a landmark church or hotel. The building, by the successor firm to Wilson Brothers, architects and engineers of the great Philadelphia train sheds, is impressive. It is also a survivor, both of a major fire in 1983 that destroyed the roof and of half a dozen floods, the latest in 2004. In addition, there were the usual miscues concerning its future use after the station closed in 1975. However, rail passenger service returned in 2003, and it appears that Main Street Station will continue to be a train station.

It was built by the C&O and Seaboard Airline railroads. The steep hip roof, tall chimneys, elaborately decorated dormers, and tower are all indicative of the French Renaissance style. A broad flight of steps ascends to five segmentally arched openings that lead to the entrance lobby. The ground story is faced with stone. The high second story, of brick with terra-cotta decoration, features a loggia with five round arches. Square-headed windows define the third story below the cornice. Two more floors lie under the red tile roof.

When the station opened, the first floor held the ticket office, waiting rooms for blacks in those segregated days, and a rear baggage room. The waiting room for whites, a ladies' lounge, and a dining room were on the second floor. Upper floors were used for

Figure 3.12

Main Street Station, Richmond, Virginia

offices—for example, the fourth floor housed the offices of the Railroad Young Men's Christian Association (YMCA; see chapter 11), which moved to a new building in 1907.

Behind the station was a large (123 by 517 feet) pitched roof train shed, open at the ends and sides, that covered six stub end tracks and had wide overhangs on either side to shelter the through tracks. Modified Warren trusses of riveted steel supported the roof, which had two central monitors running its length. Trains approached the station on a new steel viaduct—those of the C&O, a major east-west route, on one side and those of the Seaboard Air Line, running north-south, on the other.

Considering what happened following Amtrak's departure in 1975, it is a wonder that the station is still there. First it was empty and vandalized for five years before a local architectural firm announced a planned multimillion-dollar renovation to put shops and a restaurant in the head house and make the train shed into a discount mall. The firm acquired the station in 1983, not long before a six-alarm fire of unknown origin destroyed the roof. Nevertheless, the restoration work continued, and the roof was rebuilt with ceramic tiles manufactured by the same firm that had supplied the original ones. The mall opened in 1985, but it failed to attract a sufficient number of shoppers. The restaurant started serving customers two years later, just days before a major flood forced it to shut its doors. By 1988, both the mall and restaurant were closed, and the building was again vacant.

At this point, the state and city became involved. In 1989, the Commonwealth of Virginia bought the station for $7.9 million and used it to house state offices. And in 1993, the City of Richmond secured sufficient funds to pay for architecture and engineering plans, construction, and purchasing the building, which it did in 2003. The restoration, overseen by Gensler Architects, included new elevators and adding reinforcing steel to the interior.

Meanwhile, the major changes in the Shockoe Bottom neighborhood surrounding the station were the 1985 construction of I-95 through Richmond, which loops around the building's west side and pretty much overwhelms it, and the installation of a $143-million flood wall in the following decade to prevent the James River from flooding the area. Unfortunately, the wall did not prevent the damaging effects of a hurricane in 2004, when the water came not from the river but from the city's higher elevations, which had been deluged by rain.

Main Street Station now has a visitors' center on the first floor. The two-story second-floor waiting room, whose high arched windows overlook the loggia, is mostly open space, with tables and chairs under a beamed ceiling supported by tall Corinthian columns (mostly replacements for the originals that were destroyed in the 1983 fire). The beautifully restored women's lounge has an ornate fireplace mantel and upholstered chairs, and the former dining room offers comfortable furniture and historic photographs of the station. The concourse between the station and the train shed is the new waiting room, with benches.

The solid walls that had enclosed the train shed when it became a discount mall, and later state offices, were removed and replaced in 2017 with glass windows. The gable ends were also glassed in. The steel trusses have been refurbished and a new timber roof put on. The total cost was about $90 million. Current plans call for the reuse of the train shed as an event space and possible future market. An intermodal center, with buses, is also a possibility for the station complex. Main Street Station will serve as a gateway into

Figure 3.13
Main Street Station, waiting room, Richmond, Virginia

Figure 3.14
Science Museum of Virginia,
Richmond, Virginia

the city, according to the project development manager for the City of Richmond (see chapter 11).

The fortunes of the adjacent 17th Street Market (the first market on the site opened in 1736) have followed the up-and-down career of the Main Street Station in recent years. In 2017, the City of Richmond began work to turn the market area into open-air pedestrian plaza with a fountain.

SCIENCE MUSEUM OF VIRGINIA
(formerly Broad Street Station,
Richmond, Fredericksburg and Potomac
and Atlantic Coast Line Railroads)
1919, John Russell Pope
2500 W. Broad St., Richmond, VA

The architect responsible for much of the look of official Washington, D.C., John Russell Pope, built only one train station, for the Richmond, Fredericksburg and Potomac and Atlantic Coast Line Railroads. Set well back from the street, a formal exercise in the neoclassical revival style, it has a broad, barrel-vaulted Doric portico, an octagonal drum supporting a low dome over the rotunda, identical wings balancing the composition, and a lengthy rear concourse—following the cruciform plan of a cathedral. The exterior material is Indiana limestone.

The rotunda, lit by large round-arched thermal windows over tall pairs of Ionic columns along the main longitudinal axis, was the waiting room; some of the original mahogany benches are still there. It has a terrazzo tile floor and pink Tennessee marble wainscoting. Niches in the corners led to baggage and rest rooms. Entrances under cast-iron and glass canopies at the ends of the wings also led to the rotunda along the secondary axis.

A copper covering for the dome replaced the original ceramic tile in 1955. Passenger rail service ceased in 1975, and the Commonwealth of Virginia acquired the station in the following year, intending to demolish it for an office park. The same year, the state allowed the new Science Museum of Virginia to occupy the building, a use that soon became permanent.

The museum has spent millions of dollars on renovations and the creation of new galleries since then. The rotunda, with a pendulum in the center, once again has a ticket office, but the tickets are to the science museum, which receives 340,000 visitors annually. One of the wings contains an exhibit on the history of the station; the main exhibits are in the concourse. Outside, the platform canopies still stand.

UNION PACIFIC RAILROAD STATION
1925, Carrere and Hastings
2603 Eastover Terr., Boise, ID

The railroad arrived late in Boise and left early, stranding Carrere and Hastings's strikingly handsome and beautifully sited Union Pacific station, one of the finest in the West. The building was carefully restored

Figure 3.15
Union Pacific Railroad Station, Boise, Idaho

in 1993, but the last Amtrak train departed four years later. Rail service is unlikely to return to Boise any time soon, and the city-owned structure is now an event space.

Although Boise was the state capitol, because it was fenced off by steep foothills on the east, it proved unattractive to mainline railroads until 1925. Then, after substantial cajoling and local contributions, Edward H. Harriman was finally persuaded to complete his Union Pacific Railroad line to the city.

Built in the Spanish colonial revival style, the station was constructed of local sandstone faced with stucco. The tower, wrought-iron grillwork, orange terra-cotta roof tiles, curvilinear parapets, arches, and decorative stonework surrounding the secondary entrances, are all typical of the style. These crisply assembled elements, and the well-proportioned, asymmetrically arranged two-story main block housing the waiting room, separated by the campanile from the one-story freight and baggage room wing, create a very pleasing composition.

The waiting room, lit by arched windows in the upper story and ceiling chandeliers, is open to the timber Howe roof trusses, which feature painted decorations. Three large arched doorways provide access to the street and track sides. At one end of the room are the ticket windows and at the other, under a balcony and stairway, a newsstand.

The Platt Gardens in front of the station, added in 1927, were named for Howard V. Platt—general manager of the Oregon Short Line Railroad (a subsidiary of the Union Pacific)—and designed by the Spanish landscape architect Ricardo Espino. Winding walkways, benches, rock grottoes, ponds, and native vegetation provided a welcome respite from the stress of travel. The station and gardens overlook Capitol Boulevard, at the end of which is the Idaho State Capitol. The boulevard, inspired by the City Beautiful movement, was completed in 1931.

Carrere and Hastings was a renowned and prolific New York architectural firm whose first major commission was for a St. Augustine, Florida, hotel built for Henry Flagler's Florida East Coast Railway (see chapter 8). Later the firm designed Flagler's mansion

Figure 3.16
Union Pacific Railroad Station, waiting room,
Boise, Idaho

in Palm Beach, Florida (see chapter 11), the New York Public Library, the original House and Senate office buildings in Washington, D.C., and many other prestigious structures in America and Europe.

The socially well-connected principals met as students at the École des Beaux-Arts in Paris, and both were draftsmen for McKim, Mead and White before starting their own firm. John Merven Carrere and Thomas S. Hastings were imbued with the beaux arts principles of classically derived civic architecture and axial planning exemplified by the Chicago World's Fair of 1893, which gave impetus to the City Beautiful movement. Carrere worked on city plans for Cleveland, Ohio, and Baltimore, Maryland. The depot was a major component of their 1924 Capitol Boulevard master plan for Boise that aligned the station's bell tower with the statehouse dome a mile and a quarter away and provided a dramatic entrance and overview of the state's capital.

The Union Pacific ended passenger service to Boise in 1971, and the station fell into disrepair. In 1990, the Morrison Knudsen Corporation, a large engineering firm headquartered in Boise, bought the building for $2 million and initiated a $3.4-million restoration. Completed in 1993, it included replacing the roof, restoring the exterior masonry and windows, and repainting the interior in its original colors. The waiting room benches, with brass armrests, were refinished. During the process, the Barkalow Brothers Company newsstand was uncovered, restored, and turned into a buffet counter. An elevator was installed in the tower, which until then had been closed to the public; it is now open to visitors, who can enjoy views of the city. New Amtrak ticketing and passenger facilities were added at one end of the building. The company's intention, besides restoring the rail station, was to highlight its significance in the history of Boise.

The engineering firm went bankrupt in 1995, the City of Boise acquired the station the following year, and the year after that Amtrak, which had restarted passenger service in 1977, ended it. Today, the building is a popular venue for weddings and other events. It is open to the public on Sundays and Mondays; the lovely gardens, though no longer welcoming train travelers, are popular as well.

KING STREET STATION
1906, Reed and Stem
303 S. Jackson St., Seattle, WA

The second Renaissance revival style King Street Station has recently enjoyed a renaissance of its own. Its change of fortune exemplifies the shifts in priorities in urban transportation over the past fifty years.

King Street Station was built by the Great Northern and Northern Pacific Railways, controlled by James J. Hill, who also built a mile-long tunnel to reach the station. Its twelve-story tower, closely modeled on the Saint Mark's Campanile in the Piazza San Marco in Venice, Italy, briefly made it the tallest building in Seattle, until the Smith Tower was constructed in 1914 with a similar profile. The two structures are major landmarks in Seattle.

Figure 3.17
King Street Station, Seattle, Washington (courtesy of David Honan)

The architects were one half of the design team for Grand Central Terminal in New York City. The surface of their steel-frame building in Seattle was granite and brick with cast stone and terra-cotta trim; the roof was of ceramic tile. The station represented an intermediate step in the development of the steel-frame high rise: it used the metal-cage form of construction, in which the walls are load bearing, and an interior metal frame carries the floor and roof loads. The tower, located at the corner of the structure's L shape, had four large clock faces and a glass pyramid at the top that was lighted at night, creating a beacon for the city.

Inside the main entrance from King Street was the Compass Room, whose terrazzo floor was inlaid with a compass. A stairway led to an upper-level entrance plaza on Jackson Street. The two-story waiting room, overlooked by a mezzanine floor with a small balcony (from which carolers once serenaded passengers at Christmastime) was lit by chandeliers and two sets of windows. Marble wainscoting with inlaid bands of colored glass mosaic tiles and a patterned terrazzo floor set with wooden benches provided the waiting room décor. Overhead was a beamed and paneled ceiling presenting a baroque swirl of decorative plaster coffers with intricate borders and moldings, rosettes, rinceau patterns (based on a running floral motif), and Ionic columns. The third floor was office space.

In 1967, the railroads completed a $250,000 remodeling of King Street Station. The main elements were a new asphalt shingle roof and a dropped ceiling in the waiting room that obscured the upper row of windows and the ornate plaster ceiling. The decorative plaster and marble was removed from the waiting room walls. The effect, despite the addition of fluorescent lighting, was to cheapen and darken the room.

Railroad passenger service was then entering its dark age. In the following decade, only a few trains a day called at Main Street Station. Reluctant to spend money in a falling market, the railroad companies reduced the maintenance they provided, and the building deteriorated.

Figure 3.18

King Street Station, waiting room, Seattle, Washington (courtesy of David Honan)

After Sound Transit, which operates the local commuter trains and light rail service, was established in the 1990s, and voters approved a new regional transit system, King Street Station's status in the community began to rise. Later in the decade, it became the site of facilities designed by Otak, an architectural and engineering firm, to accommodate commuter rail trains.

The ten-year, $55-million rehabilitation of the station began in 2003 with the Compass Room, whose floor insignia, marble wainscoting, and chandelier were restored. The program came to a halt for lack of funds, but it accelerated in 2008 when the City of Seattle bought the station from the railroads for $10 and hired Otak and later ZGF Architects to complete the restoration.

The forty-five-foot antenna and microwave dishes that had disfigured the tower were removed, the four clocks repaired, and the glass tower lantern relit. The leaking asphalt shingle roof of the station was replaced with a green ceramic tile roof, the same type it had had initially. An escalator that had been added on the side of the building was demolished, and the stairway, which had been closed, was reopened to the Jackson Street Plaza. The plaza over the years had been turned into a parking lot; reroofed, landscaped,

Figure 3.19
Union Station, Seattle, Washington (courtesy of David Honan)

and with nighttime lighting by period reproduction lamps on tall standards, it became once again an attractive secondary entrance to the station.

The demolition of the dropped ceiling in the waiting room revealed what train passengers had been missing for fifty years: the magnificent ornamental plaster ceiling, which was painstakingly restored. New versions of the chandeliers that had originally hung in the waiting room were installed, the marble wainscoting and plaster decoration was re-created, and the terrazzo floor was refinished.

Some 1,300 tons of steel were inserted as reinforcements to stabilize the building in case of an earthquake. The station had been slightly damaged during the 2001 Seattle earthquake (which was 6.8 on the Richter scale), the most powerful in the Pacific Northwest in half a century. There are new mechanical, electrical, and HVAC systems. Green architecture features such as a ground-source heat pump for heating

and cooling (via geothermal wells) were part of the rehabilitation.

The award-winning restoration was completed in 2013. King Street Station, host to some 17,500 passengers daily, is once again a beacon for Pioneer Square, the International District, and the city as a whole. In the summer of 2017, the Seattle Department of Transportation and the city's Office of Arts and Culture opened the first art exhibits on the station's third floor, which is to become a cultural center featuring art, lectures, and performances.

UNION STATION
1911, Daniel J. Patterson
S. Jackson St. and Fourth Ave., Seattle, WA

Not be outdone, Edward H. Harriman, who was president of the Union Pacific Railroad and was jousting with Hill for dominance in the Pacific Northwest, decided to build his own station across the street from the new King Street Station. He commissioned Daniel Patterson—a San Francisco architect who designed a number of stations and other buildings for the Southern Pacific Railroad, which Harriman also controlled (see chapter 11)—to draw up the plans.

The result, a plain, three-story box whose front was marked by a balcony, clock, and stylized pediment, was not one of the architect's best efforts, but it had two distinctions. One was its structure: a steel frame covered by reinforced concrete, a relatively early use of the material, and with a brick and cast stone veneer and a terra-cotta trim. The building's central section (behind the pediment) has a pitched roof; the two wings have hip roofs. The other distinction was the great barrel-vaulted interior, a single open space lit by skylights and a large thermal window at the far end. The coffered ceiling was supported by steel trusses. The wings on either side held waiting rooms for women and immigrants, a men's smoking room, barbershop, ticket office, and baggage room. (The railroads attracted immigrants by offering jobs and land; they traveled at reduced rates in special immigrant cars and had separate waiting rooms.)

The Chicago, Milwaukee, St. Paul and Pacific Railroad (the Milwaukee Road) also used Union Station. The building was vacated after passenger service ended in 1971. Later in the decade the station became an antiques warehouse and mall. In 1997, Nitze-Stagen, developers, purchased the building and—with Paul Allen, a cofounder of Microsoft, as a partner—completed a $23-million restoration two years later. The developers have also constructed several new multistory office buildings on land formerly occupied by the rail approaches.

Union Station is now headquarters for Sound Transit. The vast waiting room is mostly empty (it serves as an event space), but it has been handsomely decorated with lights outlining the longitudinal beams and vault ribs, stenciled anthemion designs in the tympana of the side arches, a Greek meander pattern under the crown molding, wall sconces, niches topped by plaster scallop shells, and green ceramic

Figure 3.20

Union Station, waiting room, Seattle, Washington (courtesy of David Honan)

tile wainscoting. Metal tables and chairs and a few oak waiting room benches sit on the tile floor.

US COURTHOUSE
(formerly Union Station)
1911, Reed and Stem; 1992 renovation
   and addition, Merritt and Pardini/TRA;
   Bassetti, Norton, Metler, Rekevics
1717 Pacific Ave., Tacoma, WA

The former Union Station, which gives the impression after dark of a cathedral of commerce with luminous stained glass windows, was the catalyst in the rebirth of downtown Tacoma. The restored station building and its conversion to a federal courthouse led to the rehabilitation of a district of derelict factories and warehouses district across Pacific Avenue as the new home for the University of Washington–Tacoma (Charles Moore created the campus master plan) in 1997, and the creation of three new museums. They are the adjacent Washington State History Museum (designed by Charles Moore and his

Figure 3.21
US Courthouse, Tacoma, Washington (courtesy of David Honan)

architectural partner Arthur Andersson and built in 1996), whose postmodern design the station clearly inspired; the Museum of Glass (Arthur Erickson, 2002), located behind the station and the Chihuly Bridge of Glass (Arthur Andersson, 2002) that connects the two buildings; and the Tacoma Museum of Art (Antoine Predock, 2003. Over $200 million was invested in these projects. Also in 2003, the $80-million Tacoma Link light rail line began operations. It connects the centrally located Union Station to the Convention Center and the Theater District, and to the Tacoma Dome and Freighthouse Square (the former freight terminal of the Milwaukee Road).

Union Station's nighttime glow is due to Dale Chihuly, a glass artist and a native son of Tacoma. Following restoration, the building took on a new life as the frontispiece for the courthouse and an informal gallery for Chihuly's artworks. In fact, the artist claims

that his glass sculptures for the station's rotunda marked the beginning of his monumental-scale work. Thanks to enlightened business and political leadership and talented artists and architects, Tacoma is a model of urban revival–and it all began with the train station.

The Northern Pacific Railway selected Tacoma, located on Commencement Bay near the southern end of Puget Sound, as its western terminus in 1873. When the railroad completed a direct route to the town in 1887, Tacoma became known as the City of Destiny. To the company's small wooden station were added an office building (1888) and a grand château style hotel (1893). The original station is gone, but the office building and the hotel still stand: the latter rose from the ashes to become the Stadium High School.

In 1906, the year that their King Street Station was

completed, Reed and Stem were hired to design the new station in Tacoma, built by the Northern Pacific, Great Northern, and Union Pacific railways. Reed and Stem designed roughly a hundred railroad stations, most of them in the West or Pacific Northwest; several were for the Northern Pacific Railway. They worked in a conservative second Renaissance revival or beaux arts style. The resulting structures were well planned and attractive to the eye, and the station in Tacoma is one of their best.

The central rotunda, flanking symmetrical wings, and clear, biaxial plan are all major elements of beaux arts architecture. Four shallow barrel vaults surround the ninety-foot-high central dome. Arched entrances are located front and rear. The cartouches that decorate the vault spandrels below the copper-covered dome are the only exterior decoration. Brick laid in Flemish bond (courses of brick laid with alternate headers and stretchers), with a limestone base and trim, faces the reinforced concrete structure. The dome has a steel frame.

Four semicircular vaults, enclosing balconies and large thermal windows, frame the open rotunda. This area, once the waiting room, now serves as the courthouse lobby and a sculpture gallery and event space. The wings on either side that housed the restaurant and ladies' waiting room have been converted to courtrooms. Four small corner spaces, also with balconies, contain stairways. A catering area now occupies the lower-level concourse; the former concourse extension over the tracks has been replaced in part by the new courthouse.

The rich finishes—oak entrance doors with bronze hardware, marble terrazzo floor and wainscoting, and the cast-iron clock case and columns and spandrel beams that support the balconies—are

Figure 3.22
US Courthouse, Tacoma, Washington (courtesy of Scott Lothes)

as appropriate to the station building's current use as they were originally. The dome's copper roof has been replaced and the skylight reopened to bring natural light into the rotunda. The station restoration and the new courthouse, which included seismic reinforcement, cost $57 million.

The major additions to the interior are Chihuly's artworks, especially the twenty-foot tall, cobalt blue chandelier *End of the Day*, which hangs in the center of the dome; *Water Reeds*, slender glass tubes that decorate the window above the main entrance; and the beautiful and colorful *Monarch Window* over the courtroom (formerly, the track) entrance. Particularly when viewed from outside at night, the combined effect is stunning. The dome's oculus and the barrel vaults are outlined with lights; the dome coffers are also lit.

Dozens of daily trains, including those of the Union Pacific Railroad and the Great Northern Railway, called at Union Station in the early decades of the twentieth century, but by the 1980s, only six remained. The last one left in 1984, following the construction of a smaller, plainer Amtrak station nearby. The building then stood empty until the City of Tacoma acquired it in 1987, after Congress had authorized its conversion to a US courthouse.

In back of the station, Tacoma's historic industrial waterfront, which developed after the railroad's arrival along a 1.5-mile inlet of Commencement Bay, was declared a Superfund site in the early 1980s. Pulp and lumber mills, chemical plants, refineries, and ore smelters had polluted the waterway over the past century with toxic substances and heavy metals (most of these industries have left, but a major shipbuilder remains).

The City of Tacoma led the $105-million cleanup, which was completed in 2006. The Thea Foss Waterway now features a shoreline promenade, marinas, parks, shops, restaurants, the Foss Waterway Seaport (a maritime museum), and over $100 million in residential development, including a 1903 cereal factory that was converted to loft apartments. In front of Union Station is *New Beginnings*, the 1984 bronze statue of a purposeful fortune seeker arriving with

bags, created by Larry Anderson, a Tacoma native, and installed for the city's centennial.

FREIGHTHOUSE SQUARE
(formerly the Milwaukee Road freight depot)
1909
430 E. 25th St., Tacoma, WA

Notable more for its conversion to a marketplace than for its architecture, Freighthouse Square was the Milwaukee Road's westernmost freight terminal. The two- and three-story wooden building with a pitched roof extends on a sloping site for three blocks along 25th Street between D and G Streets. Rebuilt after about half of the structure was destroyed in a 1992 fire set by a serial arsonist, it now houses some fifty specialty shops and restaurants. Freighthouse Square is also a transportation center serving passengers on the Tacoma Link light rail line and the Sound Transit commuter rail service. In the summer of 2017, a new station was nearing completion at Freighthouse Square, preparatory to making it a stop for Amtrak's Cascades trains operating between Vancouver, British Columbia, and Eugene, Oregon. The 1937 timber trestle approach to Freighthouse Square is being demolished and will be replaced with a two-track bridge.

GOVERNMENT CONFERENCE CENTER
(formerly Union Station)
1912, Ross and MacFarlane
2 Rideau St., Ottawa, ON

Nowhere in Canada is there a better example of the relationship between the railroad station, the hotel, and the center of the city than in Ottawa, the nation's capital. The train traveler in the first half of the twentieth century who emerged from under the marquee in front of Union Station would have looked across the street to the Château Laurier (if he did not use the underground connection between the station and the hotel). On the left, plainly visible and within easy walking distance, were the Parliament Buildings; closer still was Confederation Square, Ottawa's civic center and the site of the National War Memorial and

Figure 3.23
Government Conference Center, Ottawa, Ontario (Wikimedia Commons)

Figure 3.24
Government Conference Center, section, Ottawa, Ontario (courtesy of Public Services and Procurement, Canada)

commemorative events. The Grand Trunk Railway built both the station and the hotel. Although Ross and MacFarlane designed both buildings, the American architect Bradford Lee Gilbert shares some of the credit (see chapter 8).

The same firm that designed Toronto's Union Station and Hotel York took advantage of a sloping site next to the Rideau Canal in Ottawa, they also clothed their station in that city in classical array. The axial plan and five-part composition, expressed as a succession of hierarchical spaces centering on the great, barrel-vaulted waiting room, were tenets of the beaux arts school.

Giant Doric columns in antis (located between the side walls of a recessed entrance) below a plain entablature defined the square, five-story head house, which contained the entrance hall with offices above. Behind it, a separate section housed the grand stairway that descended to the waiting room. This ran crosswise to the head house and was clearly marked on the outside of the building by huge arched windows under elaborate hood moldings. Next was the ticket lobby and then the segmentally vaulted concourse that led out to the tracks and Bush train sheds.

The steel-frame structure sat on a rusticated granite base, and the brick walls were faced with limestone from Bedford, Indiana. Steel Warren trusses supported the vaults over the waiting room and concourse. It was no accident that the station closely resembled McKim, Mead and White's 1910 Pennsylvania Station in New York City (since demolished). Nowadays, the best way to experience the glory of the waiting room of that station, which was modeled on the Roman baths, is to visit Ottawa's Union Station, whose waiting room is a half-scale version of it.

Marble wainscoting and plaster walls imitating Travertine were the finishes in the entrance hall, stairway, and waiting room. The last, under a coffered plaster vault and surrounded by eight thermal windows and the same number of tall Corinthian columns (plaster over a steel armature), had wooden benches with reading lights. Multiglobe lamps on high bases and standards, similar to those in the original Penn Station, provided additional illumination. A special waiting room for government officials, with a marble mantelpiece, and a restaurant were located off the waiting room.

In the ticket lobby, travelers could book passage on either the Canadian Pacific or the Canadian National Railways. The sloping floor led down to the concourse, an open room that spanned the width of the station building and was lit by large windows at either end and a central band of windows in the coffered vault above.

The railroads' tenure at Union Station ended in 1966. Highways replaced the tracks, a new suburban station was built, and plans called for Union Station to be demolished. Instead, it became the Government Conference Center in the early 1970s. A new

entrance and canopy were constructed at the rear of the building, and translators' booths (for simultaneous translation) were installed in the waiting room. Murals depicting members of the First Nations, settlers, and construction scenes of the transcontinental Grand Trunk Pacific Railway (now the Canadian National Railway)—created by Frank Brangwyn, a well-known illustrator, for the Grand Trunk's corporate headquarters in London, England—were donated to the center and placed in the ticket lobby.

While organized tours were permitted, the center was not open to the general public. That is expected to change when the Senate, which has to vacate its home on Parliament Hill so that building can be restored, moves into the former station concourse in 2018. The Senate's plan to move was timely since the Government Conference Center was in need of rehabilitation anyway, the original conversion having been hasty and less than thorough. The $269-million renovation program calls for the floors to be reconstructed in the main entrance hall, the translators' booths to be removed, the waiting room restored, and the concourse ceiling to be repaired. The building will be structurally reinforced, and new electrical and mechanical systems will be installed.

GARE DU PALAIS
1916, Harry Edward Prindle
450 rue de la Gare du Palais, Quebec City, QC

The architect Harry Prindle, taking his cue from the Château Frontenac up on the bluff, designed a château style station that achieves monumentality despite its small scale. The Gare du Palais was built by the Canadian Pacific Railway. The name refers to the nearby former Intendant's Palace—home of the administrator of colony of New France, built in the late seventeenth and early eighteenth centuries.

The entrance pavilion, with a steep hip roof and two conical-roofed towers enclosing a massive, multiarched window, is particularly effective. A pair of brief wings bracket the center block; additional sections, also with entrances, angle off in the rear of the building. The use of colorful materials—red

Figure 3.25
Gare du Palais,
Quebec City, Quebec

brick with light gray limestone trim and contrasting dark metal roofs—gives the station additional
visual impact.

The entrance lobby, an elongated octagon with
galleries on either side and skylights overhead, is
a dramatic, lofty space whose walls of varicolored
brick and contrasting decorative patterns lend it
needed warmth. A row of ticket windows (currently
unused) lines one wall, and the surrounding rooms
would have held the usual station amenities such as a
restaurant and newsstand. A low archway leads to the
concourse, whose open expanse is lit by upper-level
windows. Steel Warren trusses with curved lower
chords support the ceiling.

The Gare du Palais is the architect's only significant structure in Canada. Harry Edward Prindle
(1873–1928) was briefly in charge of the drafting room
of the Canadian Pacific Railway's superintendent of
buildings in Montreal during the time the station was
designed. Born in New York City, Prindle attended
Cooper Union, studied art and architecture at other
New York institutions, and worked in several local
architectural offices before leaving to become the supervising architect of Cochise County, Arizona. He
later returned to New York and opened his own office.

The station was closed from 1976 to 1985, and at

Figure 3.26
Gare du Palais, entrance lobby,
Quebec City, Quebec

the end of that period it underwent major renovations. Since then, $1.2 million has been spent on a new heating system and environmental upgrades to the station; an additional $1.5 million is to be invested in improving the building's air-conditioning and other systems. Food vendors occupy about half of the concourse. Ticketing and waiting room facilities have been moved into an adjacent area. A steak house and a dentist are current tenants in the entrance lobby. Passenger traffic is increasing.

4

DOWN BY THE STATION

The train station, along with city hall and the courthouse, was one of the most important buildings in smaller cities and towns. (It still is, although it has sometimes been converted to a new use.) The station created the visitor's first impression, acted as the nerve center of the community, and served as the springboard for new development. In unsettled parts of the country, it was often the first substantial structure to be erected, and the town literally grew up around it. When the train arrived, sleepy localities stirred themselves into activity; when it left again, they settled back into somnolence. Many of the small-town stations that survived the near disappearance of the passenger train in the late twentieth century are now fulfilling one of their historic functions: providing the impetus for the construction of new buildings and town centers. Henry Hobson Richardson's station for the Old Colony Railroad at North Easton, Massachusetts, has all of the architectural qualities and amenities that made these buildings so central to the life of their respective locales.

Black people lived right by the railroad tracks and the train would shake their houses at night. I would hear it as a boy and I thought: I'm gonna make a song that sounds like that.

LITTLE RICHARD,
"When John Waters
Met Little Richard"

EASTON HISTORICAL SOCIETY
(formerly the Old Colony Railroad station)
1884, Henry Hobson Richardson
80 Mechanic St., North Easton, MA

The North Easton station building, designed by one of the great masters of nineteenth-century American architecture, suggests shelter, simplicity, and strength.

The dominant feature is the flared hip roof made of slate, which is supported on plain brackets with deep overhangs that shelter the doors and windows. Two wide clipped gable dormers adorn the trackside roof. These are absent on the street side of the station, which has a broad porte cochere.

The body of the two-story building is constructed of local granite with brownstone trim. Dual Syrian arches enclosing windows, doors (facing the tracks), and benches appear on the longer sides of the rectangular structure. The heads of snarling wolves (or dragons) decorate the wooden crossbeams dividing the windows. Between the arches on the track side is the

Figure 4.1
Easton Historical Society, North Easton, Massachusetts

slightly rounded agent's bay, its window of clear glass surrounded by bull's-eye panes. A long platform canopy once fronted the station. Frederick Law Olmsted landscaped the grounds.

The large, arched windows fill the interior with light. Located on either side of the entrance lobby and the agent's office were waiting rooms for men and women. Wood floors and ceilings and tall wainscoting of white oak make up the interior finishes. The beaded wainscoting has a curved profile in the public spaces and a flat one in the private ones.

North Easton's station is one of a group of about sixty stretching from New England through the mid-Atlantic states and to the Midwest that Richardson and the successor firm, Shepley, Rutan and Coolidge, designed for the Old Colony, the Boston and Albany, and several other railroads. Many of the stations have been demolished or abandoned. North Easton, one of the finest, is also one of the best preserved.

Richardson's collaboration with Olmsted on the Old Colony station (and on numerous stations for the Boston and Albany Railroad) extended to many other architectural works in North Easton and even as far away as Sherman, Wyoming (see chapter 14). These structures were commissioned by members of the Ames family. Frederick L. Ames, who hired Richardson and Olmsted to draw up the plans for the North Easton train station and paid $19,000 for its construction, was a director of the Old Colony Railroad and resident of the town. He was also a principal of the Oliver Ames and Sons Company, manufacturers of shovels.

Frederick Ames's great-grandfather manufactured the first metal-blade shovel in the United States in 1774, in West Bridgewater, Massachusetts. Prior to the American Revolution, wooden shovels were the norm in North America. Those with metal blades were imported from England under that country's colonialist

Figure 4.2
Easton Historical Society, entrance,
North Easton, Massachusetts

Figure 4.3
Easton Historical Society, women's waiting room,
North Easton, Massachusetts

economic policy, which dictated that the products of American agriculture be exchanged in trade for British finished products, including farm implements. In 1803, the Ames shovel company moved to North Easton, where it prospered. Twenty-five years later, Ames shovels broke ground for the nation's first railroad, the Baltimore and Ohio. Wielded by thousands of Irish, German, and black laborers, the shovels dug the country's early canals and cleared the way for its first turnpikes. Prospectors took the shovels into the Sierras during the gold rush, and they were used to build Civil War embankments and fortifications.

By that time, Oliver Ames and Sons Company was in the hands of Frederick Ames's father, Oliver Ames Jr., and uncle, Oakes Ames. The brothers were major backers of the Union Pacific Railroad, the eastern segment of the first transcontinental line—which nearly proved their undoing. In 1866, Oakes Ames was a congressman, the prime advocate of the transcontinental railroad, who steered the funding legislation through Congress. Oliver Ames Jr. was president of the Union Pacific Railroad, having ousted Thomas Durant from that position.

Durant had created the Credit Mobilier of America, a secretive company designed to siphon off profits from the construction of the Union Pacific, which was heavily subsidized by the federal government through cash and land grants. Construction stopped

briefly when the Ames brothers took over, but it began again when Durant was reinstated and again diverted profits. Oliver Ames and Sons Company invested in the Union Pacific Railroad and received contracts from it.

In 1872, a major scandal, fanned by a partisan press, erupted when Oakes Ames was accused of distributing Union Pacific Railroad stock to certain members of Congress in exchange for their political support. The recipients turned on Ames, who claimed he had done nothing illegal. Nevertheless, he was censured by the House of Representatives in February 1873. He returned to North Easton the following month and, in a poignant address to his constituents, said he had sold $16,000 worth of Union Pacific Railroad stock to eleven members of Congress at the same price he paid for it, and that the investigating committee had not proved him guilty of bribery. Ames thanked the crowd for their faith in his honor, truth, and integrity. He died two months later.

Wishing to dispel the stigma of the Credit Mobilier scandal, Ames family members commissioned Richardson and Olmsted to design several civic structures for North Easton: the Oakes Ames Memorial Hall (1881); the Oliver Ames Memorial Library (1883); and the Rockery, a Civil War memorial (1884). There was also Richardson's famous rockbound Gate Lodge for Langwater, Frederick Ames's estate (1881). Olmsted's

Figure 4.4
Maine Central Railroad Station, Conway, New Hampshire

Figure 4.5
Erie Railroad Station, Tuxedo, New York

landscaping was an integral part of all these projects, which makes North Easton a showcase for the work of two of America's greatest practitioners of architecture and landscape design.

Across the tracks from the train station are the solidly constructed former stone factory buildings of the Oliver Ames and Sons Company. Workers' housing is located in the surrounding areas, and the estates of the owners are on the periphery—a classic company town (the company still exists as Ames True Temper and still makes shovels, although no longer in North Easton). The descendants of Frederick Ames still occupy Langwater, and family members remain major philanthropists. The North Easton train station was closed in 1958. The Ames family bought it in 1969 from the Pennsylvania Railroad for $15,000 and gave it to the Easton Historical Society, which restored the building as a museum. There is a plan to restore service on the line as part of the Massachusetts South Coast Rail project.

Two of Richardson's Massachusetts stations for the Boston and Albany Railroad, at Framingham (1885) and Palmer (1883), have been converted to restaurants, with much of their interiors intact.

MAINE CENTRAL RAILROAD STATION
1874, Nathaniel J. Bradlee
38 Norcross Circle, Conway, NH

Nathaniel Bradlee's station building uses a railroad station design that is rare and perhaps unique in the United States. Based on Russian rural vernacular architecture, it was allegedly inspired by a Portsmouth, Great Falls and Conway Railroad official's trip to Russia (the railroad was a predecessor of the Maine Central). The brightly painted, two-story, wood-frame building with clapboard siding has a central cross gable topped with a monitor. Bilevel stages of convex and concave mansard roofs with roof cresting crown the two end pavilions.

The ground-floor canopy, edged with bargeboards, that surrounds the building is supported by oversize brackets. The ticket office and men's and women's waiting rooms inside were finished with

black walnut woodwork. Offices were located in the towers.

A Boston architect and engineer, Bradlee is credited with designing more than five hundred buildings, mostly churches, schools, and residences. He served on the Boston Water Board and ran for mayor of Boston in 1876. His name should be better known today than it is, as much for what has been demolished of his work as for what is still standing. Bradlee's landmark Union Station in Portland, Maine (1888), with its tall clock tower—demolished in 1961 to make way for a shopping mall—led to the formation of Greater Portland Landmarks and a citywide preservation movement. Likewise, the 1975 demolition of his Jordan Marsh Department store in Boston (circa 1860s), a brownstone building also with a corner tower (and a survivor of the Boston fire of 1872), galvanized local preservationists: the creation of the Boston Landmarks Commission was a direct result.

The Conway station served vacationers from Boston and elsewhere who came to the White Mountains to ski in the winter or cool off in the summer. Passenger service ended in the early 1960s, and the station was closed a decade later. It was restored and reopened in 1974 by the Conway Scenic Railroad, for its tourist train operation. The interior spaces were turned into a gift shop, museum, and snack bar, but the original décor was retained. The trains run fifty-two miles to the Maine Central's former station at Crawford Notch (1891); built in Queen Anne style, the station is now a visitors' center. The four-stall roundhouse and freight depot at Conway, both with clapboard siding, are contemporaneous with the station.

ERIE RAILROAD STATION
1886, Bruce Price
Route 17, Tuxedo, NY

Bruce Price designed the station for Pierre Lorillard IV (see chapter 2), who owned 13,000 acres of land in the Ramapo Mountains northwest of New York City and wanted to establish an exclusive hunting resort for wealthy Manhattanites that could be reached by train. Starting in 1885, with the help of

Ernest Bowditch, an engineer, and several hundred laborers who built streets, a sewer system, and two dozen houses, Lorillard had Tuxedo Park ready for visitors in eight months.

Price's shingle style station has a low slate roof with triangular dormers and deep overhangs that extend beyond the two-story tower, which has a flared pyramidal roof. The entrances to the former men's and women's waiting rooms are on either side of the tower. The street side entrance is in the center of the building, sheltered by a porch. Panels of vertical and horizontal siding and shingles cover the exterior. The upper sashes of the windows are bordered by panes of colored glass.

Most of the original interior was removed in a 1980s renovation. The station, owned by the town, was restored in 2009 at a cost of $1 million. It received a new roof and a new interior that replicated the original one, based on the use of old photographs. A waiting room with new restrooms, a television, and a book borrowing cart is at one end of the station; the former waiting room at the other end is a meeting space. Price also designed the shopping center across Route 17 from the station in Tudor revival style, the town library in neoclassical revival style, a rustic gatehouse, and several houses. Today, Tuxedo is a gated community on an active New Jersey Transit commuter line.

Figure 4.7
Lambertville Station, Lambertville, New Jersey

LAMBERTVILLE STATION
(formerly the Pennsylvania Railroad station)
ca. 1873, Thomas U. Walter
11 Bridge St., Lambertville, NJ

Prominently situated at the end of the bridge across the Delaware River from New Hope, Pennsylvania, and backed by the scenic Delaware and Raritan Canal State Park, the Lambertville Station is a popular bar and restaurant whose success has inspired the restoration of other historic buildings and the renascence of the town itself.

The striking two-and-a-half-story stone station has a pitched roof with jerkinhead gable ends; four dormers, also with clipped gables; and a central tower and spire. The canopy that encircles the building has been extended on the track side to provide for outside dining overlooking the canal park. New owners acquired the station in 1981 and completely rebuilt the interior to accommodate the current uses on multiple levels. They later added a nearby inn and conference center. Since then other inns, restaurants, shops, and galleries have opened in Lambertville, a town over three hundred years old whose buildings exhibit a wide range of architectural styles.

Figure 4.6
Erie Railroad Station, waiting room, Tuxedo, New York

The Pennsylvania Railroad acquired the Belvidere and Delaware Railroad, which ran from Trenton to Belvidere, New Jersey, along the eastern shore of the Delaware River, in the early 1870s and hired Thomas Ustick Walter (1804–87) to design a new station. Like most of his colleagues at the time, Walter lacked formal education as an architect, but he more than made up for it with on-the-job training, and by the end of his long career he had become a consummate professional. At about the time that he was designing the Lambertville train station, Walter succeeded Richard Upjohn as president of the American Institute of Architects, the professional organization that he had helped to establish.

The son of a Philadelphia mason, Walter received an elementary education and studied painting and the physical sciences on his own. Starting in 1828, he spent a year working for William Strickland, an important early American architect who designed Philadelphia's Second Bank of the United States (1824) and Merchants' Exchange (1833). In 1833, Walter won the design competition for Girard College in Philadelphia, a charitable temple of learning and a landmark in the Greek revival style (1847).

Walter is best known for the cast-iron dome and

extensions of the House and Senate wings of the US Capitol (mid-1860s), which he designed in his capacity as government architect (he replaced Robert Mills). He retired shortly thereafter due to ill health but resumed his career to work on, among other things, Philadelphia's City Hall with John McArthur Jr.

GRAVER'S LANE STATION
Reading Railroad
1883, Frank Furness
East Graver's Lane and Anderson St.,
Philadelphia, PA

Frank Furness was a genius whose brilliant and unique designs, growing out of a boldly conceived fusion of disparate elements, both summarized and surpassed all of Victorian architecture. The suburban station at Graver's Lane on the Chestnut Hill line was one of about 125 projects that he did for the Reading Railroad. It is a modest but representative example of his work that illustrates two of the company's aims for small station architecture: the avoidance of monotony in standard designs and attractive landscaping.

In 1879, Franklin B. Gowen, the powerful president of the Reading Railroad (and ruthless prosecutor of

Figure 4.8
Graver's Lane Station, Philadelphia, Pennsylvania

the Molly Maguires), hired Furness as the company's official architect. Furness's job, like that of other railroad architects, was to give the stations an identifiable look or image. He certainly did that; in fact, his stations looked like no others anywhere. His smaller stations for the Reading were variations on a theme, described by his biographer as "lively and witty, lighthearted pavilions under complex roofs."[14]

They were also idiosyncratic versions of Andrew Jackson Downing's picturesque Italianate villa and rural Gothic cottages, whose projecting roofs, verandas, and prominent chimneys expressed domestic comfort. Furness extended his station roof planes into ample track-side passenger shelters; his chimneys suggested the waiting rooms' warmth and protection from the elements.

Graver's Lane Station is two stops north of Mount Airy, where Gowen had his estate. The projecting roof of Furness's Mount Airy station was trimmed back when the tracks were raised. The only change at Graver's Lane Station appears to have been a brief extension and porch added to the south side. The major exterior feature is a three-story tower topped by picturesque dormers that rises over the semicircular station agent's bay. Next to this, a broad set of steps descends to the tracks beneath a long shed roof that is supported by intricate wooden trusswork. The station materials, interwoven in the Queen Anne style, are stone, brick, stucco, wood, and asphalt shingle.

On the street side opposite the tower is a porte cochere. The interior follows the traditional axial plan, this time with the agent's living room and kitchen on one side, and the waiting room and toilets for the passengers on the other. With their sloping roofs and windows reminiscent of castles, the second-floor bedrooms and tower spaces must have delighted the agent's children.

In the Victorian period, before the space around train stations was devoted to parking for automobiles, railroad companies invested in landscaping and railroad gardens. The trees, shrubbery, and well-kept lawn surrounding Graver's Lane Station are still familiar and welcoming signs to the suburban riders of the former Reading line, now operated by the Southeastern Pennsylvania Transportation Authority.

STRICKLER INSURANCE STATION
(formerly the Cornwall and Lebanon Railroad Station)
1885
1912, office wing addition, G. W. and W. D. Hewitt
61 N. Eighth St., Lebanon, PA

The Hewitt brothers' wonderfully eclectic and eccentric train station might come as no surprise since the elder brother, George, was the partner of Frank Furness from 1871 to 1875, during which time the firm designed the Pennsylvania Academy of the Fine Arts—one of Philadelphia's best-known buildings and probably Furness's finest work. In the Lebanon station, stepped gables, sculptured chimneys, miniature dormers that probably act as roof vents, a variety of arch treatments, volutes, and lavish surface decoration help make the ensemble visually exciting. George (1841–1916) and William Hewitt (1847–1924) specialized in churches, which may account for the bell cotes. The influence of Furness and his penchant for dramatizing the industrial aspects of railroads and buildings can be seen in the exaggerated iron brackets and their wheel emblems under the canopy. The materials are stone and brick with terra-cotta trim, and slate for the roof.

The interior has the original maple floors, oak wainscoting, and beamed ceiling with wood panels. Fireplaces are at either end of the waiting room, and the station agent's office and ticket kiosk are still in place.

The station was built by Robert H. Coleman, owner of the Cornwall Iron Furnace located seventeen miles to the south. He built the Cornwall and Lebanon Railroad to connect the iron furnace with the Philadelphia and Reading Railroad line at Lebanon.

George and William Hewitt were prominent Philadelphia architects; besides churches, they designed numerous hotels and mansions. Before joining Furness, George had worked for William Notman, an

Figure 4.9
Strickler Insurance Station, Lebanon, Pennsylvania

early US practitioner of the Italianate style who designed a number of Philadelphia churches. After he
and Furness parted company, Hewitt set up his own
firm and brought his brother in as partner three years
later. In the 1880s, the Hewitts planned the upscale
suburb of Chestnut Hill for a director of the Pennsylvania Railroad who was developing the property.
Besides the inn and clubhouse, they designed more
than a hundred houses in Chestnut Hill.

In 1980, E. Peter Strickler, president of the Strickler Insurance Agency, bought the station building; for
the previous twenty years, it had been occupied by a
dressmaker. The restoration by John Milner Associates of West Chester, Pennsylvania, included repoint-
ing the exterior and installing the clock. The interior

Figure 4.10
Strickler Insurance Station, waiting room,
Lebanon, Pennsylvania

Figure 4.11
Illinois Central Railroad Station, Galena, Illinois

woodwork was refurbished and a new stairway added to the second floor, which has rentable space.

The elongated yellow brick Reading Railroad station (1901) across the street, designed by Wilson Brothers, presents an interesting counterpoint. It has a flared slate roof with clipped gable dormers and an octagonal tower that encloses the station agent's bay on the ground floor. A covered drive-through passageway separates this section of the building, containing the men's and women's waiting rooms, from the smaller portion, where the baggage room and offices were located.

After passenger service ended in 1963, a bank occupied the building for a decade. It is now owned by the Lebanon Family Young Men's Christian Association (YMCA; see chapter 11) across the street, which uses it for offices.

The Cornwall Iron Furnace, an eighteenth-century plantation with most of its original buildings—including the ironmaster's mansion—intact, is now a museum.

ILLINOIS CENTRAL RAILROAD STATION
1857
101 Bouthillier St., Galena, IL

Constructed at the height of the Italianate or Italian villa style (also known as the railroad style), the two-story, T-shape, brick Galena station has twin cupolas and round-headed dormers atop its hip roof. Large brackets undergird the ground-floor canopy and roof soffit. The semicircular hood moldings over the doors and windows are most likely of cast iron. The interior was divided into the customary ticket office, waiting rooms for men and women, and baggage room. Its most famous passenger was Ulysses S. Grant, who lived in Galena and was welcomed home by some twenty-five thousand citizens when he got off the train here at the end of the Civil War.

The station agent and his family lived in the six-room second-floor apartment until 1968, when the station closed its doors. The City of Galena subsequently bought the property and leased it in 1978 to the Galena Chamber of Commerce, which installed a new roof, renovated the second floor for its offices, and restored the station. The first floor was turned into a visitors' center. The Chamber of Commerce and the center have left the station building, and as of summer 2017 it stood empty.

MINERAL POINT RAILROAD MUSEUM
(formerly the Chicago, Milwaukee, St. Paul and
Pacific Railroad [Milwaukee Road] Station)
1857
Commerce St., Mineral Point, WI

This railroad station in Mineral Point is one of the oldest in the United States and is comparable in style and materials to the early stations built by the Grand Trunk Railway in Ontario, Canada. The Mineral Point Railroad was built to reach the lead- and zinc-mining district of Wisconsin. John Toay and Philip Allen, Cornish stonemasons, built the station of local limestone. Severely plain, the vernacular building is two stories high and three bays wide, with a pitched roof, semicircular arched door openings, and rectangular windows.

The railroad company, which had its offices on the second floor, was purchased by the Milwaukee Road in 1880. The station remained in operation for

Figure 4.12
Mineral Point Railroad Museum,
Mineral Point, Wisconsin

another century. In 2004, twenty years after it closed, the restored building reopened as the Mineral Point Railroad Museum.

NORFOLK AND WESTERN (N&W)
RAILROAD STATION
1902
101 Martin Luther King, Jr. Blvd., Bristol, VA

Resembling a medieval fortress, the Romanesque revival station guards the southern end of the N&W Railroad line from Roanoke, which stopped at the Virginia-Tennessee state line (the town of Bristol straddles the border). The Southern Railway continued south and west; in 1982, the two companies merged as the Norfolk-Southern.

The station is built of brick with stone trim. A square, two-story tower under a hip roof anchors one side; at the other are two cross gables and a platform canopy reaching out along the tracks almost as far as the building is long. Round-arched windows with alternating stone voussoirs, diaper-work panels, and a corbel table distinguish the tower. The pediment panels of the larger cross gables are decorated with swags.

A newsstand, lunch counter, and smoking room were located on the first floor of the tower; the railroad offices were on the second floor. Baggage and freight rooms were at the opposite end. In between was the open, two-story waiting room under a beamed ceiling, divided into sections for men and women and also containing the ticket office.

The train station was a busy place for much of the twentieth century—Bristol being a manufacturing center (producing textiles, furniture, leather goods, wagons, barrels, and boxes) and commodities shipper (of grain, coal, lumber, and iron)—but the building had been closed for some time when the Bristol Train Station Foundation bought it in 1999. The foundation's intention was to renovate it as a working train station and a stimulus for downtown revitalization.

The $5-million restoration program was completed in 2008, and the Bristol Train Station is now an event space. Rail passenger service has not yet

Figure 4.13
Norfolk and Western Railroad Station, Bristol, Virginia

Figure 4.14
Norfolk and Western Railroad Station, waiting room, Bristol, Virginia

returned, although plans are being made for that. In the meantime, the $11-million Birthplace of Country Music Museum opened in downtown Bristol in 2004, and the adjacent former Executive Plaza building is being converted into an $18-million boutique hotel.

SOUTHERN RAILWAY STATION
1908, Frank P. Milburn
215 Depot St., Salisbury, NC

Frank Milburn, a talented, prolific, and driven architect, was also an accomplished stylistic bricoleur, his Salisbury station being a good example. The red tile roof, curvilinear parapets, arcaded entrance, and buff brick walls that imitate adobe reflect the mission revival style. However, the tower's gargoyles, stylized corbel table, and multiple tall round-headed windows enclosed in recessed panels draw on the Romanesque revival tradition. These were two of Milburn's favorite architectural styles for train stations, and the fact that he combined them so successfully is a tribute to his ability as an eclectic designer.

On the track side, triple jerkinhead dormers appear in the hip roof above a broad canopy (supported by metal trusswork) that covers the open concourse. Another metal and glass canopy shelters the side

Figure 4.15
Southern Railway Station, Salisbury, North Carolina
(courtesy of Historic Salisbury Foundation, Inc.)

entrance to the waiting room. Red brick makes up the base of the station building.

Salisbury was an important cotton milling town and railroad junction. The yardmaster had his office at the top of the tower; its ground floor contained the ticket office. Wooden arches supported the lofty ceiling in the waiting room, which had an intricately patterned tile floor. The women's parlor featured furniture and a fireplace surround in the Craftsman style. The waiting room, dining room, and lunchroom were all rigidly segregated; a "colored lunch window" opened between the lunchroom and the section of the waiting room set aside for blacks.

The son of a builder, Frank Milburn (1868–1926) was born in Bowling Green, Kentucky. He gained his first practical experience as a teenager helping his father build courthouses. Milburn attended the University of Arkansas, studied architecture in Louisville, Kentucky, and started practicing there and later in

Figure 4.16
Southern Railway Station, waiting room, Salisbury, North Carolina (courtesy of Historic Salisbury Foundation, Inc.)

West Virginia, where he specialized in courthouses. Moving to North Carolina in 1893, he continued to design this type of structure, but he also designed banks, schools, hotels, and several buildings for the University of North Carolina at Chapel Hill. In addition to being a talented designer, Milburn was hard working and an aggressive self-promoter; he published several booklets illustrating his buildings for distribution to prospective clients.

In 1902, the Southern Railway appointed Milburn its architect, and he designed eighteen stations for the company. The one in Salisbury is the sole survivor of his North Carolina stations (his Southern Railway station in Danville, Virginia [1900], now the Danville Science Center, is an arresting but less successful pastiche of Dutch stepped gables and Renaissance arches).

Although the Southern Railway continued to operate its premier train—the New York to New Orleans Crescent, which stopped at Salisbury—until 1979, eight years after the formation of Amtrak, the station had been abandoned in the meantime. The structure seriously deteriorated, and a local task force was formed to save it. In 1985, the railroad essentially donated the building to the Historic Salisbury Foundation, which completed a $3-million restoration in 1993. The station is now used as an event and office space.

It is also once again an operating passenger station with an Amtrak ticket office and waiting room (the Amtrak Crescent still stops there). A brokerage firm has its offices in the former baggage room, and the old dining room is home to the Historic Salisbury Foundation. The former Yadkin Hotel next door, built in 1912 for the railroad trade, closed in 1975 and reopened five years later as housing for disabled elderly people. The rejuvenation of the train station has led to the construction of new office and retail space in the area and to the opening of the Rail Walk Studios and Gallery in a former grocery warehouse on an abandoned rail spur.

LAS VEGAS AND TONOPAH
RAILROAD STATION
1908
Rhyolite, NV

Eloquent in its silence, the mirage-like train station in Rhyolite, an odd survivor in a barren landscape, symbolizes the evanescent nature of the mining towns of the American West. In the early 1900s, high-grade gold and silver ore were discovered at Rhyolite, named for the volcanic rock in the area, and at Goldfield and Tonopah to the north. The resulting arrival in the region of thousands of miners and many others who saw opportunity in the new wealth to be created made towns of all three places overnight. They soon declined once the mines played out, but none sprang into existence or disappeared as quickly as Rhyolite, which was like a flash flood in a dry desert canyon.

Frank "Shorty" Harris and Ernest "Ed" Cross named their mine near Rhyolite the Bullfrog, because the green ore flecked with gold reminded them of a bullfrog's back. The name was later applied to the whole mining district; there was also a town of Bullfrog.

Rhyolite became a town in 1905 when prospectors flocked to the Bullfrog district. The town expanded greatly in the next few years after Charles M. Schwab, the eastern steel magnate, bought the district's richest mine and built the infrastructure needed to develop it: a mill to process the ore, rail lines to move it, and electric and water lines. By 1907, Rhyolite had a population of about four thousand, electric lights, running water, banks, a stock exchange, an opera house, two newspapers (the *Daily Bulletin* and the *Herald*), schools, churches, a miners' union hospital, and a red-light district that attracted prostitutes from as far away as San Francisco.

William A. Clark's San Pedro, Los Angeles, and Salt Lake Railroad had reached Las Vegas in 1905, and Clark wasted no time building a branch line to the mining districts (see chapter 11) Clark's Las Vegas and Tonopah Railroad reached Rhyolite in 1906 and Goldfield, 157 miles from Las Vegas, the following year. (It never got to Tonopah). One of three railroads that competed to be first to serve the region—the others being the Tonopah and Tidewater and the Bullfrog-Goldfield—Clark's line won the race.

The Rhyolite station is a supercharged mission revival style model, as if the architect sensed that its time was limited and therefore felt a bold statement was needed. Rhyolite had already reached its peak by the time the station was built; the financial panic of 1907, brought on in part by the attempt of the Butte, Montana, copper barons to corner the market in copper and the devaluation of Schwab's mine in the Bullfrog district, led to its eventual abandonment.

The hip tile roof is in two planes, its corners and ridges outlined by contrasting buff-colored tiles and roof cresting. The entrance through a portico with a shaped parapet was at one end of the long one-story main section of the building. Bisecting it at right angles was a two-story pavilion, also with shaped parapets, and with roof extensions on both sides that acted as awnings. For the passengers and spectators, a broad, deep, shady veranda ran almost the entire length of the station, giving it the aspect of a comfortable hotel. The building was constructed of concrete block, manufactured in Las Vegas and shipped by rail to the site. The ticket office was in the central portion of the building, with men's and women's waiting rooms on either side, the freight room at the far end, and the station agent's apartment overhead.

The Rhyolite newspapers stopped publishing in 1908. By 1910, Schwab's mine was operating at a loss; it closed the following year. The last train left the station (one of three in Rhyolite!) in 1914, and the population departed as well. In 1920, fourteen people remained in the town. A few of Rhyolite's buildings were moved intact to the nearby town of Beatty, others provided salvaged building materials, and some collapsed.

Starting in the 1930s, the train station first became a boardinghouse, then a bar and casino, and, in the 1950s, a gift shop. It has served as a backdrop for Hollywood movies. The building is now abandoned and fenced off, but still in remarkably good shape (the decorative terra-cotta cartouches that probably

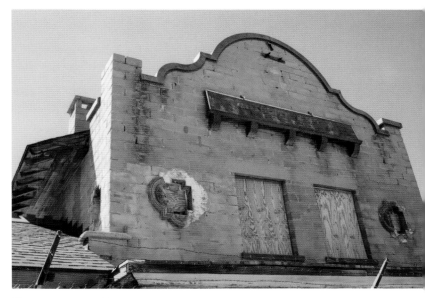

Figures 4.17 & 4.18
Las Vegas and Tonopah Railroad Station,
Rhyolite, Nevada

carried the railroad's emblem have been removed). It is owned by the federal Bureau of Land Management as part of the Rhyolite Historic District.

On the eastern edge of Death Valley, Rhyolite is about 120 miles northwest of Las Vegas on Route 95, which was built on the abandoned right-of-way of the Las Vegas and Tonopah Railroad. The town is four miles west of Beatty, on Route 374. Rhyolite is a ghost town. Just a few structures remain, including the Bottle House, built by a miner from discarded beer and liquor bottles, the slowly self-deconstructing, three-story John S. Cook and Company bank building, and

Figure 4.19
Rhyolite, Nevada

the miraculously surviving Las Vegas and Tonopah Railroad station. Goldfield and Tonopah had multiple train stations as well, but there are none left.

BOONE AND CROCKETT CLUB
(formerly the Milwaukee Road Depot)
1910, J. A. Lindstrand
Third St. and Higgins Ave., Missoula, MT

The Milwaukee Road was the last of the transcontinental railroads to reach the West Coast, which it did at Tacoma, Washington, in 1909. The railroad company then decided to electrify much of the western portion of its route through the mountains. Because the company lacked the government land grants that had benefited the other transcontinental lines, it had to buy most of the right-of-way; the $234-million cost of the Pacific extension, which did not produce the anticipated traffic, and the electrification project sent the Milwaukee Road into bankruptcy first in 1925 and again ten years later. Most of the Pacific extension was subsequently abandoned, including the main line through Missoula.

The Missoula train station is an updated rendition of the Romanesque revival style. Lindstrand the Milwaukee Road's in-house architect, incorporated some elements of the mission revival style, such as the red tile hip roof and the shaped parapets of the towers. The striking three- and-five-story towers that define the corners of the main station building have stylized bell cotes and turrets at their tops. Altogether, it is a concise combination of stylistic influences.

The two-story station has transom windows on the ground story and round arched windows above them. The separate one-story annex building was for baggage and express packages. The buildings sit on a concrete base; the brick walls are trimmed with Bedford, Indiana, limestone. The general waiting room, ticket office, and women's salon, with beamed ceilings and paneled wooden wainscoting, were on the ground floor of the station building, and the offices were on the second floor.

The Milwaukee Road ended passenger service at the station in 1960, and it became a freight station, which was closed in the late 1970s. In 1981, a connection was built between the two station buildings, and they were turned into a restaurant. Two different operators failed to make a go of it, and the station stood empty until it was purchased in 1992 by the Boone and Crockett Club as its new headquarters.

Theodore Roosevelt founded the Boone and Crockett Club in 1887. Its members—who included George Bird Grinnell, General William T. Sherman, and Gifford Pinchot—were interested in big game

Figure 4.20
Boone and Crockett Club, Missoula, Montana

hunting and the conservation of wildlife and natural lands. The club worked closely with Roosevelt to establish the US national park system.

After its move from Washington, D.C., the Boone and Crockett Club restored the station over a period of years, ending in 2004. A public exhibit area was created in the section between the two buildings.

Lindstrand also designed the Milwaukee Road station in Great Falls, Montana (1915), in a more straightforward neo-Romanesque revival style, with a 150-foot tower. It was redeveloped as an office building.

At the opposite end of Higgins Avenue is the Northern Pacific Railway station (1901), designed by Reed and Stem. With a three-story center block and one-story wings in red brick with stone trim under a red tile hip roof, the station seems to have used a generic design for the company's urban stations in Montana. Terra-cotta medallions on the track side carry the Northern Pacific logo. The restored station is now a private office building. An attractive park at one end has a Northern Pacific Railway 4-6-0 locomotive and some coaches.

AMTRAK STATION
1995, Rob Wellington Quigley
105 N. Cedros Ave., Solana Beach, CA

By adding a tower to a version of the Quonset hut, Rob Quigley, a San Diego-based architect, fashioned an offbeat and visually arresting train station for Solana Beach. He bisected the barrel-vaulted corrugated metal roof with a glass skylight and recessed the glass end walls behind the edge of the roof to create a canopy effect. Since the clock appears front and center in the façade, the tower, the traditional bearer of the station timepiece, seems to have no function (it looks more like an airport control tower) except to support a metal trellis resembling a TV antenna. The

Figure 4.21
Amtrak Station, Solana Beach, California

industrial-grade interior finishes are metal, concrete, marble, granite (for the ticket counters), and ceramic tile. Wood paneling lines the underside of the vault.

The model for the station was indeed the humble Quonset hut, produced by the thousands during World War II to meet the need for a lightweight, all-purpose, prefabricated shelter that could be easily erected. A row of wartime Quonset huts was built by a defense contractor in Solana Beach, south of the present station location. They are still there, housing shops, galleries, and restaurants in an area known as the Cedros Avenue Design District. The station design evolved in a series of public workshops, at which people expressed a desire for a station building that would express the community's importance and reflect its unique architecture. The station was also intended to serve as the catalyst for a new town center consisting of a parking garage, theaters, restaurants, retail space, apartments, low-cost senior housing, and artist's lofts.

The $6-million station was built by the North County Transit District to replace an outmoded station at nearby Del Mar. In 1995, the district initiated the Coaster commuter train service that operates between Oceanside and San Diego. The Solana Beach station is also a stop for Amtrak's Pacific Surfliner trains that run from San Luis Obispo through Los Angeles to San Diego. In the late 1990s, to reduce traffic congestion and improve safety, the tracks were lowered in front of the station, at a cost of $18 million.

SOUTHERN PACIFIC RAILROAD STATION
1894, Howard and Mathison
290 California Dr., Burlingame, CA

This station was one of the earliest to be built in mission revival style, and although the style became quite popular later on for railroad stations in other parts of the country, particularly the South, this example of it has never been surpassed. To some extent a reaction against the eastern Victorian architectural styles then prevalent in California, the mission revival style was endemic to the area. It was based on the late eighteenth- and early nineteenth-century Spanish missions in the American Southwest, of which California boasts an especially large number.

The missions were built of readily available natural materials, basically earth and timber. The walls were constructed of adobe bricks covered with a layer of adobe. Wooden beams (vigas), which sometimes extended beyond the walls, supported the ceramic tile roofs. Curvilinear shaped gables and parapets were common, as were arcaded passageways. Sometimes there was a bell tower or two. The interiors were simple: painted roof beams and walls, usually a rear balcony, a wooden altarpiece and furniture, and a tile floor.

The town of Burlingame evolved in the wake of the 1870 acquisition by the Southern Pacific Railroad of a railroad line operating between San Francisco and San Jose. The area was devoted mainly to large estates. In the succeeding decades, communities began to grow up along the railroad route. The region is known today as Silicon Valley.

The Burlingame station came about because the wealthy San Francisco members of the Burlingame Country Club (California's first country club), which they had formed in 1893, were dissatisfied with the inadequate shelter at the railroad stop nearest to their club. The Southern Pacific Railroad agreed to share the cost of a new station at Burlingame if the club members designed it.

One of the members was Arthur Page Brown (1859–96), who was largely responsible for making the mission revival a native California style. Born in New York State, Brown spent a year at Cornell University. He left for a draftsman's job with McKim, Mead and White, where he remained for three years. He came to San Francisco in 1889 at the behest of the widow of Charles Crocker, the late president of the Southern Pacific Railroad, to design a mausoleum for him. Brown stayed to pursue his architectural career. Bernard Maybeck, who was to become a well-known California architect, joined his staff in 1891.

Brown's firm won the design competition for the California state building at the 1893 Chicago World's Fair, and Maybeck traveled to Chicago to oversee its construction. The California building was based on the 1820 Spanish mission at Santa Barbara, which Brown was familiar with, and it gave the new mission revival style national exposure.

Club members George H. Howard (1864–1935) and Joachim B. Mathison (d. 1896), the station architects, were familiar both with the Burlingame site and the California state building at the Chicago World's Fair. Howard belonged to a wealthy family that owned one of the local estates; his half-brother donated the land for the station. Mathison had worked for Brown as a draftsman in 1890 and, after he went out on his own the following year, entered the competition for the California building—which he lost to Brown. He and Howard formed their own architecture firm circa 1893–94, and one of their first jobs was the Burlingame station.

The low-slung, rambling Burlingame station exhibits all of the ingredients of the mission revival style arranged in a graceful manner and incorporating a landscaped plaza, which was very much a part of the Spanish missions. Arcades line both sides of the station. On the track side, three arches, the station name, and a quatrefoil window appear under a curvilinear shaped gable. A squat tower with a low pyramidal roof on the street side marks the station's main entrance. Smaller towers and buttresses with pitched roofs are ranged around the building. The roof tiles were the genuine article, salvaged from abandoned missions in the area. At the south end of the station is a beautifully landscaped garden. An arcaded and covered outside waiting area was added to the north end in 1910.

The station contained a baggage room and the station agent's apartment on either side of the waiting room, which had a wooden ceiling with exposed beams. The construction method—diagonal redwood siding covered with stucco—was similar to that used for the Chicago World's Fair buildings, which were made of "staff," a mixture of plaster and hemp fiber applied over wood or metal framing.

Figure 4.22
Southern Pacific Railroad Station,
Burlingame, California

Figure 4.23
Southern Pacific Railroad Station, garden,
Burlingame, California

Brown died two years after the station opened, at the age of thirty-six, in a runaway horse-and-buggy accident in Burlingame. He is best known for San Francisco's Ferry Building (1898). He also helped introduce the mission revival style to the city of Santa Barbara, which adopted it wholesale. Mathison died the same year as Brown. Howard continued working as an architect, designing some seventy-five houses as well as churches and clubhouses around Burlingame.

After the Southern Pacific Railroad sought to abandon passenger rail service in the corridor in 1977, Caltrain, the San Francisco commuter rail service, took over train operations and acquired the right-of-way in 1991 for $220 million. Caltrain commuter trains run between San Francisco and Gilroy, south of San Jose. The 2007 $13-million restoration program for the Burlingame station included the addition of mission revival style shelters and landscaping. The building is now occupied by the Burlingame-Hilllsborough Historical Society.

Several of the stations along the Southern Pacific Railroad are architecturally noteworthy. Among them is the one in San Carlos (1889), a rare California train station in the Richardsonian Romanesque style; it is currently a restaurant. The station in Palo Alto (1941) is an equally unusual for the area for its art deco design; it is a train and bus station; the café has a large mural depicting Leland Stanford and the evolution of transportation in California.

NORTHWEST RAILWAY MUSEUM (formerly the Seattle, Lake Shore and Eastern Railway Station)
1890 King St., Snoqualmie, WA

When the Northern Pacific Railway spurned Seattle in favor of Tacoma as its West Coast port city, the city fathers responded by building their own railroads in an attempt to link up with the transcontinental lines. One was the Seattle, Lake Shore and Eastern Railway. Established in 1885, it headed east, hoping to meet the Northern Pacific at some point, and north toward Canada and the Canadian Pacific Railway.

The eastern line got a little beyond Snoqualmie, roughly forty miles by train from Seattle, but then construction funds ran out in 1889. The northern line reached Sumas, Washington, on the Canadian border about the same time; the Canadian Pacific Railway had extended a branch line to meet it. Shortly thereafter, circa 1890–1892, the Northern Pacific Railway acquired the Seattle, Lake Shore and Eastern Railway, probably to forestall the possibility of losing freight business to its transcontinental rival.

Figure 4.24
Northwest Railway Museum, Snoqualmie, California

The Snoqualmie line did a decent business in lumber, farm products, and tourists, the station being just a short distance from the popular, 270-foot Snoqualmie Falls. The first train into Snoqualmie was an excursion train. To persuade investors that it was fiscally solvent, to impress tourists, or both, the company ordered a special station at Snoqualmie. The result was a particularly attractive Queen Anne style building.

The wood shingle hip roof extends beyond the walls of the station to create a covered walkway whose curved wooden brackets give the effect of an open arcade. The roof fans out over the round end of the building and terminates in a gable at the opposite end, where there is a raised platform. Eyebrow dormers and a windowed octagonal tower are positioned on either side of a central cross gable. The station agent's bay is under the tower. Horizontal shiplap siding covers the exterior.

The waiting rooms inside have tongue-and-groove paneling of Douglas fir, laid diagonally. The picture rails and chair rails in the men's waiting room (in the rounded end) are kerfed and curved to fit the different radii of the walls. The freight room was located in the rear, opening onto the raised platform. The second floor served as living quarters for the agent.

The Northern Pacific Railway ended passenger service to Snoqualmie in the 1920s but continued to use the building as a freight station until 1974, during which time it was severely modified. When the Northwest Railway Museum took over the abandoned station in 1981 and began restoration work, it had to rebuild the eyebrow dormers and the tower. The museum also acquired several miles of railroad right-of-way and equipment, including a pair of geared locomotives commonly used in lumbering operations and rolling stock. Scenic train trips to the falls still attract tourists.

HISTORIC DAYTON DEPOT
(formerly the Oregon Railway and Navigation Company Station)
1881
222 East Commercial St., Dayton, WA

Dayton is located at the end of a branch line some seventy miles by railroad northeast of Walla Walla, in the high grain and orchard country of eastern Washington. At the time the depot was constructed, Henry Villard was putting together the Northern Pacific Railway, an important part of which was the Oregon Railway and Navigation Company—whose line ran east out of Portland, along the Columbia River.

The Dayton station is a gem in the combined stick and Eastlake styles, which celebrate the structural and

Figure 4.25
Historic Dayton Depot, Dayton, Washington

decorative possibilities of wood. The gable boards at the edges of the high, pitched, cross-gable roof are embellished with figured panels. Complex diagonal brackets hold up the balcony that rings three sides of the building; its railing is composed of shaped balusters. The horizontal shiplap siding on the ground floor of the two-story station is sandwiched between bordered wainscot panels of alternating vertical and diagonal boards and additional decorative woodwork under the balcony. The building is painted as it was originally: mustard-color siding with brown trim.

The two-story station agent's bay allowed the agent, who lived on the second floor, to observe the track action if he happened to be upstairs, or to step out on the balcony to do so. On the ground floor was the customary waiting room, equipped with a pot-bellied stove, a freight room, and the agent's office.

A second railroad reached Dayton in 1889, and ten years later, the Dayton depot was moved to its present location. The Union Pacific Railroad, which had acquired the Northern Pacific, closed the station in 1971 and initially planned to demolish it. Instead, the railroad donated the building to the Dayton Historical Depot Society, a nonprofit corporation established to restore the station and open a museum. The station received a new foundation, and the balcony was rebuilt. The museum, open to the public, contains an archive and artifacts. Freight trains still operate between Walla Walla and Dayton.

MCADAM STATION-HOTEL
Canadian Pacific Railway
1901, Edward Maxwell; 1911,
　　Walter S. Painter, addition
Saunders Rd., McAdam, NB

The existence of this imposing station-hotel in a remote small town in New Brunswick is a testament to the confidence of the Canadian Pacific Railway (CPR) and its dynamic president, William C. Van Horne, in the future of their enterprise. In November 1885, Van Horne had helped drive the last spike at Craigellachie, British Columbia, to complete the CPR from Montreal to Vancouver. Four years later, the 382-mile

eastward extension from Montreal across the state of Maine to St. John, New Brunswick, the line's ice-free port on the Bay of Fundy, was finished. A continuous 3,375-mile railroad now ran from coast to coast.

The village of McAdam (2011 population, 1,284), seven miles east of the Maine border and eighty-five miles west of St. John, was a junction point between the CPR and a north-south railroad. In 1898, the CPR moved its shops from near Fredericton to McAdam. Covenhoven, Van Horne's summer home, was located not far away in St. Andrews, a popular vacation spot just north of Eastport, Maine. Covenhoven (circa 1900) was designed by Edward Maxwell, who also had a summer home in St. Andrews. To accommodate the affluent vacationers and others changing trains at McAdam, Van Horne wanted a hotel.

While impressive in size and appearance—the château, or Scottish baronial, style station-hotel was two and a half stories tall and about half a block long—it was not a destination in itself, as the CPR's resort hotels were. The few hotel rooms were spartan and designed for short layovers, not extended stays; there were no mountains to explore or hot springs to soak in. Some attractive lakes were nearby, and by damming a stream behind the hotel to provide water for the steam locomotives and ice for the hotel and the trains, the railroad created a scenic pond.

The station is constructed of local granite; some of the window lintels are twelve feet long. Gabled dormers in two sizes jut from the steep hip roofs of the two pavilions, one at the end of the building and the other two-thirds of the way along its length—the latter is flanked by truncated towers. The pavilions are also decorated with finials and wooden balconies. More gabled dormers line the edge of the main red shingle roof. A deep canopy surrounds the building. The station-hotel has the picturesque silhouette typical of the Scottish baronial style.

Men's and women's waiting rooms, a dining room, large lunchroom (the sign still hangs outside), ticket office, baggage room, and small jail for prisoners being transported by rail and changing trains were on the ground floor, finished with dark wood wainscoting and trim. The second floor held eighteen hotel

Figure 4.26
McAdam Station-Hotel, McAdam, New Brunswick

rooms, a library for the guests, and the railroad offices. The dormitory for the cooks, waitresses, and hotel staff was on the third floor, with the male and female quarters at opposite ends of the building.

Maxwell (1867–1923) was born in Montreal. After four years of training with Boston's Shepley, Rutan and Coolidge, successor firm to H. H. Richardson, he returned to his hometown and opened an architectural office in 1892. Ten years later, his brother William S. Maxwell (1874–1952) joined him as a partner, having also apprenticed with an architectural firm in Boston and attended the École des Beaux-Arts in Paris. Edward and W. S. Maxwell became one of the biggest and most influential architectural firms in Canada.

Born in the United States, Walter S. Painter (1877–1957) served as chief architect of the CPR between 1905 and 1913. He designed the central tower of the CPR's Banff Springs Hotel, which opened in 1914. Later in his career, he developed a prefabricated home

construction system that used reinforced concrete (see chapters 2 and 8).

In McAdam's prime years, when the population had grown to 3,200, sixteen daily trains stopped at the station-hotel, and hundreds of passengers, mainly from Boston or Montreal, ate their meals in the dining room and lunchroom. But the mid-twentieth-century change from steam-powered locomotives to diesel engines reduced much of the activity in the shops, and the advent of the St. Lawrence Seaway meant that ships could travel directly to Montreal without having to unload their cargoes and move them by rail from St. John. McAdam, which was almost entirely dependent on the railroad, faced severe economic challenges.

Short-line railroads acquired sections of the CPR's former Montreal to St. John route. Passenger rail service to McAdam finally ended in 1994, and the station-hotel was transferred to the McAdam Historical Restoration Commission. The organization is slowly restoring the building and conducts tours during the summer for some 25,000 visitors annually.

KINGSTON AND PEMBROKE RAILWAY STATION
1887, William Newlands
Ontario and Clarence Sts., Kingston, ON

At the eastern end of Lake Ontario, halfway between Toronto and Montreal, Kingston was the site of Fort Frontenac, an important outpost during the French and Indian War; a haven for British loyalists fleeing the United States following the American Revolution; and, briefly (1841–44), the capital of Canada.

In more recent times, it was a transportation and manufacturing center. Kingston was the lake port for the Rideau Canal that ran north to Ottawa; an important stop on the Grand Trunk Railway; and the terminus of the Kingston and Pembroke Railway, a north-south line. For a little over a century, beginning in 1854, the Kingston Locomotive Works, later known as the Canadian Locomotive Company, built steam and diesel engines; the CPR was a major customer.

Many of the town's historic buildings were built of the native limestone, as was the Kingston and Pembroke Railway station, centrally located on the harbor (the railroad mainly transported natural products such as lumber and iron ore for transshipment by water, since Kingston was at the junction of the

Figure 4.27
Kingston and Pembroke Railway Station, Kingston, Ontario

St. Lawrence River and the Great Lakes). The modest, two-story building has an interesting combination hip and mansard roof, flared at the bottom, punctuated with gabled dormers, and crowned with roof cresting. The large wooden brackets supporting the deep overhang rest on stone corbels; and in general the building, with its plain round-arched window and door openings, is an excellent example of the mason's art. The interior dark wood trim and wooden ceiling are original.

The CPR acquired the Kingston and Pembroke in the early twentieth century. The last train ran out of Kingston in 1986, and the station was made into a visitors' center. Originally a market and then a railroad yard, the area between the station and the harbor is now a landscaped park. The beautiful waterfront setting of the visitors' center makes it one of the most successful of such conversions.

GRAND TRUNK RAILWAY STATION
1856
Hayward St., Port Hope, ON

Port Hope is ancient for a railroad station, and quite rare in that it has been in continuous use since it opened. It is now owned by the Canadian National Railways. VIA Rail operates the passenger service. Actually, nine Grand Trunk Railway stations from the mid-nineteenth century still stand in Ontario, but few are active. Two others still fulfilling their original function are at Napanee (the station there is quite similar to the one in Port Hope) and at Belleville (where the station has been altered).

The Grand Trunk Railway hired England's premier civil engineering firm, Peto, Brassey, Jackson and Betts, which had designed and built several major railways in the cradle of railroading, to supervise the construction of its initial Toronto-to-Montreal line, including the stations. The result was simplicity itself: a rectangular box; a low-pitched roof, whose deep overhanging eaves were supported by the exposed rafter ends and triangular brackets; four prominent chimneys; and five to seven round-arched openings in the sides and two in the ends, under oculus windows.

Figure 4.28
Grand Trunk Railway Station, Port Hope, Ontario

Port Hope had six side openings, which made it a type B station. The building material was coursed limestone masonry, again simply executed. The brick agent's bay on the track side was built in the late nineteenth century.

The interiors of these stations had wooden floors, wainscoting, and crown molding. The waiting and freight rooms were at either end, with the station agent's office in between. Assuming that the four chimneys were all attached to stoves, the spaces must have been comfortable during the winter months. The piers of regular coursed cut stone that support the viaduct approaching the station offer more examples of fine masonry.

PETROLIA LIBRARY
(formerly the Grand Trunk Railway Station)
1903
4200 Petrolia Line at Greenfield St., Petrolia, ON

Major oil wells were discovered in Petrolia in 1866, the site of an early oil boom in Ontario. The Great Western Railway's branch line from Sarnia reached the village that same year, and Petrolia became the center of oil production in Canada. Rail shipments of oil continued well into the twentieth century (oil derrick pumps are still working in the area).

The Grand Trunk Railway, which had taken over the Great Western, built the new Petrolia station to replace an outmoded facility erected in 1868 by its predecessor. It was a beautiful two-story building in the Queen Anne style, made up of brick on a stone base and with a variety of roof forms. Round towers with conical roofs stood alongside a central square tower under the pyramidal roof that held the main entrance. The men's and women's waiting rooms were in the circular towers. The station agent's bay and ticket office occupied the rear (trains backed into the station). The interior was finished with vertical wood paneling, dentiled crown molding, and a two-tone wooden ceiling.

Petrolia's oil boom had mostly subsided by 1927, and the Canadian National Railway, which in turn had taken over the Grand Trunk, closed the station.

Figure 4.29
Petrolia Library,
Petrolia, Ontario

Figure 4.30
Station Restaurant and Heritage Railway Station, Lake Louise, Alberta

Ten years later, it became the town library, an early instance in Canada of the adaptive reuse of a railroad station. The intact interior is now hung with pictures and lined with bookshelves. The rail line, active until 1994, was removed in 1997. The tracks in back of the station have been replaced by an open market shed used for a farmers' market.

STATION RESTAURANT AND HERITAGE RAILWAY STATION
1910
200 Sentinel Rd., Lake Louise, AB

The rustic building's long, low silhouette, framed by the evergreen forests of the Canadian Rockies, was the result of the CPR's rebuilding of its mountain resort stations. The one at Lake Louise, formerly known as Laggan, replaced the earlier 1890 station, a small, square log building with a flared mansard roof. Van Horne, the CPR's president, recommended building the railroad's mountain stations as log chalets (see chapter 8).

The new station was built of peeled logs, set on a stone base. A cross gable with tall windows bisected the pitched roof, one end of which sheltered a timber-frame open waiting area. The main waiting room in the cross gable had high, cathedral-like leaded glass windows through which the outside scenery was visible. A massive brick double fireplace was between the main and the secondary waiting rooms, with hearths in each room. The comparable space at the other end of the station was the baggage and freight room. After leaving the train, visitors rode in horse-drawn carriages the three steep miles to Lake Louise and its château. From 1912 to 1930, a tram operated between the station and Lake Louise.

VIA Rail took over the CPR's passenger service in 1978 and until 1990 continued to operate its transcontinental train, the Canadian, between Toronto and Vancouver, with stops at Banff and Lake Louise. In that year, VIA Rail shifted the Canadian to the Canadian National Railway's route (the service is still running).

In 1991, a small café opened in the Lake Louise station building. Two years later, new operators restored the building and opened the present restaurant.

5

ROOM STREETS
(Train Sheds)

I n the early days of the railroad, the train shed was an integral part of the station: it was an attached roof or canopy that sheltered passengers and freight. In some primitive stations, the train ran right through the building! As stations grew bigger and trains longer, train sheds expanded as well. In the larger cities, they became their own structural entities, completely detached from the station building or head house. Carroll Meeks, in his classic *The Railroad Station* called them "room streets."[15]

Based on British precedents and using what was then the latest iron and glass building technology, engineers designed enormous structures that for a brief period in the late nineteenth century came to dominate railroad architecture. There were three main types: wide-span trussed train sheds with pitched roofs, often with a monitor running the length of the roof; arched sheds, known as "balloon sheds," some of which also had a monitor; and Bush sheds and their progeny, butterfly and umbrella sheds (platform canopies).

There are several examples of the first and last of these types still in existence, but only one of the great "balloon sheds" remains standing: the Reading Terminal in Philadelphia, Pennsylvania.

PENNSYLVANIA CONVENTION CENTER
(formerly the Reading Terminal)
1893, Francis Kimball, Wilson Bros.; 1993, train shed
renovation, addition TVS Design, Vitetta
51 N. 12th St., Philadelphia, PA

The Pennsylvania Convention Center, which incorporates the Reading Terminal, is a highly successful redevelopment effort that has attracted hotels, restaurants, and jobs to the city center. It was a major factor in bringing the 2016 Democratic National Convention to Philadelphia. The famous Reading Terminal Market is a destination in itself.

The train shed is the sole survivor of the soaring balloon sheds that

Figure 5.1
Pennsylvania Convention Center, head house, Philadelphia, Pennsylvania

railroads built at major city stations to enclose the tracks in one great sweeping arc. The head house and train shed now function respectively as the entrance and grand hall of the Convention Center.

The Philadelphia and Reading Railroad began operations in 1842 and was a principal developer of the anthracite coalfields in Pennsylvania. It constructed an extensive network of rail lines in that state and New Jersey, radiating out from the Philadelphia-Reading axis. Plans for a major terminal in Philadelphia began in 1887, partly to compete with the rival Pennsylvania Railroad and its new Broad Street Station a few blocks away. However, the City Council repeatedly rejected the idea because of the increased number of street grade crossings and the disruption to the operations of farmers' markets in the vicinity that dated back to the days of William Penn.

A new Reading Railroad president, Archibald

Figure 5.2
Pennsylvania Convention Center, train shed,
Philadelphia, Pennsylvania

McLeod, proposed to elevate the rail line over the streets, eliminating the grade crossings, and to provide space in the new terminal for the farmers' markets. He even offered to pay $1 million to the displaced market owners. This won over the City Council and the downtown merchants, who approved the new plan.

Francis H. Kimball, a New York architect known for his early Manhattan commercial towers decorated with terra-cotta, was chosen to design the head house. For the train shed, the Reading turned to Philadelphia's Wilson Bros., architects and engineers, and their wealth of railroad experience. The two oldest brothers, John A. and Joseph M., were both Rensselaer Polytechnic Institute graduates who had found work with the Pennsylvania Railroad designing bridges and stations. They collaborated on the design of the main building for the 1876 Centennial Exposition in Philadelphia and that year formed Wilson Bros. Ten years later, the youngest brother, Henry W., also a graduate of Rensselaer and the Pennsylvania Railroad, joined the firm. In the meantime, Wilson Bros. designed the Pennsylvania Railroad's Broad Street Station (1881). While working on the Reading Terminal train shed, they were also busy with the new Broad Street Station train shed. When it was completed, also in 1893, with a span of 391 feet, it was

the world's largest single-span train shed (it was later demolished).

Kimball's nine-story Reading Terminal head house in the second Renaissance revival style, fronts on Market Street between 11th and 12th Streets. The metal-frame structure is faced on the first story with pink granite, and above, with pink brick and a profusion of white terra-cotta trim: rosettes, decorated panels, Ionic capitals, and raised bands that suggest rustication.

Inside, the ticket windows were on the ground floor and the waiting room on the second, separated from the tracks by a concourse. Company offices occupied the upper floors. The Reading Terminal Market was located under the train shed between Filbert and Arch Streets.

The train shed was 509 feet long, 88 feet high, and 259 feet wide, covering thirteen tracks. Eleven main arches—all three-hinged, elliptical, and made of wrought iron—carried the roof. They were fabricated as half arches in the shops of Pennsylvania's Phoenix Bridge Company and erected on site, joined with hinges at the crown and feet. One foot of each arch rested on rollers, allowing it to move in response to changes in temperature. Wrought-iron eyebars connected the arches under the tracks to resist the outward thrust. Glass skylights ran the length and sides of the train shed, whose glazed ends brought in more daylight.

With the decline of anthracite coal's use as a heating fuel, the Reading Railroad went bankrupt in 1971. The Southeastern Pennsylvania Transportation Authority (SEPTA) gradually took over its Philadelphia commuter service. In the mid-1980s, with the completion of a new commuter rail tunnel, the last train left Reading Terminal, and the City of Philadelphia bought the complex for use as a convention center. The conversion of the head house and train shed and the addition of a new structure to the north was finished in 1993, at a cost of $522 million.

A Marriott Hotel at Market and 12th Streets across from the terminal opened in 1995. Four years later the Marriott converted the former company offices in the head house to suite-type hotel rooms; the waiting room became the ballroom. In 2011, at a cost of $786 million, the Pennsylvania Convention Center opened its new building to the north that replaced the original addition. An enormous box, it covered six city blocks between Arch and Race Streets and 11th and Broad Streets, forming an L-shape structure with the Reading Terminal.

In the Reading Terminal head house, the ground floor space formerly devoted to the railroad's passenger facilities now features a lobby, a bank branch, and the Hard Rock Café (the red, twenty-five-foot high electric guitar outside points to the railroad president's former office behind the oriel window). In back of the lobby and across Filbert Street is the Reading Terminal Market, full of Amish and other traditional merchants and their food stalls, all doing a brisk business with natives, tourists, and the conventioneers that have replaced the commuters. Below the lobby are SEPTA's Market East transit station and several underground levels of The Gallery, a shopping mall.

Escalators lead to the second-level concourse, where there is an entrance to the hotel rooms upstairs and to the skywalk linking the head house with the Marriott Hotel across 12th Street. On the opposite wall are 1972 artworks by Robert Motherwell and Helen Frankenthaler, produced by Gloria Ross—a tapestry designer who brokered arrangements between contemporary artists and weavers to create wall hangings. In the center of the concourse, an informative exhibit relates the history of the Reading Railroad and its Philadelphia terminal.

In the train shed, the middle rank of skylights has been closed in, leaving those at the top and sides still open. The pylons, exaggerated versions of the end-of-track bumpers used to stop trains, contain heating and cooling equipment. A new floor has been inserted at the rear of the train shed, where another set of escalators gives access to the ballroom and meeting space above. The passageway below it connects to the convention center's main building. At a total cost of $1.3 billion, the Pennsylvania Convention Center was the largest public works project in the state.

HARRISBURG TRANSPORTATION CENTER
(formerly the Pennsylvania Railroad Station)
1887, W. Bleddyn Powell, architect; train shed,
William H. Brown, chief engineer
Fourth and Market Sts., Harrisburg, PA

Harrisburg provides a particularly fine example of the pitched-roof train shed with a glazed monitor. Bleddyn Powell, who worked off and on for the Pennsylvania Railroad, was the station architect, but the train sheds were often designed by engineers and it is likely that Harrisburg's was the work of Brown.

The shed, which is supported by Fink roof trusses, is 420 feet long, spans 90 feet, and is 24 feet from the

Figure 5.3
Harrisburg Transportation Center, train shed, Harrisburg, Pennsylvania

ground to the lower chord of the truss. A second shed was added in the early 1900s, adjacent to the original one.

By the mid-1970s, the Harrisburg facility was in a serious state of disrepair. A decade later, the station and train sheds were restored as part of a $13.4-million project. Additional improvements costing $3 million were completed in 2007. Amtrak trains and interstate buses use the station.

A similar pitched-roof shed, also with a monitor and employing the same type of roof trusses, can be seen at the former station of the Chicago, Milwaukee, St. Paul and Pacific Railroad (Milwaukee Road), in Minneapolis, Minnesota. It dates from 1899. The station, known as The Depot, is now a Marriott hotel. The shed is used for parking in the summer and as an ice rink in the winter.

Another excellent example of a reused train shed is at Union Station, Montgomery, Alabama. It was built by the Louisville and Nashville Railroad in 1898 and designed by Robert Montfort, then its chief engineer. Howe roof trusses with a curved bottom chord support the structure. The large monitor gives it a form almost like that of a basilica. The closing in of the portal trusses with woodwork and windows in the restoration also gives the shed a distinct resemblance to the Rialto Bridge in Venice. Amtrak service to Montgomery ended in 1979. The station was converted to a visitors' center, and the train shed is used for parking and events.

The same type of train shed roof appears at Mount Royal Station, in Baltimore, Maryland, through which CSX Transportation's freight trains still run. Erected in 1896, it was designed by John E. Greiner, the Baltimore and Ohio Railroad's assistant engineer and a notable bridge designer. Similar train sheds that have found new uses are at Savannah, Georgia (see chapter 1) and at Richmond, Virginia (see chapter 3).

DELAWARE, LACKAWANNA AND WESTERN RAILROAD TERMINAL
1907, Kenneth M. Murchison, architect; train shed, Lincoln Bush, chief engineer
One Hudson Place, Hoboken, NJ

The new type of train shed that ended the era of the all-enclosing pitched roof and balloon sheds was inspired by the waterfront site conditions at Hoboken: there was unstable fill on a site where several previous wooden stations had burned. Kenneth Murchison's new station in the beaux arts style was therefore to be a steel-frame structure with reinforced concrete walls clad with lightweight copper sheathing. To lessen the load on the new foundation of concrete platforms, which in turn rested on a base of timber pilings and grillage, the concrete was made with a

Figure 5.4
Delaware, Lackawanna and Western Railroad Terminal, Hoboken, New Jersey

Figure 5.5

Delaware, Lackawanna and Western Railroad Terminal, train shed, Hoboken, New Jersey

weight-reducing cinder aggregate. Lincoln Bush devised a train shed that spread the load equally over the entire track area instead of concentrating it under the walls or columns of a pitched-roof shed or the side walls of a balloon shed.

The Bush sheds, made of concrete vaults supported by steel girders, spanned just the distance between platforms, with open slots over the tracks to let the smoke from the engines escape and to bring in light. (In the pitched-roof and balloon sheds, smoke tended to collect under the roofs, which corroded the ironwork and resulted in costly maintenance.) The support columns in Bush's system at Hoboken ran down the centers of the nine platforms, the sheds covering fifteen of the eighteen tracks. The proliferation of columns helped to spread the weight out.

Abraham Lincoln Bush (1860–1940) was born in Illinois a few weeks after the election of 1860, and his parents named him for the new president; he later dropped the Abraham. Bush taught public school for several years before deciding to be an engineer. After receiving a degree in civil engineering from the University of Illinois, he went west to work on the Union Pacific and other railroads. He joined the Delaware, Lackawanna and Western (DL&W) Railroad in 1990 as a bridge engineer, later becoming chief engineer. Bush ran his own construction company after leaving the railroad in 1909 and built the DL&W Railroad's

monumental Tunkhannock Viaduct (1915), in Nicholson, Pennsylvania (see chapter 12).

The DL&W terminal at Hoboken, where ferry service was restored in 2011, is the last to remain in operation of the five such facilities that lined the New Jersey shoreline across from New York City in the early nineteenth century and made it the greatest rail-ferry terminal complex in the world (rail and highway tunnels into Manhattan largely rendered the ferries obsolete). The Hoboken terminal has been restored and the clock tower rebuilt, after it was taken down in the 1950s following storm damage. A 2016 train crash damaged the concourse between the sheds and the station.

One other Bush shed terminal still stands at Jersey City, Peabody and Stearns' 1889 Romanesque revival station for the Central Railroad of New Jersey. The 1914 Bush sheds that replaced the original train shed were the largest of the type ever constructed; they covered twenty tracks. Rail service to the terminal ended in 1967; the restored station and the sheds are now part of Liberty State Park.

Bush sheds later appeared at many train stations, one of the largest installations being at Toronto's Union Station (see chapter 2). A slightly different version, known as the "butterfly shed," or platform canopy, was subsequently developed. Instead of spanning the tracks, it branched out in leaves on either side of central columns, sheltering the platform but leaving the portion over the tracks open. Platform canopies can also be seen at many train stations.

The biggest train shed ever built (covering ten acres and thirty tracks) still stands at St. Louis Union Station, a kind of combination of the wide-span trussed shed and the balloon shed but more amply lit with longitudinal bands of skylights (see chapter 2). Variations on the theme of re-creating this type of elevated shelter, but in glass to admit the maximum amount of light—as was done in the renovation of Toronto's Union Station—can be seen at the Long Island Railroad's Jamaica Station, in Queens, New York; and at Union Station in Denver, Colorado, where Skidmore, Owings and Merrill designed a fabric-covered space frame as a track shelter.

6

THE BIG STOREHOUSE
(Freight Depots, Warehouses, Grain Elevators)

Moving goods was the first mission of the railroads. In the long run, transporting freight proved much more lucrative and less problematic than carrying passengers (a gondola car full of coal didn't complain about being left stranded on a siding for a week in the rain). Small-town stations generally included a freight room for handling and storing merchandise. In larger cities, separate freight depots and warehouses were the rule. Commodities—coal, ore, and grain, the railroads' traditional payloads—required larger, more sophisticated loading and storage facilities, such as grain elevators. Trucks today deliver most of the smaller items the railroads once carried, and many of the bulk materials as well. Obsolete freight depots and warehouses and even a few grain elevators have proved to be adaptable to current needs.

In terms of scale and architectural distinction, the Cupples Station warehouse complex in St. Louis, Missouri, is unequaled in North America. Built to handle the tremendous amount of railroad freight carried over the Eads Bridge, the technologically advanced warehouses were linked horizontally by rail spurs and vertically by hydraulic elevators. Although less than half of the original twenty warehouses are still standing, their conversion to new uses has allowed them to remain a powerful presence in the St. Louis cityscape.

CUPPLES STATION
1894–1917, Eames and Young
Clark Ave. and Spruce St., between 8th and 11th Sts., St. Louis, MO

The finest remaining railroad warehouse complex, in terms of its architectural quality and innovative functionality, was the creation of Samuel Cupples and his business partner, Robert S. Brookings. Cupples was a successful St. Louis merchant whose company manufactured wooden buckets, washtubs, butter churns, axe handles, stepladders, brooms, spoons, and other household items. He was also in the paper-making business (producing bags, envelopes, and postcards), using as raw material the wooden discards from his factories. But his greatest innovation was Cupples Station.

The first building was built in 1889 (since demolished), the same year that Jay Gould formed the Terminal Railroad Association—one of whose purposes was to remedy the lack of freight terminal facilities in St. Louis. The complex grew to twenty buildings, unified by a common architectural design and linked by rail spurs.

The Samuel Cupples Woodenware Company, most of the wholesale grocers in St. Louis, and a variety of other firms were the tenants of Cupples Station. Incoming freight was sent directly from the railroad cars to the upper floors of the warehouses (each of which had 4–7 stories) via fifty-two heavy-duty hydraulic elevators. Outgoing orders were assembled and shipped in a similar fashion. Cupples Station was the first to employ this convenient railroad freight distribution system, which eliminated drayage and saved time and labor, and it influenced the design of similar facilities in Chicago, Pittsburgh, and New York.

The separate warehouses were designed in a uniformly plain but handsome Commercial Romanesque style with very little decoration. However, subtle differences, mainly in fenestration, gave each of the buildings a distinctive appearance. William S. Eames and Charles C. Young attended different colleges in St. Louis and formed their partnership in 1885. They designed numerous residential and commercial buildings, but Cupples Station was their most notable work (Eames was the father of Charles Eames, the industrial designer).

The buildings were of brick on stone bases, with corbeled cavetto cornices. The interiors featured what was known as mill, or slow-burning, construction, with seventeen-inch square columns and beams of Georgia pine: timbers of this size tend to char in a fire, and the charcoal that forms on the outside of the beam protects it by slowing combustion.

Figure 6.1

Cupples Station, St. Louis, Missouri

Brick-enclosed stairways and elevator shafts, iron doors, and sprinkler equipment were also installed to make the buildings more fireproof.

By 1900, hundreds of warehouse employees and railroad workers were toiling at the site, which daily handled a thousand tons of merchandise. That same year, Cupples and Brookings conveyed the property to Washington University as an endowment. In the latter half of the twentieth century, as freight in sizes smaller than a railroad car load abandoned the railroads for trucks and airlines, Cupples Station went into decline. The tenants gradually departed, and the buildings stood empty. Five of them burned in 1965; others were razed for the construction of Busch Stadium and highway entrance ramps. (The last demolition occurred around 2012; the building was taken down as a structural hazard.)

The university, which had proved to be an indifferent landlord, conveyed Cupples Station to new owners in 1992. There have been a series of property transfers since then, as the site was broken down into smaller parcels that were acquired by individual developers. The nine remaining buildings have been or are being converted to office and residential use.

The first conversion, in 2001, was to create the Westin Hotel, which occupies a former coffee warehouse and three other buildings bordered by Clark Avenue and Spruce Street, between 8th and 9th Streets. One of these buildings, at 820–26 Clark Avenue, is the only one in the complex not designed by Eames and Young; the adjacent L-shape building at 808–8 Clark Avenue, built 1917, is framed in reinforced concrete. The 255-room hotel is adjacent to the Metrolink Stadium stop, which marks the entrance to the tunnel connection to the Eads Bridge (see chapter 6). Cupples Station was named a city landmark in 1971. Landmark status made the hotel project eligible for Missouri historic rehabilitation tax credits, which were critical to the roughly $59-million redevelopment.

West of the hotel, the warehouse at 900 Spruce Street is now occupied by an advertising agency and an information technology consulting firm. The Ballpark Loft Apartments, with the Wheelhouse Bar and Restaurant on the first floor, are at 1004 Spruce Street. Another ad agency is located at 1000 Clark Avenue, and the Cupples Station Loft Apartments are at 1023 Spruce Street.

SILO POINT
(formerly a B&O Railroad grain elevator)
1924, John S. Metcalf Company, engineer;
**   2008, Chris Pfaeffle, renovation architect**
1200 Steuart St., Baltimore, MD

Grain elevators, stark sentinels of the prairies, remain an indelible part of the landscape in western America and Canada, often its most prominent architectural feature—even though the adjacent rail lines may no longer be in service, and the grain moves mainly by truck. In addition to these country elevators, receiving elevators were built in urban areas, usually next to a brewery or flour mill; such elevators stored the grain until it was needed. Finally, there were terminal elevators in port cities that processed the grain and held it for shipment. The B&O Railroad grain elevator in Baltimore was one of those.

Early grain elevators were built of wood, but since they were subject to fire, around 1900 steel and reinforced concrete began to be used in their construction. The stronger materials allowed the elevators to expand in size, and some reached truly massive proportions. Despite their ungainliness, they were much esteemed by architects. Henry Hobson Richardson

wanted to design a grain elevator for Buffalo, New York. Walter Gropius and Le Corbusier, pioneers of modernism, admired the scale of the terminal grain elevators, their use of new materials and methods (reinforced concrete and slip-form construction) and of basic geometrical forms (cube and cylinder), and their complete lack of ornament—all elements of what came to be known as the international style.

A terminal elevator consisted basically of a head house, a tall rectangular structure, grouped together with nearby cylindrical silos. In a sea-rail operation such as Baltimore's, the grain, most of which arrived by rail in hopper cars, would be dumped into a pit and transferred by bucket containers to the top of the headhouse. After it was weighed, it was moved down to holding bins to be cleaned and sorted, and then sent further down for shipment or out by conveyor over the tops of the silos for storage. When a ship was to be loaded, conveyors running in a tunnel under the silos carried the grain to the head house, and then more conveyors transferred it to the pier.

Baltimore's early success as a commercial port was due in large part to the shipment of grain, plus tobacco. In 1850, the B&O Railroad extended a branch line to Locust Point, a peninsula that ends in Fort McHenry and was largely developed by the railroad. It built its first grain elevator there in the 1870s. Eventually, the railroad had three grain elevators in operation, timber-frame structures covered with sheet metal. Two of these burned in a spectacular fire in 1922 that destroyed 500,000 bushels of grain and sixty carloads of tobacco, and set ablaze several barges and ships in the harbor. Total damage was estimated at $4,000,000. The fire was caused by lightning striking the top of one of the elevators that held rye, corn, and wheat and igniting the gases inside. The railroad rebuilt, using better, and more fireproof, materials.

The B&O Railroad's grain elevator, constructed of reinforced concrete, consisted of a fifteen-story head house and—half as high—a grain drier house in front and 182 storage silos in the rear. The John S. Metcalf Company—the Chicago engineering firm that designed the grain elevator and all of its equipment, including four automatic hopper car dumpers

Figure 6.2

B&O Railroad grain elevator (circa 1930), Baltimore, Maryland (James D. Dilts Collection)

—also engineered grain elevators for Montreal, Chicago, St. Louis, and Kansas City. The builder was Boston's George T. McLaughlin and Company, which in addition operated a machine shop and ironworks. With a 3.8-million-bushel capacity, the facility could weigh, wash, dry, and store grain and move it at 800 feet per minute on 10.5 miles of belting. It was one of the largest and fastest-operating grain elevators of its time.

Baltimore's two-century run as a major grain shipping port essentially ended in 2001, after the end of the conveyor that carried the grain from the elevator to the ships collapsed and neither Archer Daniels Midland, the elevator's owner, nor the State of Maryland, the pier's owner, wanted to rebuild it. Grain

shipments shifted to other ports. In 2003, the developer Patrick Turner bought the derelict grain elevator for $6.5 million (he said it had great bones).

A major problem in converting industrial behemoths such as grain elevators to new uses, or even demolishing them, is their fortress-like construction. A substantial portion of Silo Point's $170-million project cost went to demolition. Turner and Chris Pfaeffle, his architect, decided to retain the grain elevator's unwieldy sixteen-foot structural grid and to work to express some of its strength, simplicity, and vastness in their condominium complex. In this, they succeeded.

The silos proved to be unadaptable and were demolished to make room for a 550-car parking structure, except for those left at the corners to mark the perimeter. New multistory metal and glass curtain wall structures that echoed the fenestration of the grain elevator were built surrounding the former silo section and in front of the head house, replacing the drier house. A penthouse was added, from which there are 360-degree views of the Baltimore harbor. The entrance to Silo Point is via the slot between the head house and the former silo section, where the rail cars were brought in. The lobby on one side retains the massive two-story octagonal reinforced concrete columns with spreading capitals that make it look like an industrial Temple of Karnak. The industrial feel is continued in the 228 condos on the upper floors that feature concrete ceilings, exposed ductwork, and panoramic views of the city. Some of the former equipment stands outside as sculptures on the attractively landscaped site.

Figure 6.3

Silo Point, Baltimore, Maryland (courtesy of Turner Development Co.)

Figure 6.4
South Side Railroad Depot, Petersburg, Virginia

SOUTH SIDE RAILROAD DEPOT
1854
37 River St., Petersburg, VA

Completed in 1854, Virginia's South Side Railroad —beginning at the James River at Petersburg, and running west 132 miles through Burkeville, Farmville, and Appomattox to Lynchburg—was one of the South's most important railroads during the Civil War. It carried food, troops and materiel to Petersburg and Richmond, the Confederate capital. Union General Ulysses S. Grant wanted to capture the South Side Railroad, both to deny use of the strategic supply line to the Confederate Army and to use it for his troops. After the siege of Petersburg (June 1864–April 1865), he forced Confederate General Robert E. Lee to abandon Petersburg and Richmond and march his remaining forces by night westward toward Lynchburg. Grant followed in close pursuit along the railroad. Lee, his army starving and exhausted, surrendered at Appomattox (Virginia Route 460 traces most of the route of the South Side Railroad).

The South Side Railroad freight depot was central to the war effort as a transfer point for troops and supplies; wounded Confederate soldiers were brought there for transfer to Petersburg hospitals. The historic depot, one of the oldest railroad structures still standing, was slightly damaged during the siege but emerged basically intact. It is also architecturally significant, an excellent example of the Italianate style—which became so popular with railroad companies of the mid-nineteenth century that it was known as the railroad style.

The handsome two-story brick central building has a pitched roof set with a tower and tall chimneys; the eaves are supported by brackets. The façade features an oculus window over the main entrance and tall ranks of biforate windows. The ground floor was for passengers; the second held the company offices. The 250-foot-long wings on either side were the freight depot.

Following the Civil War, former Confederate General William Mahone became president of the South Side Railroad, and from his second-floor office in the depot, he assembled several other lines that eventually stretched from Norfolk to Bristol. The system, acquired by northern interests in 1881, was reorganized as the Norfolk and Western Railroad.

A century later, a plumbing company was using the South Side Railroad Depot as a warehouse. A 1993 tornado destroyed the tower and roof of the central building and the roof of the western freight wing, and essentially leveled the eastern wing. The tower and roof of the central building and the western freight wing have been rebuilt. The eastern wing, whose walls are partially intact, will probably remain as an industrial ruin.

Work started in 2015 on a multimillion-dollar effort to turn the city-owned depot into a visitors' center operated by the National Park Service. The central building is intended to contain a museum and gallery to tell the Civil War history of Petersburg, and the National Park Service would have its offices in the adjoining freight wing. City officials believe that the visitors' center will inspire the redevelopment of surrounding commercial buildings.

A two-story addition to the freight depot with stepped gables, recessed panels, and Flemish bond brickwork was built in 1917 by the Norfolk and Western Railroad (the outlines of the roof destroyed in the 1993 tornado are visible on the walls of both depot structures). The building now houses a restaurant and loft apartments.

Nearby is the Union Station of the Norfolk and Western Railroad, built in neoclassical revival style in 1910; the former station building is now an event venue.

CENTRAL RAILROAD OF NEW JERSEY FREIGHT STATION
1891, Wilson Brothers
602 W. Lackawanna Ave., Scranton, PA

The fact that a lowly freight depot could achieve such a high level of architectural distinction is owing to its designers, the Philadelphia firm of architects and engineers responsible for that city's Reading Terminal and the Main Street Station in Richmond. The Jersey Central's three-story, red-brick, château-style building has a two-story extension. Gothic-inspired gables decorate the corner tower's conical roof, and the high hip roofs of the main building and the extension boast

Figure 6.5
Central Railroad of New Jersey Freight Station, Scranton, Pennsylvania

a number of jerkinhead gables. Round-arched openings with basketweave brickwork at the entrances define the ground story; decorative brick belt courses surround the tower. A trucking company uses the building as a warehouse.

SILO NO. 5, GRAND TRUNK RAILWAY
1906, John S. Metcalf Company, engineer;
   1913 addition, enlarged 1922; 1957 addition,
   C. D. Howe and Company, engineer
Pointe du Moulin, foot of McGill St., Montreal, QC

Silo No. 5 is altogether twenty-two stories tall and as long as five and a half football fields, with a capacity of five million bushels of grain. Since it closed in 1994, it has become Montreal's largest industrial ruin, so huge and formidable as to defy—so far anyway—viable plans for its reuse. A favorite destination of urban explorers and photographers attracted by a sense of adventure and the spectacular views of the city from the roof, it was the site of a light installation in 1997 and the "Silophone" project in 2002 (a voice from a pier side telephone connected to microphones in one of the silos produced spectral, reverberating sonic effects), and there were plans in 2005 to turn the structure into a museum of modern art.

The elevator was built as three separate structures, connected by elevated conveyors. The steel-sided central section is the oldest. The newest and largest, constructed of reinforced concrete, was built by a firm headed by Clarence D. Howe (1886–1960), a successful businessman and politician who was well known in his time. Born in Waltham, Massachusetts, Howe earned an engineering degree from the Massachusetts Institute of Technology and went to teach at Dalhousie University, in Halifax, Nova Scotia. He left academia to build grain elevators for a Canadian government agency; extending from Toronto to Vancouver, they were mostly located in the western provinces.

After his business failed in the Depression, Howe entered politics. He became a Liberal member of Parliament and was quickly appointed to the cabinet as minister of transport. He continued working for the Canadian government through World War II and afterward, as minister of trade and commerce. During his government career he was involved with everything from airlines to pipelines. It ended with the Liberals' defeat a few years before his death. Known as a plainspoken industrialist who got things done, Howe grew increasingly sensitive to criticism and once described the debate in Commons as the children's hour.

Silo No. 5 sits at the terminus of the 1825 Lachine Canal, the waterway that circumvented the rapids at Montreal. Much of the grain that came to the elevators at Pointe du Moulin was delivered by lake boats; the grain was then transferred to oceangoing ships. Grain could also be received by rail. In the 1920s, Montreal was the world's leading grain port.

The 1959 opening of the St. Lawrence Seaway reduced the need for the city's many grain elevators and

Figure 6.6
Silo No. 5, Grand Trunk Railway, Montreal, Quebec

made the Lachine Canal, which was closed to shipping in 1970, obsolete. Grain could now travel all the way from the Great Lakes and out into the Atlantic Ocean in the same ship. Containerization in the railroad industry also had an effect, because grain could be shipped from the western provinces by rail and placed directly aboard ships. However, Montreal is still a major grain shipping port; another abandoned elevator in the city was recently put back in use at a cost of $22 million, and containerized rail shipments of grain to the city are increasing.

Meanwhile, Silo No. 5 remains a looming presence in Montreal's urban landscape, with seemingly few prospects. Schemes to make it into a center for network servers, a hotel, or condominiums have come and gone. In 2010 the Canada Lands Company acquired the entire Pointe du Moulin property, including Silo No. 5. The company is a Crown corporation that acquires surplus properties and attempts to find new uses for them. The most recent redevelopment plan for the Pointe du Moulin—presented in summer 2017 by Heritage Montreal, a preservation group—calls for an enclosed glass viewing deck atop Silo No. 5, a glass-enclosed elevator to reach it, and a pedestrian bridge connecting the silo to McGill Street. New residences, shops, offices, hotels, and a sports center are part of the plan for redevelopment, which has a total cost of $175 million.

7

THE OFFICE

Railroads, the first major American corporations, created avalanches of paper. Stationmasters, yard masters, tower operators, train dispatchers, engineers, conductors, shop foremen all filled out daily forms. Divisional superintendents, departmental managers, and their underlings in traffic, operations, engineering, mechanical, financial, purchasing, personnel, and legal offices generated more reports and kept up a steady stream of letters, memoranda, and queries. For almost a century (1887–1985) railroad companies—nearly a quarter of whose employees were clerks—filed still more documents required by the Interstate Commerce Commission. The Pennsylvania Railroad reportedly spent more money per year on paper than it did on steel rails.

Early railroad offices were in the station buildings themselves, but toward the end of the nineteenth century separate office buildings were built, sometimes next to the stations. The greatest railroad office building is located appropriately in Chicago: D. H. Burnham and Company's Railway Exchange Building.

RAILWAY EXCHANGE BUILDING
1904, D. H. Burnham and Company
224 S. Michigan Ave., Chicago, IL

Built to provide office space for railroad companies at the height of Chicago's rise to power as the railroad center of the nation, the Railway Exchange was one of the Burnham firm's finest designs. Daniel Burnham was an investor in the building, had his offices on the fourteenth floor, and produced his famous 1909 plan of Chicago in an added penthouse.

The steel-frame, seventeen-story building is square and has a hollow core that forms a central light court. The wavy effect of the two street façades is due to alternating ranks of Chicago bay windows that project so slightly as to be hardly noticeable. White glazed terra-cotta forms the surface. Burnham, a modern classicist, added some subtle decoration at the top of the building, all but invisible from the street. Between the porthole windows are caryatids—winged angels—in relief. Two street entrances led to a marble lobby, surrounded by balconies under a skylight.

When the Santa Fe Railroad, an original tenant in the Railway Exchange and eventually the major one, made Chicago its corporate headquarters in the 1980s, it bought the building and renovated it. The lobby skylight, which had been blacked out, was replaced, and the light court above it was covered over with glass to form an atrium, around which corridors were constructed to provide interior circulation. The two-story lobby and its grand stairway were restored. The railroad also added a "Santa Fe" sign at the top of the building. This was replaced with a Motorola sign when, in 2012, that company acquired control of

Figure 7.2

Railway Exchange Building, lobby, Chicago, Illinois

the property, where it occupies several floors. Architectural firms and the Chicago Architecture Foundation are other tenants.

STATE UNIVERSITY OF NEW YORK ADMINISTRATION BUILDING
(formerly the Delaware and Hudson Railroad Building)
1918, Marcus T. Reynolds
353 Broadway, Albany, NY

Marcus Reynolds's magnificent railroad headquarters terminates the view down State Street from the New York State Capitol (by Henry Hobson Richardson), with which it is sometimes confused. The building's soaring, castellated central tower and widely extended arms are in the Flemish Gothic revival style. Granite and cast-stone trim make up the surface of the steel-frame and concrete structure, which has steep slate roofs; the spire atop the lower, southern tower is covered with terra-cotta tiles.

The square thirteen-story main tower and the five-story wings that angle out from it are linked by an arcade. Arched window bays rise up to richly

Figure 7.1

Railway Exchange Building, Chicago, Illinois

Figure 7.3
State University of New York Administration Building, Albany, New York

decorated dormers, and ornamental figures—coats of arms, human statues, and beavers (representing early trade with Native Americans)—add visual interest. In the dormer at the top of the central tower, flanked by turrets, is a copy of Michelangelo's statue of Lorenzo de Medici called *Il Pensieroso* (the thoughtful one). And at the very pinnacle of the ensemble sits a seven-by-nine-foot, four-hundred-pound replica of the *Half Moon*, the ship in which Henry Hudson sailed up the river to Albany. It is supposedly the nation's largest working weather vane.

The building stretches 1,013 feet from end to end, but is just 48 feet deep, forming an architectural screen. This concept evolved as the result of a plan advanced by Reynolds to create a plaza at the foot of State Street. Arnold W. Brunner, a landscape architect hired by the City of Albany, argued that the view would be not of the Hudson River, but of the

unsightly railyards and piers that lined it. He recommended a new building anchored by a picturesque tower on the axis of State Street, and Reynolds got the job of designing it.

Marcus Reynolds (1869–1937) was born in Massachusetts but raised in Albany. He graduated from Williams College and received an architecture degree from Columbia University. In 1910 he began a two-year tour of Europe to study medieval architecture, and near the end of it discovered the Cloth Hall in Ypres, Belgium, which he used as a model for his railroad office building. Reynolds designed other prominent buildings in Albany and elsewhere, but the Delaware and Hudson Railroad Building is considered his masterpiece. It was built in stages in 1914–18, with the central tower and north wing first, followed by the south wing and its octagonal secondary tower. The latter was occupied by the *Albany Evening Journal*, but the rest of the building was devoted to the railroad's offices, except for the shops that lined the arcade. A plaza fronted the building.

Following the general decline of railroads in the mid-twentieth century, the vast pile stood empty for a time until it was rescued by Governor Nelson Rockefeller, who was expanding the State University of New York and decided to make the building the university's headquarters. The university bought it in 1973 and moved in five years later, after the original interior had been removed; the space reconfigured for contemporary office use; and new electrical, plumbing, and mechanical systems added—for a total cost of $15 million.

In 2001 a two-year, $10-million restoration of the façade was completed, supervised by John G. Waite Associates, architects, whose offices are located across Broadway from the building. A detailed examination of the structure, scientific testing, and archival research using the original drawings and correspondence revealed that it had been built in four sections by four different contractors. (As a result of this investigation, Waite determined that the sections that required the most restoration work were those built by the contractors who cut corners or used shoddy materials.) The exterior masonry was cleaned, repaired, and repointed, and missing decorative elements were recast and replaced. Repairs were also made to the gables and roof.

The top four floors of the southern tower are the official residence of the State University of New York's chancellor. State University Plaza, as it is now known, was recently restored.

Two blocks to the north, at 575 Broadway, stands Albany's former Union Station, designed by Shepley, Rutan and Coolidge and built in 1900 by the New York Central Railroad; the Delaware and Hudson Railroad also used it. Albany—the hub of the New York Central System, which linked New York City, Boston, and Buffalo to points west—hosted the Twentieth Century Limited and other named trains of the day. The beaux arts station building features a granite center block with three large arched portals, similar to New York's Grand Central Terminal and to union stations

in several other major cities. In the interior, balconies with cast-iron railings overlooked the high-ceilinged waiting room.

The station closed in 1968 and was later sold, with the tracks behind it, to the New York State Department of Transportation to make way for Interstate 787. (The trains were rerouted to a remote and inconvenient station across the river in Rensselaer.) The station building, not needed for the highway, stood empty until 1984, when Norstar Bancorp acquired it for $450,000 and, at a cost of $14 million, renovated it for its operations. There have been changes in ownership and tenants since then.

RAILWAY EXCHANGE BUILDING
1914, Mauran, Russell and Crowell
600 Locust St., St. Louis, MO

The huge Railway Exchange Building, a department store topped by railroad company offices, exemplifies the expansive role of St. Louis as the nation's centrally located water-rail transportation depot, second only to Chicago.

The twenty-one-story building covers an entire

Figure 7.4
Railway Exchange Building, St. Louis, Missouri

city block, bounded by Sixth, Seventh, Locust, and Olive Streets, and its statistics are commensurate with its size. The Railway Exchange Building contains 1.2 million square feet (27.5 acres) of office and retail space, 10,000 tons of steel, and 4,142 windows. It is faced with 182,978 terra-cotta tiles. Its weight of 189,230 tons is borne by 110 steel and concrete caissons sunk 40 feet to bedrock.

The steel-frame, Commercial style structure incorporated a novel reinforced concrete floor system employing corrugated steel sheets covered with concrete. That—plus a sprinkler system and metal stairways, doors, and window frames—made it fireproof in the eyes of city officials, enabling them to waive the height restrictions on downtown buildings in this case.

The ground-floor display windows and the first five store levels are defined by string courses; their absence and subtle variations in the fenestration identify the fifteen upper stories that are devoted mostly to offices (a central light court penetrates the office floors).

The four major street entrances (there are seven entrances altogether) are highly ornamented with balustrades of S-scrolls, a variety of decorative moldings, rows of arches, and pairs of pilasters with Ionic capitals and human busts, all executed in terra-cotta. The architect, John L. Mauran—a graduate of the Massachusetts Institute of Technology who worked for Shepley, Rutan and Coolidge in Boston, Chicago, and St. Louis before forming his own firm—regarded terra-cotta as particularly appropriate for local buildings. He said it suited the St. Louis climate, and the raw material, clay, was readily available.

The Famous-Barr department store initially occupied the lower seven floors in the building, later expanding to ten floors. The first floor, overlooked by a mezzanine on one side, featured twenty-foot Doric columns and a soda fountain of Italian marble and Mexican onyx. The second had a Louis XVI style salon. On the fifth floor were an art gallery, circulating library, nursery and play area for children, and company offices. Men's and women's gymnasiums, a dance pavilion, a hospital, and a dining room occupied the sixth floor. All merchandise entered and

Figure 7.5
Railway Exchange Building, detail, St. Louis, Missouri

left the store via a ten-story annex a block away that was connected to the main building by a conveyor system in a tunnel.

Offices were around the central light court and on the perimeter of the building. Railway companies—twenty-four in all—were the major tenants, with the Wabash and the Missouri Pacific each taking up several floors. Doctors, dentists, lawyers, insurance and construction companies, detective agencies, real estate agents, and hair dressers also had offices in the Railway Exchange Building.

In 2006, Federated Department Stores acquired the May Company, of which Famous-Barr was a part, and installed a Macy's department store in the building. The store closed in 2013, and the other major tenant, a technology firm, also left. The building has stood empty since then.

One City Center, a four-story mall with a twenty-five-story office tower developed by the May Company that cost $95 million, had opened on an adjacent block in 1985. One City Center was anchored at one end by the Railway Exchange Building and connected to it by sky bridges. Facing competition from suburban malls in the mid-1990s, One City Center closed in 2006. In 2010, it was converted to a parking garage and given a new façade; the sky bridges to the Railway Exchange Building were demolished.

FRISCO BUILDING
1904; 1906, Eames and Young
906 Olive St., St. Louis, MO

The St. Louis–San Francisco Railroad (the Frisco) was an 1870 combination of the Pacific Railroad (later the Missouri Pacific)—the first railroad west of the Mississippi River—and another early trans-Mississippi line, the Atlantic and Pacific Railroad. Around 1900, when Benjamin F. Yoakum, who owned the Chicago, Rock Island and Pacific and other railroads, took over the Frisco, a new headquarters building was called for.

It was the work of the designers of Cupples Sta-

Figure 7.6
Frisco Building, St. Louis, Missouri

tion, the St. Louis railroad warehouse complex. The Frisco building is a thirteen-story, steel-frame, Commercial style structure faced with brick and trimmed with Bedford limestone and terra-cotta. A matching addition to the west along Olive Street was completed in 1906. Above the storefronts, lion heads, cartouches, and plain and vermiculated bands decorate the piers and apron panels below the windows. The Frisco monogram (FS) appears at the top level. An interior court brought daylight into the building—which, besides the railroad, housed other commercial firms and physicians' offices.

After the Frisco merged with the Burlington-Northern Railroad in 1980, the building's occupancy rate declined. The Burnham Development Corporation and Hastings and Chivetta Architects completed a $14-million renovation in 1984. The interior was rebuilt, and new elevators and electrical and mechanical systems were installed. The windows were replaced with energy-efficient ones similar in appearance to the originals. A bank and police station are now located on the ground floor, and health care systems, construction companies, and legal and accounting firms occupy the upstairs offices.

PARK PACIFIC APARTMENTS
(formerly Missouri Pacific Building)
1928, Mauran, Russell, and Crowell
1226 Olive St., St. Louis, MO

The twenty-two-story, steel-frame building in the modernistic style is faced with terra-cotta tiles; railroad iconography appears over the Tucker Boulevard entrance. Above the gray granite base are New York–style zoning setbacks (Hugh Ferris, a native of St. Louis and the influential delineator of New York skyscrapers, sketched an early version of the building). The U-shape plan ensures that the maximum amount of light reaches the interior.

In contrast to the gleaming white exterior, the lobby is quite colorful, with a black-and-white checkerboard floor of terrazzo tile, light brown marble walls, and a coffered ceiling decorated with floral and pine cone motifs.

Figure 7.7

Park Pacific Apartments, St. Louis, Missouri

Figure 7.8

Park Pacific Apartments, lobby, St. Louis, Missouri

The Missouri Pacific (MoPac) Railroad, which built the building, operated the first train west of the Mississippi River in 1852. The company later expanded—partly under the aegis of Jay Gould, who bought a controlling interest in 1879—into a vast network that reached north to Chicago, south to New Orleans, west to Colorado, and southwest to Texas.

Before moving to its new headquarters, MoPac was the largest single tenant of the Railway Exchange Building, designed by the same architects. In 1982, MoPac merged with the Union Pacific Railroad, and when the new company made Omaha its corporate headquarters in 2004, the building became vacant. New owners renovated it for residential use in 2006 at a cost of $109 million. The lobby was restored, but the upper floors have been altered.

HELMSLEY BUILDING
(formerly New York Central Building)
1928, Warren and Wetmore
230 Park Ave., New York, NY

An office tower was part of the original plans for Grand Central Terminal. The New York Central Building was the belated physical result, shifted a few blocks north. Designed by the architectural firm that was responsible for the headhouse, it became a major element of "Terminal City," the air rights development planned for the nearby area that was inspired by the City Beautiful movement.

One of the few drive-through skyscrapers, the steel-frame, brick-faced, thirty-four-story building has a lavishly decorated entrance and lobby and an equally ornate crown. The two portals carry Park Avenue traffic around the Met Life Building (formerly the Pan Am Building) and Grand Central Terminal. The main entrance is under a clock and flanking sculptural figures that closely resemble Jules Coutan's statuary group fronting Grand Central Terminal. The marble-lined lobby serves as a passageway between the cross streets. Topped by a tall, fanciful lantern and spire that look as if they might have been lifted from a baroque cathedral in France and dropped down in

Figure 7.9
Helmsley Building,
New York, New York

Manhattan, the copper-covered pyramidal roof is festooned with oval dormers. At night, when additional light was projected through the dormers, the lantern was illuminated, creating a beacon for Grand Central Terminal, known as the Gateway to the Continent.

The construction of the Pam Am Building in 1963 blocked the view of the New York Central Building from the south, and when seen from the north it tends to be overwhelmed by the façade of its much larger neighbor. The Helmsley real estate firm bought the building in 1977 and changed its name. It has had several other owners since then.

GERALD GODIN BUILDING
(formerly Grand Trunk Railway Office Building)
1902, Richard A. Waite
360 McGill St., Montreal, QC

Its main exterior element, decoration, and magnificent central staircase compensate somewhat for the Grand Trunk Railway's flagship headquarters in Montreal being an imperfectly integrated architectural composition, due primarily to the disjointed window treatments. The entrance pavilion resembles a tall grandfather clock: it has a doorway and a balcony, then a two-story oriel and a stone grill separating the name and date of the building, and finally a clock six feet in diameter that is under a classical pediment

Figure 7.10

Gerald Godin Building,
Montreal, Quebec

bordered by antefixae. The whole constitutes a re-minder that time ruled the railroads (and their passengers and workers).

The five-story, U-shape building with corner towers sits on a granite base and is finished with Indiana limestone, a softer material that allowed extensive sculptural modeling. A closer look is rewarding, for the ornamentation of the three façades is quite striking. Winged lions and cornucopias mark the corners of the right-hand tower, and various scrollwork, ribbons, and stylized keystones and capitals decorate the areas around the windows.

The panels of ceramic tile from England in the vestibule present figures of Hermes, the Greek god of commerce and travel, and angels, as well as masks. The main feature of the lobby is the central staircase. Guarded by a pair of cast-iron griffons, it has wide marble steps and wrought-iron railings decorated with palmettes, scrolls, and human heads. The staircase rises through five floors of the building in an open light court that takes up 20 percent of the interior space. The marble for the lobby walls came from several European countries and Africa.

Due to his training, the decorative use of iron was familiar to the architect. Richard A. Waite (1848–1911) was born in London and grew up in Buffalo, New York. Family circumstances forced him to cut short his schooling and go to work. At the age of eighteen, he moved to New York City. Waite first served as an apprentice to John Ericsson—a maritime engineer and designer of the ironclad *USS Monitor*, of Civil War fame. He then worked as a draftsman with John Kellum, the architect of several of New York's cast-iron-front buildings. Kellum's work included the 1862 landmark A. T. Stewart Department Store (later demolished), which featured a grand central staircase under a light court. Returning to Buffalo, Waite designed iron-front commercial buildings there as well as schools, churches, hotels, and houses. He also worked in several Canadian cities, designing the Ontario Legislative Building in Toronto. One of his employees was Louise Blanchard Bethune, America's first professional female architect.

A particular challenge in designing the Grand Trunk headquarters was the St. Pierre River that ran under the site and made it difficult to find adequate

Figure 7.11
Gerald Godin Building, staircase, Montreal, Quebec

footings for the foundation. The St. Pierre flowed into the St. Lawrence; used mainly as a sewer, it gradually became part of Montreal's sewer system and is today known as a ghost river.

The Grand Trunk Railway occupied its headquarters until 1919 when, overextended financially, it became part of the Canadian National (CN) Railways.

After CN moved elsewhere in 1961, the Government of Quebec acquired the building, later turning it over to the province's Ministry of Immigration. Restored in 1988 and again in 2013, it was named for Gerald Godin, a Quebec journalist, poet, and politician who was minister of immigration in the 1980s.

8

GRAND HOTELS

I n 1885, William Cornelius Van Horne, then general manager and later president of the Canadian Pacific Railway (CPR), saw completed through the Rocky Mountains the final section of a nearly 3,000-mile transcontinental railroad line extending from Montreal to Vancouver. And he foresaw the tourist potential of the spectacularly beautiful mountain wilderness. If we can't export the scenery, we'll import the tourists, said Van Horne.

The railroad's dining cars were too heavy to drag up the steep mountain grades, so in 1886 the company built in the Swiss chalet style three eating house–hotels in British Columbia (all later demolished). The CPR built the first Banff Springs Hotel in Alberta, designed by Bruce Price, and the first Hotel Vancouver in its brand-new West Coast destination city in 1888 (both later demolished). Price's Château Frontenac in Quebec City opened in 1893. It was the railroad's first hotel in the château or Scottish baronial style that not only became the model for the company's later hotels, but would also set the pattern for government buildings in Ottawa for the next fifty years.

In the following decades, the CPR built more luxury urban and resort hotels. The Grand Trunk and Grand Trunk Pacific Railways and the Canadian National Railway (CNR) followed suit. By the 1930s a string of railway hotels in the major cities extended across Canada from the Atlantic (in Halifax, Nova Scotia) to the Pacific (in Victoria, British Columbia). The CNR's Queen Elizabeth (1958) in Montreal was the last of the grand railway hotels. Thirty years later, the CPR acquired ownership of all of Canada's railway hotels. In 1999, it bought the American Fairmont chain and renamed the company Fairmont Hotels and Resorts, which is the operator of the greatest collection of railway hotels in North America. Expanded and upgraded, the hotels have maintained their status as luxurious places to stay.

Van Horne's optimistic vision of the tourist potential of the Canadian Rockies has been more than justified. Railroads were instrumental in establishing the system of national parks in the United States and Canada. Banff National Park—Canada's first, created in 1885 and patterned on Yellowstone National Park (1872) in the United States—is now one of the most popular national parks in North America. Banff and the adjoining Jasper National

Park draw five million visitors annually, although the tourists arrive these days primarily by airline and automobile rather than by rail.

Many railroad resort hotels are likewise located in the national parks of the American West and Southwest. The Northern Pacific Railway and Jay Cooke, who financed its construction, publicized the Wyoming Territory's bizarre geology and provided key support for the political movement to make Yellowstone America's first national park. The railroad built the Old Faithful Inn there in 1904 in a combination of Swiss chalet and Craftsman styles.

Farther south, in Las Vegas, New Mexico, the Santa Fe Railway created the classic Fred Harvey railroad hotel-restaurant, the Castaneda Hotel, in mission revival style in 1899. But the railroad departed radically from architectural regionalism in its Montezuma Hotel at Montezuma (Las Vegas Hot Springs), designed by Burnham and Root in the Queen Anne style. From a distance, the hotel resembled a French castle; nothing like it had ever before been seen in the American Southwest.

In Arizona, Mary Colter—the Santa Fe's in-house architect and stylist—employed the Pueblo style to design some of the structures of the El Tovar Hotel complex (1905) in Grand Canyon National Park. Traditional Southwestern architectural styles again came into play when the railway and its architect, along with the Fred Harvey Company (discussed below in this chapter), created La Posada in Winslow, Arizona (1930), which Colter designed in a combined Spanish colonial–mission revival style. It is the one of the few remaining Santa Fe–Harvey-Colter collaborations in which railroad hotel hospitality, as originally conceived, is still extended to passengers when they get off the train.

Montana's Glacier National Park has two great railroad hotels: the Glacier Park Lodge and the Many Glacier Hotel, both in the Swiss chalet style. James J. Hill, founder of the Great Northern Railway, helped create Glacier National Park in 1910. His son and successor, Louis W. Hill, built these hotels, and one at Waterton Lakes, Alberta, in the same style.

Schools and colleges have been the saviors of

several former railroad hotels: the Montezuma (Las Vegas Hot Springs) in New Mexico; Frank Furness's former Bryn Mawr Hotel, near Philadelphia; and two in Florida. The first in Florida, built by Henry Flagler's Florida East Coast Railway in 1888, was the Hotel Ponce de Leon in St. Augustine, designed by Carrere and Hastings in a Spanish Renaissance revival style. The second, the Tampa Bay Hotel (1891) was a magnificent Moresque palace built by Henry B. Plant, whose railroad system on the Gulf Coast rivaled Flagler's on the East Coast.

CHÂTEAU FRONTENAC
1893; 1899, Bruce Price; 1909, Walter S. Painter, wing; 1924, Edward and William S. Maxwell, wing, tower; 1993, Arcop Group, wing, restoration
Rue St. Louis, Quebec City, QC

Cape Diamond, the site chosen by Van Horne and his associates for their new hotel, was one of the most historic in Quebec City. The settlement's earliest forts were built there, and the French and British governors had their residences there for two hundred years. Close by was the Citadelle, the fort built by Louis de Buade, comte de Frontenac, greatest of the governors of New France in the late 1600s. It overlooked

Figure 8.1

Château Frontenac, Quebec City, Quebec

Figure 8.2
Château Frontenac, Quebec City, Quebec

the Plains of Abraham, where British and French forces fought the decisive battle in 1759 that led to the creation of British Canada.

The model for Price's hotel was the Château de Jaligny, a castle in the Loire Valley of France (Price described his work at the Château Frontenac as "the early French château adapted to modern requirements.")[16] His building was fortress-like: the main façade consisted of a large round tower under a conical roof with Gothic-style dormers, a central section, and a semi-octagonal tower with a pyramidal roof and turrets. Wings angled off from both towers forming a faceted structure, roughly horseshoe-shape, with the entrance in the rear through an enclosed courtyard. The materials were red brick and gray stone.

The public and dining rooms on the ground floor and the 170 hotel rooms above, with fireplaces and sixteenth-century-style oak furniture, all faced the St. Lawrence. To make sure that the hotel appeared majestic enough when seen from the river, Van Horne and Price went out in a small boat and looked back at the completed building. Evidently satisfied, Van Horne decided to replicate the Château Frontenac across Canada. One of the first such structures was the Place Viger Station-Hotel in Montreal, which opened in 1898 (see chapter 2). All of the additions to the Château Frontenac, with the exception of the main central tower, were extensions of Price's first plan. Price added a wing on the western side in 1899, and ten years later Walter Painter extended it, using reinforced concrete; the wing culminated in a square pavilion under a high-reaching hip roof.

The counterpart to Painter's addition was the eastern wing; it and the great central tower were designed by the Maxwell brothers, Edward and William,

Figure 8.3
Château Frontenac, stairway to the Palm Room, Quebec City, Quebec

and opened in 1924. The square seventeen-story tower's top four floors expanded slightly outward and were surrounded by corner turrets below a steep hip roof with many dormers. The tower unified the scattered collection of wings and gave the hotel its distinctive profile of a mountain peak surrounded by foothills. The steel-frame tower had reinforced concrete floors, and the walls were constructed of fire-resistant clay tiles. Two of the hotel's finest interior features were the double stairway at one end of the lobby and its destination—the Palm Room, with its frescoed ceiling. The Maxwell brothers designed the Hotel Palliser (1914) in Calgary, Alberta, and other hotels and stations for the CPR. The upper portion of their Château Frontenac tower bears a distinct resemblance to Henry Hobson Richardson's landmark Trinity Church tower (1877) in Boston.

In 1926, a fire destroyed Price's initial hotel structure. It was rebuilt according to the architect's plans, but nothing remains of the original interior. The hotel was the site of conferences in 1943 and 1944 when President Franklin D. Roosevelt and British Prime Minister Winston Churchill, their chiefs of staff, and other dignitaries met with Canadian Prime Minister Mackenzie King to plot military strategy in the midst of World War II. British royalty and Hollywood stars have also stayed at the hotel over the years.

In 1993, to celebrate the Château Frontenac's centennial, the CPR opened its $65-million final addition to the hotel. Designed by the Arcop Group, it extended Painter's eastern wing in a compatible style and incorporated a swimming pool, fitness center, and convention facilities. The Château Frontenac became part of the Fairmont chain of hotels in 2001. In 2007, the

Quebec Deposit and Investment Fund, a Crown corporation that manages several pension funds, and its real estate affiliate, Ivanhoe Cambridge, acquired the hotel. The current owners completed a $75-million restoration in 2014 that included new copper roofs and exterior masonry repairs, a renovation of the guest rooms, an expansion of the banquet areas, and three new restaurants. Behind the reception desk in the lobby, a blue onyx panel was installed that represents the St. Lawrence River. And in the rotunda of the grand passageway leading from the lobby to the restaurants facing the river, a fifteen-foot glass stalactite was hung, a reminder of the icy Quebec winters. The hotel has 611 guest rooms and a staff of 700.

The Dufferin Terrace, the historic boardwalk in front of the Château Frontenac, serves as a broad promenade (and toboggan slide) from which to view the building that has become the symbol of the city, as well as the oceangoing ships gliding by on the river below. The spectacle is especially impressive at night.

CHÂTEAU LAURIER
1912, Ross and MacFarlane; 1929, Archibald and Schofield, east wing
1 Rideau St., Ottawa, ON

The British-owned Grand Trunk Railway, Canada's first important railroad, opened its initial line between Montreal and Toronto in 1856. At the end of the nineteenth century it was the dominant railroad in Ontario and Quebec. But the CPR was becoming a serious competitor in the home territory of the Grand Trunk, which envied its rival's transcontinental line and growing collection of resort hotels. Furthermore, the Grand Trunk's financial performance was lackluster. To deal with these problems, in 1896 the company brought Charles Melville Hays in as general manager (he was named president in 1909).

Hays was born in Rock Island, Illinois; started in the railroad business as a teenage clerk; and worked his way up to become vice president of the Wabash Railroad. After he arrived in Montreal, Hays increased profits by improving the Grand Trunk's physical plant and general operations. He also got a new company

headquarters built and began planning to construct the Grand Trunk Pacific, part of a new transcontinental line, in partnership with the Canadian government. In addition, he wanted to build several railroad hotels. The first was to be in Ottawa, in conjunction with a new railroad station (see chapters 3 and 7).

In 1906, the Grand Trunk hired Bradford Lee Gilbert (1853–1911) to design both the station and the hotel. A railroad architect, Gilbert designed roughly seventy-five train stations and related structures for some twenty-five major railroad companies during his career. Among these were an earlier version of New York's Grand Central Terminal, and the Illinois Central Station in Chicago (both later demolished). Based in New York City, Gilbert was talented and prolific, and judging by his writings, he thought deeply and critically about his profession.

The reasons for replacing Gilbert with Ross and MacFarlane on the Ottawa project are not entirely clear, but there was evidently a dispute over costs. According to published reports at the time, Gilbert designed a classical-style train station for a different location than the one that was chosen. When the current site was selected, he redesigned the station in the château style to match his hotel, because the two buildings would stand opposite each other on Rideau Street. Gilbert's estimated costs were $1 million for the station and $1.5 million for the hotel. Hays told him to cut the hotel cost to $1 million, but when Gilbert did so by removing several floors from the building plans, he was accused of exceeding his instructions and dismissed.

Hays later admitted at a city council hearing that the Ross and MacFarlane hotel was essentially the same as the one designed by Gilbert. This is borne out by the rendering of Gilbert's hotel published at the time. Ross and MacFarlane cut the costs as Hays requested by reducing the budget for the station to $500,000 and reportedly adopted Gilbert's classical design for that building as well. Gilbert sued for nonpayment of fees, alleging plagiarism, but the case was settled out of court.

The façade of the Château Laurier, with its recessed central block between two tower-like pavilions,

Figure 8.4
Château Laurier, Ottawa, Ontario
(courtesy of Fairmont Hotels and Resorts)

recalls that of the Château Frontenac. The longer leg of the roughly L-shape building follows the same pattern. It faces the Rideau Canal, again according to Gilbert's plan. Linking the two sections is a circular medieval stair tower under a conical roof that also contains a water tank. A porte cochere with a ceiling of Guastavino tile fronted the building.

Clad with Indiana limestone on a granite base, the fourteen-story, steel-frame hotel cost $2 million to construct. The steep hip roofs and ornamental dormers and finials, hallmarks of the château style, were present, but the pale monochrome walls were plainer than the rugged multicolored masonry of Price's hotel in Quebec City, perhaps more in keeping with the Château Laurier's more formal setting in the nation's capital. The open, lofty, and rather chilly interior public spaces—lobby, ballroom, and dining room—were finished in imitation Caen stone, marble, and dark woodwork.

Gilbert died the year before the hotel was completed. In 1912 Hays, whose Grand Trunk Pacific Railway was proving to have been a costly misadventure, was in London soliciting funds for the project. He died in the sinking of the *Titanic* on his way back to Ottawa to open the hotel officially. Prime Minister Sir

Wilfred Laurier, for whom the hotel is named, did attend the opening ceremony.

The transcontinental line, completed in 1914, was a financial failure that led to the Grand Trunk's bankruptcy five years later. In 1923, it became part of the new Canadian National Railway, which today operates coast-to-coast passenger trains in Canada through the Canadian Rockies to Prince Rupert, Hays's original destination in British Columbia.

Archibald and Schofield's 240-room addition to the Château Laurier, facing Mackenzie Avenue, was crowned with a high pyramidal roof. The 1929 east wing doubled the size of the hotel and made it U-shape. New public spaces were created on the ground floor. The lobby, which retains its balcony and paneled ceiling, was made warmer with the installation of oak wainscoting. The Flemish style was chosen for the nearby lounge, whose fanciful columns, bracket-formed shoulder arches, and decorative beams are still in place. The ballroom was designed in elegant Adam style, with a Palladian motif and stenciled ceiling. Distinguished guests used the new arched entryway from Mackenzie Avenue. Echoes of the lobby's grand marble staircase occur throughout the hotel, in smaller corner stairways with fancy ironwork railings.

John Archibald, a Scotsman, and John Schofield, an Irishman, both emigrated to Canada and ended up in Montreal. Archibald found employment as a draftsman for Edward Maxwell, whose railroad work includes Windsor Station and the Château Frontenac; he later went into business for himself and designed numerous stations and hotels for the Canadian National Railway. Schofield went west to Winnipeg and worked as a draftsman for another railroad before coming to Montreal as the Canadian National Railway's chief architect.

In the 1960s, a parking structure was built in the rear of the hotel. The porte cochere was enlarged, but it lost its Guastavino tile ceiling in the 1980s when the interior was renovated once again. The hotel's copper roof was replaced in the early twenty-first century.

The Château Laurier has hosted its share of heads of state and real and stage royalty (in the early days,

Figure 8.5
Château Laurier, dining room, Ottawa, Ontario
(courtesy of Fairmont Hotels and Resorts)

the hotel manager stood in the lobby and personally greeted guests). The photographer Yousuf Karsh had his studio and residence in the hotel for nearly twenty years. Pierre Trudeau lived there in the 1960s, before he became prime minister. Much parliamentary business has been conducted in the hotel's restaurants, lounges, and hallways.

BANFF SPRINGS HOTEL
1914, Walter S. Painter, center section;
   1928, John W. Orrock, wings; later additions
405 Spray Ave., Banff, AB

So expansive has this hotel building grown over the years, and so vast and magnificent is the surrounding mountain scenery, that it is impossible to take everything in at once. The Banff Springs Hotel is the western flagship of the CPR's resort hotels.

Bruce Price designed the original Banff Springs Hotel, which opened in 1888. It was an amalgam of the shingle and château styles. The three-story hotel, made of timber and faced with wooden shingles, consisted of a center section and two wings. It had tall hip roofs and chimneys and lots of dormers, but the last were more in the Swiss chalet than the château style. Critics had trouble describing the incompletely integrated elements. Terraced porches were available for relaxing and viewing the outdoor scenery. Inside, an open rotunda, overlooked by balconies, rose through all the floors to the ceiling. This feature later became a staple of nearly all the Western railroad resort hotels.

Banff Springs proved popular, and two additional wooden wings were added to house the hotel's growing clientele. The next big expansion was actually a reconstruction that required the demolition of the center section of Price's building. Later substitutions and a fire resulted in its complete disappearance.

Painter, the CPR's chief architect, was the author of the new central portion of the hotel: an eleven-story, steel-frame tower in true château style — with which the architect was familiar, through his earlier work on the Château Frontenac. It was of reinforced concrete construction, covered with Rundle stone — a blue-gray limestone from nearby Mount Rundle that turns reddish brown on exposure to the sun, giving it a color similar to that of red brick. It had a steep pitched roof with three ranks of dormers, above which a pyramidal roof rose to a sharp point, also with several sets of dormers. Painter's plans called for two wings to be added to the central section, terminating in pavilions with tall octagonal roofs.

The wings were not built until 1928, and they were in a slightly different configuration than that proposed by Painter. They replaced the wooden wings of Price's hotel, one of which was destroyed in a 1926 fire. John W. Orrock, the CPR's engineer of buildings, designed the new wings and also significantly enlarged Painter's central section, to which he added a new roof. Orrock was an engineer rather than an architect, but he evidently knew a great deal about construction and wrote a book on the subject, *Railroad Structures and Estimates*, that discussed everything from bridges to section houses.

Orrock's eight-story wings in the château style also were constructed of concrete faced with Rundle stone and had a steel frame. Their roofs were enriched with dormers; steep pyramidal roofs rose

Figure 8.6
Banff Springs Hotel,
Banff, Alberta

Figure 8.7
Banff Springs Hotel, Mount Stephen Hall, Banff, Alberta
(courtesy of Fairmont Hotels and Resorts)

over the angled end pavilions. Orrock rearranged the basic elements of Painter's roof over the central section of the hotel. He also added a new entrance and lobby, so the building today primarily represents Orrock's work.

The Banff Springs Hotel both celebrated its rugged surroundings by inviting guests to explore the Bow River Valley and Canadian Rockies by foot, canoe, or horseback (Swiss guides were available for the more adventurous) and demonstrated that urban luxury and sophistication were transferrable to the wilderness, via the railroad. Hotel guests could also relax in the nearby hot springs.

While the hotel exterior was unified in terms of style, the interior spaces reflected a range of influences and a variety of exotic materials. Mount Stephen Hall, named for the CPR's first president, Lord Mount Stephen, is a two-story room with an L-shape balcony that resembles the hall of a castle. Marble elliptical arches support the oak-beam ceiling. Crowned heads and torsos holding provincial crests decorate the corbels supporting the beams. The room is lit by a wall of windows and wrought-iron chandeliers that hang from the ceiling; the floor is Bedford, Indiana, limestone. Overlooking Mount Stephen Hall is the lantern-lit Spanish Walk, featuring the same décor.

The Riverview Lounge boasts a huge mantelpiece of carved Tyndall stone (a soft limestone from Manitoba that contains fossils), decorated with ram's heads. The lounge offers classic views of the evergreen trees, river valley, and mountains through large round-headed picture windows. On the same level is the Grapes Wine Bar, the former library and writing room. It has a flowing grape vine motif in the plaster crown molding, head-high dark paneled wainscoting, an oak floor, and painted glass windows. Rundle Hall, the former lobby, is now a bar and lounge. Heritage Hall, off the main stairway, tells the story of the railroad and the hotel in photographs and text; most of the railroad hotels have a similar room or space devoted to their history.

A new wing (1987) and a conference center (1991), built in a complementary style, roughly doubled the size of the 1928 hotel. In the courtyard formed by the new additions stands a bronze statue of Van Horne, pointing to his 770-room hotel and the mountains conquered by his railroad.

EMPRESS HOTEL
1908, Francis M. Rattenbury; 1914, Walter S. Painter, north and south wings; 1929, John W. Orrock, addition
921 Government St., Victoria, BC

In Victoria, the capital of British Columbia and some 3,200 miles by railroad from Quebec City, the CPR built the Empress Hotel in the same style as the Château Frontenac, which had been completed fifteen years earlier. The Canadian Pacific Line steamship pier was conveniently near the Empress (visitors today arrive via ferry from Vancouver). Superbly sited overlooking Victoria's inner harbor, the Empress has become the city's signature building.

Francis Rattenbury—the hotel's architect, whose scandal-filled personal life ended tragically—also designed the British Columbia Parliament Buildings (1898), a short distance away, in a ponderous, multidomed, neobaroque style. Though a very large building, his hotel, opened a decade later, was buoyant by comparison.

The Empress was a six-story, steel-frame structure; brick and stone (for the trim) were the exterior materials. The façade was the conventional arrangement: a recessed central section between two pavilions. All three parts had steep hip roofs, the middle one adorned with Gothic type dormers and roof cresting. The architect incorporated one unusual feature: a pair of domed stairway towers at the inside corners. Front and center was a broad, five-bay entrance portico. Tall Ionic columns supported the beamed ceiling of the lobby inside.

Asked to make two minor changes in the interior plan, Rattenbury resigned at the end of 1906. Since the hotel was to be built in stages, he had already drawn up preliminary plans for the north and south wings; Walter Painter was brought in to design these. The south wing faced a rose garden. Two of Painter's outstanding interior spaces were the ballroom, with

Figure 8.8
Empress Hotel, Victoria, British Columbia
(courtesy of Fairmont Hotels and Resorts)

a segmentally arched coffered ceiling, and the Palm Court—in neoclassical revival style, with a large saucer dome skylight of painted glass.

John Orrock's $2.5-million addition in 1929 nearly doubled the size of the building. The hotel went through some difficult times after World War II and came close to being torn down in the1960s, but instead it was restored. The conservatory-like Victoria Conference Center was added in 1989 near the rose garden, part of a $45 million-renovation. A $40-million program to rehabilitate the guest rooms and some of the public spaces is ongoing under new owners.

The main entrance was moved to a lobby pavilion fronting the north wing, and the former lobby is now the Empress Tea Room. The long hallways between the ground-floor public rooms are lined with carved paneling in dark wood and have high beamed ceilings.

In his prime, Rattenbury (1867–1935) was the lead-ing architect of British Columbia. He designed banks, courthouses, and private residences, and at one point he was chief architect for both the CPR and the Bank of Montreal. The Empress is the sole survivor of his CPR hotels. Rattenbury's falling out with the CPR led to his designing a number of hotels for the rival Grand Trunk Railway, but none were constructed due to the death of Hays, the Grand Trunk's president, and the company's subsequent bankruptcy. If Rattenbury's name is known these days, it is as much for the tragic trajectory of his life as for his architecture.

Rattenbury was just twenty-five when he arrived in Victoria from his native England, having trained in his uncles' architectural firm. After he won the competition for the Parliament Buildings, commissions poured in. He married Florence Nunn, the daughter of a retired British Army officer, and mingled with the social elite of the city. He lived in a beachfront home with his wife and their two children.

But Rattenbury was a heavy drinker and could be overbearing and hard to deal with, as indicated by his early departure from the Empress Hotel job. His marriage was in difficulty. At a dinner in his honor at the Empress Hotel in 1923, Rattenbury met Alma Pakenham, a beautiful and bohemian musician from Vancouver who was in town to give a recital. She stayed on to become a music teacher, and they began a very public affair.

He was fifty-six and married; she was twenty-seven and had already had two husbands. The first had been killed in World War I, and Alma Pakenham received the Croix de Guerre for her work behind French lines with a Scottish ambulance unit; her second marriage ended in divorce. The lovers' open carryings-on—fueled, according to rumor, not just by liquor but also by cocaine—scandalized the ultraconservative British social set of Victoria. Rattenbury and Pakenham were ostracized. His wife refused to divorce him, and Rattenbury began to entertain his mistress in their home.

Florence Nunn relented and granted him a divorce. He and Pakenham married and had a child, but they were not welcomed back into Victoria society. In 1929, they moved to Bournemouth, England. With no clients and beset with financial problems, Rattenbury sank further into alcoholism. His wife, bored, took up with their chauffeur-handyman, George Stoner, an eighteen-year-old dropout. One spring night in 1935, as Rattenbury sat in his chair in an alcoholic haze, his head was beaten in with a carpenter's mallet.

Alma Rattenbury and Stoner were charged with murder. After a sensational trial at London's Old Bailey, she was found innocent, but he was declared guilty and sentenced to death. When she left the courthouse, she was booed by a large crowd. A few days later, convinced that Stoner would hang, she committed suicide by stabbing herself in the heart.

Public sympathy lay with her teenage lover, the immature chauffeur-handyman, whom people thought had been seduced and led into committing a foul act by a calculating older woman. A petition with over 300,000 signatures was presented to the home secretary, who commuted Stoner's sentence to life imprisonment. Given time off for good behavior, he was released seven years later. Stoner served in World War II, lived the rest of his life in Bournemouth, and died in 2000 at age of eighty-three. John, the son of Francis and Alma Rattenbury, also an architect, studied under Frank Lloyd Wright at Taliesin and worked on several of Wright's projects, including the Guggenheim Museum.

The Rattenbury affair was the subject of Terence Rattigan's 1975 radio play, *Cause Célèbre*, which was produced in London two years later. A 1987 television version starred Helen Mirren. In 1988, Sir David Napley, a lawyer, wrote a book based on the case, *Murder at the Villa Madeira*. Rattigan's play was successfully revived at London's Old Vic in 2011, the playwright's centenary. A reviewer said that it covered "such classic Rattigan themes [as] the inequality of passion, the power of youth over age and the corrosive effects of English sexual puritanism."[17]

Figure 8.9
Empress Hotel, Palm Court, Victoria, British Columbia (courtesy of Fairmont Hotels and Resorts)

Figure 8.10

Old Faithful Inn, Yellowstone
National Park, Wyoming

OLD FAITHFUL INN
1904; additions, 1914 and 1927, Robert C. Reamer
Yellowstone National Park, WY

Yellowstone's Old Faithful Inn is the ur-hotel of the US national park system. Established in 1872, Yellowstone was America's first national park. The Northern Pacific Railway was instrumental in its creation. Jay Cooke paid for the artist Thomas Moran and the photographer William Henry Jackson to accompany the 1871 Hayden Geological Survey, whose team members explored the region. Their images and Ferdinand Hayden's report were critical factors in making Yellowstone Park a reality. In 1903 the Northern Pacific became the first railroad to access the park by rail, through Gardiner, Montana.

Robert Reamer's architectural response to Yellowstone's otherworldly landscape and natural phenomena, primarily Old Faithful, became a prototype for national park hotels. El Tovar at the Grand Canyon, in Arizona (Atchison, Topeka and Santa Fe Railroad, 1905); Montana's Glacier Park Lodge (Great Northern Railway, 1913); and the Prince of Wales Hotel at Waterton Lakes, Alberta (Great Northern Railway, 1927), are all variations on the theme begun by the Old Faithful Inn: the rustic mountain camp lodge.

The Old Faithful Inn is an especially grand version. Its center section rises dramatically via a high, steeply sloped roof, punctuated with dormers, to a widow's walk with flags flying. Lower wings on either side culminate in cross gables and make for complementary bookends. A large porte cochere extends out in front, supporting on its roof an open deck for viewing Old Faithful. The log-frame structure, covered with cedar shingles, sits on a foundation of concrete and native stone.

Beyond the red entrance doors is an interior forest, where light from the strategically placed windows filters through a tangle of wooden posts, beams, struts, and trusses as it would through the branches of the pine trees outside—at least, that was the architect's intention. The seven-story space is ringed by balconies and split-log stairways that lead to guest rooms and quiet areas for reading, writing, or viewing the ground-floor activity. One corner is anchored by a freestanding, four-sided fireplace built of volcanic rhyolite, whose chimney flows upward to the ceiling like a geyser (it also serves as a support column for the trusswork). Facilities such as a reception counter, dining room, lounge, and gift shop occupy the ground floor.

Constructed largely of lodgepole pine by railroad carpenters experienced in building timber trestles, there is no other interior like the inn's. The fact that it survived an earthquake that registered 7.5 on the Richter scale in 1959 and forest fires that burned over a million acres in Yellowstone and came perilously close to the building in 1988 only adds to its value. (The Crow's Nest at the top, from which musicians used to serenade the guests at dinner, was closed in the aftermath of the earthquake.)

The architectural antecedents of the Old Faithful Inn are the Swiss alpine chalet and the camps of New York's Adirondack Mountains of the late 1800s and early 1900s. They shared some characteristics, such as log construction and a generally rustic appearance. The Swiss chalet typically had a front-facing pitched roof with deep eaves supported on ornamental brackets, a balcony or gallery, and lots of windows. The roofs sometimes had clipped gables.

The Adirondack Mountain camps used native fieldstone and wood in the form of peeled logs and branches to create rustic getaways for the well-to-do. Mission style furniture and mounted fish and game trophies were the preferred interior décor. The publications of Andrew Jackson Downing and Calvert Vaux on country houses and rural cottages, and of Charles Eastlake on interior decoration, popularized

Figure 8.11
Old Faithful Inn, lobby, Yellowstone National Park, Wyoming

the rustic style. The Arts and Crafts movement of the late nineteenth century, inspired by John Ruskin and William Morris, promoted traditional building methods using local materials; it also had an influence. When the National Park Service was created in 1916, it adopted the rustic style for its lodges.

The multistory hotel atrium, surrounded by galleries where guests and visitors can enjoy the passing scene, dates from the early 1800s in the United States. It has remained a staple of hotel design, from Frank Edbrooke's Brown Palace (1892) in Denver to John Portman's Hyatt Regency (1971) in Atlanta, where people ride up and down in glass-enclosed elevators.

In the Old Faithful Inn, Reamer accomplished what every architect hopes for but few achieve: he made a unique personal statement. This is all the more remarkable because at the same time he was redesigning the nearby Lake Hotel in a conventional neoclassical revival style more suited to Eastern resort hotels.

Reamer (1873–1938) was twenty-nine when he received the commission for the Old Faithful Inn. Born in Oberlin, Ohio, he had worked with a Detroit architect as a draftsman when he was a teenager and later moved to San Diego, California, where he opened an architectural office with a partner. He then met Harry W. Child, president of the Yellowstone Park Association, which was controlled by the Northern Pacific Railway.

Reamer designed the Northern Pacific's depot (1903, demolished in 1954) in Gardiner, Montana, in the same rustic style, using a base of native rock, log walls and roof, and a large stone fireplace. He also designed Gardiner's Roosevelt Arch, a fifty-foot-high triumphal arch of coursed rubble masonry that formally marked the north entrance to Yellowstone. President Theodore Roosevelt, a conservationist who created several national parks while he was in office, laid the cornerstone in 1903. The inscription at the top of the arch reads "For the Benefit and Enjoyment of the People." At Gardiner, visitors boarded carriages and later buses for the trip into Yellowstone.

Reamer designed the Canyon Hotel for Yellowstone National Park (destroyed by fire in 1960) before moving to Cleveland, Ohio, where he continued his work for other railroads. His 1914 east wing for the Old Faithful Inn is a three-story, flat-roofed addition sheathed with cedar shingles that angles off from the main hotel axis and faces Old Faithful; it contains 100 guest rooms. Then in 1927, he designed the Y-shape west wing (with 150 guest rooms), four stories with a faux mansard roof and dormers. The year before, after relocating to Seattle, Reamer had designed the Lake Quinnault Lodge in Olympic National Park, west of Seattle, Washington.

The Old Faithful Inn was constructed during Yellowstone's severe winter weather, which brings heavy snowfalls and subzero temperatures. The rhyolite for the fireplace and the lodgepole pine for the lobby interior, including gnarled pieces handpicked by the architect for their decorative value, were found within a ten-mile radius of the hotel. This was in keeping with the principles of rustic architecture—that buildings should harmonize with their surroundings and be made of local materials. It was also considerably faster and less expensive than hauling building materials long distances. Almost everything in the hotel, with the exception of the mission style furniture, was fabricated on site, including the wrought-iron strap hinges and the locks for the front doors.

The spaces in the central section of the inn have been expanded and rearranged several times over the years. In 2012, a $30-million restoration of the inn under the direction of A&E Architects of Missoula, Montana, was completed. It included rebuilding the widow's walk, adding steel reinforcement for seismic stability, installing new mechanical systems, laying a new maple floor in the lobby, restoring the fireplace and chimney, and renovating the guest rooms.

Other railroads later made their way to Yellowstone, most notably the Union Pacific Railroad at West Yellowstone in 1907. Rail passenger service to the park ended in 1960. Today the 3.4 million people who visit Yellowstone each year arrive by automobile, but the joys and rewards of experiencing the American landscape at its most sublime from the deck of the architectural wonder that the Northern Pacific Railway and Robert Reamer created remain unchanged.[18]

CASTANEDA HOTEL
1899, Frederick Louis Roehrig
524 Railroad Ave., Las Vegas, NM

How the West was tamed, according to one Hollywood legend, was by the Atchison, Topeka and Santa Fe Railroad and the Harvey Girls, who brought a civilizing graciousness to a beautiful but violent land. This was not far from the truth in the case of Las Vegas, New Mexico. In 1879, Doc Holliday briefly practiced dentistry there and ran a saloon; after he killed a man, he fled to Dodge City. Billy the Kid left town a year later, going by train from the Las Vegas depot to a jail cell in Santa Fe, courtesy of Sheriff Pat Garrett. Just twenty years later, Fred Harvey's new Castaneda Hotel opened.

The impact of Fred Harvey and the Harvey Girls on the traveling public in the West can only be imagined. In the pre-Harvey era, railroad passengers and other itinerants ate hurriedly in eating houses at train stations and stagecoach stops. The menus typically contained little except beans, bacon, ancient eggs, and black coffee. The plates of food were flung down by former miners or loggers eager to live up to their new reputations as "hash slingers." Often travelers' twenty minutes were up and they were called to reboard their trains before they were even presented with these wretched meals. The only alternative—box lunches or sandwiches purchased on the train—was equally bad.

Harvey admonished his employees to maintain the standard, but first he had to establish it. Frederick Henry Harvey (1835–1901) was born in London, immigrated to America at the age of fifteen, worked as a busboy in a New York restaurant (he didn't like it), journeyed to New Orleans and contracted yellow fever, and then traveled to St. Louis and got married. He opened a restaurant with a partner, who later absconded with their funds. Harvey fell ill with typhoid. His next job was with a packet boat company; after that, he became a railroad mail clerk. By 1876, the Harveys were living in Leavenworth, Kansas, and Harvey was the western freight agent for the Chicago, Burlington and Quincy Railroad. This required him to travel throughout the Midwest and experience firsthand the abysmal eating places and lousy hotels of the time. His ailments doubtless made the conditions in these places seem even worse. In any case, he determined to improve the situation.

In 1875, Harvey and a partner began operating two widely separated cafés on the Kansas Pacific Railway. Supervision proved to be a problem, the partners disagreed on how to run the establishments, and the business soon folded. Harvey's employer, the Chicago, Burlington and Quincy, was not interested in his idea of a chain of restaurants, so he took it to the Santa Fe, whose superintendent, Charles F. Morse, decided to give the tall, distinguished-looking Englishman a chance by leasing him the Topeka depot lunchroom.

On their handshake in 1876 was constructed an amazing business edifice. When Harvey died at the turn of the century, it consisted of fifteen hotels, forty-seven restaurants, thirty dining cars, and the food service on the San Francisco Bay ferries and in the huge St. Louis Union Station. (Since 2006, the Harvey House Diner at Kansas City's Union station has re-created the ambiance of the original Harvey House Grill, which closed in 1968 and was replaced by the ubiquitous food court.)

Harvey started out at the Topeka lunchroom by expanding the menu and providing good food and fast service at moderate prices. Business improved to the extent that the Santa Fe's management asked him to open more restaurants. The first, in 1878, was an existing hotel and restaurant in Florence, Kansas, that Harvey acquired with borrowed funds and then sold to the railroad. Harvey managed the operation. He brought in the former chef of Chicago's Palmer House at a salary of $5,000 a year, and the menu came to include pheasant, quail, and prairie hen, along with the best regional produce.

Word of the venture spread, and Harvey quit the railroad business to become a restaurateur. As the Santa Fe expanded south and west, stagecoach service moved out ahead of the advancing trains, and Harvey Houses followed in their wake. A half-hour before the train was due at the next station that had a Harvey House restaurant, conductors passing through the cars took orders from the passengers. These were telegraphed ahead, and when the train arrived, the first course was already on the tables. Nobody was rushed through a meal.

Courteous and efficient Harvey Girls, dressed in black with starched white aprons, attended to the diners. The Harvey Girls debuted at the Raton, New Mexico, Harvey House in 1883, replacing the male waiters who tended to fight among themselves and pick fights with the customers. Selectively recruited in the Midwest and the East, the young women were ages 18–30, attractive, intelligent, and well trained. They were also well chaperoned, boarding in dormitories with a 10:00 PM curfew. The one-year agreement the Harvey Girls signed required them to remain single during that time. Nevertheless, their impact on the cowboys, trainmen, and other males in the communities where they worked was quite powerful, and vice versa. Employee turnover was high.

Harvey personally enforced the strict standards he set for his establishments, whose table linens came from Ireland and place settings were from Europe. Whenever Harvey inspected one of his restaurants and found a chipped or cracked plate, he smashed it on the floor. Badly set tables were overturned.

In a mutually beneficial and profitable arrangement, Harvey managed the restaurants and hotels, and the Santa Fe Railroad hired (or provided) the architects and built the buildings. The railroad also provided free transportation for Harvey's employees, the ingredients for the meals from all over the country, and the restaurant supplies. Its privately owned dairy facilities (the largest was at Las Vegas) produced fresh milk to drink and to use in the Harvey House homemade ice cream.

After Harvey's death, the Santa Fe Railroad and the family-run Fred Harvey Company expanded their symbiotic relationship into cultural tourism. Together, they recruited the architect Mary Colter to design a new series of more elaborate hotels and restaurants, designed for longer stays. Colter combined elements of Spanish colonial revival and mission revival style and Pueblo Indian motifs into a

Figure 8.12

Castaneda Hotel,
Las Vegas, New Mexico

signature style. The hotel gift shops featured Native American arts and artifacts. Thomas Moran, William Henry Jackson, and other well-known artists, photographers, and writers were given railroad passes and dispatched to record the sublime scenery, particularly the Grand Canyon; the results were used in advertising and other publicity material. Charming and informative hostesses in Western garb called couriers led bus tours to visit the pueblos and admire the landscape (the first "Indian Detours" excursion left the Castaneda Hotel in 1926). The program was designed to identify the Santa Fe Railroad and Fred Harvey with the American West, and to promote the idea that the newly tamed land was ready for tourists and even settlers. It worked.

The Fred Harvey Company extended its restaurant operations to some other railroads and many other cities, airport and bus terminals, and even the Illinois Tollway, before being sold in 1968. Its major association, however, was with the Santa Fe Railroad. Most of the Fred Harvey restaurants that occurred every 100 miles and the hotels scattered along the Santa Fe's 2,250-mile route between Chicago and Los Angeles have closed, and many have been demolished. Three notable hotels that survive and continue to operate are La Fonda in Santa Fe; El Tovar at Grand Canyon, Arizona; and La Posada at Winslow, Arizona.

The Castaneda Hotel was designed by a practitioner of many styles and something of a pasticheur. Frederick Roehrig—a thin, dapper man with a mustache—was trained in architecture at Cornell University where his father, a German immigrant, was a professor of Oriental languages. Roehrig settled in Pasadena, California, and built several houses there and in Los Angeles. His best-known building in Pasadena is the Moresque Castle Green, an addition to a resort hotel. It opened the same year as the Castaneda.

Roehrig's plan for the Castaneda was unusually straightforward for him: a plain mission revival style hotel. It is a two-story, U-shape brick building that embraces a landscaped courtyard. Shaped parapets terminate the arms of the U, and a short tower marks the center. Surrounding the railroad front of the hotel is an arcaded porch. The ground-floor corner conveniently closest to the railroad station housed a bar and lunchroom; behind them, facing the street, was the lobby. It had cast-iron columns, a tin ceiling, a registration desk and newsstand, and a handsome wooden stairway leading to the forty guest rooms above. An upright radiator of the type used in railroad stations originally surrounded the central cast-iron column. The existing newsstand counter on the street side dates from circa the 1940s. Double doors led to the dining room. The hotel's bakery occupied the far corner of the building, across from the bar and lunchroom.

Teddy Roosevelt's Rough Riders held their annual reunions at the Castaneda Hotel from 1899 to 1948, when it closed. The Santa Fe Railroad sold the building to a private developer, who auctioned off most of the furnishings and converted the hotel rooms into apartments. In 1972, new owners opened a bar and discotheque in the former lunchroom and rented out the lobby and dining room for catered events, weddings, and dances. Gradually, the apartment tenants left, the events ceased, and only the bar remained.

In 2014 Allan Affeldt—who restored La Posada, the former Harvey House in Winslow, Arizona (see below)—bought the Castaneda Hotel for $450,000. On completion of a planned $2.5-million restoration, it will be a twenty-room boutique hotel with a dining room, lounge, museum, and art gallery.

Across the street from the hotel, at 515 Railroad Avenue, is the 1899 Rawlins Building. The former home of the Las Vegas Harvey Girls, its second floor has a sheet-metal front.

UNITED WORLD COLLEGE
(formerly the Montezuma Hotel)
1886, Burnham and Root
Route 65, Montezuma (Las Vegas Hot Springs), NM

Actually, there were three Montezuma Hotels, all opened within just a few years of each other in the period 1882–86. The first two burned; the third—the existing building—was rebuilt using the stone walls that survived the final fire. The size of these hotels (three and a half stories high and several hundred feet wide, with picturesque towers and broad verandas) and their "modern" design (Queen Anne style) were a radical departure from the small adobe hotels in territorial style that were customary in that time and place.

The hot springs at Las Vegas have been known for hundreds of years. The Indians and the Spanish sampled their medicinal and restorative properties long before the US Army acquired land at the site in 1846 and built a hospital for Mexican War veterans. Around 1862, the Army decamped, and the former hospital became the Adobe Hotel. Its single story had a sod roof, and log columns supported the front veranda. Jesse James reportedly signed the hotel's guest register. The Adobe Hotel burned circa 1882.

Meanwhile, the Hot Springs (Old Stone) Hotel —three stories topped with a mansard roof, and a two-story wing—had been erected in 1879. It was constructed of sandstone and had 40–50 rooms. A two-story veranda fronted the main section. The building still stands, minus the mansard roof, and is the administration headquarters for United World College. A small community sprang up around this hotel and the bathhouses at the hot springs.

In 1879–80, the Atchison, Topeka and Santa Fe Railroad, which had completed its line to Las Vegas in the summer of 1879, bought the Hot Springs property, including the existing buildings and eight hundred acres of land. The railroad decided to build a much larger destination resort hotel on the scale of those familiar to its travelers from the East and Midwest.

The first Montezuma Hotel was designed by a firm of Kansas City architects. It was E-shape, and a tall, square tower with a pyramidal roof and dormers anchored its central pavilion. The 270-room hotel had a sandstone foundation and a timber frame faced with wooden shingles. When it was completed in 1882, at a cost of $200,000, Fred Harvey was on hand to greet the guests arriving via the six-mile narrow gauge railroad from Las Vegas. The specialty of the dining room was fresh seafood delivered by rail from Mexico. In front of the hotel was a landscaped park with bluegrass lawns, rare flowers, and trees surrounding a central fountain. The Sangre de Cristo Mountains and the Gallinas Canyon, renowned for trout fishing, provided the backdrop (the Gallinas River emerges from the foothills here and enters the fertile lowlands —Las Vegas in Spanish).

In 1884, a clogged gas main caused a fire that destroyed the hotel, leaving only the stone boiler house and its ninety-foot chimney. The Santa Fe Railroad immediately planned to rebuild and hired Burnham and Root, the well-known Chicago architects. (The selection of this renowned Chicago architectural firm may have been related to the fact that the Atchison, Topeka and Santa Fe was at this time extending its line from Kansas City to Chicago, its future headquarters; the line was completed in 1887.) On a visit to the the location, Daniel Burnham determined that the previous hotel had been poorly sited near the river and oriented the wrong way, so that the sun struck only the back of the building. Burnham's site for the new hotel was at a higher elevation, where the Hot Springs reservoir was located, and where it would be much more prominent.

John Wellborn Root designed the new Montezuma Hotel in a fresh Queen Anne style, but in an L-shape (with extensions), and this time in masonry as a fireproofing measure. The brick walls, three feet thick, were faced with local red sandstone on the lower stories and red and black slate shingles from Oklahoma on the upper ones. The roof was of gray slate. A round five-story tower resembling a medieval French fortress, topped by a cantilevered observation platform and a candle-snuffer roof, marked the angle of the L. There were two subordinate towers: a square one with a pyramidal roof near the primary tower (the main entrance to the lobby was between them); and an octagonal tower, also with a belvedere, at one end of the L, where an extension angled off to partially enclose an inner courtyard. The two main façades caught the morning sun, the wooden verandas and balconies offered fine views of the canyon, meadows, and pine-covered slopes.

The lobby's major feature was a huge fireplace with a Tudor Gothic arch and decorated chimney-breast of terra-cotta. The room itself was finished in white ash, used in the beamed and paneled ceiling, columns, floor, wainscoting, reception desk, and latticework screening for the central oak staircase. The adjacent dining room also had a beamed ceiling, multicolored windows with small panes, and a large buffet that included three stained glass panels. Behind the dining room in this functional side of the hotel was the kitchen wing. The other leg of the L with the angled extension housed the 250 hotel rooms. A basement bar, bowling alley, and "Mongolian curiosity bazaar" offered other distractions.

The second Montezuma Hotel opened in April 1885. Only four months later it too was nearly destroyed by fire, probably due to an electrical short circuit. Once again the hotel was rebuilt, reopening a year after the fire. The exterior changes were minor: a standing seam metal roof replaced the slate roof, and a gable was substituted for a monitor dormer.

Figure 8.13

United World College, Montezuma
(Las Vegas Hot Springs), New Mexico

The latter signaled a change in the roofline and reconfigured space and fenestration above the dining room. Nearly all of the original interior woodwork had survived the fire.

The Santa Fe Railroad spent several hundred thousand dollars to give the Montezuma Hotel a new lease on life and ran several trains a day for tourists on its narrow-gauge line between Las Vegas and the hot springs. Nevertheless, the enterprise lasted less than twenty years. Starting in 1893, the hotel was open only during the summers. It closed for good in 1903, following a downturn in the economy and the railroad's decision to make El Tovar (1905)—the new Fred Harvey hotel at Grand Canyon, Arizona, which was also accessible by a branch line—its prime tourist attraction.

Ten years after it closed, the railroad donated the Montezuma Hotel to the Las Vegas Young Men's Christian Association (YMCA; see chapter 11), which could not find a viable use for it and turned it over to the Southern Baptist Convention. Between 1922 and 1930, the hotel housed the Montezuma Baptist College. The narrow-gauge branch line, converted to an electric railway, ceased operations in 1937. The Catholic Church bought the building that year and opened a Jesuit seminary that trained Mexican priests. The Jesuits left in 1972. The building then stood empty, open to vandals and the weather—with several thousand bats its only residents.

But the story had a happy ending. Ten years later, Armand Hammer acquired the property, including the derelict and badly deteriorated Montezuma Hotel, for the US campus of United World College, an institution that brings together two hundred scholarship students, ages 16–19, from all over the world for a two-year program featuring academics and community service.

The restoration of the hotel was completed in 2001, after a two-year, $15-million program overseen by the Albany, New York, architects Einhorn, Yaffee, Prescott. Exterior work included replacing the veranda and the roof. Inside (once the bats were gone), the failed timber trusses that spanned the dining room, supporting the ceiling and the floor of the former ballroom overhead, were reinforced with steel. The woodwork in the lobby and dining room was restored (the lobby's reception desk is a reproduction). The dining room, with the addition of a pair of green glass chandeliers by Dale Chihuly, has resumed its original function. The hotel rooms were converted into student rooms, and administrative offices and classrooms occupy the rest of the building, which is open for scheduled public tours.

Figure 8.14
United World College, staircase, Montezuma (Las Vegas Hot Springs), New Mexico

EL TOVAR
1905, Charles F. Whittlesey;
1905–32, Mary Colter, park structures
South Rim, Grand Canyon National Park, AZ

The hotel, train station, Hopi House, and other picturesque structures built for the Grand Canyon National Park represent the first creative collaboration of the trio that would transport millions of people to see one of the world's great scenic wonders, immerse them in the local culture, and publicize the existence of these treasures far and wide. The collaborators were the Santa Fe Railway, the Fred Harvey Company, and Mary Colter (one of the first female American architects, who designed the park structures at Grand Canyon). Their work was commercially motivated to entice upper-class tourists to ride their trains and stay in their resort hotels, and exploitative of the native Hopi and Navajo Indians. But it was also highly beneficial in terms of exposing multitudes to the glories of the natural resources and native cultures of the American Southwest and the need to safeguard them for future generations.

In 1901, the Santa Fe Railway extended its branch line from Williams, Arizona, originally built to haul ore from local mines, to the Grand Canyon. The present train station, designed by the Santa Barbara, California, architect Francis W. Wilson, was completed in 1910. The Craftsman style log building consists of a center block with two and a half stories and one-story wings. The eastern wing housed the baggage room; the western, the waiting room and ticket office. Outside is a covered, open-sided passenger shelter. The gable bears the Santa Fe logo and the name of the station, and the station agent's bay is a miniature version of the main façade. The railway ended passenger service to the Grand Canyon in the mid-twentieth century, but new owners reinstated it in 1989.

Grand Canyon tourists arriving by train could stay at the El Tovar Hotel, up a short flight of steps from the station and within feet of the south rim of the Grand Canyon. The hotel was named for Don Pedro de Tovar, one of Francisco Vazquez de Coronado's lieutenants on his legendary 1540 expedition in search

Figure 8.15
Santa Fe Railway Station and El Tovar, South Rim, Grand Canyon
National Park, Arizona (courtesy of Xanterra Parks and Resorts)

of the mythical Seven Cities of Cíbola; they were the first Europeans to see the Grand Canyon.

The wide, low-slung building had a broad entrance portico that enclosed a veranda and was anchored by stone arched corner supports. A hip-roofed cross gable fronted by a balcony was above the portico, with an octagonal tower behind it. The gambrel roof of wood shingles had a row of dormers lighting the fourth-floor rooms. Built of native limestone and Douglas fir from Oregon, the rustic hotel was covered with log slab siding (the logs were milled with a hewn or rough-sawn surface to make the hotel resemble a log cabin) on the lower stories and regular siding on the upper ones. The style was described in a 1910 promotional pamphlet as a combination of Swiss chalet and Norwegian villa.

A gray sandstone corner fireplace, Craftsman style furniture, and Navajo rugs on the floor awaited visitors to the two-story lobby, called the Rendezvous. It had the atmosphere of an Adirondack Mountain camp. The cathedral ceiling was of peeled logs, and the log-paneled walls were lined with trophy moose, elk, and deer heads. The Fred Harvey dining room opposite the entrance was similarly furnished. A women's lounge on the mezzanine surrounded the octagonal rotunda. The 100-room hotel cost $250,000.

Charles F. Whittlesey—who was born in Alton, Illinois—was working as a draftsman for Louis Sullivan in Chicago when he was named the Santa Fe Railway's chief architect in 1900. He designed the railroad's Alvarado Hotel in Albuquerque, New Mexico (1902, later demolished), as well as several of its stations. He was also the architect for the Pacific Building (1907, still standing) in San Francisco, an example of the early use of reinforced concrete.

Mary Elizabeth Jane Colter (1869–1958) spent virtually her entire career in the employ of the Santa Fe Railway and the Fred Harvey Company. Born in Pittsburgh, Pennsylvania, to Irish immigrant patents, she was raised in St. Paul, Minnesota, and then went

Figure 8.17
El Tovar, lobby, South Rim, Grand Canyon National Park, Arizona
(courtesy of Xanterra Parks and Resorts)

west with her family after her father died. She graduated from the California School of Design in San Francisco, where she met Bernard Maybeck, an eclectic and eccentric architect of the California Arts and Crafts school. The English Arts and Crafts movement, from which the American version was derived, was a reaction to industrialization and machine-made products. Inspired by the theories of John Ruskin and William Morris, it championed handicrafts, the use of traditional building methods and native materials, and the careful integration of architecture and interior design. In her seven Grand Canyon National Park structures, Colter put these principles into practice.

Her first assignment for the Santa Fe–Harvey organization in 1902 (a year after Harvey died) was setting up and decorating the Indian Building at Albuquerque's Alvarado Hotel. This was a combined museum and salesroom for Indian blankets, pottery, jewelry, baskets, and other items suitable for home furnishings or gifts. Visitors could watch Native American weavers, potters, and silversmiths producing these items on site.

Interspersed with periods of teaching school and working at other jobs, Colter extended her design career in the Southwest, beginning at Grand Canyon in 1904. Her last park structure, the Watchtower at Desert View, was finished in 1932. In the interim, she designed three Santa Fe–Harvey hotels, culminating in La Posada in Winslow, Arizona, 1930, for which she was the architect as well as the interior designer. Colter also designed restaurants for the union stations of four major cities: Chicago, St. Louis, Kansas City, and Los Angeles. At the age of eighty, she was called out of retirement to redo a restaurant, La Cantanita, and an entrance lobby at La Fonda Hotel, in Santa Fe, New Mexico.

Colter was a serious student of Native American ruins and culture, scouring out-of-the-way places in the countryside for inspiration. She traveled to Mexico to study its architecture and search for furnishings. She collected Native American art, especially jewelry. Colter designed the readily identifiable and strikingly beautiful Mimbreno china (based on artistic motifs from ancient tribes of the Mimbres Valley) that was used on the Santa Fe's premier train, the Super Chief, for thirty-five years. A horseback-riding, chain-smoking "incomprehensible woman in pants" who never married and was obsessed with details, Colter left a body of work that has been restored and is finding a new audience.[19]

HOPI HOUSE
1905, Mary Colter
South Rim, Grand Canyon National Park, AZ

Hopi House (opposite the hotel), the first building Colter designed at Grand Canyon, was based on an ancient Native American pueblo she had visited. Built by Hopi Indians, it is a three-story structure with setbacks, the roof of one unit forming a terrace for the next, and so on. Local limestone and sandstone were used in its construction. The roof beams were the traditional vigas, interwoven with small branches, but modern methods and materials, such as cement floors, were incorporated as well.

The low-ceilinged interior, lit by small windows, was filled with displays of Native American artistry and craftsmanship (part of the collection toured

Figure 8.18
Hopi House, South Rim, Grand Canyon National Park, Arizona (courtesy of Xanterra Parks and Resorts)

Figure 8.19
Lookout Studio, South Rim, Grand Canyon National Park, Arizona
(courtesy of Xanterra Parks and Resorts)

American and European museums). Several of the native artisans lived in the building. They demonstrated their skills at weaving blankets, making pottery, and creating silver jewelry for visitors during the day and performed ceremonial dances at night. Their products were sold (the Hopis received only room and board for their work), and other Native Americans were hired to do menial jobs in the park. The Fred Harvey Company ran the business. It and the Santa Fe Railway often used images of Native Americans in the very effective advertising and promotional materials developed for their growing and lucrative hospitality industry in the Southwest. The Hopi came to resent these exploitative practices and the commercialization of their culture, and the dances came to an end in the 1970s.

Hopi House was restored in 1995. The interior ambiance seems much the same today as it was in Colter's time, minus the artisans. The gift shop takes up two floors.

LOOKOUT STUDIO
1914, Mary Colter
South Rim, Grand Canyon National Park, AZ

Situated on a point a short walk from the hotel and the Hopi House, and appearing to rise out of the rock of the canyon rim, is a stone structure that was a combination social center and Fred Harvey souvenir and gift shop. The exterior is of coursed rubble masonry. Inside, the stone walls and the log posts and vigas are exposed. The small fireplace no doubt helped keep the tales of vacation adventures circulating around the hearth. A balcony that literally overhangs the canyon and an outdoor observation deck with telescopes invited viewers. California condors, reintroduced into the canyon in recent years, are occasionally seen soaring above.

HERMIT'S REST
1914, Mary Colter
South Rim, Grand Canyon National Park, AZ

A destination, rest stop, and carriage turnaround was needed at the western end of the recently opened seven-mile scenic drive from the train station that followed the rim of the canyon past several observation points (the 4.5 million people who visit Grand Canyon National Park each year now ride out to Hermit's Rest on park buses). Colter's response was a stone hut announced by a primitive arched gateway and bell— and a story to go with it.

The organic, free-form structure of uncoursed rubble masonry and the whimsical chimney added to the fairy-tale character of this supposed castle for a humble man. A timber porch marked the entrance. Inside, framed by a huge elliptical arch, was a stone apse containing not an altar but a fireplace and a cottage-style inglenook. The two-story main room was open to the wood-beam ceiling and lit by windows just below it. An adjacent space held a gift shop.

Colter's fanciful Hermit's Rest was based on the true story of Louis Boucher, a Grand Canyon prospector and guide originally from Sherbrooke, Quebec, who arrived in the area in 1891. Tall and bearded, he rode a white mule named Calamity Jane. Boucher's actual camp was at Dripping Springs, down in the canyon close by, where he had a mine. Mining failed to pay off, so Boucher took to showing tourists around to make a living. Due to his solitary lifestyle, he was nicknamed "the hermit," although he really wasn't one. Hermit Trail and Boucher Trail in the Grand Canyon, and Hermit's Rest at its edge, are his legacy.

Figure 8.20
Desert View Watchtower, South Rim, Grand Canyon National Park, Arizona (courtesy of Xanterra Parks and Resorts)

DESERT VIEW WATCHTOWER
1932, Mary Colter
South Rim, Grand Canyon National Park, AZ

At the other end of the scenic road, on a promontory overlooking the south rim and the Painted Desert near the eastern end of Grand Canyon National Park, Colter designed a round, seventy-foot-high watchtower, modeled on the ones built by the ancestral Pueblo Indians. Santa Fe Railway bridge builders erected the steel frame. Sandstone forms the outer surface, in uncoursed rubble masonry for the ground floor and range masonry for the upper floors, which incorporate decorative elements. Randomly placed openings appear below a row of uniform rectangular windows at the top. Adjoining the tower and connected to it is a single-story sandstone building that is supposed to resemble a Pueblo Indian kiva, or ceremonial space.

The tower closely resembles those build by the Anasazi, such as the ruins at the Hovenweep National Monument in the Four Corners area, circa 1250. The purpose of such towers—whether for defense, storage, living space, or astronomical observations—remains unclear. Colter studied the structures at Hovenweep in preparation for designing the Desert View Watchtower.

The tower's interior is open to the ceiling, ringed by balconies at three levels linked by stairways; the top floor is an observation level. The colorful murals, including the ground floor *Snake Legend*, whose subject is the Hopis' cultural connection to the Grand Canyon, are by Fred Kabotie, a Hopi artist. Colter's aim was to surround the visitor literally with Native American lore and mythology.

Colter designed two other structures in Grand Canyon National Park: Phantom Ranch, a rustic lodge at the bottom of the canyon (1922), and Bright Angel Lodge and cabins (1936), near El Tovar.

LA POSADA
1930, Mary Colter
303 East Second St. (formerly Route 66),
   Winslow, AZ

La Posada was the last of the Santa Fe–Fred Harvey railroad resort hotels and Colter's magnum opus. Winslow, in the high desert in eastern Arizona, is on the Santa Fe's main line and close to several tourist attractions: the Petrified Forest, Painted Desert, Meteor Crater, and Native American lands. The successful formula was well-established—feature Southwestern lore and native arts and crafts, and provide comfortable lodging and fine dining—and Colter this time imagined a mid-nineteenth-century Mexican hacienda.

The result was a low, rambling two-story structure, incorporating an inn and train station. It combined the styles of the Spanish colonial revival (with decorative iron balconies and window grilles) and the mission revival (with pitched tile roofs and multiple arches). Constructed of reinforced concrete covered with stucco (the walls are eighteen inches thick) the building was roughly E-shape. It faced the tracks, since that was where the guests would arrive. Connecting the station to the hotel was a covered walkway that segued into an arcade, deep and shady enough for reading, relaxing, or watching trains. The surrounding gardens—planted with elm, cottonwood, poplar and juniper trees—were made for strolling or sitting. Colter's landscape plan included a sunken garden with fountains set at the rear of the hotel, between its two wings.

As Stanford White and his Eastern colleagues (or their agents and dealers) ransacked the abodes of a declining aristocracy in Europe for tapestries, mantelpieces, and entire rooms to furnish the mansions of railroad magnates, so Colter traveled to Mexico and throughout the American Southwest in search of appropriate furnishings for her railroad hotel interiors. Antique Mexican chests, benches, tables, chairs, beds, and rugs acquired from ranches, churches, and hotels or imported from Spain were deployed in the interior of La Posada. What the architect could not find, her

Figure 8.21
La Posada, Winslow, Arizona

crew of woodworkers fabricated as period reproductions, down to an ironwork lamp with a painted shade that was then treated to look like a genuine antique.

The ground-floor public spaces—lobby, dining room, lunchroom, and lounge—were separated by Colter's parabolic arch entryway (some of the fireplaces also employed this type of arch, one of her favorite devices). Here the floors were flagstone or quarry tile; the seventy guest rooms had oak floors. Colorful ceramic tile wainscoting lined the walls of the lunchroom. Other walls were brightened with the floral murals of Earl Altaire, a Santa Fe artist. Decorative wrought-iron work appeared in stairway and balcony railings. The hotel's cool, dim interior, with its comfortable furniture and secluded corners, was meant to evoke the home of the owner of a ranch.

The train station waiting room was a large open space with a timber cathedral ceiling hung with

Figure 8.22
La Posada, bookstore entrance, Winslow, Arizona

chandeliers. The entrances were again framed with Colter's signature parabolic arches.

The hotel's opening coincided with the onset of the Depression. More prosperous times followed, and Hollywood stars and international celebrities stayed at the hotel, but it closed in 1957. Four years later, the Santa Fe Railway decided to make the building into offices, since Winslow was a division point on the railroad. The furnishings were sold off, and the eastern half of the hotel was renovated with drop ceilings and drywall partitions. In 1993, the railroad declared the building surplus and announced plans to get rid of it.

Local citizens fought to keep it. In 1997 Allan Affeldt and his wife, the artist Tina Mion, bought La Posada for $158,000, moved in, and began to restore it. The tile roof and shell of the building were in good shape, but the interior, said Affeldt, was a wreck. They did much of the work themselves, removing the drywall that had covered the original openings, and called on their artist and craftsman friends to produce new artworks and decorative ironwork. A 900-piece collection of hand-painted furniture was acquired from the La Fonda Hotel in Santa Fe.

After a seven-year, $6-million effort, financed by Affeldt and his friends and city, state, and federal money, La Posada was once again "the resting place" that Colter and her employers strove to create. It has a healthy occupancy rate, an award-winning restaurant (the Turquoise Room, in the former lunchroom), and grateful townspeople, who in 2005 elected Affeldt mayor of Winslow. He and his wife, whose paintings are displayed in the hotel, and the light artist James Turrell, are now turning the railroad station into the Route 66 Art Museum. Outside will be a Santa Fe Railway Super Chief dome car that Affeldt acquired and is restoring.

The former head of a California institute that dealt with the social responsibility of architects, designers, and planners, Affeldt has made something of a career of rescuing Harvey House hotels. He is also working on La Castaneda in Santa Fe (see above).

"I believe we save great buildings in the same way we save families, cities and nations: one day at a time, with constant investment and courage, undaunted by naysayers and long odds. I believe in the sacredness of place, and in the power of great architecture to inspire creativity, kindness, and civic responsibility," said Affeldt.[20]

BRYCE CANYON LODGE
1925, Gilbert Stanley Underwood
Bryce Canyon National Park, UT

The Union Pacific Railroad, which joined the Central Pacific Railway at Promontory, Utah, in 1869 to form the nation's first transcontinental line, was the last of the transcontinental railroads to enter the resort hotel business. In 1925, the Union Pacific opened the Bryce Canyon Lodge at what later became Bryce Canyon National Park and the Zion Lodge at Zion National Park, both in Utah. Three years later, the Grand Canyon Lodge on the North Rim in Grand Canyon National Park, Arizona, was ready for business.

All three hotels were designed by Gilbert Underwood (1890–1960). Born in Oneida, New York, Underwood worked as an architectural draftsman in Los Angeles, earned architecture degrees at Yale and Harvard Universities, and returned to Los Angeles to open his own office. He designed some twenty Union Pacific Railroad stations, including the art deco Union Station (1931) in Omaha, Nebraska, and several lodges in the rustic style for the National Park Service and private clients.

His Bryce Canyon Lodge is the finest architecturally of the three railroad resort hotels and the only original one—the other two have been rebuilt following fires. It is U-shape with two wings enclosing a courtyard, a nice effect. The variety of roof planes adds to its attractiveness. The materials are stone and timber.

The dark wood interior, casual and homelike, centers on a lobby with a fireplace under a low timber ceiling, from which are suspended Underwood's unusual log lighting fixtures. The restaurant occupies one wing and the auditorium–recreation room the other. The latter has a large uncoursed rubble stone fireplace and a scissor-truss ceiling.

Figure 8.23
Bryce Canyon Lodge, Bryce Canyon National Park, Utah

Figure 8.24
Bryce Canyon Lodge, cabins,
Bryce Canyon National Park, Utah

The lodge, facing the canyon, has a large front porch whose roof is supported by a single fifty-two-foot beam. Between the lodge and the canyon are forty two-story cabins (1927), designed by Underwood and Daniel R. Hull, a landscape architect. Grouped like a little village in the pines, they have steep pitched roofs, stone corners and chimneys, and vertical and horizontal log slab siding. A few yards beyond the cabins is the rim of Bryce Canyon and its fantastic hoodoos. The lodge is located midway between Sunrise and Sunset Points, two popular stops

on the rim trail. Access to all three lodges was via Cedar City, Utah, the end of a Union Pacific Railroad branch line, where passengers detrained and boarded buses for the trip of several hours to the parks.

GLACIER PARK LODGE
1913, Samuel L. Bartlett
East Glacier, Glacier National Park, MT

In 1907, Louis W. Hill (1872–1948) took over from his father—James J. Hill, known as the empire builder —as president of the Great Northern Railway. The railway had completed its transcontinental line from St. Paul, Minnesota, to Seattle, Washington, via Montana's Marias Pass in 1893 (see chapter 14). In Montana, the route traced what became the southern boundary of Glacier National Park, established in 1910 with the strong support of the railway.

Louis Hill was a promoter who understood the value of public relations. As the heads of the Canadian Pacific, the Northern Pacific (now controlled by the Great Northern), and the Santa Fe Railways had before him, he saw an opportunity to bring tourists to an intermediate tier of North American geography, a formerly almost inaccessible area that was rich in mountain scenery. He set about building hotels to accommodate the visitors the trains would transport to the area known as the Alps of America. The style, appropriately, would be Swiss chalet.

The first hotel was in the town of Belton, the main entrance to the park for tourists arriving by rail. The Belton Chalet (1910) is the finest example at Glacier

National Park of the Swiss chalet style, encompassing all of its major elements. The wide, low-pitched roof has deep overhangs and decorated brackets. The center section, festooned with antlers, presents two balconies and numerous windows. The open front porch, which runs the full width of the chalet, rests on stone pillars; the building itself is made of wood. For a time, the tap room was reputed to be the wildest in northwest Montana. Restored in 2000 under new owners, the Belton Chalet still operates as a hotel. The 1935 train station across Route 2 from the hotel was also recently restored. The National Park Service has a bookstore and gift shop in the building. The Amtrak stop is now known as West Glacier.

Hill's major hotel in the park was Glacier Park Lodge, visible across a broad expanse of lawn from the 1912 train station, a structure with one and a half stories, a pitched roof, a cross gable, and log slab siding. The central portion of the building was the waiting room, located between a covered porch for passengers and an enclosed baggage and freight room. The community was originally known as Midvale, then Glacier Park Station; the current Amtrak stop is East Glacier.

Louis Hill had seen the Forestry Building at the 1905 Lewis and Clark Exposition in Portland, Oregon, whose main interior space was outlined by forty-eight-foot log columns supporting a pitched roof with a skylight. Hill obtained the plans for the building and forwarded them to the architect to use as the model for Glacier Park Lodge.

Samuel Bartlett of St. Paul, Minnesota, was a

friend of James Hill. He had been named architect of the Great Northern Railway in 1905, having previously worked for the Chicago, Burlington and Quincy Railroad in Chicago. Bartlett designed ten or so stations and other structures for the Great Northern as well as several buildings in Glacier National Park. His associate for some of the park buildings, including Glacier Park Lodge, was Thomas D'Arcy McMahon, who had worked for Bartlett in Chicago, went with him to St. Paul when he changed jobs, and succeeded him as architect for the Great Northern.

The main entrance to Glacier Park Lodge lies under a broad shed dormer and between two pavilions in the classic Swiss chalet style. The hotel's elongated hip shingle roof has clipped gables and three skylights. The cathedral-like great hall inside is open to the ceiling. Supporting the log trusses that hold up the roof are twenty-four Douglas fir logs, four feet in diameter and forty-eight feet high—the height of a four-story building. A natural version of an Ionic capital appears at the tops of the timber columns. The reception desk and a lounge are located on either side of the lobby on the ground floor, which has Craftsman style furniture and chandeliers. Two balconies where the guest rooms are located ring the room; the railings of the upper one step back from the log columns. Of the Western American railroad resort hotels, perhaps only the interior of the Old Faithful Inn at Yellowstone National Park equals Glacier Park Lodge in rustic grandeur.

Louis Hill purchased the land for Glacier Park Lodge from the Blackfeet Indians, whose reservation abuts Glacier National Park. The huge logs, sixty in all, arrived by rail from the Pacific Northwest. The Blackfeet erected their teepees on the grounds for the opening of the hotel, which they called Big Tree Lodge.

Hill also built eight back-country chalets, a day's trip from the hotel by horseback, along three tour routes. These were designed as basic masonry and timber structures with spartan overnight accommodations, although some had dining halls. Guests could experience the wilderness, sometimes traveling by launch on the many lakes, then return to the

Figure 8.26

Glacier Park Lodge, lobby, East Glacier, Glacier National Park, Montana

relative luxury of the hotel. Only two of the back-country chalets remain: Sperry Chalet and Granite Park Chalet, both accessible by trail. The present camp store at Two Medicine Lake is the former dining hall of the Two Medicine Chalet.

Many Glacier Park visitors preferred the more civilized amenities of the hotel to the primitive chalets. In 1915, a four-story addition to the sixty-one-room lodge was built that provided 111 more guest rooms. The design—a central pavilion in Swiss chalet style, with balconies under a clipped gable roof and flanking wings—emulated the main hotel building. Connecting the two was a long, glass-enclosed passageway with a timber-truss ceiling and lined with comfortable chairs and writing desks.

The year the hotel opened, Hill introduced a new form of transportation that was to have a profound effect on the national parks, the railroads that provided access to them, and society at large. He was one of the sponsors of a cross-country auto race from St. Paul to Montana. After a week-long trip of 1,245 miles over mostly unpaved roads, the drivers ended their race in front of Glacier Park Lodge.

In 1914, backed by the Great Northern Railway, White Motor Company tour buses that had been painted a fire-engine red made their appearance in the park. By 1930, after Route 2 (which follows the railroad and the southern boundary of the park) and the Going to the Sun Road (which crosses Route 2 at its midpoint) were built, 90 percent of the visitors were arriving by car. Eight of the famous "red jammers" (so-called because of their drivers' tendency to grind the gears), restored by the Ford Motor Company, still ferry tourists around Yellowstone and Glacier National Parks.

MANY GLACIER HOTEL
1915–17, Thomas D. McMahon
Grinnell Point, Glacier National Park
  near Babb, MT

The place Louis Hill chose for his second major hotel was in a remote area facing Swiftcurrent Lake, with Grinnell Point (elevation 7,652 feet) looming above. It might be the most strikingly beautiful hotel site in Glacier National Park. The lake level was raised artificially with a dam, to create the final scenic effect.

The hotel is in many ways a replica of Glacier Park Lodge. The four-story, wooden main building has a multiplaned shingle roof with dormers. Two front-facing pavilions with clipped gable roofs and balconies bracket a wide central section. Wings were added in the succeeding years.

The interior is quite similar to that of the earlier hotel. The four-story open lobby is surrounded by massive logs that support three balcony levels and a pitched timber roof with skylights. A freestanding circular fireplace with a large copper-clad hood and chimney stack is the main feature of the lobby, which has Craftsman style furniture and lanterns.

The massive log columns were brought in from the Pacific Northwest, but local stone and timber were used in the construction of the hotel, which had some two hundred rooms and cost $500,000. It was renovated in the 1950s, when the porte cochere was built, and again in the 1980s, the early 2000s, and 2016.

The Western landscape paintings of John Fery (1859–1934) are another feature of the hotel. As a western artist in the employ of the railroads, Fery was a journeyman compared to Thomas Moran or William Henry Jackson, but he clearly was their superior in productivity.

Fery was born Johann Levy in Austria. He attended the Vienna Academy of Art and was recruited as one of a large group of German artists by a Milwaukee, Wisconsin, firm to come to America and produce traveling panoramas of historical scenes. He later returned to Europe and got married. He emigrated to the United States in 1886, settling in the East and Americanizing his name.

Five years later, on a trip to the West, Fery became enraptured by the magnificent mountain scenery and wildlife. He began a new career of leading hunting parties for wealthy European sportsmen, but that did not work out financially. Neither did his subsequent attempt to make a living as a landscape artist, after he moved his growing family to a remote cabin in the area around Jackson Hole, Wyoming.

The family returned to Milwaukee, where Fery's artistic career was rescued by Louis Hill and the Great Northern Railway. Hill, whose love for the Rocky Mountain West equaled Fery's, wanted a series of large landscape paintings for the "See American First" publicity campaign that he inaugurated in 1910. The paintings would be displayed in his station buildings and elsewhere to promote rail travel to the West on the Great Northern. He found the right man in Fery.

The artist must have been grateful, in light of his previous misadventures, to receive a salary of $200

Figures 8.27 & 8.28
Many Glacier Hotel, Grinnell Point,
Glacier National Park, near Babb, Montana

per month, a studio in St. Paul, a railroad pass, and an allowance for sketching trips to Glacier National Park. After the trips, he would return to his St. Paul studio to complete the artworks. In four years, Fery produced an astonishing 347 paintings, or roughly seven per month—some as large as four by sixteen feet. At his salary, that would come to about $29 apiece.

Evidently having a sufficient supply of landscapes, Hill farmed Fery out to the Northern Pacific Railway to paint scenes in Yellowstone National Park, but brought him back in 1915 to make a painting of the Many Glacier Hotel. Fery did similar work for other railroads until the late 1920s, when Hill called on him one last time to paint his new hotel at Waterton Lakes, Alberta, and other scenes. Fery had moved to Orcas Island, Washington, and was still working on these in 1929 when his studio burned down, destroying a year's worth of finished paintings owed to the railroad. He asked to be kept on at a reduced salary until he could replace them. Hill agreed to pay $600 for seventeen paintings, but no more. The Depression essentially ended the artist's career.

Besides the Many Glacier Hotel, Fery's paintings of the Western landscape hang in several other buildings in Glacier National Park and in museums in the surrounding area. At auction, they generally sell in the five figures, but one large painting went for $117,000.

PRINCE OF WALES HOTEL
1927, Thomas D. McMahon
Waterton Lakes National Park, AB

Louis Hill may have been a calculating businessman, but he had a vision that extended beyond national borders. He conceived of Glacier National Park and Waterton Lakes National Park in Alberta, Canada (established 1895), as a continuous wilderness entity and helped to make that happen. His hotel would play a leading role in the endeavor.

There was another, more mundane factor involved. Prohibition had been in effect in the United States since 1920, and Great Northern executives saw in a Canadian hotel a secondary reason, besides the scenery, for people to board their trains to the West: Americans could drink legally in Canada (Prohibition ended in 1933).

Figure 8.29
Prince of Wales Hotel, Waterton Lakes
National Park, Alberta

The spot Hill selected, possibly even more dramatic than that of the Many Glacier Hotel, was a natural bench at the head of Upper Waterton Lake in the shadow of 7,800-foot Mount Crandell. It was a pastoral stage waiting to be occupied. But completing the building proved to be a monumental task: of the Great Northern Railway hotels, the Prince of Wales was by far the most difficult to construct.

Thomas McMahon's early sketches showed a modest four-story Chalet style building quite similar to his Many Glacier Hotel. What emerged, after many design changes initiated by Hill or the St. Paul architects he called in to assist McMahon, was a seven-story, cruciform hotel with a tower at the crossing and the maximum possible number of windows and balconies—a Swiss chalet that had taken the Charles Atlas bodybuilding course.

Erecting the hotel took just a year after ground was broken in July 1926, but it must have seemed like a century to Douglas Oland and James Scott, the contractors from nearby Cardston. To begin with, the excavation by horse-powered equipment was extremely hard work; beneath the thin topsoil, Oland and his laborers encountered huge boulders immured in clay. Removing them proved to be extremely difficult. The unpaved road from Cardston that was used to transport lumber, other supplies, and equipment was fine

in the summer, but rain and snow in other months made it nearly impassable.

The hotel was a complex structure to begin with, and the constant alterations in the plans made constructing it much more difficult. The building shrank and then grew in size according to the shifting ideas of the railroad executives. The contractors pushed their men hard to meet their July 1927 deadline. Meanwhile, new sets of architectural plans kept arriving. In December, Oland had to tear down the superstructure he had erected and start over. He later claimed that altogether, he rebuilt much of the hotel's framework four times.

Then there was the wind—notorious in the region, since the lakes functioned as a wind tunnel. Later in December, a storm almost blew the hotel away. The resident engineer estimated the wind speeds to be 85 miles per hour, with gusts up to 100 miles per hour. The framework was blown eight inches off

Figure 8.30
Prince of Wales Hotel, lobby, Waterton Lakes
National Park, Alberta (courtesy of Glacier Park, Inc.)

center, and lumber stockpiled at the site was found two miles away. Oland and his workers winched the timbers back into place (or almost) and carried on. The contractor added wind bracing of his own design that was not included in the drawings. Heavy snowfalls also slowed the progress of the contractors and their crews.

Nonetheless, the ninety-room, $300,000 Prince of Wales Hotel opened on time. The four wings have steep roofs, two-story pitched-roof dormers, and smaller shed-roof dormers. Balconies with elaborate brackets surround the building. The exterior finishes are stucco and wood siding in horizontal, vertical, and diagonal arrangements.

The building's main interior attraction is an open central court, ringed by balconies braced with wooden piers and struts, and lit by three metal wagon-wheel chandeliers that recede in size as they approach the apex, seven stories up. In the lobby, picture windows eighteen feet high overlook Waterton Lake. It is a welcome departure from the tree-lined lobbies of the two previous Great Northern Railway hotels in Glacier National Park. Renovations in the 1990s included replacing the original cedar shingle roof with one of composite material.

The Prince of Wales Hotel was the venue for a 1931 meeting of Rotarians from Alberta and Montana, who approved a resolution to establish an international peace park. The following year the United States and Canada passed legislation creating the Waterton-Glacier International Peace Park. Located on the longest unfortified boundary between two countries in the world, it was the first of 170 such parks now in existence worldwide.

BALDWIN SCHOOL
(formerly Bryn Mawr Hotel)
1890, Frank Furness
701 West Montgomery Ave., Bryn Mawr, PA

Frank Furness has joined the ruling triumvirate of nineteenth-century American architects—Henry Hobson Richardson, Louis Sullivan, and Frank Lloyd Wright—in the eyes of some critics. (Sullivan worked

Figure 8.31
Baldwin School, Bryn Mawr, Pennsylvania

in Furness's office early in his career and absorbed some of his ideas.) Furness's best-known work is probably the Pennsylvania Academy of the Fine Arts, in Philadelphia. He also did a great deal of work for the railroads (see chapter 3).

Furness's summer resort hotel for the Pennsylvania Railroad in Bryn Mawr, whose station is located conveniently nearby, replaced an earlier railroad hotel that burned. The site is adjacent to Bryn Mawr College, established in 1885. The hotel was part of the railroad's plan to develop an attractive commuter suburb along its Main Line between Philadelphia and Lancaster. By the beginning of the twentieth century, there were three hundred homes within a mile of the station, as prominent Philadelphians made Bryn Mawr their permanent residence rather than a summer vacation spot.

The approach to the building from the corner of Montgomery and Morris Avenues is along a winding road lined with trees and skirting a broad lawn. Only at the last minute is the architect's variegated, sprawling façade revealed, with the powerful projecting semicircular bay at its center marking the entrance. This has a conical roof, two levels of dormers, an arcade, and a ground floor with transom windows. Secondary towers, more dormers, and lots of chimneys enliven the roofline. Open porches extend to one side of the entrance bay. The five-story, L-shape château-esque structure, with an angled wing, is built of local stone and brick.

A set of steps leads to the lower lobby, the focus of which is a fieldstone fireplace; stairways are on either side. The main lobby a half-level above features a central staircase that branches at the overhead landings; a desk; and another fireplace, this one of sandstone.

The wooden stairway's riveted steel stringers are a characteristic Furness touch, referring to the technology of the industry that built the hotel. The lobby's original steel columns were later given coatings of classical plaster to reflect the more genteel nature of the building's new use as a private school for girls. Hardwood floors and oak wainscoting complete the interior finishes.

Hallways off the main lobby lead to the dining room at one end and a multipurpose space at the other. The former hotel rooms upstairs are now offices, apartments, and studios.

Figure 8.32
Baldwin School, staircase, Bryn Mawr, Pennsylvania

The Bryn Mawr Hotel lasted only a dozen years. In 1896, Florence Baldwin leased the building from the railroad during the winter months for Miss Baldwin's School for Girls, a preparatory school for Bryn Mawr College that she had started in 1888. No longer attracting a sufficient number of guests, the hotel was leased year-round to Miss Baldwin's School in 1912. A decade later, the school acquired it outright, together with twenty-five acres of land (including a golf course), for $240,000.

Since then several buildings have been added to the property without affecting the overall appearance of the main building, which was restored and renovated in the 1980s and 1990s. Over the years, four thousand young women have graduated from the Baldwin School and gone on to college.

FLAGLER COLLEGE
(formerly Hotel Ponce de Leon)
1888, Carrere and Hastings
74 King St., St. Augustine, FL

About the same time in the late nineteenth century that William Van Horne grasped the tourist potential of the Rocky Mountain scenery along the route of his Canadian Pacific Railway and began to build hotels, Henry Morrison Flagler foresaw the attraction that Florida's warm weather and sandy beaches would hold for frigid Northerners. He started with a hotel—the railroad would come later.

Flagler (1830–1913) was initially an oil man, not a railroad man, although he was privy to the operations of railroads: he had perfected a system of secret rebates to help weaken competitors and consolidate the power of his company. At the beginning of his Florida adventure, he was the multimillionaire partner of John D. Rockefeller in Standard Oil and living in New York with an ailing wife. The Flaglers spent a winter in Florida at their doctor's suggestion, taking the train and stopping in Jacksonville because of a dearth of transportation and hotels farther south.

Flagler's wife died in 1881. He married her nurse two years later, and they honeymooned in Jacksonville, again taking the train. On a side trip by boat to

Figure 8.33
Flagler College, St. Augustine, Florida

St. Augustine, Flagler still found transportation and hotels lacking. At the time, Florida was mainly a subtropical wilderness. Flagler met Franklin W. Smith, a Boston millionaire and architecture enthusiast, who was building a winter home in St. Augustine. Called Villa Zorayda, the house was in the Moorish revival style, based on the Alhambra Palace in Granada, Spain. Smith was using poured concrete, at that time a novel application of the material in residential construction.

Flagler and Smith discussed building a hotel together in St. Augustine. Smith later backed out, but he convinced Flagler to adopt the Villa Zorayda architectural style and construction method for his hotel. Located almost across the street from the Villa Zorayda, the Hotel Ponce de Leon was one of the first big buildings constructed of poured concrete. It was also innovative in its use of electricity for lighting, having its own dynamos to produce power. The style is actually Mediterranean, a pastiche of influences from Byzantine to Moresque, with a particular emphasis on the Spanish colonial and mission revival styles.

The architects John M. Carrere (1858–1911) and Thomas S. Hastings (1860–1929) met as students at the École des Beaux-Arts in Paris in 1882 and then

Figure 8.34
Flagler College, rotunda, St. Augustine, Florida

worked for architects McKim, Mead and White for two years. They formed their own firm in 1885 after Flagler approached them to design his hotel, and the Hotel Ponce de Leon was their first commission. Hastings's father (like Flagler's) was a Presbyterian minister, and Flagler attended his church, which is how the commission came about.

Carrere and Hastings designed other buildings for their first client: the Alcazar Hotel (1888, now the Lightner Museum) across the street from the Hotel Ponce de Leon and planned as an adjunct to it, and the Flagler Memorial Presbyterian Church (1887), also in St. Augustine, both in the same Mediterranean style; and Whitehall, the 1902 Flagler mansion in Palm Beach (see chapter 11). Well connected socially, Carrere and Hastings went on to become civic architects par excellence in the beaux arts style. They worked on city plans for Cleveland, Ohio; Baltimore, Maryland; and Hartford, Connecticut, and they designed the initial House and Senate Office Buildings in Washington, D.C.; and the New York Public Library, their crowning achievement. They also drew the plans for the Union Pacific Railroad depot in Boise, Idaho (see chapter 3.)

The main entrance to the U-shape Hotel Ponce de Leon, which occupies a city block, is set well back from the street behind a landscaped courtyard with palm trees and a fountain, framed by two-story arcaded wings. The arched entrance is enclosed in a domed central pavilion between a pair of five-story towers with conical roofs. (They contained the water tanks for the hotel.) The sculpted brick chimneys, red tile roofs, and decorative terra-cotta balconies, window lintels, and door surrounds provide a welcome contrast to the tan concrete.

The architects' beaux arts training is seen in the axial plan centered on the lobby rotunda: the primary axis leads to the dining room in the rear, and a cross axis leads to a series of salons. The lobby is a condensed version of the potpourri of styles juxtaposed in the interior. As young jazz musicians are sometimes faulted by their elders for playing too many notes, so the neophyte architects, anxious to display their technique, might have been carried away by youthful enthusiasm—as Hastings later admitted.

As the designer member of the team, he was able to indulge his penchant for elegant ornament. Flagler, anxious to create the emblem of his American Riviera, in Florida, was a willing client with an open checkbook. He had largely withdrawn from the daily operations of the Standard Oil Company, which was increasingly under attack in the press for its business practices, to pursue his new real estate and transportation ventures in the South. When the 540-room hotel was completed at a cost of $2.5 million, it was significantly over budget.

The three-story rotunda, open to the domed ceiling decorated with murals, looks as if it could have been inspired by a sixth-century Byzantine-Romanesque church in Ravenna, Italy. The colorful mosaic tile floor is inlaid with geometric figures. Four-sided caryatid columns of hand-carved oak (Hastings referred to them as Spanish dancers) support the upper-level arcades. The second floor is in the Renaissance mode; the third, actually the drum under the dome, has Italianate style arches.

The rotunda ceiling and the dome are decorated with the murals of George W. Maynard (1843–1923),

Figure 8.35
Flagler College, dining room,
St. Augustine, Florida

an American painter who studied at the National Academy of Design in New York and apprenticed with John La Farge. Maynard also painted the murals in the Library of Congress's Jefferson Building, in Washington. His rotunda murals in Florida depict the figures representing adventure, discovery, conquest, and civilization, as well as cupids, sailing ships, and explorers. Topping off this eclectic ensemble, the dome lantern is covered with stained glass by Louis Comfort Tiffany.

Tiffany also designed the windows, and Maynard the murals, for the dining room. This is contained in a circular pavilion and had a central rectangular dining area, surrounded by coupled columns, that is flanked by semicircular wings overlooking the grounds at the rear of the hotel. A gallery for musicians is at one end of the room.

The salons, more monochromatic but just as ornate, were designed in the Adam style: they feature elaborate white plaster columns, crown molding, and ceiling medallions. As in the rotunda and dining room, the ceilings were decorated with frescoes and murals.

To move the materials to build the hotel and bring the tourists when it opened, Flagler needed a railroad. He began by assembling short-line railroads and melding them into what became the Florida East Coast Railway. He extended the line in 1894 to Palm Beach and two years later to Miami, whose citizens wanted to name their unincorporated area in his honor. Flagler convinced them to adopt the traditional Native American name for the place instead. He added hotels as he went. The only original one that remains is the Hotel Ponce de Leon; the Breakers (1926), at Palm Beach, is the third hotel on the site, succeeding two that burned down.

Then Flagler undertook an endeavor that seems quixotic in hindsight, but was militarily strategic at the time. He built a 128-mile railroad, much of it over open water, from the end of the Florida peninsula to Key West—which was halfway to Cuba and the closest US port to the Panama Canal, then under construction. It took seven years, and the cost was fearful. A 1906 hurricane killed more than a hundred laborers, and hurricanes in 1909 and 1910 destroyed much of what had been built. But the Over-Sea Railroad was completed, at a cost of some $12 million, and Flagler rode the first train to Key West in 1912. The man who was in many ways responsible for the creation of modern Florida died a year later.

A 1935 hurricane washed away a third of the Key West extension of the Florida East Coast Railway, and

Figure 8.36

Plant Hall, University of Tampa, Tampa, Florida

it was not put back in service by the then-bankrupt railroad. The concrete causeway and other parts of the infrastructure were later reclaimed and rebuilt as a highway, the present US 1 to Key West. The Florida East Coast Railway operates today as a freight line between Jacksonville and Miami; however, as of the summer of 2017 a portion of it between West Palm Beach and Fort Lauderdale was scheduled to open to passenger service soon.

The Ponce de Leon Hotel closed in 1967. The following year, Lawrence Lewis, head of the hotel branch of the Flagler companies, created Flagler College, donated the hotel building to the college, and spent $14 million converting the hotel. Flagler College began as a liberal arts college for women; it became

coeducational in 1971. The hotel rooms now serve as dorm rooms for freshwomen, who eat their meals in one of the most sumptuously decorated college dining halls in the country.

PLANT HALL, UNIVERSITY OF TAMPA
(formerly Tampa Bay Hotel)
1891, John A. Wood
401 W. Kennedy Blvd., Tampa, FL

Henry B. Plant (1819–99) put together a system of railroads and steamships and a collection of hotels that brought growth and development to the central peninsula and Gulf coast of Florida, just as Henry Flagler's enterprises had done for the Atlantic coast.

Plant had also visited Florida, though much earlier than Flagler, for his wife's health and had spent several months at Jacksonville. He too saw opportunity.

A farmer's son from Connecticut, Plant began his business career as a steamboat deckhand; one of his tasks was handling the express parcels. This led to a job with the Adams Express Company, where he became a superintendent. He went South at the start of the Civil War to open his own express company in Georgia. Around 1880, Plant started buying bankrupt short-line railroads with a variety of gauges. He standardized them and welded them into a network. To facilitate this project, he formed the Plant Investment Company, and Henry Flagler was one of the investors. By 1884, the Plant System of railroads, as it was called, extended from Charleston, South Carolina, through Savannah, Georgia, to Tampa, Florida —which Plant developed as a deepwater port for his line of steamships to Havana.

With his hotel, Plant sought to outdo his rival, Flagler. Plant's four-story building, in a flamboyant Moorish revival style, was a quarter-mile long. Although it appears larger, it contained fewer rooms (511) than the Hotel Ponce de Leon. The Tampa Bay Hotel was also built of poured concrete and faced with brick and cast concrete trim, but the floors were reinforced with salvaged steel rails. It was meant to be fireproof, and it would be lit by electricity.

Six round towers resembling minarets—they culminated in bulbous roofs and onion-dome belvederes—outlined the two end pavilions and the long middle section of the I-shape building (the crescent forms that rose above them were more Islamic than Moorish). The central main entrance passed through a lobby and exited in the rear between two semicircular pavilions that contained the hotel's grand salon, music room, and other spaces. A deep, two-story wooden porch, defined by Moorish style horseshoe arches and elaborate jigsawn trim, extended on either side of the main entrance.

John A. Wood (1837–1910), the architect, was from upstate New York. He designed churches, an armory, and a hotel in Kingston, New York, and several more hotels in other towns. In 1887, having moved his office to New York City, he designed a handsome, six-story, cast-iron storefront for a merchant at 687–691 Broadway.

The hotel cost $3 million, including $500,000 in furnishings. Plant and his second wife attended the 1889 Universal Exposition of Paris and then went shopping for statues, paintings, tapestries, mirrors, vases, and marble columns for the hotel's public rooms. They bought 30,000 yards of red carpeting decorated with blue dragons from Christie's in London and ordered some eighty carloads of furniture for the hotel rooms. The treatment for the hotel's surroundings was equally lavish: the 150-acre grounds were planted with palms, cacti, banana and citrus trees, and orchids. Plant subsequently added a casino, race track, and exhibition hall.

In 1898, Tampa was selected as the port of embarkation for the Spanish-American War, and the Tampa Bay Hotel served as staff headquarters. Theodore Roosevelt and his Rough Riders trained and paraded on the manicured hotel grounds.

The City of Tampa bought the hotel in 1904, five years after Plant died, and operated it until the early 1930s. In 1933, the Tampa Municipal Museum, established to preserve the building, occupied a portion of it; additional space was leased to the Tampa Bay Junior College for offices and classrooms. The college evolved into the University of Tampa, which holds a long-term lease on the former hotel, renamed Plant Hall. The museum, now the Henry B. Plant Museum, still occupies the south wing and exhibits the original hotel furnishings.

Plant built eight Florida hotels altogether, but only the Tampa Bay Hotel remains. The Plant System of railroads was acquired by the Atlantic Coast Line in 1902. Following two mergers, the line became part of CSX Transportation, which—along with Amtrak— operates trains over sections of Plant's original routes.

9

THE BACK SHOP

Everything that rolled on rails and more could be made and repaired in the large shop complexes operated by the major railroads. Forges and foundries produced the metal components for building locomotives, cars, switches, and even bridges. New locomotives were built and old ones taken apart and rebuilt in huge erecting sheds. Separate shops were needed for building passenger and freight cars. There were blacksmith, boiler, axle, wheel, machine, carpentry, pattern, and paint shops. The hundreds of skilled workers employed in the railroad shops could make whatever was needed, whether that was upholstered seats for the coaches or furniture for the president's office.

Roundhouses (engine houses), and turntables or transfer tables were necessary at shop complexes to maneuver, house, service, and repair the huge steam locomotives and the many different types of rolling stock. Coal and water towers supplied the basic ingredients for making steam, the driving force. Power stations were sometimes part of the shop complex. Interlocking (signal) towers were often present there, and they were ubiquitous out on the line—primarily at rail junctions.

When the railroads switched over to diesel locomotives in the 1950s, most of the shop complexes became obsolete and were closed or consolidated with newer facilities. The more fuel-efficient diesel locomotives required less frequent servicing and fewer repairs than steam locomotives, and the shops and technology for maintaining the two types of motive power were quite different. This left derelict some of the largest buildings the railroads ever constructed. Of the approximately three thousand roundhouses that once stood in North America, just a few hundred remain. Coal and water towers likewise became obsolescent; only a few linger on, stark sentinels in the railroad landscape. Interlocking towers are also almost gone, having been replaced by centralized traffic control systems. Of the thousands of such towers that once operated in the United States and Canada, fewer than a hundred are still in use.

Some of the former shop complexes—the Pennsylvania Railroad shops at Altoona, Pennsylvania; the Delaware, Lackawanna and Western Railroad shops at Scranton, Pennsylvania; the B&O Railroad Mount Clare complex at Baltimore, Maryland; and the Southern Railway shops in Spencer, North Carolina—have been turned into museums. The huge Santa Fe Railroad shops at Albuquerque, New Mexico, have been put to use recently by the film industry. One of the few places in America where the engines and equipment from the age of steam still run essentially as they did a century ago (except that the current payload is tourists rather than copper ore, miners, and schoolchildren) is on the Nevada Northern Railway in Ely, Nevada.

The oldest roundhouse in America is in Aurora, Illinois. Built in 1855 for the Chicago, Burlington and Quincy Railroad, it was converted to a bar and restaurant. In Toronto, Ontario, the John Street Roundhouse has been given over mainly to commercial uses, while the surrounding area has been made into a railroad park. A few interlocking towers that were left standing in their original locations have become museums. One of the great artifacts of the railroad age—the Glenwood Power Station at Yonkers, New York, built by the New York Central Railroad and designed by the architects of Grand Central Terminal—stands tall, empty, and abused.

NEVADA NORTHERN RAILWAY MUSEUM
(formerly Nevada Northern Railway shop complex)
1906
1100 Ave. A, Ely, NV

"Much of Nevada was built on dreams," according to Mark Bassett, director of the Nevada Northern Railway Museum and president of the Nevada Northern Railway.[21]

The Nevada Northern Railway complex is significant not for any individual structure, but because it is a remarkably intact and functioning early twentieth-century railroad, now in a museum context. The fifty-six-acre site has the necessary administrative, repair, and storage buildings; the locomotives, rolling stock, and other equipment; and, most important, the knowledgeable and skilled staff to run the museum and railroad.

The Nevada Northern was built to connect the extensive copper mines at Ely with the Southern

Figure 9.1
Nevada Northern Railway shop complex, Ely, Nevada

Pacific Railway at Cobre, Nevada, 140 miles to the north. The mines and railroad were developed by Mark Requa, a mining engineer who was the son of a Comstock Lode silver magnate. He formed the White Pine Copper Company, with financing by the Guggenheim family and their associates, who controlled both the mines and the railroad by 1906.

When the Nevada Northern arrived, Ely was a stagecoach and Pony Express stop, with a population of 307. By 1910 the population had mushroomed to 7,441. Nevada had a late, but long-lasting mining boom: the good times ebbed and flowed with the price of copper until 1978, when the ore trains stopped running. In the following decade, Kennecott Copper, then the mine owner, closed the mills and smelters. In 1986, the company donated the railroad to the City of Ely and a nonprofit corporation, and the Nevada Northern Railway Museum was born.

The museum collection consisted of fifty-odd buildings, some steam and diesel engines and passenger coaches, and several miles of track, all pretty much as the railroad had left it. The museum's goals were to keep it that way and give visitors an authentic experience of the gritty, oil-soaked, clangorous operation of a steam railroad shop complex that almost all towns and cities of any consequence once had—something that has almost completely vanished.

Figure 9.2
Nevada Northern Railway
shop complex, engine house,
Ely, Nevada

Among the more important buildings and structures are a station in the mission revival style, on one
side of which is an office building (both have second-
story station agent's bays), and on the other, an elongated one-story, clapboard freight shed with a canopy
over the platform. The engine house (circa 1920),
where locomotives are serviced, maintained, and repaired, is a particularly active shop building; historic
coaches are restored in the adjacent coach house. The
supersize saws and other tools in the carpenter's and
blacksmith's shops are a good indication of the scale
of the engine components and other items needed
to run the railroad. Rising above the high desert landscape are the coal and water towers (an owl still lives
in the former).

Bassett, who has a background in newspaper publishing and direct-mail marketing, started with the
Nevada Northern Railway Museum in 1999 as a volunteer and became director in 2002. In 2006, Secretary of the Interior Dirk Kempthorne announced the
designation of the museum as a National Historic
Landmark, referring to it as "the best-preserved, least
altered, and most complete main yard complex remaining from the steam railroad era."[22] The 26,000
visitors who are attracted each year to this remote location take guided tours of the buildings and seasonal
train rides. The museum has a staff of eleven and a
large number of volunteers to orient the visitors.

Figure 9.3
Nevada Northern Railway shop complex,
coal and water towers, Ely, Nevada

The Nevada Northern shop complex and the rail
line between Ely and Cobre are now jointly owned
by the City of Ely and the Nevada Northern Railway
Foundation. Copper mining is still an active industry
in the area; in fact, new mines are still being developed, and almost half of the rail line is still in operation to serve the mines. Bassett's aim is to raise $18–20

million to restore the rest of the rail line and put it into operation. If he succeeds, he and his colleagues at the museum and in the City of Ely will have created what may be the only combination of a railroad museum and working short-line railroad.

EAST BROAD TOP RAILROAD
SHOP COMPLEX
1874
Route 994 west of Route 522, Rockhill Furnace, PA

The East Broad Top Railroad is an intact industrial artifact, accessible though not capable of being fully appreciated since the tourist trains no longer run and the buildings are closed (visitors are free to wander among them).

They include a two-story train station (1906) with a pitched roof and canopies extending on both the street and track sides; a two-story residence (1885) with a wide front porch across the street from the station, built by the railroad for its general superintendent (now the Iron Rail Bed & Breakfast); and numerous shop buildings. There is a turntable and an eight-stall brick roundhouse; a wood-frame foundry; blacksmith, carpenter, locomotive and car, and machine shops; sand house; and several other wooden buildings, most with pitched roofs and vertical board-and-batten siding, painted red.

Figures 9.4 & 9.5
East Broad Top Railroad shop complex, station, Rockhill Furnace, Pennsylvania

The narrow-gauge railroad, located in the bituminous coal country of south-central Pennsylvania, ran thirty-three miles between Robertsdale and Mount Union, where it connected with the Pennsylvania Railroad. It hauled coal, lumber, and iron ore (there was an iron furnace in Rockhill) until 1956, when the railroad was shut down and sold to the Kovalchick Corporation, a railroad salvage company. But instead of scrapping the railroad, the corporation's owner, Nick Kovalchick, rehabilitated several miles of track and ran tourist trains for the 1960 Orbisonia–Rockhill Furnace bicentennial. The East Broad Top Railroad opened as a tourist railroad the following year and had a successful fifty-year run until the funds ran out in 2011. Since then, the Friends of the East Broad Top Railroad, a volunteer group, has worked to maintain the buildings. The complex is for sale.

RAILROADERS MEMORIAL MUSEUM
(formerly Pennsylvania Railroad Office Building)
1882
Ninth Ave. and 12th St., Altoona, PA

Located at the eastern base of the Allegheny Mountains, Altoona was the staging point for the Pennsylvania Railroad's mountain crossing. The first shop buildings there were constructed in 1850. Seventy-five years later, Altoona had become one of North America's largest railroad shop complexes: its 122 buildings covered 242 acres and employed 16,500 workers. The shops were divided into four sections: the Altoona machine shops, Altoona car shops, Juniata shops, and South Altoona foundries. Thousands of steam locomotives, freight cars, and passenger coaches were produced there, and the shops maintained and repaired the railroad's vast fleet of rolling stock.

The 1968 merger that created the Penn Central and the company's bankruptcy two years later resulted in a drastic reduction of the Altoona shops. Most of the buildings, including three roundhouses, were razed in 1972. The thirty-acre Juniata Locomotive Shop is still in operation as part of the Norfolk Southern Railway. Altoona's population, which had grown with the railroad to a peak of 90,000, fell to almost half that.

Figure 9.6

Railroaders Memorial Museum, Altoona, Pennsylvania

In 1998, the Railroaders Memorial Museum, established a few decades earlier, moved to the office building formerly occupied by the master mechanics and other departments such as the railroad police. The long three-and-a-half-story brick building has a pitched roof lined with wide shed-roof dormers. Vertical rows of segmentally arched windows are set in recessed panels topped with corbel tables. The building is an example of the railroad esthetic at its most basic: it is a warehouse for offices. The renovation by Philadelphia architects Wallace, Roberts and Todd (1998) rearranged the interior to provide museum display spaces, an auditorium, and a gift shop. Other shop buildings from Altoona's railroad age remain in the vicinity.

The presence in the region of the Pennsylvania Railroad's famed Horseshoe Curve and the Allegheny Portage Railroad (see chapter 12) and a vigorous state industrial tourism program have helped bring more people to the area.

B&O RAILROAD MUSEUM
(formerly the Baltimore and Ohio Railroad
Passenger Car Shop)
1884, Baldwin and Pennington
Pratt and Poppleton Sts., Baltimore, MD

The railroad in America began in Baltimore. In fact, the Baltimore and Ohio (B&O) was the world's first long-distance, general-purpose railroad—that is, the first modern railroad. Before the B&O, there were mostly rudimentary tram roads, operations that were powered by gravity and horses and associated with mines. The only line that used locomotives to haul freight and passengers, England's Stockton and Darlington Railroad, extended just twenty-five miles between the two towns. In 1827, the civic leaders of Baltimore proposed to build a railroad 250 miles long over a range of mountains, to connect their city's port with the Ohio River and the inland trade and travel. No one had ever done anything like that before.

Baltimore's inventiveness and self-reliance are reflected in the architecture of the B&O's passenger car shop, commonly known as the roundhouse—which is often referred to as an industrial cathedral. Described as "the largest circular (actually 22-sided polygonal) industrial building in the world,"[23] the roundhouse is 235 feet in diameter, 123 feet high (to the top of the cupola), and has a 60-foot turntable.

The lower roof, originally carried on wrought-iron truss girders, was supported by the brick perimeter walls and twenty-two interior wrought-iron columns. Assisted by a tension ring, the columns also carried the weight of the upper roof (in effect, a dome) plus the lantern. Light entered the building at three levels—ground, clerestory, and lantern—through glass windows that could be opened to provide ventilation.

The firm of Baldwin and Pennington was the house architects for the B&O Railroad, designing many of its utilitarian structures and stations, including the much-photographed ones at Point of Rocks and Oakland, Maryland. One of Baltimore's leading architectural firms, Baldwin and Pennington was also responsible for some of the city's most important buildings, including the addition to Latrobe's Cathedral.

Ephraim Francis Baldwin (1837–1916) was born in Troy, New York, the son of a civil engineer. He attended Mount St. Mary's College in Emmitsburg,

Figure 9.7
B&O Railroad Museum, Baltimore, Maryland
(courtesy of B&O Railroad Museum)

Figure 9.8
B&O Railroad Museum, interior, Baltimore, Maryland
(courtesy of B&O Railroad Museum)

Maryland, and then became a draftsman at the Baltimore architectural firm of Niernsee and Neilson (the principals of the firm had been engineers for the B&O Railroad and designed some of its earliest structures). Baldwin was in a partnership with Bruce Price in 1869–73, when the latter was working in Baltimore. Josias Pennington (1854–1929), a native of Baltimore, attended St. John's College in Annapolis before interning with Baldwin; the two became partners in 1883.

The B&O Railroad roundhouse was one of their first assignments. There were European precedents for it, including plant conservatories and Robert Stephenson's 1847 Camden roundhouse in London (now an arts center), but the size of the Baltimore building, dictated by the length of the passenger cars and the turntable, distinguishes it from the rest.

With the contemporary annex building and the 1851 Mount Clare Station, the roundhouse now houses the exhibits of the B&O Railroad Museum. The motive power and rolling stock in the rail yards, the huge 1871 L-shape car shop next door (now used for the repair and restoration of the engines and coaches), and a few other buildings on the site are what remain of the nation's earliest railroad shop complex, dating to 1835. At its zenith in the 1920s, the three thousand workers in its machine shops, foundries, bridge shops, and repair facilities—which collectively covered thirty acres—could produce eighteen new and rebuilt locomotives a week, and just about anything else the railroad needed.

In 1953, the roundhouse became the heart of the B&O Railroad Museum, its twenty-two stalls housing the most important of the roughly two hundred locomotives and cars in the collection. After the Mount Clare shops ceased operation in 1974, most of the buildings were demolished. The museum complex was renovated at a cost of about $1.5 million.

During a 2003 snowstorm that set a record in Baltimore, half of the roundhouse roof collapsed, damaging about a third of the engines, cars, and full-scale models of early equipment on exhibit. The museum reopened in late 2004 following the complete rebuilding of the slate roof with steel trusses and glue-laminated timbers, replicating the original design. SMG Architects and Century Engineering supervised the $15-million restoration.

A forensic engineering examination largely exonerated Baldwin, the original architect. His wrought-iron trusses were found to have design flaws, but they also had features that meant the building was less badly damaged than would otherwise have been the case. Baldwin designed the roof to bear a load of snow about a foot deep—a not uncommon specification for railroad buildings at the time, before structural engineering was an exact science. About twenty-eight inches of snow fell during the 2003 storm, and the drifts that formed on the section of the roof that collapsed were estimated to have been twice that high.

TWO BROTHERS ROUNDHOUSE
(formerly the Chicago, Burlington and Quincy Railroad roundhouse)
1856, Levi Hull Waterhouse
205 N. Broadway, Aurora, IL

The oldest roundhouse in North America became a bar and restaurant in the late twentieth century and still operates as one. Once part of a sixty-acre railroad industrial complex, the largest such facility in the Midwest, the roundhouse closed in 1974; the shop buildings around it were subsequently demolished. After standing vacant for twenty-one years, it was acquired and renovated by a Chicago Bears football star and his partners and reopened in 1996 as Walter Payton's Roundhouse, a pub and restaurant. New owners took over in 2011; the premises include a brewery and a bakery.

The initial line of the Chicago, Burlington and Quincy, which was formed in 1855, extended from Aurora to Chicago. The roundhouse was the first of the support facilities to be built. It was designed by Levi Hull Waterhouse (1824–1905), an Aurora architect. The first section was constructed as a semicircle; additional sections were added in 1859 and 1866 to form a complete circle. A machine shop, blacksmith

Figure 9.9
Two Brothers Roundhouse, Aurora, Illinois

shop, and other facilities were added in back of the roundhouse.

The exterior walls were built of native limestone. The forty locomotive bays of the inner walls were framed with cast-iron columns and arches, stone impost blocks, and brick spandrels, and a drum reached up to the roof, eighteen feet above the ground. Wrought-iron trusses supplied by Pennsylvania's Phoenix Iron Works supported the roof. The ceiling was yellow pine.

The turntable area in the center of the roundhouse has been made into a landscaped courtyard from which the structure of the building is plainly visible. The Metra station next door marks the last stop on the BNSF Railway's Aurora commuter rail line to Chicago.

NORTH CAROLINA TRANSPORTATION MUSEUM
(former the Spencer shops, Southern Railway)
late nineteenth and early twentieth centuries
1 Samuel Spencer Dr., Spencer, NC

In 1894 J. Pierpont Morgan reorganized several bankrupt and decrepit railroads in Virginia and neighboring states, combining them into the Southern Railway, and installed his railroad expert, Samuel Spencer, as its new president. Shortly afterward, planning began for extensive shops at a location three miles north of Salisbury, North Carolina (see chapter 4). The 263-acre site of open farm and woodland was roughly halfway between the Southern's ends at Washington, D.C., and Atlanta, Georgia. The shops, adjacent to extensive rail yards, grew into the largest locomotive repair facility in the Southern Railway system. They were named for the railroad president, as was the surrounding town—almost all of whose residents were shop workers or their family members. Spencer died in a 1906 railroad accident when his private railroad coach, the last car in a train that was stalled on the tracks, was rear-ended by a following train.

The earliest shop buildings at Spencer, designed by the railroad's engineers, went into operation in 1896 (a few of them remain standing). The largest

Figure 9.10

North Carolina Transportation Museum, Robert L. Julian Roundhouse, Spencer, North Carolina

and most important structures were built in the first decade of the twentieth century. In 1905 the huge machine and erecting shop (the back shop), designed to build and repair locomotives, was constructed. Built of brick and steel, 150 by 600 feet, and four stories high, it was lit by a double rank of large windows plus skylights. A row of steel columns divided the interior lengthwise; overhead, an intricate array of metal trusswork supported the pitched roof. The master mechanic's office next door (1911) was a smaller version of the back shop.

The centerpiece of the shop complex, the Robert L. Julian Roundhouse (named for its foreman) was added in 1924, replacing an earlier similar structure. A hundred-foot turntable stood in front of the thirty-seven-stall roundhouse, which was built of reinforced concrete. Locomotive servicing and minor repairs took place inside. At the Spencer shops' peak in the 1930s, 2,200 workers staffed them, performing daily maintenance and heavy repairs on steam locomotives.

Dieselization took a heavy toll on the shops. The Southern Railway was a pioneer in the process, having introduced the world's first diesel freight engine in 1941 and completing the conversion to diesel locomotives a decade later—the first of the major railroads to do so. The Spencer shops were converted to handle diesel engine repairs and manufacture engine components, but in 1960 the facility was closed. Several of the shop buildings were demolished, and the rest were abandoned. The railyard was relocated to nearby Linwood.

The slow, arduous struggle by a hardy and committed group of state employees and volunteers—rail enthusiasts and preservationists, including several of the former shop workers—to rescue the derelict turntable, roundhouse, and shop buildings began in the late 1970s. The concept of adaptive reuse was then becoming a factor in historic restoration. An initial proposal for a shopping mall was quickly replaced by the idea of a transportation museum. The museum was founded in 1977, when the Southern Railway donated the initial three acres and three buildings to the State of North Carolina. Two years later, the railroad donated another fifty-three acres, the site of the remainder of the shop buildings. Volunteers went to work cleaning up the site.

The first big renovation project was a new roof for the back shop. The state paid the $1.25-million cost, but legislators were reluctant to commit more funds without knowing whether the museum would succeed. It opened in 1983, with its first exhibit, *People, Places and Times*, in the master mechanic's office. Ten years later, the North Carolina Transportation Museum was the third most visited tourist site in the state. It currently has 80,000 visitors annually.

One of the most popular attractions is the turntable: various locomotives are regularly brought out of the roundhouse, one of the largest in the United States, to pirouette on the turntable before an appreciative audience. The museum's collection of rolling stock and exhibits on shop workers and the African American community at Spencer are housed in the roundhouse. The restored back shop, opened in 2009, offers general transportation exhibits. More exhibits and a gift shop are located in the master mechanic's office. Heritage trains for tourists continually circle the museum site. The Southern Railway's former Barber Junction station (1898), moved to the museum grounds and restored in 1996, is a visitors' center.

ATCHISON, TOPEKA AND SANTA FE RAILWAY SHOPS
1914–25, Edward A. Harrison, architect;
  C. F. W. Felt, A. F. Robinson, engineers
Second St., between Atlantic and Cromwell Aves.
  SW, Albuquerque, NM

When the Atchison, Topeka and Santa Fe Railway (AT&SF) arrived in Albuquerque in 1880, it created a new linear town paralleling Second Street that replaced the old town surrounding the plaza located along the Camino Real. (The railroad had a similar effect on Las Vegas, New Mexico.) Over the next fifty years, the Santa Fe Railway remade Albuquerue from a farming village into an industrial center and the state's chief city. The major north-south route through town—Interstate 25, Albuquerque's new commercial corridor—parallels the railroad line.

Albuquerque was a division point on the Santa Fe's 2,250-mile main line between Chicago and Los Angeles. Once the primary employer in the city, the railroad built some of its most important structures. Although the mission style Alvarado Hotel (1902, designed by Charles F. Whittlesey) that marked the beginning of the remarkably creative and successful collaboration among the Santa Fe Railway, Fred Harvey, and Mary Colter was demolished in the 1970s—to be replaced thirty years later by a look-alike bus and rail terminal—other important buildings remain (see chapter 11).

Albuquerque's AT&SF Railway shops began to take shape in the 1880s (the early shop buildings, located on a different site than the present complex, no longer exist). The Santa Fe Railway went bankrupt during the panic of 1893; after it was reorganized in 1895, Edward P. Ripley took over as president. Ripley concentrated on expansion (to California), corporate identity, and efficiency. The mission revival style stations and Fred Harvey hotels were important elements of the railroad's image, but efficiency was the keyword for operations—including the maintenance and repair of the rolling stock. The company's Albuquerque shops represented a radically different approach to architecture than its Alvarado Hotel.

Figure 9.11
Atchison, Topeka and Santa Fe Railway Shops,
Albuquerque, New Mexico (photo by Adric Menning)

The boiler and machine shops were the main components of the twenty-seven-acre shop complex, which contained some seventeen buildings. The 1921 machine shop, the larger of the two, was 600 feet long, 235 feet wide, and four stories in height. It was a steel-frame building, with glass curtain walls. The ends facing the street and the tracks were built of cast concrete—structurally superfluous, but evidently meant to give the utilitarian structure a more presentable public face. The building was in four sections: the main part; the erecting bay; and three extensions, which had a lower profile. The façade of the erecting bay, replicated by the extensions, was a stylized temple front, composed of columns supporting a pediment that contained the Santa Fe Railway logo.

The erecting bay interior resembled an industrial cathedral, but the nave and side aisles were lit by clerestory windows whose ceiling consisted of steel trusses, not Gothic rib vaulting. Overhead, traveling on steel guideways, a 250-ton bridge crane ran the

length of the room, strong enough to lift a locomotive boiler off its frame. The floor consisted of a six-inch concrete slab topped with wooden pavers three inches thick, set with the end grain showing. This helped reduce noise, absorb the omnipresent oil, and serve as a shock absorber if parts were dropped.

The smaller, lower bays for heavy and light machinery and bench work expanded from one side of the erecting bay. Lit by sawtooth skylights, they were also equipped with cranes to handle heavy components such as wheel sets, to be worked on once the locomotives were disassembled. A ventilating room above the heavy machinery bay that was equipped with steam radiators and circulating fans could completely change the air in the huge space several times a day. Windows could also be opened to provide ventilation. A factory washroom on the mezzanine allowed the workmen, many of them immigrant Mexicans or Native Americans from the area, to clean away some of the dirt and grease before going home.

In 1923 a narrower version of the machine shop was built parallel to it: the boiler shop, also lit by skylights and with an overhead bridge crane. Between the two buildings a transfer table, which operated on tracks similar to those of the traveling cranes inside, delivered locomotives to the proper bay doors that opened along the lengths of the two buildings.

The enfilade of long, low railroad shop buildings separated by the transfer table was remarkably similar to the Ford Motor Company buildings at Highland Park, Michigan, that were designed by Albert Kahn and opened in 1910. They marked the introduction of the moving assembly line that halved the production time of a Model T Ford and transformed the automobile industry. The only difference was that Kahn's buildings were of reinforced concrete rather than steel, and a roadway lay between them. Another architect with the same surname, Louis Kahn, adopted a comparable arrangement of buildings in his Salk Institute at La Jolla, California, in 1965. Their serrated façades, which frame a view of the Pacific Ocean, regard each other across a water feature.

Just as the moving Ford assembly line was inspired by the technology of the meatpacking industry, it is likely that the in-house design team for the Albuquerque railroad shops knew about and sought to emulate the production practices of the industry that was destined to have such a profound impact on their own.

At any rate, their buildings were set up to apply the Ford emphasis on high-quality parts, a rapid work flow, division of labor, and efficiency. Even though taking apart a twenty-five-ton steam locomotive, repairing or replacing its major elements, and putting them back together was on a different scale than assembling a Model T Ford, the general procedure was the same—and the thousand craftsmen in the Albuquerque shop could turn out at least one rebuilt locomotive a day.

Edward A. Harrison (b. 1869), the railroad's staff architect, was originally from Hamilton, Ontario. Beginning as a draftsman for a California subsidiary of the Santa Fe Railway, he spent virtually all of his career with the company. Harrison designed numerous Santa Fe depots and office buildings, remodeled some of Fred Harvey's restaurants, and worked with Mary Colter on the El Navajo Hotel in Gallup, New Mexico.

His colleague, C. F. W. Felt (b. 1864), the Santa Fe's chief engineer, was from Salem, Massachusetts. After graduating from an agricultural college, he too spent most of his life working for railroads, starting in 1886 with the Santa Fe as an ax- and rodman on survey crews, and then as a bridge engineer. Felt continued his survey crew work with other railroads, including one in Mexico, as a leveler, instrument man, and transit man. Returning to the Santa Fe, he was a division and resident engineer before becoming chief

Figure 9.12
Atchison, Topeka and Santa Fe
Railway Shops, machine shop,
Albuquerque, New Mexico
(photo by John Mulhouse)

engineer in 1913. The third member of the team, A. F. Robinson, was the Santa Fe's bridge engineer.

Another notable building is the one-story brick blacksmith shop (1917) that adjoins the boiler shop; its pitched roof is supported by steel Warren trusses with curved lower chords. The sheet metal shed (circa 1918), which houses an intricate array of overhead tracks for moving and storing large sheets of metal, is the only timber-frame shop building; it is covered with vertical wooden siding. The firehouse (1920) is an aberration in style as well as materials: a two-story, sandstone structure built in Mediterranean style, the tower was used to dry hoses. Otherwise, the sixteen or so buildings that make up the shop complex represent a straightforward industrial expression of materials and structure. In addition, the major ones develop the concept of universal space that Ludwig Mies van der Rohe proposed and rendered perfectly decades later in his Crown Hall (1956), for the Illinois Institute of Technology in Chicago.

The Santa Fe, like the Southern Railway, was an early convert to diesel engines. Following World War II, the Albuquerque shops were demoted to an equipment repair facility. After the complex closed in the 1970s, it stood vacant and was vandalized. In 2000, the railroad sold the property to a private developer for $2.5 million, but early plans for a convention center and other uses ended in recriminations and lawsuits after the buyers defaulted on a loan. The City of Albuquerque bought the shop complex in 2007 for $8.5 million. Subsequent studies have recommended mixed-use development, including housing.

Meanwhile, the film industry has taken over several shop buildings, and the Wheels Transportation Museum—the city's partner in the redevelopment of the Albuquerque shop complex—displays its exhibits in the former storehouse next to the machine shop. The shops are fenced off and closed to the public except for Sundays, when a farmers' market is held in the blacksmith shop and the Wheels Transportation Museum is open.

JOHN STREET ROUNDHOUSE
Canadian Pacific Railway
1931, John M. R. Fairbairn, engineer
255 Bremner Blvd., Toronto, ON

Although it is almost lost among the ambient high-rise towers, the John Street Roundhouse was one of the largest ever constructed in Canada. It has been renovated and partially rebuilt over the past thirty years to house mainly commercial space (a brewery and retail and entertainment establishments) and a railroad museum. The immediate area is Roundhouse Park, the new home of several railroad structures moved from their original locations.

The semicircular, two-story, thirty-two-stall roundhouse, which replaced an earlier similar structure, was a timber-frame building faced with brick. Large windows in the inner and outer walls and clerestory windows in the central roof monitor admitted more light than was customary for such buildings. The roundhouse faced a turntable 120 feet in diameter— also one of Canada's largest (it was restored in 2009).

Its roundhouse's designer was the CPR's chief engineer, John M. R. Fairbairn (b. 1873) from Peterborough, Ontario. Fairbairn graduated from Toronto's School of Practical Science in 1893, having spent his summer vacations working for the CPR's chief engineer of construction. He then conducted topographical surveys in Alberta and right-of-way surveys for various Canadian government agencies. Fairbairn was a city engineer in British Columbia for a time, and a railroad construction engineer. He joined the CPR's construction department around 1900 and rose gradually through the ranks, moving back and forth several times between the Montreal and Toronto offices, before he was named chief engineer in 1918.

The John Street Roundhouse was the centerpiece of the CPR's sixteen-acre complex of shops and yards that stretched for two miles near the lakefront and consisted of some forty-three buildings. It was built on landfill near the contemporary Union Station, which the shop complex was set up to serve (see chapter 2). Steam and diesel engines were maintained and

Figure 9.13
John Street Roundhouse,
Toronto, Ontario, from the
CN Tower (courtesy of Michael
Mayer, Wikipedia)

repaired in the roundhouse; passenger coaches and dining and sleeping cars were cleaned and readied for service in the extensive coach yards.

To the west were the Canadian National Railway's Spadina Roundhouse and shops (see chapter 14). Together, the two facilities were known as "the railway lands." With the changes in motive power technology and the decline of railroad passenger service in the mid-twentieth century, the shops and yards became excess property—and some of the most valuable real estate in Canada. Almost all of the buildings except for the John Street Roundhouse were demolished in the succeeding years, and some of Toronto's landmark buildings constructed on their site, including the CN Tower in 1976 and the Rogers Centre (formerly the Skydome) in 1989.

The John Street Roundhouse was spared. The CPR closed the facility in 1986 and donated it to the City of Toronto for a railroad museum. A decade later, several bays on the left-hand side of the roundhouse were demolished and rebuilt to facilitate construction of the underground expansion of the Metro Toronto Convention Centre, which had opened in 1984 on former railway lands. As part of the expansion project,

the 1930 reinforced-concrete coal tower, with a 350-ton capacity (actually, two circular silos plus a brick access tower with stairs), was moved six hundred feet from one side of the roundhouse to the other.

Roundhouse Park was created in 1997. In 2000, Steam Whistle Brewing opened a brewery in the rebuilt roundhouse bays, and the following year the Toronto Railway Historical Association was established to create the museum. The Toronto Railway Museum now occupies three bays in the center of the roundhouse, one for its exhibits and the others for the restoration of engines and cars. Leon's furniture and appliance store moved into the right-hand half of the roundhouse in 2009 (a Cineplex entertainment center replaced Leon's in summer 2017). The striking timber-frame interior of the roundhouse is readily accessible.

Several historic railroad structures have been moved to Roundhouse Park over the past twenty years, including the Don Station, an 1896 CPR station building originally located in the east end of Toronto; and Cabin D, a Toronto interlocking tower built by the Grand Trunk Railway, which was formerly located in the area west of the roundhouse. A miniature railroad circumnavigates Roundhouse Park.

Figure 9.14
Huntingdon County Chamber of Commerce, Huntingdon, Pennsylvania

HUNTINGDON COUNTY CHAMBER OF COMMERCE
(formerly the Pennsylvania Railroad Hunt Tower)
1900
500 Allegheny St., Huntingdon, PA

The simplest way to control the traffic at railroad intersections where two lines cross one another (called "the diamonds") is to have each train stop first before proceeding. But this is inefficient, since stopping and starting a train is not easy. So basic signal towers were installed at intersections to inform train engineers in advance whether it was safe to proceed without stopping.

However, most railroad crossings involved switches, so the signal function was combined with that of aligning the switches to enable trains to negotiate the more complex track configurations safely. This was done manually at first, and later by a mechanical interlocking system. Developed in England in 1856 and

first installed on an American railroad in 1870, an interlocking system was operated by a row of tall levers in the tower that were connected to the switches by an extended array of metal pipes, which sometimes ran for several hundred feet along the rails. It required a good deal of strength to shift the levers (the interlocking towers were sometimes called "strong arm" or "Armstrong" towers), and weather and other factors could affect the movement of the connecting pipes. Later, pneumatic, hydraulic, or electrical operation all but eliminated the physical effort required to move the pipes and turn the switches.

The interlocking system correlated the signals with the aligned switches to ensure the safe passage of trains moving through junctions; when the levers were sequentially lined up, conflicting routes could not be established. The system was universally employed by railroads until quite recently. When Cabin D, now at Roundhouse Park in Toronto, was an active interlocking tower on the Grand Trunk

Railway, switch tenders on the ground outside the tower manually turned the switches in response to instructions relayed by loudspeaker, an anachronistic method that lasted until the 1980s.

Centralized traffic control (CTC), first employed in 1927, shifted the local functions of the interlocking towers to a remote location. Train dispatchers at modern CTC centers can regulate traffic flow and operate interlocking systems throughout a vast territory. In the 1980s, CSX Transportation began dispatching trains over its system, which contained thousands of miles of track, from a single building in its Jacksonville, Florida, headquarters.

Although a small number of the obsolete interlocking towers are still in use routing trains, most of them were boarded up and abandoned. The great majority were eventually demolished, some were moved to new locations such as railroad museums, and a few are still visible from passing trains. Fiber optic cables, advanced electronics, and computers have enabled the mechanical signaling and switching functions of the interlocking tower to be replicated in small, pitched-roof metal boxes called bungalows, which are located at signals and usually accompanied by a solar panel to generate power.

The interlocking towers were compact, straightforward pieces of vernacular railroad architecture built of wood or masonry. They were generally two stories high, with an outside access stairway. The ground floors housed equipment, utilities, and sometimes the interlocking machine, which might be the size of a small automobile and weigh several tons. The upper floors, with windows on three sides to provide clear views of the track and switching action below, were the domain of the tower operator, connected by telegraph (and later by telephone) with the train dispatcher in a central office. The operator also delivered written orders to passing trains "on the fly"—placing the orders on a pole so the locomotive engineer could grab them through his open window as he went by.

The Pennsylvania Railroad's interlocking tower at Huntingdon, Pennsylvania, is an admirable example of its type. Set on a stone foundation, the brick ground floor has a set of windows enclosed in recessed panels. The exterior of the second floor is almost all glass; the bay window, analogous to the agent's bay of a train station, gave the operator even more of an advantage in seeing approaching trains.

When the Hunt Tower was closed in the 1980s and scheduled for demolition, a group of local railroad enthusiasts managed to save it and turn it into a transportation museum. The Huntingdon County Chamber of Commerce now has its offices in the building. The nearby Huntingdon depot (1872), which served the Pennsylvania Railroad and the Huntingdon and Broad Top Mountain Railroad (a short-line coal hauler) is in commercial use.

ALTO TOWER
1880

Tenth Ave., near the 17th St. Bridge, Altoona, PA

Alto Tower guided trains entering and leaving the busy Altoona terminal on the Pennsylvania Railroad's main line for over 130 years, before it was closed in 2012. The wooden building's second story is cantilevered over the first. Lending relief to the

Figure 9.15

Alto Tower, Altoona, Pennsylvania

Figure 9.16
Chesapeake and Ohio Railway coal tower, Thurmond, West Virginia,
at night (courtesy of Scott Lothes)

horizontal wooden siding is some decoration in the style of Charles Eastlake: wheel-shape scrolls, fish-scale shingles, and a dentiled cornice of pointed slats. The tower is abandoned, and its future is uncertain.

CHESAPEAKE AND OHIO RAILWAY COAL TOWER

1922, Fairbanks Morse and Company
Thurmond, WV

Located deep in the New River Gorge, Thurmond was a railroad and coal town. The Chesapeake and Ohio (c&o) Railway completed its line through the gorge in 1873. About that time, Captain William D. Thurmond, who had been a Confederate officer in the Civil War, arrived in the area as a surveyor and acquired seventy-three acres of land on the north side of the river. He built several houses and rented them to miners and railroad workers. By the next decade, a dozen coal mines in the area were shipping their product through the town that had been named after Thurmond, which by then had two general stores, telegraph and express companies, and a post office. The first depot in Thurmond opened in 1888. A few years later, Captain Thurmond built a hotel, but because of his strict Baptist beliefs, he refused to allow drinking or gambling on the premises. The town of Thurmond was incorporated in 1903, and the sale of liquor was outlawed.

Across the river at Glen Jean, Thomas G. McKell —who owned coal mines, railroads, and the town it-self—built his own hotel, the Dun Glen, which offered everything the Thurmond Hotel did not: liquor, gambling, and prostitution. It was reputed to host the longest-lasting poker game on record (it went on for fourteen years). The south side of town near the Dun Glen Hotel was the red-light district.

At the beginning of the twentieth century, several hundred people lived in Thurmond, fifteen passenger trains a day stopped at its station, and the stores, banks, and boardinghouses were prospering. So was the railroad. Due to the coal shipments, the annual receipts from Thurmond were greater than those from Cincinnati and Richmond combined.

Figure 9.17

Chesapeake and Ohio Railway coal tower, Thurmond, West Virginia, in daytime (courtesy of Scott Lothes)

The main street was the railroad line, which provided the only connection to the world outside; the paved road from Glen Jean did not reach Thurmond until 1921. By then the boom was over. The Dun Glen Hotel was destroyed by arson in 1930, and the banks and other businesses pulled out during the Depression. The conversion to diesel locomotives meant that Thurmond was no longer needed as a coal and water stop.

Essentially a ghost town, most of Thurmond is now owned by the National Park Service, which restored the 1905 station building in 1995 and made it a National Park Service visitors' center and museum. Coal mining is largely a thing of the past in the New River Gorge, but a new tourism industry has developed in recent decades, with white-water rafting on the New River. Thurmond was the location for *Matewan*, a 1978 film directed by John Sayles about the lives of West Virginia coal miners.

Only three commercial buildings are left in the town center. The major railroad structure, besides the station, is the five-story reinforced-concrete coal

Figure 9.18
Glenwood Power Station, Yonkers, New York
(courtesy of Peter Field Peck)

tower that carries the legend "C&O 1922" over the locomotive bay. The fully automated tower, with its 500-ton capacity, could load the tender of one of the company's mammoth H-8 Mallet engines with 25 tons of coal in minutes. It also supplied the locomotives with sand (to increase traction on slippery rails), through a system of outriggers maneuvered by the pulleys that hang midway on the tower.

Before the locomotive tenders could be loaded with coal, the tower had to be filled. This was accomplished by bringing loaded bottom-dump hopper cars into the central bay. The coal fell into an enclosure twenty-two feet below ground level. From there it went to a crusher and then was hoisted by buckets on a conveyor belt to the upper part of the tower and dropped into bins. Chicago's Fairbanks Morse and Company built more than 700 such railroad coaling stations.

Coal towers take many forms. Their enormity makes them ungainly, even otherworldly, but startling and unmistakable presences in the railroad landscape. Their size also protects them. Like the railroad grain elevators, they are so huge and solidly constructed that it is prohibitively expensive to

demolish them. The C&O Railway abandoned the Thurmond coal tower in 1960.

Directions to the coal tower: take Route 19 to the Glen Jean exit; then follow signs to Thurmond, seven miles away via Route 25.

GLENWOOD POWER STATION
1906, Reed and Stem
Yonkers, NY

The Glenwood Power Station was built as part of the electrification program for the new Grand Central Terminal to supply electricity via a third-rail system to the trains (see chapter 2). The New York Central Railroad's Hudson River line (now operated by Metro North) fostered the suburban growth of Westchester County and the City of Yonkers. Abandoned, the power station has stood empty and been vandalized since it closed in the mid-1960s (there is a smaller substation building in use to the north).

Its imposing size (it has the form of a double basilica and is five stories high, with two very tall chimneys) and impressive site (on the banks of the Hudson, almost halfway between the George Washington and Tappan Zee Bridges and opposite the Palisades) make it a prime prospect for creative reuse, but a daunting one.

The power station, designed by the architects of Grand Central Terminal, is built of brick and steel in what might best be described as an industrial Romanesque revival style. Between the row of multistory round-arched windows and the stylized corbel table is a rank of small rectangular windows. A pair of large, metal and glass central monitors create clerestories over the two main interior spaces: the turbine hall, which resembles a cathedral, and the boiler room.

In 1936, the railroad sold the building to Con Edison, having found that it was cheaper to buy power than produce its own (the Glenwood Power Station

Figure 9.19 *(opposite)*
Glenwood Power Station, turbine hall,
Yonkers, New York (courtesy of Peter Field Peck)

Figure 9.20
Glenwood Power Station,
Yonkers, New York (photo
by Michael Tiranoff and
Megan Haungs)

was built—like several others by different railroads —because it was felt at the time that the utility companies could not generate enough electricity to run the trains). Glenwood continued to produce power for the county until 1968, when, its turbines having become obsolete, it was closed and the machinery scrapped. Ten years later, a private individual bought the power plant to use it as a storage facility for his construction company. Various redevelopment schemes were proposed as the new owner marketed the property, but concerns about environmental issues prevented them from moving forward.

In 2013, the Goren Group acquired control of the building, planning to turn it into an art-focused event and entertainment complex that would eventually include a hotel, restaurant, and marina. The first step, since it is a brownfield site, was to clean up the contaminants produced by sixty years of burning fuel. A physical cleaning was also necessary: after standing open and neglected for fifty years, the structure had become a favorite destination for urban explorers and, supposedly, a gang initiation site. The building was secured from vagrants, and some repairs were made, including to the roof. The estimated cost of the conversion, which is dependent on tax credits, is $150 million; the completion date is uncertain.

10

WHERE THEY LIVED
(Railroad Towns and Suburbs)

I n the settled East, the comparatively fast and reliable transportation provided by the railroads in the nineteenth century facilitated people's moving to the suburbs. And in the wide open spaces between the Mississippi River and the Rocky Mountains, the railroads created a whole galaxy of new towns and cities. Most of this development occurred naturally as a result of the railroad's arrival, but a few of the new communities were planned and built by the railroad companies or their subsidiaries. These included Mount Royal, in Montreal, Quebec; and Rancho Santa Fe, in California.

As early as 1834, South Carolina Canal and Railroad Company engineers drew up the plan for Aiken, South Carolina. This was a summer retreat accessible by rail from Charleston, with rectangular blocks separated by broad, tree-lined parkways, that offered a healthy environment with plenty of open space.

Several mid-nineteenth-century communities claim to be the first planned suburb (or the first planned railroad suburb) in America. Kirkwood, Missouri, got started in 1853 when the Pacific Railroad (predecessor of the Missouri Pacific Railroad) arrived from St. Louis and developers auctioned off town lots. In 1855 some gentlemen wanting to have summer residences there established Glendale, Ohio, fourteen miles north of Cincinnati on the Cincinnati, Hamilton and Dayton Railroad. In 1854 the developers of Mount Washington, Maryland, offered a picturesque location on the Northern Central Railroad within easy commuting distance of Baltimore, and at a safe remove from city rowdies (this was at the height of the Know Nothing period in Baltimore, when it was earning a reputation as Mobtown). Llewellyn Park—in West Orange, New Jersey, fifteen miles from New York City on the Delaware, Lackawanna and Western Railroad —was founded in 1857; the brilliant and influential architect Alexander Jackson Davis designed the gatehouse and several villas.

Frederick Law Olmsted planned Riverside, Illinois (1870), on the Chicago, Burlington and Quincy Railroad west of Chicago and Sudbrook, Maryland

(1889), outside Baltimore. In the latter case, the land's original owner worked with the Western Maryland Railway in designing the suburb. Quite different in origin and outcome was Rancho Santa Fe, California (1922 and later), which was developed by a subsidiary of the Santa Fe Railway as a re-creation of a Spanish village. The architect was Lilian Rice, and it is now one of the wealthiest communities in the United States.

By the end of the nineteenth century, large American cities from Philadelphia to San Francisco had strings of suburbs radiating outward from their centers along the major rail lines. Chicago, the railroad capital of America, had eleven such lines and hundreds of satellite communities.

In much the same fashion, but spread out over a vast territory, the railroads populated the plains and mountain states with new towns and cities. A diagram of a section of North Dakota as it appeared in 1910 reveals small and moderate-size towns, as well as larger communities such as Minot, distributed at regular intervals along the railroad routes. As shown by a current highway map, this dispersal pattern of settlements, formulated and executed by the railroads, still remains despite subsequent decades of paving and the imposition of the Interstate Highway System. Cities ranging widely in size and geography—including Miami, Florida; Albuquerque, New Mexico; and Vancouver, British Columbia—came to life as a result of the railroads.

RIVERSIDE, IL
1870, Frederick Law Olmsted,
Calvert Vaux, landscape architects

Commutation tickets offering a reduced rate for train travel over the same route for a limited period of time, and the term "commuters" for people who used them, both came into popular use in the mid-nineteenth century. At the same time Chicago, soon to become the fastest growing city in the West, was emerging as the quintessential commuter town. From Wilmette in the north and Hyde Park in the south on the shores of Lake Michigan to Aurora

and Elgin on the open prairie to the west, and the surrounding suburbs, the business and professional men of Chicago made their diurnal procession by rail to the Loop. The suburbs were considered clean, healthy, wholesome—good places to raise a family—in contrast to the big city, with its primitive sanitation, unpaved streets, and other assorted evils.

Riverside, nine miles west of Chicago, would become "the most pleasant, healthful and desirable place of residence attainable anywhere . . . in all respects a model suburban neighborhood," promised its promoters.[24] To that end, they hired America's foremost landscape planner.

Frederick Law Olmsted created the profession of landscape architecture in America. He believed that carefully sculpted landscapes could have a civilizing effect on society. Olmsted and his partner, Calvert Vaux, designed Central Park in New York City and several other major urban parks (such as the chain of parks in Boston collectively known as the Emerald Necklace), parkways (including the Martin Luther King, Jr. Drive, formerly the Grand Boulevard, in Chicago), residential communities (for example, Druid Hills, in Atlanta, Georgia), university campuses (such as that of Stanford University, in California), and private estates (including Biltmore, in Asheville, North Carolina). Olmsted was the site planner for the 1893 Chicago World's Fair. Riverside, Illinois, was his first planned community.

Riverside was the creation of Emery E. Childs, a sharp real estate speculator from the East; and David A. Gage, the wealthy owner of Riverside Farm, an 1,100-acre horse farm and oak and hickory forest on the Des Plaines River. Gage was treasurer of the City of Chicago. Their idea for a commuter suburb began to take form in 1868, when Childs bought Riverside Farm from Gage for $300,000, payable in installments as the lots sold (the Chicago, Burlington and Quincy Railroad had constructed its line through the area five years earlier).

Childs quickly brought in the landscape architecture firm of Olmsted and Vaux, and by the time he had formed the Riverside Improvement Company in 1869, the landscape architects had their plan ready. It

Figure 10.1
Train station and water tower,
Riverside, Illinois

outlined 700 acres of parks, forty miles of carriage drives, eighty miles of paved walks, playgrounds, a train station, and a water tower. The last two components defined the town center. The wide roadways on either side of the arrow-straight railroad right-of-way were not laid out like an urban grid but were curved to follow the natural contours of the land and the winding of the river (an Olmsted trademark).

Thanks to the efforts of some five hundred laborers, Riverside began to emerge from the prairie in 1870. However, the improvement company, which had taken on substantial debt to pay for construction, was in poor financial shape—80 percent of the lots were still unsold. With his fees unpaid, Olmsted quit (he had earlier referred to the project as a purely speculative venture).

Devising several obscure schemes, Childs maneuvered desperately to raise funds. However, the Chicago fire of 1871, which placed great demands on the available capital for rebuilding, and the financial panic of 1873 spelled the end for the Riverside Improvement Company. In 1873 it expired under the weight of bankruptcy and litigation that dragged on for decades. That same year, Gage, who had evidently been lending himself city funds in an attempt to recoup his investment, was tried for embezzlement. He was acquitted, and some people felt the $400,000 in question was a disappointingly small amount for a man of Gage's position to make off with, given the customary level of municipal graft in Chicago.

The town of Riverside survived, owing to the strength of its plan and its continuing attraction for members of the business and professional class, who would live harmoniously with their peers, according to the town's promotional literature. In the aftermath of the Chicago fire, an increasing number of people who could afford to live there saw the benefits of combining country charm with city convenience. Riverside, incorporated in 1875, inspired several other rail-oriented suburbs, such as Brookline, Massachusetts, and Forest Hills Gardens in Queens, New York. Riverside was not unique in other ways, either: Childs and Gage were not the last suburban real estate developers to promise more than they could deliver.

To supervise the construction of Riverside, Olmsted had hired William Le Barron Jenney—a Chicago architect and engineer who was to become famous as the architect of Chicago's Home Insurance Company Building (1885), regarded as America's first modern skyscraper. Jenney designed the landmark water tower in Riverside. Completed in 1871, the Swiss Gothic tower, which contained a water tank, was built of cream-colored brick with decorative accents of red brick on a stone base. Several stories tall, it culminated in a slate roof shaped like a flared inverted funnel. Circling the top story was an iron balcony from which prospective buyers could survey the town of Riverside and glimpse Chicago in the distance. Jenney also designed several houses in Riverside.

The linear, one-story train station (1901), which replaced an earlier one built at the same time as the water tower, was designed by architects on the staff of the Chicago, Burlington and Quincy Railroad. The hip roof of red tile covers the waiting room and an extended outdoor passenger shelter. The materials are brick with a limestone trim. The attractive interior has quarter-sawn oak paneling, classical crown molding, and a patterned terrazzo floor. The station building was restored in 1978. On the opposite side of the tracks is a covered passenger shelter.

Other significant buildings in the immediate vicinity include the Riverside Historical Museum, located in the former Water Tower Pump House (circa 1871), at 10 Pine Avenue; the Riverside Improvement Building (1871), across the street from the train station; the Riverside Town Hall (1895); and the Riverside Public Library (1930). Another landmark is Frank Lloyd Wright's Coonley House (1908), one of his finest prairie style houses. About nine thousand people live in Riverside now, and it has an active Frederick Law Olmsted Society.

RANCHO SANTA FE, CA
Atchison, Topeka and Santa Fe Railway,
1922 and later, Lilian J. Rice

Lilian Rice, one of California's first professional women architects, commented that "with the thought early implanted in my mind that true beauty lies in simplicity rather than ornateness, I found real joy in Rancho Santa Fe."[25]

Rancho Santa Fe started with three thousand acres of eucalyptus trees planted in the coastal hills of southern California and became one of the oldest, wealthiest, and most exclusive communities in the state. It was built by a subsidiary of the Atchison, Topeka and Santa Fe Railway, and the initial buildings were designed by Rice.

In 1906, the Santa Fe Land Improvement Company bought 8,450 acres of land in the hills east of Delmar and Solana Beach for $100,000. The property was conveniently close to the rail line between Los Angeles and San Diego that the Santa Fe Railway had assembled from some existing routes twenty years earlier (now called the Surf Line, the line parallels ocean beaches for much of its length; see chapter 4). Formerly known as the Rancho San Dieguito, the land

had belonged to Juan Maria Osuna, the first mayor of San Diego; he had obtained it as a land grant from the Mexican government in the 1840s.

The railroad's original purpose in buying the land was to grow eucalyptus trees that it could use to make railroad ties. The company imported thousands of seedlings from Australia and planted them in groves on the property, but the wood was found to be inappropriate for making railroad ties (or much of anything else), so the railroad looked for other uses for the property.

The fast-growing blue gum eucalyptus, which could shoot up ten feet per year, was native to Australia. In the 1870s, it was introduced to the treeless coastal hills of southern California, mainly given over to sage and chaparral, as a potential source of lumber and a way to beautify the landscape. The trees proved disappointing if used as lumber; the wood split and twisted when it dried. But they adapted well to the local climate, and ranchers and farmers planted them as windbreaks or ornamental trees. Current public opinion in the region is divided as to whether eucalyptus trees are an asset or a nuisance.

In 1915, the Santa Fe Land Improvement Company leased the ranch to a San Diego land developer, Colonel Ed Fletcher, who proposed that a dam be built to supply water to the ranch and surrounding county. The $2-million dam was completed in 1918 and named for Walter E. Hodges, vice president of the Santa Fe Railway and president of the improvement company (the water company was another subsidiary of the Santa Fe Railway).

Leone G. Sinnard was hired in 1920 to advise the improvement company on subdividing the property. A San Francisco land expert, Sinnard had worked in advertising and promotion for the Southern Pacific Railroad. He recommended that the owners develop a permanent community of gentleman farmers who would practice horticulture by growing citrus trees. The new residents would travel by train and ship their fruit by rail, which would increase the railroad's business.

An equally high-class residential subdivision was called for. Sinnard prepared a site plan whose curving streets enclosed multi-acre residential lots (the development was planned for automobiles). The focal point was the civic center, a rectangular area of roughly ten blocks, where the hotel, business section, school, and several streets of private homes would be built. The hotel, with streets radiating from it, sat at the center of one half of the area; the remaining half contained the other elements. The town center had an axial plan, and the residential streets were divided by a landscaped boulevard. At the end of the year, the Santa Fe Land Improvement Company filed a subdivision plan for Rancho Santa Fe.

To develop the plan and design the buildings for the town center, the company hired the San Diego architectural firm of Requa and Jackson in 1921. Richard S. Requa, the senior partner, had apprenticed with Irving Gill, a leading California architect who had evolved an individual style that had several influences, including the mission revival style. Requa was very interested in the regional architectural heritage of the Native American pueblos and Spanish missions, a passion he communicated to his assistant, Lilian Rice —who later took over the Rancho Santa Fe project.

Lilian Rice (1889–1938) was born in nearby National City, California. In 1910, she became one of the first women to graduate with a degree in architecture from the University of California, Berkeley. She worked as a draftsman in an architectural office and taught mechanical drawing and geometry at the high school and college levels for a time in San Diego before joining the office of Requa and Jackson in 1920.

Rice chose the site for the town center, refined the plan, and designed the first buildings in a combination of the Spanish colonial revival and mission revival styles. Her intention was to create a replica of a Spanish village. First came the inn: La Morada (1922) was a rambling, one-story structure surrounded by landscaped gardens. In 1923, at the corner of the business block, the Santa Fe Land Improvement Company's office building was erected, with an arched corner entrance and arcades that faced Paseo Delicias, the central landscaped boulevard, and the Avenida de Acacias. The first residence Rice designed was at 6036 La Flecha (1923), now the headquarters of the Rancho Santa Fe Historical Society. About this time, her employers sent Rice to Spain, Portugal, and Cuba to research and study the architectural styles used there.

Perhaps the finest of Rice's many buildings at Rancho Santa Fe, and the best examples of her understated rendition of the Spanish styles she combined so effectively, are the four so-called rowhouses at 6112–6126 Paseo Delicias (1927). Their red tile pitched roofs alternately face and parallel the street. Stark entrances and windows are decorated with wrought-iron railings, grilles, and lamps; tile house numbers mark the doorways. The fronts of the houses, which

Figure 10.2

La Morada, Rancho Santa Fe, California

are set back in an irregular pattern from the street, are landscaped with cacti and colorful native plants. The interiors are equally plain, and the front gardens are repeated in rear patios. Rice's Joers/Ketchum Store (1927), at the corner of Paseo Delicias and La Granada, is one of her best commercial buildings: it consists of a two-story main block with a one-story wing, and there is a handsome wrought-iron balcony over the main entrance.

While continuing to supervise the design work at Rancho Santa Fe, in 1928 Rice opened her own architectural office in San Diego and designed residences and schools in the region. In 1931 she became a member of the American Institute of Architects, one of the few women at the time elected to the national professional organization.

The last member of the Rancho Santa Fe design team was Charles H. Cheney, a San Francisco architect and city planner, who arrived around 1928. One of the leaders of the city planning movement in California, he helped establish city planning commissions in such cities as Berkeley, Palo Alto, and San Rafael. Cheney devised the restrictive covenants in the deeds and set up the Rancho Santa Fe Association in 1928 to oversee them. The deed restrictions governed such things as the appearance of existing and future architecture, use of buildings, and general attractiveness of property. They were designed to preserve and maintain the character of the community and its rare landscape features. The homeowners' association is in effect the governing body of the town, providing building, planning, and security services.

Figure 10.3
Rowhouses, Rancho Santa Fe, California

Figure 10.4
Joers/Ketchum Store,
Rancho Santa Fe, California

Rancho Santa Fe has attracted its share of the rich and famous over the years (Bing Crosby, Geena Davis, Howard Hughes, and Bill Gates have lived there), and today it is a community of about three thousand people with a median annual income of $172,000. House prices are in the range of $1–10 million. Estate homes, amid groves of orange and lemon and eucalyptus trees, are mainly invisible behind locked gates.

MOUNT ROYAL, QC
Canadian Northern Railway
1912–17, Frederick G. Todd, landscape architect

Near the end of the nineteenth century, two energetic and entrepreneurial individuals from Ontario, William Mackenzie and Donald Mann, began to piece together a system of existing branch lines in western Canada and to build others. Mackenzie and Mann learned the railroad business as contractors constructing the Canadian Pacific Railway (CPR) across the prairies and into the Rocky Mountains.

Their original intention, supported by the western provinces, was to counter the CPR's monopoly in the region. In 1899 they established the Canadian Northern Railway and began buying and building their way east. The Canadian Northern reached Port Arthur (then known as Thunder Bay) at the western edge of Lake Superior in 1902. This gave the railroad access to Great Lakes shipping for its cargoes of western grain. The following year, the Canadian Northern entered Quebec Province and aimed for Montreal.

Mackenzie and Mann had difficulty finding a route into the city because the CPR and the Grand Trunk Railway had already taken the most convenient ones. The two men therefore decided to tunnel under a low mountain, Mount Royal, that lay between their rail line and downtown Montreal. They would construct a new underground terminal topped by air rights development in the city. The tunnel and terminal were to be electrified. Together with Mackenzie and Mann, Henry K. Wicksteed, the Canadian Northern's chief engineer, played a key role in developing the overall plan, based on the recently completed Grand Central Terminal in New York City. On the north side of the mountain, to help pay for the project through the sale of lots, the men planned to build a model city. Thus began the planned community of Mount Royal.

To design the new town, the Canadian Northern hired the man now considered Canada's first landscape architect. Frederick Todd (1876–1948) was born in Concord, New Hampshire; attended an agricultural college in Massachusetts; and apprenticed with the Olmsted Brothers firm in Brookline, Massachusetts. After moving to Montreal in 1900, he started his own landscape architecture practice and designed parks and garden cities. The latter were based on the work of Ebenezer Howard and the Garden City movement in Great Britain, which was just then coming into vogue.

The first step was to acquire the land, and around 1910 the Canadian Northern bought 4,800 acres of farmland north of Montreal for $120,000. Todd laid out a new town that combined aspects of several approaches to city planning. The rectangular plan was centered on a landscaped park and a train station. Four diagonal boulevards, along which the retail and commercial establishments were to be located, radiated out from the central square, forming an X-pattern through the town. The residential streets were laid out in a gridiron pattern, but around the edges was a meandering circular parkway that enclosed a series of parks and playgrounds. Bisecting the whole was the rail line. Stone from the tunnel's excavation was to be used to pave the streets, and trolleys would link the new town with nearby communities.

Both the plan for Washington, D.C., and the City Beautiful movement influenced the plan for Mount Royal, with its central square and diagonal boulevards. (Some of Frederick Law Olmsted's plans for other places included a winding circumferential parkway.) Wicksteed, the chief engineer, also had a hand in the early planning for the town. The gridiron street pattern was common to most cities. Other features of the Mount Royal plan were the availability of public transit, a variety of housing types, and commercial and retail establishments within walking distance of the residences.

Construction began in 1912. The tunnel (the estimated cost for its three and a quarter miles was $3–4 million), delayed by World War I, was completed five years later. However, little development had taken place at Mount Royal during that time. In 1917, despite the infusion of substantial government bond money and land grants over the years, Mackenzie and Mann were in financial difficulty—due in large part to the high construction costs of the project. The government took over the Canadian Northern that year (Mackenzie and Mann were forced to resign) and six years later made it part of the Canadian National Railway.

The town of Mount Royal grew slowly, with development occurring in waves. Schools and churches began to appear in the 1920s. The greatest period of growth took place in the 1950s. Although the initial idea was to attract upper-income residents, in recent decades Mount Royal has become economically and

Figure 10.5
Train station, Mount Royal, Montreal, Quebec

Figure 10.6
Connaught Park, Mount Royal, Montreal, Quebec

ethnically diverse. The train station—a one-story brick building with a flared hip roof and large triangular dormers—is now a pizza restaurant; passengers board the Agence Métropolitaine de Transport (AMT) commuter trains for the ten-minute ride to Montreal's Central Station at a trackside shelter. Across the street from the station is Connaught Park, a beautifully landscaped central green space. The boulevards leading out from its corners are lined with stores and apartment buildings, and between the boulevards are quiet residential streets. In 2011 the population was 19,500.

With their Canadian Northern Railway and its tunnel entrance into Montreal, Mackenzie and Mann created a third transcontinental railroad, built a new town, and established the pattern of development in the center city. Besides long-distance and commuter-rail transportation, the present Central Station (1943) offers a wide variety of stores and restaurants and connections to Montreal's vast underground pedestrian network, including Windsor Station and the Metro system. Built on the air rights over the station, the Canadian National Railway's Queen Elizabeth Hotel opened in 1958, with direct access to the station concourse. Place Villa Marie (1962; a cruciform, forty-seven-story office tower) and Place Bonaventure (1967; an office, exhibition, and hotel complex) were also part of Central Station's air rights development.

11

HOW THEY LIVED

The railroad barons of the nineteenth century lived and traveled on a plane of luxury unimaginable to most people at that time or today. The owners' mansions could be extremely sumptuous, a prime example being the one built in Baltimore for Robert Garrett, president of the Baltimore and Ohio (B&O) Railroad.

The barons also traveled in style. To move the Garretts and their small entourage by private railroad car from Baltimore to Chicago for the 1893 World's Fair—where they had a suite at Adler and Sullivan's magnificent new Auditorium Hotel, with adjoining rooms for the servants (and the accommodations could not be above the second floor, because of the danger of fire)—required logistics on the scale required for a military operation. It was all smoothly planned by Mrs. Mary Frick Garrett's confidential secretary, Amzi B. Crane.

The California counterpart to Baltimore's Garrett-Jacobs Mansion, now a private business club (but one that welcomes the public for tours), is Leland Stanford's spectacular mansion in Sacramento, restored as a state historic park and official reception center.

Asa Packer, owner of the Lehigh Valley Railroad and founder of Lehigh University, built one mansion for himself and another for his son in Jim Thorpe, Pennsylvania. Both are open to the public—the former as a museum, the latter as a bed-and-breakfast. Packer also built sixteen stone rowhouses nearby for his engineers and foremen. They are still used as residences, with some storefronts on the ground floors.

But generally the laborers at the bottom of the railroad pay scale, even if they lived in the same town or city, were in a different world. The typical housing for workers was flimsily built and for the most part has not lasted.

Railroad companies sometimes provided housing for their employees. This was occasionally free, but more often it was merely subsidized. While construction workers were building the railroads, they lived in house cars that rolled along the rails or in tents or shanties erected beside them.

When the line was finished, maintenance-of-way crews responsible for particular sections of track stayed in section houses. As a rule, these were individual wood-frame structures built along the right-of-way so the trackmen could respond quickly to an emergency, but there could be whole camps of these buildings.

Railroad companies used stock designs for various sizes of section houses, just as they did for small-town stations. The Great Northern Railway's standard section house was a two-story building in the form of a New England saltbox, with the extended pitched roof in the rear enclosing an extra room. It had a roof of cedar shingles, horizontal siding, and a privy out back. The ground floor contained a combined living and dining room, a bedroom, and a rear kitchen. The second floor had two bunk rooms. There was a single woodstove for cooking and heating, but the upstairs bunk rooms were unheated. The structure could accommodate a dozen section men. The section foreman sometimes had a separate dwelling.

Station agents and their families sometimes occupied an upstairs apartment in the station building, especially in remote areas where there was little other housing available. Some stations had dormitories on the upper floor where track gangs or train crews could lay over. Train crews generally found housing in the local railroad Young Men's Christian Association (YMCA).

Not much physical evidence is left of the transitory railroad construction camps, although some of their former sites in British Columbia have become campgrounds. A few section houses still stand, such as those at Chama, New Mexico, and Osier, Colorado.

One of the largest providers of railroad workers' housing was the YMCA. In the late nineteenth and early twentieth centuries, railroad branches of the organization were the universal home away from home for thousands of railroad men. The railroad companies and the YMCA shared the cost of building and operating these facilities.

The idea for the American railroad YMCA may have begun in Cleveland. There, Henry W. Stager, a train dispatcher at the city's Union Station in the early 1870s, watched the body of a railroad employee who had been killed in an accident as it was carried through the crowded station. Someone asked who it was. Only a railroad man, was the response from another bystander. Overhearing this derogatory reference to a fellow railroad worker, Stager decided to do something about it. Perhaps bettering the lives of railroad men would elevate their status in the public mind.

Stager organized the first railroad YMCA in America, which began modestly with a reading room in Cleveland's Union Station. The year was 1872. A few years later, Cornelius Vanderbilt Jr. opened a similar reading room in New York City's Grand Central Depot (Vanderbilt became a major backer of the railroad YMCA movement). Another early railroad YMCA was established in Stratford, Ontario.

The YMCA was founded in London in 1844. By the time Stager set up his reading room in Cleveland, the American branch of the YMCA was already proselytizing along the line of the Union Pacific Railroad, then under construction. As the railroads extended their reach, the YMCA saw an opportunity for expansion. The station reading room soon evolved into separate facilities that provided a full range of YMCA services. In 1879, the YMCA created a railroad department that worked with railroad companies to establish YMCA branches at division points where train crews laid over.

The companies liked the idea because of the safety factor. The customary haunts of off-duty train crews were the local saloons, gambling dens, and houses of prostitution. Consequently, the men were sometimes not in the best shape when they reported for work, thus endangering themselves and passengers. By offering an alternative, the railroad branch YMCA played a major role in improving the safety of American railroads.

Railroad employees appreciated the clean beds, hot showers, decent meals, libraries, and healthy recreation (along with a dose of spiritual inspiration) that the railroad branch YMCAs provided. By the early 1900s, over two hundred railroad branch YMCAs were operating in the United States, with an annual budget of $1 million, about 40 percent of which was borne by the railroad companies.

The Depression and the decline in railroading after World War II, along with changes in the industry, drastically reduced the number of railroad branch

YMCAS. Diesel locomotives could travel greater distances with less servicing than steam engines, so fewer division points and their accompanying shops and yards were needed. Although new consolidated railroad branch YMCAS were being built as late as the 1950s, the last one closed in 1970.

The railroad YMCA in Richmond, Virginia, is unusual in that it was designed by an architect; the building was recently converted to loft apartments. Like Richmond's YMCA, the Drury Inn in St. Louis, a former railroad YMCA, is located close by the train station. Although no longer a railroad branch, New York City's Vanderbilt YMCA (1932), on East 47th Street, still offers low-price rooms and meals and is one of the best hotel bargains in Manhattan. Besides trainmen, a number of well-known writers and actors have stayed there over the years.

Along with subsidized housing, the railroads offered other benefits to their employees, including medical care. They built hospitals, mostly in the Midwest, South, Southwest, and West. The former Atchison, Topeka and Santa Fe Railway Hospital in Albuquerque, New Mexico, was recently renovated as the Hotel Parq Central. San Francisco's Southern Pacific Railroad Hospital is now the Mercy Terrace Apartments.

ENGINEERING SOCIETY OF BALTIMORE
(formerly Garrett-Jacobs Mansion)
1884–93, McKim, Mead and White;
**   1905–16, John Russell Pope**
11 West Mount Vernon Place, Baltimore, MD

John Work Garrett (1820–84), a dynamic nineteenth-century president of the B&O Railroad, provided the property by giving 11 West Mount Vernon Place (not the present mansion) to his eldest son and his bride as a wedding present in 1872.

In 1884, when Robert Garrett II (1847–96) took over from his father as B&O Railroad president, he and his wife, Mary Sloan Frick (1851–1936), demolished the existing houses on the site and began to construct a new one. When the mansion was finally finished in 1916, it was the largest, most costly townhouse ($2.5

million) ever built in Baltimore. And it was mostly the creation of Mary Garrett, who reigned there as the grande dame of Baltimore society for four decades.

As railroad men, John and Robert Garrett could not have been more different. John, a shrewd, driven businessman, kept the strategic B&O Railroad firmly in Union hands during the Civil War, despite the depredations of Robert E. Lee and Stonewall Jackson on its lines and rolling stock. President Abraham Lincoln once referred to him as the federal government's right arm. In the postwar years of expansion, Garrett extended his rail network to Pittsburgh and Chicago and set his sights on New York, but the B&O Railroad was outmaneuvered by the Pennsylvania Railroad. Due to overexpansion and heavy borrowing, the company was mired in debt.

However, Garrett kept dividends high and stockholders happy. This was in his personal interest, since he owned more stock in the B&O than the president of any other major American railroad owned in his company. Garrett found ways to reduce costs, but his wage cutting on the B&O precipitated the Great Railroad Strike of 1877. When he died, he left the railroad, which he had made into one of the East's four major trunk lines, in the hands of Robert Garrett. He also left 30,000 shares of B&O stock to Robert and his other two children, T. Harrison and Mary Elizabeth. The stock was worth about $5.6 million in 1884, roughly $138 million in today's dollars.

An affable, well-dressed socialite, Robert lacked his father's drive, business acumen, and autocratic mien. John Garrett had expressed reservations about his son's taking over the railroad and said that he wished his daughter, Mary, had been a boy so that she could have succeeded him as B&O president.

Mary Garrett attended business meetings with her father, acted as his private secretary, and developed a keen business sense. She could well have run the B&O Railroad, but it was unthinkable in that era for a woman to assume control of a large corporation. Instead, she found other outlets for her energy and intelligence and substantial fortune. One of the first American female philanthropists, she was a major benefactor to Bryn Mawr College and, through a

Figure 11.1
Engineering Society of Baltimore, Baltimore, Maryland
(courtesy of Alain Jaramillo)

strategic gift to establish the Johns Hopkins University medical school, forced it to admit women on the same terms as men.

To his credit, Robert Garrett did extend the B&O line to Philadelphia and expanded the company's telegraph system. In December 1885, Garrett was at the Manhattan townhouse of William H. Vanderbilt, president of the New York Central Railroad, discussing terminal arrangements, when Vanderbilt suddenly pitched forward, dead of a stroke. Two years later, while Garrett was in Europe trying to raise money, the B&O Railroad Telegraph Company was sold against his wishes to Jay Gould and Western Union in a deal brokered by J. P. Morgan. These two events reportedly contributed to Garrett's mental illness and physical decline. He resigned as B&O's president in 1887 and died nine years later.

Railroad money built the mansion—the B&O had been the main source of the Garrett family's wealth ever since the family firm of investment bankers, Robert Garrett and Sons, began buying B&O stock in the 1850s. The mansion is really a New York townhouse transplanted to Baltimore. In scale and style, architects and artisans, and location and purpose, it closely resembles McKim, Mead and White's Villard Houses, which were under construction in New York

in 1884 as work began on the Garrett home in Baltimore. The Villard Houses and the Garrett home were large brownstone mansions built for railroad barons in the most fashionable parts of town. They inaugurated the new second Renaissance revival style.

Henry Villard, president of the Northern Pacific Railroad in 1881–84, completed that northern transcontinental line in 1883. He and Robert Garrett lasted just three years as presidents of their respective railroads, resigned following business reverses, and took long trips abroad to recuperate. Villard later regained control of the Northern Pacific Railway, but Garrett never returned to the business world.

Villard's twin townhouses in midtown Manhattan, separated by an open courtyard, looked across Madison Avenue to the rear of St. Patrick's Cathedral, designed by James Renwick (the townhouses are now the frontispiece and entry to the New York Palace Hotel). Garrett and his wife, Mary, built their townhouse on the site of two former houses at 9 and 11 West Mount Vernon Place—Baltimore's premier residential location, which overlooked the Washington Monument. The mansion was designed for opulent living and entertaining in the Gilded Age.

Almost immediately a general controversy arose over the building's modern appearance and excessive size. Henry P. Janes, the neighbor to the east, objected to the monstrous vestibule that projected several feet beyond the building line, depriving him of light and air and his first-floor view of the monument. Janes filed suit to stop work on the building and won his case, but the decision was overturned on appeal the following year. The first phase of the mansion, designed by Stanford White, was completed in 1886.

White's 1892 alterations created some of the mansion's most distinctive spaces. His two-story entrance hall incorporated a fireplace and inglenook, a Venetian lantern, a richly carved oak arcade, and an elliptical spiral staircase under a Tiffany glass dome. From a second-floor gallery overlooking this social barbican, screened by thin vertical spindles fronting a plate-glass window, Mary Garrett could discreetly monitor the arrival and attire of her guests (her dressing room adjoined the space).

Figure 11.2
Engineering Society of Baltimore,
entrance hall, Baltimore, Maryland
(courtesy of Alain Jaramillo)

Figure 11.3
Engineering Society of Baltimore, gallery,
Baltimore, Maryland (courtesy of Alain Jaramillo)

In the oval room next to the staircase (the Red Room), she took her afternoon tea. Behind this space was the family dining room, hung with seventeenth-century European tapestries. White's double parlor occupied the eastern (now the center) section of the house. It closely resembled the parlor of Mrs. William P. Astor's Fifth Avenue mansion that accommodated and therefore defined "the 400"—the most fashionable members of New York Society. Referred to in the local press as "the Mrs. Astor of Baltimore's 400," Mrs. Garrett's invitations to the mansion guaranteed the recipients' social arrival. The Garretts' separate bedrooms were on the second floor; the twenty house servants lived on the third.

New York artisans were responsible for most of the interior décor, a prime example of the visual pleasures afforded by the aesthetic movement. New York's Herter Brothers, decorators to America's wealthiest families, produced the vestibule and entrance hall.

Their clients on both coasts included members of the Vanderbilt, Gould, Morgan, Stanford, Crocker, and Huntington families. Few Herter Brothers interiors remain intact.

In 1902, Mary Garrett married her deceased husband's physician, Henry Barton Jacobs, and bought the property to the west of the mansion (No. 7). In 1905, John Russell Pope designed an addition. He extended the brownstone façade in the same style and behind it arranged a library, a Caen stone hall and grand marble staircase, and, in the rear, a ballroom that measured thirty by seventy feet. The largest of the mansion's forty rooms, it also had a stage. The staircase led down to a lower-level supper room, which had a musicians' gallery. Pope also designed a picture gallery to run across the rear of the property. Completed in 1913, it enclosed the courtyard, in which Mary. Jacobs later installed an iron and glass conservatory containing exotic plants, a monkey, and a trickling stream. The mansion was solidly constructed in true railroad fashion, with brick walls and structural iron; the picture gallery was made of steel and concrete.

Pope also converted White's double parlor into a Louis XV rococo style drawing room (a recent restoration included the regilding of the fourteen-carat gold decoration). Finally, in 1915, Mary Jacobs bought the offending neighbor's house to the west (No. 13) and promptly demolished the rear of it for light and air for her staircase. She was an imperious and remarkably tight-fisted patron, and the correspondence concerning the mansion at the Maryland Historical Society is full of repeated requests from artists and tradesmen seeking to be paid. White, frustrated by the Garretts' incessant requests for cost reductions, said at one point that they could wait—he was going fishing.

Mary Jacobs died in 1936, and most of her $5.6-million estate was devoted to establishing children's medical facilities in Baltimore. Her art collection, containing paintings by van Dyck, van Ruisdael, Rembrandt, Hals, Chardin, and Canaletto (and a number of French fakes), went to the Baltimore Museum of Art. It is housed in a special wing (1937) designed by Pope and built with Works Progress Administration funds.

Robert Garrett began the art collection. He also contributed the basin and fountain to the west square in front of the mansion and W. W. Story's statue of George Peabody to the east square before the Peabody Institute. Mary Garrett and her second husband viewed these artistic additions to Mount Vernon Place, one of the nation's great urban spaces, every Sunday morning on their way to church when, at precisely 10:45 AM, their limousine, with a uniformed chauffeur and footman, would pick them up in front of the mansion, drive east, circling the Washington Monument, then travel in the opposite direction along the north side of the square before depositing them at Grace and St. Peter's Church, one block to the west.

Henry Jacobs died in 1939, and the mansion was sold the next year. It had a couple of occupants before 1958, when the City of Baltimore acquired it with the intention of demolishing it for a proposed expansion of the Walters Art Gallery. The resultant controversy ended in 1962 when the Engineers Club (now the Engineering Society of Baltimore) bought the building for $155,000 for its headquarters and began to restore it.

In 1994, the Engineering Society of Baltimore formed a separate endowment fund to raise money for major restoration projects; since then, the organization has evolved into a general businessmen's club. The society, which has now been in residence longer than the original occupants, has invested nearly $8 million over the years to restore the façade and the major interior spaces and install a new kitchen and steel and glass roof over the courtyard, making it usable in all seasons.

LELAND STANFORD MANSION

Leland Stanford Mansion State Historic Park
1857, Seth Babson; 1872, renovations, additions,
Nathaniel Goodell (?)
800 N St., Sacramento, CA

The Stanford mansion is a superb physical manifestation of the enormous wealth, power, and influence the railroads created, particularly for their owners. Consider the timeline. On June 19, 1861, Republicans nominated Leland Stanford, a lawyer turned merchant, as their candidate for governor of California. Two days later, he was named president of the newly incorporated Central Pacific Railroad. A month after that he bought from another local merchant for $8,000 a brick, two-story, five-bay Renaissance revival mansion designed by Seth Babson, a Sacramento architect. It was the nucleus of the present building.

Stanford won the election handily, and his two-year term as governor began with a natural disaster. Flooding rivers in Sacramento in January 1862 forced him to return from his inaugural in a rowboat to his inundated home. But the skies cleared, and a year later Stanford broke ground for the Central Pacific —the railroad he had started with other Sacramento businessmen, including Collis P. Huntington, Mark Hopkins, and Charles Crocker.

The men became known as the Big Four, and their line formed the western end of the transcontinental railroad. On May 10, 1869, at Promontory, Utah, Stanford and Thomas C. Durant of the Union Pacific Railroad drove the ceremonial last spike, signaling (by telegraph) the completion of a 1,900-mile rail line extending from the Missouri River opposite Omaha to Oakland on San Francisco Bay. The Central Pacific Railroad was an immediate financial success, and with its transcontinental connection, it revolutionized life in the West.

In the meantime, Leland and Jane Lathrop Stanford had had a son. In 1871, they decided they needed more room for the family and for entertaining on a scale that reflected their increased social status. As governor, Stanford had steered public funds to the Central Pacific. He now turned to the railroad to help pay for his palatial mansion—and later on to establish Stanford University.

The house, plus a one-story brick office building that Stanford had added to the east, was jacked up to make room for a new ground floor. Another floor was added under a new mansard roof that featured round-headed dormers, urns, decorative chimneys, and cast-iron roof cresting. The recessed panels under the cornice, the elaborate window hood moldings, and the portico's Corinthian column capitals are also cast iron. A grand curved double staircase in front led to the raised main entrance of the house, which had doubled in size and was now in the fashionable Second Empire style.

A transverse wing, mainly for entertainment, was constructed in the rear. A second wing for the servants, aligned with the main entrance axis, extended in back of that. The entire mansion was covered with stucco.

A ballroom and billiard room occupied the ground floor of the new wing. Upstairs was the dining room, furnished (in case any of the dinner guests needed to be reminded of where they were) with a wooden cabinet topped by a cartouche illustrating a railroad train and a sideboard in the shape of a foreshortened locomotive, including boiler, headlight, cab, and cow-catcher. Pocket doors separated the library at one end of this floor from the men's lounge and Stanford's private office at the other end.

These new rooms connected with the second-floor formal spaces of the original mansion, where there were a large parlor on the west side and a smaller parlor and music room, also separated by pocket doors, on the east. In between was the central hall and main staircase, with a walnut handrail. The bedrooms, both in the initial house and the new wing, were on the third floor. The bathroom in the master bedroom still has the original zinc tub made by Sacramento's Central Pacific Railroad locomotive works. The other interior features include gas chandeliers, plaster ceiling medallions, highly detailed crown molding, rosewood and mahogany woodwork, and numerous paintings.

The 1870s renovations and additions to the mansion were similar to later works in Sacramento by Nathaniel Goodell, the architect: mansions for Albert Gallatin (still extant) and for the widow of Judge E. B. Crocker (later demolished). Babson and Goodell were both native New Englanders who came to California with the gold rush, but they soon grew disillusioned with mining and decided to put their carpenter and builder skills to better use as architects. Babson designed Sacramento mansions for E. B. Crocker, Charles's brother (now the Crocker Art Museum), and Llewellen Williams (now a youth hostel).

The Stanfords opened their new forty-four-room home in early 1872 to several hundred guests, who dined on a service of solid silver and danced to the music of two orchestras. However, when the railroad headquarters was moved to San Francisco in 1874, the Stanfords followed, constructing an even more grandiose home on Nob Hill (destroyed in the 1906 earthquake).

Ten years later, while on a grand tour of Europe with his parents, fifteen-year-old Leland Stanford Jr. died of typhoid fever in Florence, Italy, where he was being cared for by Catholic nuns. Sitting at his son's bedside shortly before he died, Leland Stanford had had a dream in which his son told him it was not true

Figure 11.4
Leland Stanford Mansion, Sacramento, California
(courtesy of California State Parks)

Figure 11.5
Leland Stanford Mansion, parlor (circa 1872),
Sacramento, California (courtesy of California
State Parks)

Figure 11.6
Leland Stanford Mansion, parlor (circa 2005),
Sacramento, California (courtesy of California
State Parks)

that he had nothing to live for: he should live for humanity. The following year, the Stanfords endowed Leland Stanford Junior University for the children of California with $30 million. Unusual at the time in that it lacked a religious affiliation and was coeducational, the university opened in 1891.

Leland Stanford, who had remained president of the Central Pacific Railroad and its successor, the Southern Pacific Railroad, was elected a US Senator in 1885 and was reelected in 1891. He died in 1893. Toward the end of his life, Stanford had come to favor workers' cooperatives that would own their own businesses and industries, believing that this would lessen the inequality between laborers and wealthy capitalists such as himself.

Meanwhile the Sacramento mansion, although furnished, had remained empty, overseen by a caretaker. In 1900, Jane Stanford gave the mansion and its furnishings, with an endowment, to the Catholic church in Sacramento to use as an orphanage—which it remained, with minor interior changes, for most of the twentieth century.

The State of California acquired the mansion in 1978 for use as a state park. In 1987, the Stanford Home for Children moved to a new facility. The Leland Stanford Mansion Foundation was created in 1991 to raise the money to restore the building.

In 2005, the Leland Stanford Mansion State Historic Park opened, following a $22-million restoration that was based to a large extent on Eadweard Muybridge's 1872 photographs of the mansion. A racing enthusiast, Stanford had hired Muybridge that year to prove his theory that a trotting horse sometimes has all four feet off the ground. Muybridge, who was already well known for his photographs of Yosemite, did so by successfully photographing Stanford's favorite trotter, Occident, airborne. Muybridge's later innovations in equipment and photographic studies of human and animal motion made important contributions to the development of motion pictures.

Besides being a public museum, the mansion now serves as the State of California's official reception center for visiting dignitaries. About 50 percent of its furnishings are original.

COPPER KING MANSION
1888, Carroll H. Brown
29 West Granite St., Butte, MT

Although extremely modest in size and appearance compared to what he built later in Manhattan, William A. Clark's thirty-four-room Butte mansion was still the most expensive house in town; it cost some $250,000, the equivalent of about $6 million in today's dollars. Clark (1839–1925) was one of the three Butte "copper kings" (the others were Marcus Daly and F. Augustus Heinze). Their combined legacy was Anaconda Copper, by 1920 the world's fourth largest company and producer of most of its copper. In addition to his many other careers—he was a miner, merchant, and banker—Clark was also a railroad man. He built the San Pedro, Los Angeles and Salt Lake Railroad, which later became part of the Union Pacific system. The line is still in operation, running from Los Angeles to Salt Lake City, with an extension into Butte. One of its products was Las Vegas, in Clark County, Nevada, which began as a railroad water stop.

The three-story château style mansion is built of brick with decorative stone and terra-cotta trim; the steep roofs, dormers, roof cresting, and tall sculptured chimneys are hallmarks of the style. Much of the cost went into the exotic woods that Clark imported and had installed in the interior: rosewood in the entrance hall; cypress and cherry in the billiard room; and Philippine mahogany in the octagonal reception room, which features a hand-carved fireplace mantel, and the main staircase, lit by a stained-glass

Figure 11.8
Copper King Mansion, Butte, Montana

window. The ceilings are frescoed; the one in the dining room (separated from the parlor by pocket doors) is gold-embossed tooled leather, bordered with hand-painted murals.

The second-floor master bedroom and bedrooms for two of Clark's daughters, Andree and Huguette, and other spaces are similarly furnished: the library woodwork is quarter-sawn oak, and the octagonal sitting room features bird's-eye maple. The ballroom and rooms for five servants are on the third floor. Carroll Brown, a California architect, went on to design houses and clubs for the wealthy in Los Angeles.

Clark hailed from Connellsville, Pennsylvania, a coal and railroad town. In the 1850s, his family moved to Iowa, where he taught school for a time and studied law. Clark enlisted in an Iowa regiment when the Civil War broke out, was discharged in 1862, and went west to become a miner—first in Central City, Colorado, and later in Montana. When he wasn't mining, he ran supplies to the mining camps, opened stores, operated a mail route, and lent money to other miners. He started banks in Deer Lodge and then in Butte, Montana, where—although he was already financially successful—he found his real fortune. Clark

was the quintessential frontier entrepreneur: smart, driven, and acquisitive in the extreme.

He purchased several mines in Butte in 1872 and built stamp mills and smelters. Then, realizing that the day of the lone prospector was over, he took a year off to attend the Columbia University School of Mines. Luck always played a part in the legends of the early prospectors in the West, but for Clark another element proved crucial—his timing could not have better.

Valuable gold and silver came out of the Butte mines, but it was copper that made it the so-called richest hill on earth. Of all the metals, copper is by far the best conductor of electricity. In 1844, Samuel F. B. Morse's famous first words to be transmitted by telegraph—"What hath God wrought?"—traveled over copper wires strung between Baltimore and Washington, D.C. (the B&O Railroad provided the testing ground). In 1876, Alexander Graham Bell patented

Figure 11.9
Copper King Mansion, dining room, Butte, Montana

his acoustic telegraph, or telephone, and in 1880, Thomas Edison began marketing his incandescent light bulb. The first commercial power plant came on line two years later. The continent and the world began to be wired in earnest. The wire was made of copper, and the copper came mostly from Butte.

When Clark arrived in the early 1870s, Butte's population was 241. By 1900, it had grown to 30,000, and Butte was the biggest city in Montana, served by three railroads. A third of the population was foreign-born, mostly English and Irish. They were later joined by Scandinavians, Eastern Europeans, and Chinese who came to work in the mines. The first strike in Butte's long, bloody, and literally explosive labor history occurred in 1890.

The miners' unions (there were several) fought not only management but each other. Copper ore is extracted by means of deep, hard-rock mining, and the mines in Butte extend hundreds and sometimes thousands of feet below the surface. Mining copper was particularly grueling, unhealthy, and dangerous work. Dynamite was used extensively in the process. In 1914, the Butte Miners' Union Hall was demolished by some twenty blasts of dynamite and a few months later, a mine company office was dynamited.

Clark ably traversed the rough terrain of Butte's feuding mine owners and unions. Although evidently more respected by organized labor than some of his colleagues, in case of emergencies he installed a call box in a closet in the mansion's master bedroom so he could summon the police, the fire department, or the hospital ambulance (he did receive death threats).

Clark expanded his operations and control in the city to include a newspaper, the *Butte Miner*, the waterworks, and a streetcar line. In 1889 in a denuded landscape punctuated with mine head frames (the miners called them gallows frames) and overcast with a yellow haze laced with arsenic from the smelters, he created a twenty-one-acre amusement park—Columbia Gardens, which had a lake, dance pavilion, and picnic grounds—and paid to operate it for the people of Butte.

That was the year when Clark, who used his newspaper to further his political ambitions, was elected to the US Senate after a bitter fight with his major rival in mining and politics, Marcus Daly. State legislatures then elected US senators, and Clark ensured his victory by distributing thousands of dollars in bribes to the members of the Montana legislature. This was not an uncommon practice at the time—railroads routinely bribed politicians at all levels to get what they wanted—but Clark's corruption scandal quickly metastasized, and he was forced to resign his Senate seat a few months after he was sworn in. Undeterred, he ran again, was reelected, and served a single term as senator, from 1901 to 1907.[26]

Mark Twain said of Clark, "He is as rotten a human being as can be found anywhere under the flag; he is a shame to the American nation, and no one has helped to send him to the Senate who did not know that his proper place was the penitentiary, with a chain and ball on his legs." Twain wrote his comments in 1907, although they were not published until 1940 (it is unclear whether he ever intended them to appear in print).[27] Two recent authors have speculated that Twain may have been motivated less by personal animosity than by the prospect of personal gain: His acid portrait of Clark might have been an attempt to curry favor with a principal of the Standard Oil Trust, who was then in the process of acquiring the Butte copper companies. Twain was obligated to the man for rescuing him from bankruptcy, had invested his nest egg with him, and stood to profit from the takeover of the mines, which was completed a few years later.[28]

Clark's private life was every bit as scandalous as his other escapades. He was a randy old rip. After his wife, with whom he had had five children, died in 1893, he took up with a young woman he met in a Butte boardinghouse, Anna LaChapelle. He was in his mid-fifties; she was sixteen. Clark sent her to Paris, where she could absorb the culture of a world capital, study the harp, and learn French. He had sent a previous protégée, another teenage girl he met in a boardinghouse, to New York to further her acting career. While Anna was in Paris, Clark had dalliances with other young women, one of whom filed a paternity suit.

Figure 11.10

William A. Clark Mansion, circa 1925 (later demolished),
New York, New York (photo: New-York Historical Society)

Andree, Clark's first child with Anna, was born in
1902. Two years later, he announced that he and Anna
had been secretly married the previous year. Huguette, their second child, was born in Paris in 1906.
Meanwhile, determined to take his rightful place
among the Astors and the Vanderbilts on Manhattan's Fifth Avenue, known as Millionaire's Row, Clark
had shifted his base of operations to New York and
started to build the grandest mansion of them all—
or at least the biggest. In this, he succeeded, and as
usual, there was plenty of controversy along the way.

Planning for the mansion really began at a Christmas gathering in 1895, where Kenneth M. Murchison
Jr.—a talented architect who subsequently designed
several railroad stations, including ones in Baltimore,
Maryland, and Scranton, Pennsylvania—introduced
Clark to James M. Hewlett, a member of the architectural firm Lord, Hewlett and Hull. The firm, with
which Murchison was associated, was brand-new and
anxious for work. They got the job of designing both

a mausoleum for Clark in Woodlawn Cemetery and
his residence. The mausoleum was a simple, neoclassical revival structure in white marble; the mansion turned out to be anything but simple.

The townhouse at Fifth Avenue and 77th Street
(on which it fronted) took fifteen years to complete.
Numerous design changes were made during this period to suit Clark's whims, and there was a falling
out among the architects that ended in a court case
(it concerned the nonpayment of Murchison's commissions; he won the case). Clark later brought in a
second architect, from Paris: Henri Deglane, one of
the designers of the Grand Palais, the iron-and-glass
exhibit hall built for the Paris Exposition Universelle
of 1900.

No particular style was discernible in the gaudy
six-story granite pile that resulted. The mansard roof
was plastered with decorations of indeterminate origin and topped by an ungainly three-story tower, also
of murky provenance: Hindu baroque? It was, as a
critic said of his former school, "an object of indeci-
pherable bastardy—a true monster."[29]

Contemporary critics were not kind. Montgomery Schuyler, the astute and influential author of the
"Architectural Aberrations" column in the *Architectural Record* said: "What of course strikes everybody
first about the house is its huge pretentiousness. . . .
A more meaningless and fatuous feature than this
steeple it would impossible to find . . . the Copper
King and his architect seem unaware that boldness
and brassiness are going out of fashion in house
building."[30]

But it was indeed the biggest mansion in New York,
and the tower could be seen from Central Park. The
cost was as mammoth as the structure: an estimated
$7 million, or roughly $170 million today. Among its
120 rooms were four galleries to display Clark's collection of French paintings (by Delacroix, Millet, and
Corot), sculpture, tapestries, and faience; a grand
salon, in which was installed the Salon Doré (circa
1770) created by the Count D'Orsay for the Hotel de
Clermont, in Paris; a Gothic library; a banquet hall;
26 bedrooms; 25 guest rooms; 31 bathrooms; Turk-
ish baths; and a swimming pool. Clark and his family,

attended by seventeen servants, lived and entertained there in palatial luxury until he died in his bedroom in 1925.

His estate, estimated at the time at $150 million, put him in a class with the Rockefellers, Fords, and Mellons. However, no university, museum, or other institution today bears his name, which may be why it is relatively unknown compared to those of his peers. Clark was not much of a philanthropist; his art collection (including the Salon Doré) went to the Corcoran Gallery of Art in Washington, D.C., but almost all of the rest of the estate was distributed to the members of his family. Huguette, the youngest and his favorite, received special treatment.

Anna and Huguette (Andree having died at sixteen of meningitis) moved to an apartment. In 1927, after just sixteen years of existence, the grandiose mansion was sold and demolished to make way for an apartment building, the tons of New England granite and Tennessee marble and the acres of plaster decoration and exotic woodwork distributed among other buildings or dumped in the landfill.

Huguette died in 2011 at the age of 104, leaving a fortune of $300 million. She spent the last twenty years of her life as a recluse, living in a Manhattan hospital surrounded by her collection of dolls. Her estate included empty apartments in Manhattan and mansions in New Canaan, Connecticut, and Santa Barbara, California, kept in constant readiness by caretaker staffs for visitors who never arrived. The estate was distributed, after a court fight, to family members and charity. The main charitable beneficiary was the Bellosguardo Foundation, an arts organization that will occupy the Santa Barbara mansion.

There is very little copper mining today in Butte, which has become the nation's largest Superfund site. The population has declined to its 1900 level. Mine head frames still dot the landscape, but students and tourists rather than miners walk the streets. The stations of the Northern Pacific Railway (1906; Reed and Stem), the Great Northern Railway, and the Chicago, Milwaukee, St. Paul and Pacific Railroad (1917) have been converted to other uses or stand empty. The Butte Labor History Center tells the sobering but fascinating story of workers' organizations in the town once known as the Gibraltar of unionism. The World Museum of Mining, at the abandoned Orphan Girl Mine, presents an equally engaging history of mining in Butte. And the Mineral Museum at Montana Tech has a collection of 13,000 specimens.

ASA PACKER MANSION
1861, Samuel Sloan (?); 1878, renovations and additions, Addison Hutton
Packer Hill Ave., Jim Thorpe, PA

In a bizarre exchange in 1954, which later proved controversial, Mauch Chunk (Lenape for "sleeping bear") became Jim Thorpe. But the charming and historic Pennsylvania town should really be named Packerville, since it is largely a monument to Asa Packer (1805–79), president of the Lehigh Valley Railroad and founder of Lehigh University, in nearby Bethlehem.

Packer, who lacked a formal education, left his native Mystic, Connecticut, at seventeen and walked to northeast Pennsylvania to apprentice as a carpenter with a cousin. In 1828, he married Sarah Blakslee. After farming for four years without much success, Packer went to Mauch Chunk, where his entrepreneurial drive and acumen found richer soil. The town still bears his strong imprint.

After being a canal boat captain, Packer went into storekeeping, boatbuilding, coal mining, canal construction, and railroads. His career path paralleled the development of the anthracite coal industry in eastern Pennsylvania.

In the 1790s, Mauch Chunk produced the first anthracite coal that was regularly mined in America. When Packer got there, a nine-mile railway powered by gravity and horses brought the coal from the mine to the almost unnavigable Lehigh River. There it was loaded into boats and sent down the Lehigh Coal and Navigation Company's forty-six-mile canal to Easton, on the Delaware River.

Packer clearly saw that railroads would be the coal haulers of the future. His Lehigh Valley Railroad, laid out by the engineer Robert Sayre, opened in 1855; it ran from Mauch Chunk to Easton, competing with the Lehigh Coal and Navigation Company—which by then had its own railroad. At the end of the nineteenth century, the Lehigh Valley Railroad, through its connections with other lines under the control of the Central of New Jersey and Reading Railroads, extended from Jersey City, New Jersey, to Buffalo, New York, and was one of the most prosperous railroads in the country.

Meanwhile, Packer had become one of the richest men in Pennsylvania (he left an estate worth $54 million when he died). He was also a politician, having served two terms in the state legislature in the 1840s and two terms in Congress in 1853–57. He was unsuccessful in his bid for the Pennsylvania governorship in the following decade.

As an industrialist, Packer may have had a hand in the design of his house. It has a partial iron frame, an early and rare domestic use of this material (a pair of fluted cast-iron columns are visible in the ground-floor entry hall). Lower wings flank the three-and-a-half-story Italianate mansion, topped by a lantern and belvedere. Prominent brackets support the wide eaves of the roof, which is raised to a peak over a large central window with a balcony. Curved hood moldings decorate the second-story windows. It is very much in the tradition of Samuel Sloan's picturesque residences.

Sloan (1815–84) also began his career (in Philadelphia) as a carpenter and builder. He designed schools, courthouses, jails, and hospitals as well as churches and houses, but he may be best known for his publications. These include *Sloan's Architectural Review and Builders' Journal*, the first of its type in the United States. It offered design drawings, articles on such practical subjects as ventilation and heating, stained glass, and fireproof construction, plus the author's trenchant observations on the state of architecture. Sloan also wrote several design books, such as *City and Suburban Architecture*, *American Homes*, and *The Model Architect*.

Although the Asa Packer Mansion does not appear in these books, circumstantial evidence points to Sloan as the architect. He had just finished Longwood (1860), an extravagant Oriental revival mansion for

Figure 11.11

Asa Packer Mansion, Jim Thorpe, Pennsylvania
(courtesy of Rebecca Haegele)

Figure 11.12

Asa Packer Mansion, parlor, Jim Thorpe, Pennsylvania
(photo by Victor A. Izzo)

Haller Nutt, near Natchez, Mississippi. Sloan probably arranged for the rococo black walnut furniture destined for Longwood, whose railroad shipment was interrupted by the Civil War, to go instead to the Packer mansion. It can be seen there in the parlor. The drawing room suite was by George J. Henkels, Philadelphia's leading furniture maker and a contributor to *Sloan's Architectural Review and Builders' Journal*.

The coal and railroad baron undoubtedly spent much of his time at home in his library-office, located in one of the wings and lit by windows in a semi-octagonal bay. Japanese leather wallpaper (made in Japan and embossed to resemble Spanish leather) covers the walls. The ungainly bronze and terra-cotta sculpture on the desk was presented to Packer as a memorial in 1870; its elements—a coal mine, canal boat, and mansion—summarize his career.

An ornate chandelier that was copied for the film *Gone with the Wind* hangs from the coved Elizabethan ceiling in the parlor. Packer imported several Italian wood-carvers to decorate the oak wainscoting in the center hall under a beamed and paneled ceiling. The swirling designs in the plaster "wallpaper" were executed using gravel.

An archway divider separates the center hall from the rear stairway. When the rooftop lantern windows were opened, the center hall and stairway served as a thermosiphon, amplified in the summer by cakes of ice (Sloan recommended this functional arrangement in his books).

The spectacular wainscoting and paneled ceiling in the dining room are of Honduras mahogany; pocket doors open to the ladies' sitting room in the front of the house. The small, utilitarian kitchen and butler's pantry are adjacent to the dining room in the mansion's other wing, with a servants' stairway leading up to the maid's and butler's bedrooms overhead.

The master bedroom is in the opposite wing (over the space that served as library and office). It has a view of St. Mark's Episcopal Church, designed by Richard Upjohn Jr. Packer was instrumental in having Upjohn's office design the Victorian Gothic church, which opened in 1869. In addition to his other achievements—in 1865, he had established Lehigh University—Packer was Mauch Chunk's leading architectural patron.

To celebrate their fiftieth wedding anniversary in 1878, an event attended by several hundred guests, the Packers renovated the mansion. A two-story porch was added at the front and a carriage entrance at the rear. A new main stairway was installed, lit between the second and third floors by Franz Mayer's stained-glass windows. The parlor and entrance hall received new woodwork. The renovation architect, Addison Hutton, had supervised the construction at Longwood and was briefly Sloan's partner in the mid-1860s.

The Packers' two sons, Robert and Harry, also career railroad men, died a few years after their father—in 1883 and 1884, respectively. The daughter, Mary Packer Cummings, inherited the family fortune. She lived in the mansion until she died in 1912. In the philanthropic tradition of Asa Packer, she willed the house and its contents to the borough of Mauch Chunk.

The Packer Mansion remained closed for forty-four years. In 1954, the newly named Jim Thorpe Lions Club became its trustee and two years later reopened the nineteenth-century time capsule to the public. In 2009 the state awarded a $500,000 grant to the Lions Club for repairs that included modernizing the heating and cooling systems and installing carpeting.

Tourism began in Mauch Chunk in the 1870s, when the railway that brought coal to the river from the mine was made obsolete by other railroad improvements in the area. The railway's length had been doubled in 1845 by the construction of a pair of inclined planes and additional trackage to facilitate the return of the empty cars. In 1872, it became a tourist railroad, one of the nation's first. Thousands of people rode Lehigh Valley trains to Mauch Chunk to experience the Switchback Gravity Railroad in the Switzerland of America.

On a darker note, the same decade saw the demise of the notorious Molly Maguires, the secret organization of Irish miners and labor terrorists in the anthracite coalfields. The Pinkerton Detective Agency's James McParlan had infiltrated the Molly Maguires and subsequently testified against them at what some historians consider show trials. On June 11, 1877, while policemen with rifles patrolled the streets outside, four of the Molly Maguires were hung in the Carbon County Jail, in Mauch Chunk.[31]

The Switchback Gravity Railroad was scrapped in the 1930s, and the tourism and anthracite coal industries began a slow decline. Joseph Boyle, editor of the local newspaper, decided that the way to lure tourists back to Mauch Chunk was to fund a project for that purpose. He began by collecting nickels, and the fund grew to several thousand dollars. In a roundabout way, it came to the attention of Jim Thorpe's widow.

Jim Thorpe, a Native American, has been called the country's greatest all-round athlete. A gold medalist in the 1912 Olympics decathlon and pentathlon, he later played football and major league baseball. Thorpe died in 1953.

His family wanted him to be buried near his birthplace in Shawnee, Oklahoma, but his widow was convinced that the state would not provide a proper memorial, and she made other arrangements. In the dark of night, escorted by state troopers, she took Thorpe's body from the Indian lodge where it was awaiting burial. Eventually hearing of the Mauch Chunk fund to attract tourists, she struck a deal with town officials to have the burial there, provided that they build a memorial to her husband and change the town name, which they did.

The scheme proved less than successful as a tourist attraction and something of a local embarrassment (a 2010 suit filed by Thorpe's sons to have his remains moved back to Oklahoma was rejected by a federal appeals court in 2014). A better idea was the municipality's 1977 hiring of Philadelphia architects and planners Venturi, Rauch, and Scott Brown. Their study recommended repurposing the town's exceptional collection of nineteenth-century buildings.

This the town has done successfully. The Wilson Brothers' striking 1888 Jersey Central Station—with its broad canopies and round, conical-roofed tower—was refurbished in 1994 as the visitors' center. Upstairs are the offices of the sixteen-mile-long Lehigh Valley Scenic Railway. The Lehigh Coal and Navigation Company's office building across the street was restored and converted to apartments for the elderly in the 1970s. The Switchback Gravity Railroad has become the Switchback Trail for hikers. Tourists now ride rented bicycles on the town's main streets, and the Lehigh River has become popular with whitewater rafters.

HARRY PACKER MANSION
1874; 1881, additions, Addison Hutton
Packer Hill Ave., Jim Thorpe, PA

Asa Packer had an equally imposing mansion built for his youngest son, Harry, as a wedding present. Harry got married in 1872, became president of the Lehigh Valley Railroad in 1883, and died of a liver ailment the following year, at the age of thirty-four.

The three-story high Victorian brick mansion has stone trim, an octagonal corner pavilion, and a mansard roof with a variety of dormers. Addison Hutton's study wing ends in a tall, eye-catching tower with a square dome roof. The veranda of New York bluestone has a mahogany ceiling and tile floor.

The study interior features hand-carved mahogany paneling, stained-glass windows featuring English poets, and a paneled ceiling. On one side of the main hall is the dining room (at the rear), with stained glass windows; on the other is a double parlor, whose sections are separated by pocket doors. The Herter Brothers provided the interiors. The mantelpieces, mirrors, and chandeliers are original.

The mansion was in a terminal state of disrepair when the present owners purchased it in 1983 and restored it as a bed-and-breakfast. Guest accommodations include the adjacent Italianate carriage house.

FLAGLER MUSEUM
(formerly Whitehall)
1902, Carrere and Hastings
One Whitehall Way, Palm Beach, FL

A reporter for the *New York Herald* wrote in 1902: "More wonderful than any palace in Europe, grander and more magnificent than any other private dwelling in the world is Whitehall, the new home Henry M. Flagler has built in the land of flowers for his bride. The Vatican, the forests, the quarries, the old salons, the art shops and the looms have contributed some of their choicest treasures to deck this marvelous structure. It is in nature's garden spot on the banks of Lake Worth, at Palm Beach, Florida."[32]

Henry Flagler's second wife (the nurse) developed serious mental problems and was institutionalized in

Figure 11.13

Harry Packer Mansion, Jim Thorpe, Pennsylvania (photo by Rebecca Haegele)

1897 (see chapter 8). At the time Flagler was courting a woman he wanted to marry, Mary Lily Kenan. He was unable to obtain a divorce, since adultery was the only ground for divorce in New York and Florida and he did not have a case for that. However, he was able to convince the Florida legislature (with the use of money, it was rumored) to pass a bill making insanity another ground for divorce. The bill passed in 1901 (it was later repealed), and Flagler remarried the same year.

Meanwhile, he had begun building his new Palm Beach mansion with the same architects who had designed the Ponce de Leon Hotel. Flagler demanded that they lower the ceiling by eight feet in the grand entrance hall because he wanted "a house to be lived in."[33] It was that and also the social center of Palm Beach—which then as now was a magnet for the wealthy and well-connected, especially during the winter season.

An alley of tall palm trees helped focus the gaze of arriving guests on the three-story mansion, all white except for the red tile roof. It was in the neoclassical revival style, with a center block and a pair of abbreviated two-story wings. The brick walls were covered with stucco. Steel beams were used in construction; the roof structure was timber. An arched ornamental wrought-iron gateway gave access to a set of steps and a broad portico paved with marble. The capitals of its five giant fluted Doric columns carried rosettes that indicated the four corners of the compass.

Coupled white marble Doric columns surrounded the grand entrance hall, with white marble walls (striped with verde antique marble) and floor (outlined with bands of darker marble). The architects' beaux arts training was evident in the baroque ceiling and the formal axial plan.

The deeply molded ornamental plaster ceiling was organized around a central shallow oval dome that

Figure 11.14
Flagler Museum, Palm Beach, Florida

contained a painting titled *The Crowning of Knowledge*. The frame was a festoon gilt molding. Smaller panels on either side held more paintings. Huge volute keystones marked the ends of the oval frame, and the corners were decorated with scallop shells and lilies.

The grand marble staircase opposite the main entrance rose five steps to a landing and then divided right and left, with straight-run stairways (also with landings) that ascended to the second floor. Lyres decorated the bronze railings. A window in back of the lower landing overlooked the courtyard, the central organizing space of the mansion. The entrance hall cross axis led to the library and salon, located in the wings of the building, and to a series of rooms lined up in back of them that flanked the courtyard and the mirrored ballroom, the entrance hall's counterpart space. Flagler's office and the service areas were in the rear. Upstairs were thirty bedrooms for family members and guests.

Figure 11.15
Flagler Museum, entrance hall, Palm Beach, Florida

Figure 11.16

Flagler Museum, dining room, Palm Beach, Florida

The interior décor was provided by Pottier and Stymus, whose New York factory and its 750 employees could produce furniture in a variety of period styles—Neo-Grec, Egyptian, or Gothic or Renaissance revival—to suit the tastes of Gilded Age industrialists and their architects. One of the principals, Auguste Pottier, who had apprenticed in France with a wood sculptor, had a brief early partnership with Gustave Herter of Herter Brothers.

It was the practice of the owners and designers of such grandiose mansions to have different rooms reflect different period styles, thereby offering an artistic and educational as well as social experience. The dining room at Whitehall, for example, was French Renaissance, from its oak parquet floor and Savonnerie carpets to the papier-mâché decoration of the embossed, coffered ceiling that was hung with bronze and crystal chandeliers. Aubusson figured tapestries covered the walls, and the curtains were of Colbert lace. A full-height, hand-carved fireplace surround, a long satinwood table, and a set of tapestry-covered chairs added luster to the dining experience. The library in the opposite wing of the house was Italian Renaissance, the music room Louis XIV, the billiard room Swiss, and so on.

Flagler died at the age of eighty-three from the aftereffects of a fall on a stairway at Whitehall. The property eventually passed to his widow's niece, who sold it to a group of investors in 1925. They turned it into a hotel and built a ten-story, 300-room hotel tower in the rear. The hotel operated until 1959, when the ten-story tower was demolished. Flagler's granddaughter, fearing that Whitehall might be razed as well, formed a nonprofit corporation that bought the building. The Flagler Museum opened in 1960. Flagler's restored private railroad car—No. 91, the one in which he rode to Key West on his Over-Sea Railroad (see chapter 8)—is exhibited in the 2005 Kenan Pavilion adjoining the mansion.

STONE ROW
(also known as Packer Row)
1848, James L. Blakslee, superintendent
27–57 Race St., Jim Thorpe, PA

The sixteen three-story stone rowhouses erected by Asa Packer for his Lehigh Valley Railroad engineers and foremen are not just survivors, but rare specimens of multiple railroad employee accommodations in a small-town setting. James Blakslee, Asa Packer's brother-in-law, superintended their construction. Blakslee's career as a canal boatman, store clerk, and canal and railroad man resembled Asa Packer's; he began as a conductor on the Lehigh Valley Railroad and ended up on the board of directors.

The buildings still function as housing, but new owners over the years have added some storefronts on the ground floors and a variety of door and window trims.

SECTION HOUSE, DENVER AND RIO GRANDE RAILWAY
1881
Osier, CO

Located in a remote area of the San Juan Mountains, Osier had first a construction camp and then a coal and water stop and crew facility for the Denver and Rio Grande, which extended its three-foot, narrow-gauge railroad into the mining territory of southwestern Colorado in the early 1880s. Today Osier is

Figure 11.17
Stone Row, Jim Thorpe,
Pennsylvania

a convenient lunch stop on the Cumbres and Toltec Scenic Railroad, a tourist line that operates between Chama, New Mexico, and Antonito, Colorado.

The L-shape, one-story, pitched-roof section house had a kitchen in the back and an extension that housed the section foreman and his family. The workers ate in the main portion of the building; some slept in a log bunkhouse nearby that has since disappeared. The section house is one of a group of railroad structures at Osier—there is also a water tank and tiny station —all carefully restored by the tourist railroad's dedicated volunteers and employees. More section houses on the line are located at Cumbres and Sublette.

On its meandering sixty-four-mile journey between Chama and Antonito, the Cumbres and Toltec Scenic Railroad wanders back and forth across the state line, loops around to gain altitude, and detours miles off course to find water, looking on a map like a lost river of steel. The Denver and Rio Grande pioneered narrow-gauge railroad construction in the West. Because it was smaller than standard gauge (four feet eight and one-half inches) everything— rails, engines, and rolling stock—could be made lighter and cheaper to construct: the bridges could be more economical in their use of materials, the tunnels narrower, and so forth. In addition, curves could be sharper and grades steeper. The Cumbres and Toltec climbs a 4 percent grade (quite steep for a

Figure 11.18
Section house, Denver and Rio Grande Railway,
Osier, Colorado

Figure 11.19
Section house, water tank and station, Denver
and Rio Grande Railway, Osier, Colorado

railroad) and negotiates some tight curves as it makes its way north from Chama to cross the 10,000-foot Continental Divide at Cumbres (Route 17 parallels part of the rail line).

The tourist railroad operates from May through October. The fall mountain scenery alone—dark green conifers contrasting with golden aspens—is enough to make the trip worthwhile. And to see the town of Chama wake up in the morning to the sound and smoke of steam engines being readied for the day's work, as was customary a century ago, and be able to wander unchallenged amid all the activity is a unique and wonderful experience.

The living railroad museum evolved gradually after the Denver and Rio Grande abandoned operations in 1969, when large-scale mining and lumbering operations ceased in the region. Viewing a scenic railroad as a way to create jobs, the states of New Mexico and Colorado jointly purchased the right-of-way between Chama and Antonito. They also acquired nine steam locomotives, more than a hundred railroad cars, and the yard and structures at Chama—which include a station, water tank, coal tipple, and various shop buildings. The scenic railroad has had several operators. The current one, the Rio Grande Railway Preservation Corporation, was formed in 2000 from the volunteer group that had long supported the tourist railroad.

The Durango and Silverton Narrow Gauge Railroad, also a tourist operation, runs on another branch of the former Denver and Rio Grande Railroad, in southwest Colorado.

RAILROAD YMCA APARTMENTS
1907, Wilson, Harris and Richards
1548 E. Main St., Richmond, VA

When the railroad YMCA outgrew its quarters in the Main Street Station next door, the station's architects employed the same French Renaissance style and materials—reddish-tan brick with terra-cotta trim and a red tile hip roof—in their solid, durable railroad branch YMCA (so designated in engraved lettering over the doorway between Corinthian columns).

Figure 11.20
Railroad YMCA Apartments, Richmond, Virginia

Figure 11.21
Drury Inn, St. Louis, Missouri

The building was described as nearly ruined in 2002, before Richmond's Historic Housing converted it to loft apartments. The City Bar and Chophouse on the ground floor has since closed; a catering firm operates in the space.

Figure 11.22
Hotel Parq Central,
Albuquerque, New Mexico

DRURY INN
(formerly the railroad YMCA)
1907, Theodore Link
201 S. 20th St., St. Louis, MO

Helen Gould, Jay Gould's daughter, was instrumental in getting the members of the Terminal Railroad Association to agree to build a railroad YMCA for St. Louis. Theodore Link's design, in contrast to his eye-filling Union Station nearby, is plain neoclassical revival style, executed in brick with stone trim.

On the lower level were a bowling alley, barbershop, swimming pool, and meeting rooms. Billiard and game tables and desks for reading and correspondence occupied the ground-floor lobby, while upstairs were 114 single rooms, a library, and an auditorium.

The St. Louis railroad YMCA closed in 1970. In 1988, Drury Hotels opened the Drury Inn, after spending $11 million to renovate the building and construct a new, seven-story addition in the rear. The lobby's tile floors, fireplace, painted glass windows, oak paneling, faux marble columns, and metal stairway were restored. The lower level now houses a restaurant.

HOTEL PARQ CENTRAL
(formerly the Atchison, Topeka and Santa Fe
   (AT&SF) Railway hospital)
1926; 2010 renovation and restoration,
   Studio Southwest Architects
806 Central Ave., Albuquerque, NM

The AT&SF established its Employee Benefit Association, supported in part by payroll deductions, in 1881. In 1906, the railroad constructed Albuquerque's first hospital (remnants of which have been incorporated into a Catholic boys' school). It was one of several hospitals spread out along the line to serve the AT&SF's five thousand employees.

In 1926 the railroad built a new, four-story, reinforced-concrete hospital consisting of a central block and two angled wings. It is in the neoclassical revival style, but the wide-arched windows and the red tile roofs—are mission style. The building is faced with stucco; minimal decoration is provided by wreaths and swags in the architrave and New Mexican ceramic tiles in the window apron panels. The 2.3-acre site included the chief surgeon's residence and a power plant with a tall chimney; nurses lived on the second floor.

After the railroad ceased using the building, it functioned for twenty-five years (1982–2007) as a psychiatric treatment facility known as Memorial Hospital. When that closed, new owners acquired the property and undertook its $21-million conversion to a hotel.

The interior was stripped down to the underlying concrete, and new finishes were applied—including decorative tiles for the lobby columns that replicate those on the exterior of the building. The former ambulance entrance at the rear of the ground floor was made into a conservatory whose glass-topped tables display AT&SF memorabilia. Outside is an enclosed, landscaped patio. A new heating, ventilating, and air-conditioning system and an elevator were installed.

Additional guest rooms are located in the former surgeon's residence and power plant; the old boiler room is now a fitness center. The fourth-floor Apothecary Lounge and roof deck of the seventy-four-room Parq Central Hotel have become the ideal places to watch the Albuquerque sunset.

MERCY TERRACE APARTMENTS
(formerly the Southern Pacific Railroad hospital)
1908, Daniel J. Patterson
333 Baker St., San Francisco, CA

The Central Pacific Railroad, precursor to the Southern Pacific, reportedly set up basic railroad hospitals when it was building the western half of the first transcontinental railroad in the 1860s. The Southern Pacific's previous hospital in San Francisco, on another site, burned in the 1906 earthquake and was dynamited. The railroad's new building incorporated the latest fireproofing methods. The four-story, H-shape building is constructed of reinforced concrete faced with brick and stucco. It has ceramic tile floors; wood was used only for the doors and window frames.

The architect avoided the sterility of some neoclassical revival buildings by adding colorful decorative ironwork columns and railings around the windows in the wings that connect the central section with the two end pavilions. Daniel Patterson (1857–1926) was an experienced railroad architect who designed several stations for the Southern Pacific and Union Pacific Railroads (both owned in the

Figure 11.23
Mercy Terrace Apartments, San Francisco, California

Figure 11.24
Mercy Terrace Apartments, window frames, San Francisco, California

early twentieth century by Edward H. Harriman) in several styles, ranging from the mission revival to the Second Empire (see chapter 3).

The son of a carpenter from New York State, Patterson graduated from the University of Minnesota and moved to Seattle to work as a draftsman in an architectural office. He specialized in courthouses and public schools before moving to San Francisco, where he became the house architect for the Southern Pacific. He designed three hospitals for the company, two of them in Texas; the one in Houston, a smaller,

Figure 11.25
Mercy Terrace Apartments, portico,
San Francisco, California

plainer, brick version of San Francisco's, survives as the Thomas Street Health Center.

The San Francisco hospital complex, in the Panhandle District, covers the entire block bounded by Fell, Lyon, Hayes, and Baker Streets. Besides the hospital building, there are a nurse's annex, social hall, utility building, and powerhouse with a tall chimney. The main hospital entrance on Fell Street was up a flight of steps to a grand three-bay, three-story portico whose giant Corinthian columns supported a classical pediment. The architect's uniform use of ground-floor rustication, quoins, and a plain entablature throughout the complex helps make the five separate buildings appear as one, stylistically.

When the railroad ceased running hospitals, the building was briefly a private hospital (1968–74) and then stood vacant and was vandalized. Mercy Terrace Apartments, providing affordable housing for seniors, opened in 1981 with 158 subsidized apartments after an extensive interior renovation, restoration of the exterior, and earthquake retrofitting. The main entrance was moved to Baker Street.

A 1998 proposal to demolish the ancillary buildings and replace them with low-rise apartments caused a neighborhood controversy. In the end, the buildings were saved and converted to Mercy Family Plaza, with thirty-six affordable housing units. The two-year project cost $6 million.

12

CROSSING OVER AND UNDER

A poet walked across Brooklyn Bridge and saw "the naked soul of a building."[34] Bridges are raw architecture, pure structure. Yet their inner logic is not always obvious, and their crucial support systems are often hidden, as a tunnel is invisible to the outside viewer. But unlike tunnels, bridges are very photogenic.

Railroads led the development of nineteenth-century bridge technology. First came the great masonry viaducts, such as Benjamin H. Latrobe Jr.'s Thomas Viaduct for the Baltimore and Ohio (B&O) Railroad at Relay, Maryland, which opened in 1835. The oldest major railroad viaduct in North America, it still carries trains.

A century later another brilliant engineer, William Barclay Parsons, and the architects McKim, Mead and White created the steel vertical-lift bridge at Bourne, Massachusetts, which is also still in railroad use. The period in between witnessed the introduction and evolution of metal bridge design, largely sponsored by the railroads—which were then the dominant form of transportation and the bearers of the heaviest loads that moved on land. Masonry bridges continued to be built during this era, but by 1915, when the Delaware, Lackawanna and Western Railroad constructed the Tunkhannock Viaduct at Nicholson, Pennsylvania, the material of choice was reinforced concrete.

By the mid-nineteenth century, railroads had begun to explore the use of metal in bridges. The B&O Railroad was one of the first, and its cast- and wrought-iron Bollman Truss Bridge (1869) at Savage, Maryland, is the last remaining one of its type. In 1874, James Eads used steel to build the great bridge across the Mississippi River at St. Louis that was to have such a profound effect on the young Louis Sullivan.

Timber was commonly used for the early trestles, or trestle bridges, which were sometimes called viaducts. When the railroads were first constructed, timber trestles were relatively fast and cheap to erect high over mountain streams or across broad river valleys. Some of the most spectacular examples were in the Canadian Rockies.

But being subject to fire and rot, they were soon reconstructed in metal or replaced by fill. Only a few timber trestles still stand unaltered, mostly in remote locations. More readily accessible is a group built by the Camas Prairie Railroad in the early twentieth century between Culdesac and Cottonwood, southeast of Lewiston, Idaho. And in Lethbridge, Alberta, stands the Lethbridge Viaduct (1909), built of steel and concrete, the longest and highest railroad trestle in the world.

In the timber country of the Northeast and the Pacific Northwest, the railroads built wooden covered bridges. Some of these have been preserved, though they are no longer in railroad use. The Boston and Maine Railroad's Town lattice truss bridges at Contoocook and Newport, New Hampshire, are particularly fine examples.

When a low-level bridge was called for to serve local industries, or where site conditions made it impractical to build a bridge and approaches high enough to clear water-borne traffic, movable bridges entered the picture. There were three types: vertical-lift bridges, bascule bridges, and swing spans.

In vertical-lift bridges, the movable span is raised by counterweights located in the towers on either side. There are particularly good examples on Cape Cod and on Cleveland's serpentine Cuyahoga River.

The bascule bridge, a mechanized version of the medieval drawbridge, is tilted vertically by counterweights. In Chicago, the St. Charles Air Line Bridge was based on principles developed by Joseph B. Strauss, a civil engineer; numerous bascule bridges of his design still operate in the city.

Swing bridges pivot horizontally. The Petaluma River Swing Bridge, also known as the Black Point Bridge (1911), was built by the Northwestern Pacific Railroad near Novato, California, and has recently been put back in service.

Tunnel faces marking the entrance to a bore through a mountain or under a river can have architectural merit and even be considered ornamental features in a landscape. They also commemorate the enormous expenditure of time, money, and human lives that went into the creation of these invisible but essential elements of railroad infrastructure. The Hoosac Tunnel in the Berkshires of western Massachusetts, four and three-quarter miles long, took nearly a quarter of a century to complete, at a cost of roughly $10 million and the loss of 195 lives. The late railroad historian William D. Middleton considered it "the nineteenth century's greatest railroad engineering feat."[35] Three prime examples are near Johnstown, Pennsylvania; Waynesboro, Virginia; and Talcott, West Virginia.

EADS BRIDGE
1874, James B. Eads, engineer
Washington Ave., St. Louis, MO

This gracefully arched, low-profile, technologically innovative bridge spanning America's mightiest river at its midpoint, symbolically united the nation's eastern and western railroads. After the launch of the Lewis and Clark Expedition in the early 1800s, St. Louis became the traditional jumping-off point for the West (a fact commemorated by Eero Saarinen's 1965 soaring stainless steel Gateway Arch). When the railroads arrived in the mid-nineteenth century, the rapidly growing city, situated at the confluence of the nation's inland waterways, already commanded the river traffic. It was the country's second-largest port, after New York City, and on an average day, over a hundred steamboats lined its cobblestone levee.

St. Louis was also second to Chicago—already the terminus of two of the four eastern trunk lines and connected to the western transcontinental line—in railroad primacy. The Mississippi may have the main avenue of commerce for St. Louis, but it was also a barrier to the city's railroad development.

Passengers and goods crossed the river between Illinois and Missouri courtesy of the Wiggins Ferry Company, a politically powerful monopoly that specialized in railroad freight and was naturally opposed to the idea of a bridge. But in wintertime, ice in the river could halt ferry operations, and then nothing moved.

To speed up freight shipments by connecting the railroad lines on either shore, and to challenge Chicago's position as the railroad capital of the United States, the St. Louis merchants wanted a bridge. Charles Ellet and John A. Roebling proposed

Figure 12.1

Eads Bridge, St. Louis, Missouri (courtesy of Bi-State Development)

suspension spans (in 1839 and 1857, respectively), but the city rejected these and other designs. Then came the Civil War, which damaged the maritime commerce and economy of St. Louis, while benefiting Chicago. At the end of the conflict, St. Louis city fathers renewed their efforts to build a bridge.

Bridge companies were chartered in Illinois and Missouri in 1864–65, but due to the maneuvering among the various interested parties, construction did not begin for three years. The political machinations during this period, which involved the Wiggins Ferry Company, the steamboat interests, and several rival bridge companies, were exceedingly opaque (one company, under the influence of Chicago forces, was allegedly working to prevent the construction of any bridge at St. Louis). Moreover, the local politicians, from the mayor to the aldermen, were reported to be remarkably duplicitous and open to bribery.

The Mississippi River at St. Louis is 1,500–1,600 feet wide and 30 or so feet deep at the high-water mark, when the surface flotsam rolls by the levee at nine miles per hour. The river bottom is a thick, swirling carpet of silt, below which are several dozen feet of mud and sand extending down to bedrock. The riverbed's depth varies with the season. An area with a thick cover of mud and sand at one time could at another time be bare stone. One of the few people who had actually seen this close up was James Eads, and with his appearance on the St. Louis bridge scene in 1867, things began to come together.

Indiana-born James Eads (1820–87) knew the Mississippi River as well as any man, including Mark Twain. Eads had arrived by steamboat in St. Louis with his family as a teenager. As the steamboat approached the levee, it caught fire—destroying all of the family's possessions. Poor, and with little schooling, Eads got a job as a clerk with a dry goods merchant, who gave him access to his library of books on mechanical engineering and boat design. At the age of nineteen, Eads was working as a purser (sometimes called a mud clerk) on a steamboat. Three years later it hit a snag and sank, but in the interim, Eads had picked up a great deal of river lore.

Intrigued with the idea of salvaging and reselling the valuable cargoes of wrecked steamboats, he found a pair of St. Louis boatbuilders to back him. He designed and patented a diving bell that they assembled and equipped, along with a salvage boat called a submarine. Eads did most of the diving himself, gaining an intimate knowledge of and respect for the river's hydraulics—particularly its silt-depositing and scouring capacity.

By 1851, Eads was operating four salvage boats and making a great deal of money. When the Civil War broke out, he went to Washington and discussed strategy for warfare on the western rivers with President Abraham Lincoln. Eads advocated the use of ironclad gunboats and eventually signed a contract with the federal government to build seven of them. He organized the production facilities, put together a workforce of four thousand men that worked around the clock, and launched the first boat in a little over sixty days. In 1862, the *St. Louis* became America's first ironclad to engage in a naval battle. Eads's ironclad flotilla, equipped with his steam-operated rotating gun turrets, was a major factor in the Union's dominance of the Mississippi River system.

In 1867, Eads was a successful St. Louis businessman with interests in banks, real estate, and railroads, and with recognized organizational and money-raising skills. He was small in stature but wiry and exceptionally strong, once placing second in a weight-lifting contest with the city's blacksmiths. Eads had clear ideas about his projects and the ability to present them logically and convincingly. Probably due to his railroad investments, he wanted to build a bridge at St. Louis. The quarrelsome local merchants eventually united behind him, even though he was not a trained engineer and had never built a bridge before.

To satisfy the steamboat interests, Congress mandated that the bridge at St. Louis have a 50-foot clearance over the river's main channel and a center span of 500 feet, an unprecedented length at the time. The center span ended up being 520 feet long with two side spans, each 502 feet long. Having just two piers minimized the bridge's obstruction to navigation.

The consolidated Illinois and St. Louis Bridge Company named Eads its chief engineer in early 1867. He soon presented his design for a bridge composed of steel arches. Eads chose the arch form, he said, because he thought it more commodious and attractive than a truss bridge. He also cited its strength, durability, and beauty with economy. Not trusting the readily available wrought iron to support such a structure, he wanted to build it of steel, then a new and untried structural metal in America. The railroad bridge at Koblenz, Germany (1864), composed of three low wrought-iron arches, was likely the model for the St. Louis bridge; Eads may have seen an illustration of it in an engineering magazine.

Eads estimated the total cost of the project at about $5 million: $3 million for the bridge itself and $2 million for land acquisition and the approaches, including a necessary tunnel under the downtown streets of St. Louis. He hired a pair of talented assistant engineers trained in Germany, Henry Flad and Charles Pfeifer.

The financial and construction team of J. Edgar Thomson and Thomas A. Scott, officers of the Pennsylvania Railroad (and Eads's fellow investors in midwestern railroads), and their associate, Andrew Carnegie, was soon in place. Eads began raising money in St. Louis; an important ally in this task was William Taussig, a St. Louis physician turned financier. In fact, besides being its designer, Eads became the bridge's chief financial backer and a major owner. The structure, appropriately enough, soon became known as the Eads Bridge—a unique instance in the United States of a bridge being named for its creator—and it still has that name.

Carnegie was a partner in the Keystone Bridge Company, a prominent firm that later won the contract for erecting the superstructure of the St. Louis bridge. However, when Eads's plans were shown to Jacob Linville, Keystone's engineer, he said that the bridge would not stand and instead proposed a three-span truss design of his own. But the citizens of St. Louis retained their faith in Eads and terminated Linville as a consulting engineer.

First the bridge abutments and piers had to be built. Eads had determined (again against the advice of consulting engineers) that these must be founded on bedrock; if not, they would be undermined by the scouring action of the river. In 1868, Eads went to Europe for his health. While there, he talked to British and French engineers about the use of steel and the pneumatic caissons that Europeans were employing to build bridge piers. Eads decided to use this type of caisson, even though it too was largely untried in the United States.

Work began on the west abutment in August 1867. Since bedrock was forty-seven feet below the high-water mark at this location (the bedrock sloped down from west to east under the river), Eads decided to build the abutment with a cofferdam. This consisted of a row of sheet piling driven into the riverbed, so that when the enclosed area was pumped out, the excavation and masonry work could take place in relatively dry conditions. However, regular flooding of the cofferdam and the need to cut down through the wrecks of several steamboats and barges that had been scuttled at the site delayed the work. Eads devised a giant chisel, a six-by-ten-inch oak beam several feet long with a steel tip, that was driven down with a steam-powered pile driver as far as it would go and then replaced with a timber pile. The workers reached bedrock in seven months, laid the cornerstone, and began construction of the west abutment and its arcaded approach of limestone faced with granite.

In the spring of 1869, at the Carondelet shipyard where Eads had had the ironclads built, the caissons for the river piers were taking shape. These were huge structures of oak timbers covered with riveted sheet iron in the shape of elongated hexagons. The caisson for the east pier was about sixty-eight feet wide, eighty-two feet long, and nine feet high; it weighed 437 tons. It was open on the bottom, and the metal covering extended below the timber—forming a cutting edge to ease its descent through the riverbed. The heavy timber roof, reinforced with iron girders, had openings for access (through airlocks) to the interior working chamber, which was divided into three compartments. There were other openings in the roof to remove the excavated material. These were the largest caissons yet built in America, although they were soon to be eclipsed by those for the Brooklyn Bridge, which was also under construction. Eads and Washington Roebling—meeting in St. Louis and in Brooklyn, New York—compared notes on their use and the strange disease that had appeared among the caisson workers (discussed below).

In October 1869 the east pier caisson was launched at the shipyard, towed upriver to the site, and anchored to the river bottom with pilings. Barges were brought in on either side and also anchored. They carried steam engines and other equipment and were rigged with derricks and travelers spanning the caisson to move the stone. As the limestone and granite blocks were placed on the caisson's roof, it began to sink. When it reached the river bottom, twenty or so feet down, compressed air was pumped in. About thirty laborers—mostly Irish and German immigrants—at a time descended a spiral staircase in the middle of the pier, went through the airlocks to enter the compartments, and went to work excavating the muck (they later became known as sandhogs). The excavated material was sent up through side shafts in the pier that were filled with water. Eads devised a water-powered sand pump that speeded up the process.

The lower the caisson sank, the greater the interior air pressure had to become to equalize the water pressure outside. Normal atmospheric pressure is about fifteen pounds per square inch. As the air pressure inside the compartments rose to twice that, some of the workmen began to experience abdominal cramps, joint pains, and partial paralysis after they emerged. One had to be hospitalized. Eads cut the work shifts to two hours, which temporarily improved matters. Five months after they started, the caisson reached bedrock, at ninety-five feet below high-water mark. The air pressure was up to forty-four pounds per square inch. One of the new hands, James Riley, climbed the stairway after his two-hour shift, said he felt fine, and fell dead—the first fatality caused by caisson disease, or the bends.

Meanwhile, construction was proceeding on the west pier, which reached bedrock—eighty-six feet below the high-water mark—in April 1870 after four months of work. The deaths continued; there were ninety cases of the bends, and fourteen fatalities; a few others were crippled for life. Eads and his personal physician, Walter Jaminet, experienced the disease—and in Brooklyn, Washington Roebling was severely crippled by it. The doctor discovered the right treatment, although it was insufficiently applied.

Nitrogen bubbles forming in the blood and body tissues after rapid decompression causes the bends; the remedy is to decompress slowly. To counter the symptoms, the caisson workers should have spent some hours in a decompression chamber while the air pressure was gradually reduced. This procedure was tried at the Eads Bridge but did not slow the process down enough to have much effect. For one thing, it hindered progress on the work.

With the caissons resting on bedrock and the stone rising high above the river, the compartments and the access openings in the piers were filled with concrete to create a solid mass of masonry. This allowed for another round of fund-raising, because the financing for the bridge was tied to construction benchmarks. In 1869, Eads, Taussig, and their allies had sold $3 million in stock subscriptions in St. Louis and New York. And in 1870, Carnegie sold $2.5 million in bonds to Junius S. Morgan and Company in London.

The east abutment, begun in late 1870, was built using an enormous timber and iron caisson with a roof 4 feet thick. Bedrock was reached in March, 1871, at the unheard-of depth of 136 feet below the high-water mark. There was just one death from the bends. However, a springtime tornado that was strong enough to pick up a nearby locomotive and shove it over an embankment killed one worker and injured several others, destroyed equipment, and flooded the caisson.

Meanwhile, Eads had been assembling the components of the superstructure. This proved to be no less difficult than building the piers and abutments, mainly because the producers were unable to meet his demanding specifications.

Eads proposed to build the arches of steel tubes, a quarter inch thick, eighteen inches in diameter, and twelve feet long. Each tube would be filled with six chrome steel "staves" (like the staves of a barrel, Eads said) to give it strength. Two arches so constructed —one twelve feet above the other and connected to it by diagonal, wrought-iron bracing—would form a trussed arch with curved top and bottom chords. Four of these trussed arches would be spaced out across the width of the bridge. Rising from their tops,

vertical wrought-iron girders, also internally braced, would support the bridge's lower railroad level and top deck for vehicles.

In early 1870, the Keystone Bridge Company was given the contract for building the superstructure for $1.5 million. Keystone subcontracted with the William Butcher Steel Works in Philadelphia, which manufactured steel wheels for locomotives, to produce the steel elements. The contract for the wrought-iron work went to Carnegie's own firm, Kloman, Carnegie and Company.

Eads, an engineering genius and a perfectionist, was unyielding in his refusal to accept tubes, staves, and other parts for the bridge that did not meet his strict qualifications—and not many did. He set up testing machines at St. Louis and at the mills to verify the strength of the metal components, which consistently failed. It became apparent that the Butcher Steel Works was incapable of making all of the chrome steel elements, so some of the work was given to the Brooklyn Chrome Steel Works.

Two years after the contract with Keystone was signed, Eads was still testing, and finally accepting, the metal elements of the bridge. Some of the parts ended up being made of iron rather than steel. In defense of the manufacturers and fabricators, who built rolling mills and other facilities in their attempts to satisfy the imperious engineer, steelmaking was a new technology at the time; the mass production of steel in the United States was still a few decades off. Eads was finally satisfied, but his demanding standards delayed construction and drove up costs.

Work on the superstructure began in April 1872, the foundation for the bridge having taken four years to complete. Normally, arched bridges are built by means of timber centering erected between the piers to support the pieces of the arch from below; when the arch is completed and can stand on its own, the timber is removed. At St. Louis, such centering, besides impeding navigation, would have been very difficult to build over the river, especially considering the tremendous length of the arch: over five hundred feet.

Instead, Flad, an assistant engineer, devised a way

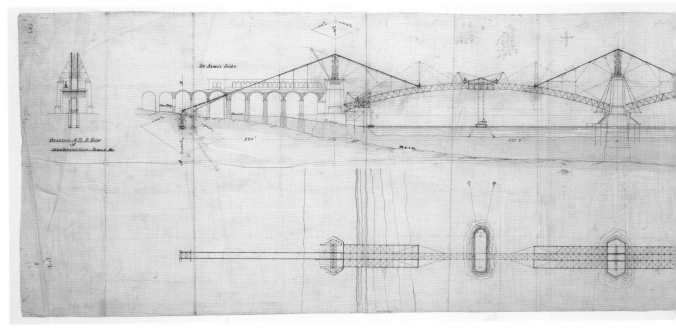

Figure 12.2

"General Plan of Erecting Ill. & St. Louis Bridge by Keystone Bridge Co.
Pittsburgh, Pa," circa 1872 (courtesy of American Bridge Co.)

to construct the arches from above, using cantilevers with backstays. Tall wooden towers were erected atop the piers and abutments. Metal skewback plates to receive the arches were attached to the masonry with long anchor bolts. The steel tubes began creeping out over the Mississippi, east and west from each abutment and in both directions from the piers, supported by suspension chains and backstays consisting of wrought-iron eyebars. The work at each location had to proceed simultaneously to equalize the tension forces on either side of the towers. Derricks hoisted the tubes and couplings from barges at the site and maneuvered them into position, where they were assembled by crews of ironworkers overseen by Theodore Cooper, the engineer supervising the erection of the bridge. Gradually, the halves of the three arches grew toward each other.

Eighteen months after work on them began, the arches were ready to be closed. Eads was in Europe negotiating a $500,000 bond deal, but the bankers would not release the money unless the arches were successfully joined by September 19, 1873. It was unseasonably hot in St. Louis, and the metal had

expanded so much that the last tubes could not be inserted. Flad packed the tubes with tons of ice, but the gap remained too small by five-eighths of an inch. Eads had prepared adjustable tubes for just such a problem, and these were used to close the arches by the deadline.

The Eads Bridge—1,630 feet long, 88 feet above the high-water mark, and 54 feet wide—was officially opened July 4, 1874. It had cost $10 million, twice Eads's original estimate. The bridge was widely praised. Among its admirers was Louis Sullivan, who developed an early fascination with bridges and was particularly inspired by Eads's use of steel—which Sullivan incorporated in his pioneering skyscraper, the Wainwright Building in St. Louis (1891). Sullivan said the bridge crossed a great river and formed the portal of a great city. He described it as sensational and architectonic.

But it was a financial failure. Railroad rivalries, the lack of passenger and freight terminals in St. Louis, the constantly shifting commercial alliances of the political and business leaders, and competition from the Wiggins Ferry Company (which now had the

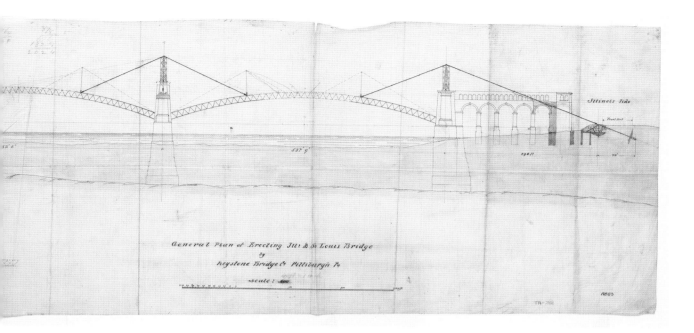

General Plan of Erecting Ill: & St. Louis Bridge
by
Keystone Bridge Co. Pittsburgh Pa.
Scale:

ability to move whole railroad cars across the river) forced the bridge company into bankruptcy the year after it opened. It took Jay Gould to get things organized in the following decade. Having taken over several local railroads and acquired control of the bridge, in 1889 Gould formed the Terminal Railroad Association of St. Louis to coordinate rail operations and interchange traffic. Taussig was made president. Later the association acquired the Wiggins Ferry Company. Freight terminal facilities took shape and in 1894, the association (which still exists) built St. Louis Union Station.

In the twentieth century, at last fulfilling its function, the Eads Bridge carried substantial railroad and vehicular traffic. But it could not accommodate the new larger railroad locomotives and cars. The last train (Amtrak) crossed it in 1974, and the bridge fell into disrepair. In 1991, it was closed for safety reasons.

In 1993, Metrolink, the St. Louis light rail system, began using the bridge and the nearly mile-long downtown approach tunnel for its trains. The city led the effort to repair the bridge's top deck, and after $35 million had been spent in 1999–2003, the bridge reopened with four lanes of vehicular traffic plus a bicycle or pedestrian lane. The bridge is jointly owned by the City of St. Louis and Bi-State Development, an Illinois-Missouri interstate compact agency specializing in transportation. In late 2016, a $48-million restoration of the bridge was completed. It included repairing the masonry approaches, replacing 580 tons of support steel, and sandblasting and repainting the superstructure.

THOMAS VIADUCT
Baltimore and Ohio (B&O) Railroad
1835, Benjamin H. Latrobe Jr., engineer;
John McCartney, builder
Relay, MD

Designed by a twenty-six-year-old surveyor who had never built a bridge or taken a formal course in civil engineering, the Thomas Viaduct has stood the test of time and use. The trains of today weigh up to 150 times as much as they did when the bridge was opened. The oldest major railroad viaduct in North America, it was the first to be built on a curving alignment.

Why the company assigned its biggest and most important bridge of the time to a relatively inexperienced engineer is something of a mystery, but

Figure 12.3
Thomas Viaduct, Relay, Maryland (courtesy of James Thomas)

Benjamin H. Latrobe Jr. (1806–78) came highly recommended. His father was the famous architect of the US Capitol and Baltimore's Cathedral. His brother, John H. B. Latrobe, was the railroad's lawyer.

The bridge was located where the B&O's branch line to Washington, D.C., diverged from the main line, which followed the Patapsco River to the west. Its configuration was dictated by the alignment's 4.5-degree curve at that point, the sharpest on the Washington branch line. Latrobe had surveyed the route for the line. He was also involved in selecting the location for the viaduct, vetoing a proposed location nearby that called for a lower and straighter bridge. This turned out to be the right decision: an 1868 flood destroyed the railroad's lower stone viaduct upstream but left Latrobe's bridge intact. Entries in the engineer's journals make clear that he regarded the Thomas Viaduct as his personal monument.

Due to the curved shape of the bridge, the convex, upstream side was longer than the downstream side, which meant that its arches would be larger than those on the opposite side. Latrobe solved the problem of having to construct funnel-shape arches by laying out the sides of the piers on radial lines, which made them wedge-shape and thus equalized the size of the arches on either side of the bridge. Latrobe gave what is essentially a Roman structure additional esthetic appeal by choosing elliptical rather than the customary semicircular arches.

Built mainly by Irish and German workmen, the viaduct was completed in two years. The material was Ellicott City granite: 63,000 tons of it were delivered to the site by rail from quarries six miles up the line. John McCartney, the hard-driving, hard-drinking Irish contractor, first erected a temporary timber trestle across the river to carry the stone cars. Shears (two-legged rudimentary cranes) were placed at intervals along its length to lower the stone.

Laborers first dug excavations for the abutments and piers. A few of the latter were in the river itself, so cofferdams had to be built to keep out the water. Latrobe once watched McCartney and a hundred men inside one of the cofferdams bailing, pumping, and scraping out the river bottom to lay the foundation.

When the piers had reached the proper height, the carpenters fabricated timber frames called centers and used the shears to raise them to the tops of the piers. Overlaid with boards, the centers supported the stones that made up the arches. After these were completed, the centers were removed, and the eight arches, each spanning fifty-eight feet, stood by themselves.

The arch spandrels were filled in and three courses of masonry added, followed by the coping stones. Massive battered-wing walls stood at either end of the bridge. The piers were faced with engaged columns and capitals. Above the latter stood the anchor blocks for the neoclassical style cast-iron railing that Latrobe had designed. The insides of the piers and the spaces over the arches were filled with rubble stone and concrete, and the bridge was ready for the tracks to be laid.

At his own expense, McCartney built a monument, designed by Latrobe, at Relay. It lists the important dates and names of the principals (see chapter 14). The bridge cost roughly $200,000; two men died and several were injured during its construction.

Named for the railroad president, Philip E. Thomas, the viaduct in its parklike setting became a favorite subject of artists and photographers in the following decades. In 1844, it carried the first telegraph message —the famous "What hath God wrought?" sent from the US Capitol in Washington to the B&O's Mount Clare depot in Baltimore, on wires strung along the Washington branch, which served as a testing ground. During the Civil War, the only railroad from the north into the nation's capital was protected by Union soldiers at the bridge.

In 1873, the B&O added the Relay Station-Hotel. Designed by the railroad's house architect, E. Francis Baldwin, in a Victorian Gothic style, it was built of the same granite as the bridge and trimmed with red Seneca stone. Beautifully sited, the building was backed by a landscaped garden in the English style that surrounded the monument. The three-story hotel section in the rear had a porch and balcony oriented so people could watch trains on the two rail lines.

The hotel enjoyed a brief vogue as a respite for passengers and weekend vacationers from Baltimore and Washington, but it shut down after just sixteen years; the station closed in 1938. Trains continued to stop at Relay until 1950 when the building, vacant and vandalized, was demolished. Today, nothing remains of this sylvan railroad retreat. CSX Transportation's freight trains and MARC commuter trains continue to cross the Thomas Viaduct, which is structurally sound but looking definitely the worse for wear.

The bridge took a frightful toll on its young engineer's health, which declined severely during the period of construction. Latrobe functioned as the project engineer, almost daily monitoring the progress of the work at the site and making on-the-spot decisions. The mental anxiety that resulted caused him to suffer chest pains, particularly around the heart; shortness of breath; indigestion; and fainting spells. These symptoms were remarkably similar to those experienced by soldiers after hard combat, a psychosomatic condition that would now be diagnosed as post-traumatic stress disorder. For Latrobe, the two years of building the viaduct was similar to going through a war. His health returned gradually after the bridge was finished, and he went on to become the B&O Railroad's chief engineer and served as a consultant to the Roeblings on the Brooklyn Bridge. He is now considered the foremost railroad engineer of the nineteenth century.

His viaduct of rustic masonry stands 704 feet long, including the approaches; 26 feet wide, and 66 feet above the surface of the river. "This masterpiece of the mason's art," said the architectural historian Carl Condit, "is a superb work of architecture as well as of engineering."[36]

STARRUCCA VIADUCT
Erie Railroad
1848, Julius W. Adams and James P. Kirkwood,
    engineers
Lanesboro, PA

The tall, slender, tapering piers; graceful arches; and slim profile make this perhaps the most beautiful of all the masonry railroad viaducts. It has an appearance of lightness, and in fact internal structural innovations did reduce the weight.

The viaduct spans Starrucca Creek, a tributary of the Susquehanna River in the northeast corner of

Pennsylvania. Like the Thomas Viaduct, it was built in just two years, but in this case under the pressure of a construction deadline. The railroad had two years to complete its line in New York State between Port Jervis and Binghamton, or risk losing its state charter. December 1848 was the deadline.

Getting the railroad across the quarter-mile-wide, 100-foot-deep Starrucca Valley was the hardest part of the project. Julius Adams, the Erie Railroad's construction engineer, rejected the idea of an embankment and decided on a viaduct. Several contractors passed up the job as being too difficult, and the one who started construction in August 1847 was soon let go for lack of progress. Adams then brought in his brother-in-law, James Kirkwood, to speed up the work and get the job done on time. With the help of some 800 workmen (most of whom were Irish immigrants), he did.

Adams (1812–99), a Bostonian, attended the US Military Academy but left in 1831 to join his uncle, George W. Whistler, one of the B&O Railroad's original West Point-trained engineers, as a railroad surveyor. In 1845, Adams started work with the New York and Erie Railroad, predecessor to the Erie. He later turned to waterworks engineering, was wounded as a Union colonel during the Civil War, and was one of the engineering consultants on the Brooklyn Bridge, along with Benjamin H. Latrobe Jr.

James Kirkwood (1807–77) was born in Edinburgh, Scotland. He took up land surveying and emigrated to America in 1832, with letters of introduction to William Gibbs McNeill—another of the B&O Railroad's early engineers who had trained at West Point. Kirkwood located railroad routes with McNeill and then worked for various railroads as a resident engineer—including the Western Railroad in Massachusetts in the early 1840s, when Whistler was chief engineer of that line. In his later career Kirkwood also specialized in waterworks engineering.

Adams designed the viaduct, and Kirkwood supervised its construction. The bridge was 1,040 feet long and 26 feet wide, and it stood 100 feet above the floor of the valley. It was built of local gray sandstone, known as bluestone. Most of the piers rest on

Figure 12.4
Starrucca Viaduct, Lanesboro, Pennsylvania

concrete footings. There were seventeen segmental arches, each spanning 51 feet (the projecting stones at the tops of the piers were probably the supports for the centers).

To compensate for the twelve-foot difference in elevation at either end of the viaduct, Adams raised each arch slightly higher than the preceding one, so the bridge appears level. And instead of filling the voids between the spandrel walls with rubble stone and concrete, as Latrobe had done at the Thomas Viaduct, Adams devised a system of lateral brick walls and longitudinal relieving arches to support the deck, which was built of flagstone and concrete. The idea was to both lessen the dead load of the bridge and transfer the weight of the passing trains more directly from the crowns of the arches to the piers and the ground.

Kirkwood opened the bridge, and the line, before the deadline—the first locomotive crossed the viaduct on December 9, 1848—but at a high price. The most expensive bridge of its time, the Starrucca Viaduct cost about $320,000 (roughly $7.4 million in today's dollars). Like the Thomas Viaduct, it proved popular with artists. Jasper Cropsey, originally an architect and later a famous landscape artist of the Hudson River school, was a colorist who specialized in autumnal scenes. His *Starrucca Viaduct, Pennsylvania* (1865), with the smoking locomotive crossing the bridge in the middle distance in a picturesque (and fanciful) setting, has become an emblem of the incursion into the wilderness of nineteenth-century technology.

The Starrucca Viaduct, now part of the New York, Susquehanna and Western Railway, is still in railroad service.

Some other notable masonry arch bridges are Whistler's seven surviving stone structures (circa 1842) for the Western Railroad (later the Boston and Albany Railroad, now CSX Transportation) in the Berkshires near Chester, Massachusetts, that still carry trains; the Great Northern Railway's long, curved Stone Arch Bridge (1883) in Minneapolis, Minnesota, today a hiking and biking trail; and the Pennsylvania Railroad's straight-line Rockville Bridge (1902) in Harrisburg, Pennsylvania — at 3,820 feet, the longest stone arch bridge in the world, and still in use by the Norfolk Southern Railroad.

BOLLMAN TRUSS BRIDGE
Baltimore and Ohio Railroad
1869, Wendel Bollman, engineer
Foundry St., Savage, MD

The mid-nineteenth century evolution of the metal truss railroad bridge in North America was a fairly rapid process. The B&O Railroad was then completing its line over the mountains from Cumberland, Maryland, to Wheeling, West Virginia, on the Ohio River, and this line provided the theater of experiment.

Besides large stone bridges such as the Thomas Viaduct, the B&O also built wooden truss spans, which were much quicker and cheaper to erect. One was the Potomac River bridge at Harpers Ferry, West Virginia, designed by Lewis Wernwag and Benjamin H. Latrobe Jr. and completed in 1836, just a year after the Thomas Viaduct. Problems soon appeared, however (with the masonry piers, not the superstructure), and the man brought in to rectify the situation had been with the railroad from its very beginning.

Wendel Bollman (1814–84) was born in Baltimore, but his parents had been born in Germany. At the age of fourteen, he marched in the July 4, 1828, parade that marked the B&O's groundbreaking. The following year, as a carpenter, he helped lay the first tracks. He pursued an independent carpenter's career but returned to the B&O in 1838, when he was hired to rebuild the bridge at Harpers Ferry. He was later made foreman of bridges and in 1849 was named master of road. By that time, Latrobe had become the B&O's chief engineer.

The third member of the team was the German-born Albert Fink (1827–97). Whereas Bollman was an engineering autodidact and an empirical designer, Fink was a trained engineer. He graduated from the Polytechnic Institute at Darmstadt, Germany, in 1848 with a degree in architecture and civil engineering. The following year, unhappy with the political situation in Germany, he emigrated to the United States, found his way to Baltimore, and was hired by Latrobe as a draftsman at the end of 1849. His timing could not have been better, for over the next few years this engineering triumvirate redesigned the American railroad truss bridge in iron.

Their early efforts were awkward composite structures — stone piers, wooden posts and beams, and metal connections that combined truss and suspension forms. The first true, all-metal truss that was adopted for general use on a major railroad was devised by Bollman.

The Bollman truss was adapted from the timber truss bridge designs of Wernwag and Latrobe that made use of diagonal struts. Bollman reengineered these in metal and turned them upside down, as it were, to create his truss system, which he called a suspension truss. The bottom chord was nonfunctional; the load was transferred to the tops of the cast-iron columns at the portal frames of the bridge by a series of wrought-iron diagonals extending from the foot of every post. The diagonals were in tension. The cast-iron beam that formed the top chord of the truss and kept the columns from inclining toward each other (Bollman called it a "stretcher") was in compression. According to Condit, "Bollman's intention

Figure 12.5

Bollman Truss Bridge, Savage, Maryland
(courtesy of Lawrence Biemiller)

in this highly redundant and bewildering array of separate pieces was undoubtedly to combine the truss with a mode of support comparable to that of the suspension bridge."[37]

The earliest example was a 76-foot span erected in 1850 on the B&O's Washington branch to replace a stone bridge that had been washed away by a flood; the cost was a modest $20,000. The next year, following accidents caused by the deteriorating timber trusses of the Harpers Ferry bridge that sent engines and cars into the river and injured crew members, one of its spans was replaced with a 124-foot Bollman truss. Eventually, the entire bridge was rebuilt using Bollman trusses.

Meanwhile, Fink had developed a variation of the Bollman truss, also based on the suspension principle. It used less metal because the diagonals extended from the portal frame columns only to the center post, rather than all the way to the opposite end of the span; and being more symmetrical, it was easier to keep in alignment. In 1852, Latrobe and Fink designed the crossings of the steep ravines in the Cheat River Valley on the B&O's line to Wheeling, the country's first iron railroad viaducts. When the

B&O's monumental bridge over the Monongahela River at Fairmont, West Virginia, opened in 1853—six hundred feet long, made up of three spans of Fink trusses—it was the largest iron bridge in America.

Bollman patented his bridge truss in 1852. He left the B&O six years later to form one of the nation's first bridge-building firms, with clients in the East, Midwest, and South America. He continued to build bridges for the B&O, including all but the channel span of the railroad's one-and-a-half-mile bridge over the Ohio River at Bellaire, Ohio, below Wheeling, which opened in 1872. By that time the Bollman truss had pretty much run its course, having been supplanted by other truss forms that used less metal. Its use was confined mainly to the railroad that sponsored it.

Fink supervised the construction of bridges and buildings on the B&O's Parkersburg branch before leaving the company shortly before Bollman did, to become construction engineer for the Louisville and Nashville Railroad. Fink also received a patent for his truss design and built several remarkable bridges, including one in Peru. He then turned from engineering to railroad administration. He wrote a report on transportation in 1874 that is regarded as the foundation of railroad economics, and he later served on a commission that tried to make peace among the Eastern trunk lines that were then engaged in disastrous rate wars. According to an autobiographical sketch among his papers, he was proudest of his work with Latrobe on the B&O. Very few of his bridges still stand.

The only remaining Bollman truss bridge of the hundred or so that once existed is the one at Savage, Maryland. Its location is quite close to where the first bridge to use Bollman's truss design was built in 1850. The bridge at Savage, with two eighty-foot spans, was constructed in 1869 for service elsewhere and moved in 1888 to its present site, on a branch line to Savage Mill.

WALKWAY OVER THE HUDSON
(formerly the Poughkeepsie-Highland
    Railroad Bridge)
1873–89, Charles MacDonald and Thomas
    C. Clarke, engineers; 2009, Bergmann
    Associates, rehabilitation engineers
Poughkeepsie, NY

The great bridge over the Hudson River at Pough-keepsie was built to create a direct railroad route between the Pennsylvania coalfields and the industries of New England and to improve east-west rail connections generally, since there was no railroad crossing of the Hudson below Albany. It was also designed to circumvent the Vanderbilts and the New York Central Railroad, which controlled the northern rail access to New York City via its lines on either side of the river. The Pennsylvania Railroad promoted and invested in the project.

The original charter granted to the Poughkeepsie Bridge Company in 1871 provided for a suspension bridge, with no piers in the river. The steamboat interests had a hand in this, since they viewed bridge piers and the bridges themselves as hazards to navigation. But despite the success of John Roebling's 1855 railroad suspension bridge at Niagara Falls, this type of bridge—being less rigid than a truss bridge—proved unsuitable for the ever-increasing weights and pounding forces generated by railroad traffic (Roebling's bridge at Niagara Falls, one of the few railroad suspension bridges, was taken down in 1897).

In 1872, the New York State Legislature amended the charter to authorize a pier bridge, with four river piers. The river spans were to be 525 feet long and 135 feet above the high-water mark. The span length was taken from the Eads Bridge in St. Louis (which ended up being 88 feet above the high-water mark). Construction started, but problems with the caissons and the panic of 1873, due primarily to rampant speculation in railroads, caused the company to go bankrupt.

The backers regrouped and tried again a few years later with a different bridge company. But the renewed effort also stopped after a few years, having resulted in only two partially completed piers.

The obstacles recalled those that faced James Eads at St. Louis. The Hudson at Poughkeepsie (which was chosen because it was roughly midway between Albany and New York City) was about half a mile wide and sixty or so feet deep. The Hudson was tidal up to Albany, so the current moved both ways.

In 1886, the promoters contracted with a third group, the Union Bridge Company—two of whose partners ended up designing the Poughkeepsie bridge. Charles MacDonald (1837–1928) was born in Ontario, worked for an engineer on the Grand Trunk Railway as a teenager, and graduated from the Rensselaer Polytechnic Institute in 1857. He was appointed assistant engineer on the Philadelphia and Reading Railroad. After the Civil War—he was captured by Confederate cavalry when he was a corporal in the Union infantry—he returned to the Reading and then became superintendent of bridge construction for the Delaware, Lackawanna and Western Railroad. In 1884, MacDonald, Thomas Clarke, and others formed the Union Bridge Company. They designed a cantilever crossing of the Ohio River at Louisville, Kentucky, shortly before starting work on the bridge at Poughkeepsie.

Clarke (1827–1901) was from Massachusetts. He earned a bachelor of arts degree from Harvard in 1848 but turned to engineering, obtaining jobs on railroads in the United States and Canada. Clarke returned to his native country in 1866 and became chief engineer for one of the first iron railroad bridges built across the Mississippi River (it was constructed at Quincy, Illinois). Recruited by the Phoenix Iron Company, of Pennsylvania around 1869 to set up a bridge-building subsidiary, he and his partners designed hundreds of bridges—including Pennsylvania's Kinzua Viaduct and several elevated railways in New York City—over the next fifteen years.

Clarke and MacDonald made two major design changes in the Poughkeepsie bridge: it was to be a steel cantilever span, and the pier foundations would be laid through the open dredging method. This was the first trial of a new system for setting deep-water bridge foundations. To reach a solid base under the Hudson, the engineers had to go down 135 feet

Figure 12.6

Walkway over the Hudson, Poughkeepsie, New York

—through 60 feet of water and 75 feet of mud and clay—as deep as the excavations for the St. Louis bridge piers had been. Eads had used closed pneumatic caissons, but Macdonald and Clarke decided on open ones.

These were cribs made of 1-foot-square timbers. The cribs measured 60 by 90 feet and were up to 115 feet tall, open at top and bottom. The lower edge was sharpened to cut through the mud and clay, and the caisson was weighted with gravel (enclosed in pockets lining the crib's sides) to drive it down. There were dredging shafts to remove the spoil, all without pumping the water out of the caisson. When the required depth was reached, concrete was loaded into the dredging shafts, and the caissons were filled with rock to form a solid base. From about 20 feet below the surface of the river, limestone piers were raised to some 30 feet above it, creating a platform for the steel support towers.

As they sank down through the river bottom, the open caissons were anchored with timber gabions filled with stone. The system worked well, except for the time when a towing cable snapped as a 5,000-ton caisson was being positioned in midstream, and the

caisson, three steamboats, and the anchor were carried three miles down the river on the spring flood tide before being brought under control.

The five river spans of the Poughkeepsie bridge can be seen as reading A-B-A-B-A across the Hudson, the As being the cantilever spans and the Bs the full truss anchor spans. The center cantilever span was in the middle of the river, where the highest clearance was needed for water traffic. Whereas Eads had constructed his entire superstructure from the tops of the piers, only the cantilever spans were built that way at Poughkeepsie.

Clarke and MacDonald decided to erect the two anchor trusses on a forest of tall timber pilings sunk into the river bottom. A platform built atop the pilings carried the traveler used to assemble the anchor trusses. When these were completed, travelers moving along their top chords raised from barges anchored below the steel used to construct the cantilever arms (which reached out simultaneously from the four river piers and the two land-based piers at either end). The suspended spans at their centers were constructed in the same manner. The Poughkeepsie bridge was 6,768 feet long, including the lengthy overland approach viaducts. The deck was 30 feet wide and stood 212 feet above the Hudson River. The first train crossed it on January 1, 1889.

The bridge's principal early user was a subsidiary of the New York, New Haven and Hartford Railroad, which ended up carrying most of the traffic over the bridge: anthracite coal moving east to the mills and factories of New England and general freight moving in both directions. The railroad also ran passenger trains between Boston and Washington over the bridge, avoiding New York City, but the service did not last long. The bridge itself had a lengthy and useful life. The engineer Ralph Modjeski strengthened it by adding a central line of trusses and support columns in 1907 (he also designed the 1930 Mid-Hudson Bridge at Poughkeepsie, a handsome suspension span). A 1974 fire atop the eastern approach viaduct put the Poughkeepsie bridge out of service. The damage was not repaired, and the railroad abandoned the bridge in 1981.

It took longer to restore the Poughkeepsie bridge and open it to the public as a state park than it took to build it, and the restoration proved almost as challenging as the original construction. The process began in 1991 with Bill Sepe, a resident of Poughkeepsie and an unassuming Vietnam War veteran who had been a Marine and a dairy farmer. Inspired by his walks on the bridge and the theories of Frederick Law Olmsted, Sepe envisioned turning the derelict span into a pedestrian path where people could enjoy views of the Hudson River. Sepe founded the nonprofit Walkway over the Hudson, obtained quitclaim deeds from private and public owners of the bridge, and began making repairs using volunteer labor. His idea attracted attention, and the organization grew. But the volunteer effort was halted by court order in 2000, after a worker was seriously injured while installing lights on the bridge.

In 2004, Fred W. Schaeffer—a local lawyer and bicyclist, and one of the many hundreds of people who had enjoyed the view from the bridge—became head of Walkway over the Hudson. The group continued Sepe's strategy of taking people out on the bridge to see it and the view for themselves and raised

the necessary funds from private and public sources to restore the structure and open it as a trail for hikers and bikers in 2009. The total cost was $38 million.

The rehabilitation engineers examined the bridge from bottom to top. The underwater timber caissons were found to be in good shape, except for one whose damage was repaired. The steel superstructure was likewise found to be basically sound. Several hundred precast concrete panels weighing several tons each were installed to form the walkway, and new guardrails and lighting were added. *Rails to Trails* magazine called it "an impressive example of architectural reclamation."[38]

QUEBEC BRIDGE
1917, Ralph Modjeski, Charles C. Schneider, and Charles N. Monsarrat (board of engineers)
St. Lawrence River, six miles west southwest of Quebec City, QC

At the beginning of the twentieth century, the Canadian government encouraged various railroads to build a northern transcontinental line to open up new territory in the West and to counter the monopoly of the Canadian Pacific Railway (CPR). William Mackenzie and Donald Mann of the Canadian Northern Railway did not want to participate, but Charles Melville Hays of the Grand Trunk Railway did, and he started building his railroad in the West. In the East, the line—known as the National Transcontinental Railway—passed through northern Ontario and Quebec, crossed the St. Lawrence River at Quebec City, and continued in a more or less straight line to Moncton, New Brunswick.

Quebec City had had rail service since 1879 via the CPR, but the railroad's main line from Montreal to its Atlantic port (St. John, Nova Scotia) ran well to the south. Sandford Fleming, chief engineer of the Intercolonial Railway, completed that line in 1872, but it passed by Quebec City on the other side of the river, as it traced the St. Lawrence on a circuitous route from Montreal to Halifax, Nova Scotia (VIA Rail's Ocean trains follow this route today).

Besides being a critical link in the National Transcontinental Railway, the Quebec Bridge would give Quebec City a direct rail connection between the Atlantic ports and the rest of Canada and allow it to challenge Montreal's dominance as a railroad center and port. The National Transcontinental was finished in 1913 except for the Quebec Bridge, but the railroad was not a financial success—partly because it traversed great stretches of unoccupied territory that generated little or no traffic. Within a decade of its completion, the National Transcontinental, the Grand Trunk Pacific Railway (and its parent company, the Grand Trunk), the Canadian Northern Railway, and the Intercolonial Railway—most of which had undergone individual but interrelated fiscal crises—were nationalized and made part of Canadian National Railways.

Serious plans for bridging the St. Lawrence at Quebec City began in 1889 with the formation of the Quebec Bridge and Railway Company, which hired Theodore Cooper as consulting engineer. Cooper was to review the proposals from bridge-building companies, advise his employers which was the best design, and have ultimate responsibility for the bridge.

Cooper (1839–1919) was at the top of his profession when he took on the Quebec Bridge assignment. Born in Coopers Plains, New York, he graduated from the Rensselaer Polytechnic Institute in 1858 and went to work on the Hoosac Tunnel. After joining the US Navy, he served on a gunboat during the Civil War and later was an instructor at the US Naval Academy, in Annapolis, Maryland. He resigned in 1872 and began an association with the Eads Bridge at St. Louis —first as an inspector at the Keystone Bridge Company, which was erecting the superstructure, and then on the bridge itself as supervisor of erection. He later succeeded Eads as engineer. After that, Cooper designed railroad shops and several bridges, including those for New York City's elevated railroads. His 1894 system of measuring the weight of trains crossing railroad bridges, based on the axle loading of locomotives and cars, is still in use today.

Four companies submitted proposals and designs to build the Quebec Bridge. In 1900, the superstructure contract was awarded to the Phoenix Bridge Company, which had the best and cheapest plan for a 1,600-foot steel cantilever bridge; the plans were drawn up by Peter L. Szlapka, the firm's designing engineer.

The St. Lawrence River narrowed at the bridge site upriver from Quebec City, but it was still half a mile wide and 190 feet deep, with a current of seven miles per hour. This was enough to make Cooper decide to broaden the main cantilever span, placing the two main piers closer to the shore, and thus reducing the time, expense, and difficulty involved with the use of deepwater caissons. Thus, the main span was lengthened from 1,600 to 1,800 feet, making it then the longest bridge in the world.

Construction began in 1900 with the piers. Even though they were near the shore, they required large caissons, 49 by 150 feet and 25 feet high. The piers were built of granite filled with concrete. Due to various problems, work on the superstructure was delayed until 1905. Cooper appointed Norman R. McClure resident engineer at the site. Work started from the south shore. Once the anchor span was in place, the cantilever span would be erected by a traveling crane.

In June 1907 the cantilever arm was complete, and the initial panels of the suspended span were in place, but McClure noticed that there was something seriously wrong with the bridge: the curved bottom chords were deflecting. He notified Cooper, and a discussion ensued about the possible causes. The situation worsened; McClure sent telegrams to Cooper and the Phoenix Bridge Company, and there were more conferences. In late August, McClure telegraphed Cooper that he was going to stop the work on the bridge unless he heard from him and the company. Receiving no response, McClure took the train to New York City to meet with the consulting engineer. After they talked, Cooper telegraphed the Phoenix Bridge Company to suspend the work in Quebec and sent McClure to Phoenixville, Pennsylvania, to meet with company officers. There was more procrastination. In the meantime, work at the bridge continued, no official notice having been received to stop it.

In the late afternoon of August 29, shortly before quitting time, with a reverberation that was felt six miles away in Quebec City, the bridge collapsed, sending 18,000 tons of steel, a train delivering materials to the job site, and eighty-six bridge workers —including thirty-three Mohawk Indians, renowned for their skill in working with steel at great heights —into the St. Lawrence River. Eleven of the workers survived, including the locomotive engineer; he was rescued by boat.

There was plenty of blame to go around. The Quebec Bridge and Railway Company was undercapitalized, which caused delays and other problems; its engineer, Edward A. Hoare, who had allowed the work at the bridge to continue after being warned of its dangers, had no experience in overseeing such large projects. Szlapka, the designing engineer, had failed to update his calculations to account for a longer bridge and the additional weight of the steel required to build it. By the time the oversight was detected, the components had already been fabricated according to the old specifications and were being assembled in the bridge. Szlapka and Cooper decided that the increase in weight was within tolerance. In addition, some of the components—notably, the lower chords—were underdesigned and poorly engineered even for the shorter bridge.

Theodore Cooper, who was nearly seventy and in poor health, had not visited the site since construction started, but he insisted on retaining full control and making the final decisions. Cooper vehemently objected to a recommendation that a consultant be hired to check the engineering work because, he said, it would make him a subordinate, which he could not accept. At the same time, he complained that his fee was too low to allow him to maintain an office staff and provide proper oversight. The Phoenix Bridge Company was also lax in this area. McClure, the man assigned to supervise the work, was a 1904 Princeton graduate with a degree in civil engineering, but he was young and relatively inexperienced.

The government commissioners appointed to investigate North America's worst bridge disaster made their report to the Parliament of Canada in March 1908. It said that the bridge had fallen due to the failure of the lower chords, whose design (by Szlapka) had been defective and had been approved by Cooper: "The failure cannot be attributed to any cause other than errors in judgment on the part of these two engineers. [Their] ability was tried in one of the most difficult professional problems of the day and proved to be insufficient to the task."[39] The commissioners found that there had been insufficient studies and tests during the course of construction, and a general lack of engineering supervision on the part of everyone involved.

"The professional knowledge of the present day concerning the action of steel columns under load is not sufficient to enable engineers to economically design such structures as the Quebec Bridge," the commissioners said. "A bridge of the adopted span that will unquestionably be safe can be built, but . . . a considerably larger amount of metal would have to be used than might be required if our knowledge were more exact."[40]

The engineers of the replacement bridge at Quebec took the commissioners at their word. Whereas the span that fell had appeared spindly, the new bridge would be massive, which was what was called for.

One of the models for the new Quebec Bridge was the Firth of Forth bridge near Edinburgh, Scotland (1890), an enormous steel cantilever railroad bridge designed by Sir Benjamin Baker and Sir John Fowler. It was built in the wake of an 1879 bridge disaster that bore an eerie resemblance to the subsequent events at the Quebec Bridge.

Three days after Christmas 1879, while a train was crossing it, the bridge over the Firth of Tay in Scotland collapsed in a gale, sending seventy-five passengers to their deaths in the water below. Its engineer, Thomas Bouch, was later blamed for the bridge's failure, due to his insufficient allowance for wind loading. (The Tay bridge was composed of lattice girders supported by cast-iron columns that in turn were braced with wrought-iron struts and ties; the investigation found the cross bracing and connections inadequate.)

Bouch was then at work on the design for the bridge over the Firth of Forth, but in the wake of the failure of his Firth of Tay bridge, he was replaced by Baker and Fowler, who developed a different design for the Firth of Forth bridge based on the cantilever. Bouch died the year following the fall of his bridge; the Firth of Forth bridge is still in service.

The former bridge companies wanted to take up where they left off with the Quebec Bridge, but the Canadian government wisely chose to start afresh, with a new company and a different set of designers. A board of engineers was established to review the proposals and oversee the work. The members of the board changed during the course of the project (Charles MacDonald, engineer of the Poughkeepsie cantilever bridge, was called out of retirement to serve on the board for a time). When a contract was signed with the St. Lawrence Bridge Company (a joint venture with two other bridge firms) and construction of the new Quebec bridge began in the spring of 1911, the board consisted of Charles Monsarrat, Charles Schneider, and Ralph Modjeski.

Charles Monsarrat (1871–1940) was born in Montreal, became a draftsman for the CPR, and in 1902 became its chief engineer of bridges.

The German-born Charles Schneider (1843–1916), a technical school graduate, came to the United States after the Civil War and found employment with railroad and bridge companies. He designed some of North America's early high cantilever bridges, including one for the Michigan Central Railroad over the Niagara Gorge in 1883, and another for the CPR over the Fraser River in British Columbia in 1887. When the latter span was replaced in 1910, it was moved and put back up over Niagara Creek on Vancouver Island, about ten miles west of Victoria in what is now Goldstream Provincial Park. As of 2016, it was still carrying the occasional freight train. Schneider also designed the anchorage and interior steel framework for the Statue of Liberty (1886) and was the engineer for the Pennsylvania Railroad's massive train shed at Jersey City, New Jersey (1892; later demolished). Around 1895, during the early planning for the Quebec bridge, Cooper—pleading advanced age and declining health—had asked Schneider to replace him as consulting engineer.

Modjeski (1861–1940), the only original member of the board of engineers who was still there when the Quebec bridge was completed, later became world renowned as a bridge builder. He was born Rudolph Modrzejewski in Cracow, Poland. His mother was a famous actress. She and her family emigrated to the United States in 1876 and ended up in San Francisco —where a theater owner insisted on a name change for her American debut. Thus, her son became Ralph Modjeski. As a teenager, he expressed aspirations to be an engineer, but he was also a talented pianist. Finally choosing the former career for his life's work, he went back to Europe to attend the École Nationale

Figure 12.7
Quebec Bridge, detail (circa 1916), six miles west southwest of Quebec City, Quebec (courtesy of Library and Archives Canada Dominion Bridge Co. Pennsylvania 135835)

Figure 12.8
Quebec Bridge, Quebec City, Quebec

des Ponts et Chaussées in Paris. He graduated at the head of his class in 1885.

Returning to the United States, Modjeski apprenticed with George S. Morison, a leading designer of steel truss bridges. Modjeski's 1905 bridge over the Mississippi River, built (with Alfred Noble) for several railroads at Thebes, Illinois, brought him particular notice. He designed the Chicago, Burlington and Quincy Railroad bridge over the Ohio River at Metropolis, Illinois, which was completed the same year as the Quebec bridge. Altogether Modjeski designed some forty bridges over some of the largest bodies of water in the United States, culminating with the San Francisco–Oakland Bay Bridge (1931). The Quebec bridge qualifies as one of his greatest.

Before workers could begin to build the new bridge, several thousand tons of tangled steel had to be cleared from the river at the bridge site. The operation was tedious, but the crumpled bridge was finally blasted apart with dynamite and hauled away in chunks. New piers were constructed, the old ones being deemed unusable. There were more problems with the caissons, particularly on the north shore where huge boulders had to be dragged or blasted

out of the way to enable the caisson to sink to the proper depth. When completed, the granite and concrete main piers measured 32 by 160 feet across their tops.

Erection of the steel superstructure began in 1913. The bridge was again to be an 1,800-foot cantilever, and it employed K-trusses. However, the critical lower chords were straight rather than curved. They were also several times larger and stronger than their predecessors, as were other components of the bridge. A different approach was taken for the suspended center span, which was to be constructed off site, floated into place by barge, and hoisted up to be joined to the cantilever arms, rather than being built out from them as before.

In September 1914, as the span was being lifted, tragedy struck a second time: a casting failed and the center section crashed into the river, killing eleven bridge workers. This time the accident was witnessed by several hundred spectators who had lined the riverbanks and the decks of excursion steamers to watch the bridge being completed.

A replacement center span was assembled and successfully raised three years later, and the Quebec

Bridge was finished at last. At 1,800 feet, it remains the longest railroad cantilever span ever built. Its total length, including the approach spans, is 3,238 feet. It is 340 feet high and 95 feet wide, and its center span rises 150 feet above the surface of the St. Lawrence River —in whose depths the remains of the first bridge and the initial center span of the second still lie.

Cooper's career never recovered. A few days after the prince of Wales dedicated the Quebec bridge in 1919, Cooper died, alone, in his New York City home.

On the eve of its hundredth anniversary, the Quebec Bridge—which carries a rail line, three highway lanes, and two pedestrian walkways, is in dire need of restoration. Following the government's transfer of the bridge to Canadian National Railways in 1993, maintenance has declined. More than half of the bridge is covered in rust, and it needs to be repainted —which would cost of some $200 million.

Other outstanding steel railroad bridges include Young's High Bridge over the Kentucky River at Tyrone, Kentucky, which was built in 1889 by the Louisville Southern Railroad (John McLeod was chief engineer). This steel cantilever that has begun an interesting new life since it was bought in 1993 by Vertigo Bungee. Three spans that all opened in 1917 are also noteworthy: Gustav Lindenthal's Sciotoville Bridge, built by the Chesapeake and Ohio (C&O) Railway (an overpowering continuous through truss crossing the Ohio River at Portsmouth, Ohio); the same engineer's monumental steel arch Hell Gate Bridge, for the New York Connecting Railroad over the East River in New York City; and the Chicago, Burlington and Quincy Railroad's bridge over the Ohio River at Metropolis, Illinois, that incorporates the longest single truss span of 720 feet (designed by Modjeski).

CAMAS PRAIRIE RAILROAD TRESTLES
1908
Culdesac, ID

In terms of size and number, the greatest extant collection of timber railroad trestles is on the Camas Prairie Railroad, an obscure short line centered in Lewiston, Idaho, and reaching into the surrounding high timber country and farmland. The trestles are concentrated on the railroad's second subdivision between Spalding, on the Clearwater River, and Grangeville, on the rich Camas Prairie. In this sixty-seven-mile stretch, there are forty-three bridges and trestles—most of them timber.

The largest of these, and the most visible and accessible, are in the section of the railroad running in a southeasterly direction from Culdesac to Cottonwood, which for the most part parallels Route 95. Here, the railroad climbs two thousand feet out of the Lapwai Canyon to the edge of the prairie at Winchester before continuing to Craigmont, Cottonwood, and Grangeville. In just twelve miles between Culdesac and Winchester, there are eighteen trestles and six tunnels as the railroad loops around to gain elevation.

In the early twentieth century, the Northern Pacific Railway was starting to construct the branch line to Grangeville at great expense when its major competitor, the Union Pacific Railroad, reached Lewiston from the west, ending the Northern Pacific's ten-year monopoly in the area. The Union Pacific planned to extend its own branch line to the Camas Prairie, but in a rare show of cooperation, the two rivals agreed to jointly own and operate one line for the benefit of both. This solution avoided the cost of building a second branch line across the canyons and through the ridges. In addition, the railroads doubted that there would be sufficient freight revenue to support two lines.

Construction in the Lapwai Valley began in 1906 and was completed in 1908. Tunnel 1 made a horseshoe bend inside the mountain. The timbers for the trestles were cut on the prairie, hauled to the edge of the canyon, and skidded to the site or were sent by rail from Culdesac to the end of track. Assembling and erecting the bents and cross bracing to create these forests of timbers must have been a Herculean task. The Camas Prairie became known as the railroad on stilts.

The first major trestle south of Culdesac was Bridge 17 over Rock Creek, 483 feet long and 99 feet

Figure 12.9

Half Moon Trestle, Culdesac, Idaho (courtesy of Blair Kooistra)

high (the bridge numbers correspond to railroad mile-posts, beginning at Spalding; the distances between bridges in highway miles on Route 95 are fairly close to the railroad miles). The Rock Creek Trestle is opposite a historical marker, titled "Railroad Tunnels."

Bridges 19 and 20 cross the highway. The first of these is a composite of wood and metal, with timber approaches and steel plate girder spans over the road.

The next large trestle, and one of the best known, is Bridge 22—called the Half Moon Trestle because it is built on a curve. Located high up on the hillside, and measuring 684 feet in length and 141 feet in height, it is visible from several points in this stretch of the highway, but not readily accessible.

Farther along, Bridge 38 presented a special challenge: Lawyer's Canyon was the widest and deepest of the valleys to be crossed. The engineers decided on a steel viaduct here. Built by the American Bridge Company, it is 1,520 feet long and 280 feet high, and twelve towers support its plate girder spans. Another historical marker, titled "Railroad Trestles," is at this location.

Bridge 40, a timber trestle 493 feet long and 122 feet high, can be reached via old Highway 95.

Bridge 46, five miles north of Cottonwood and west of the highway, is a timber trestle 646 feet long and 86 feet high. Sandspur Road leads to a good view of the bridge.

In the town of Cottonwood, at Front and Pine Streets, is Bridge 50—542 feet long and 51 feet high. The timber trestle crosses the road before reaching a grain elevator.

Lumber products and grain were the mainstays of the Camas Prairie Railroad, segments of which are still in operation under new ownership (passenger service ended in 1955). Service on the second subdivision lasted almost a century; it saw its last train in 2000. The trestles remain—except for Bridge 213, which burned in a 2011 wildfire—rare examples of a once-common type of structure that, on the slenderest of supports, carried heavy trains through the air with the greatest of ease.

Other outstanding timber trestles are the Goat Canyon Trestle (1933), one of the largest in the United States (750 feet long and 200 feet high) built by the San Diego and Arizona Eastern Railway in what is now the Anza-Borrego Desert State Park, California; and the 1,415-foot-long Meskanaw Trestle (1930) near Melfort, Saskatchewan, one of the longest in Canada.

LETHBRIDGE VIADUCT
Canadian Pacific Railway
1909, John E. Schwitzer, engineer
Lethbridge, AB

A bent is a structure with at least two legs, usually inclined toward each other and cross-braced. It can be made of timber, iron, steel, or reinforced concrete. Deployed in series, bents form a trestle and are used to support bridges. Often the entire composition is called simply a trestle, or trestle bridge, or viaduct.

The Lethbridge Viaduct was built as part of a realignment of the Crowsnest Route, the CPR's second main line in southern Alberta and British Columbia. Completed in 1897, the line had avoided the broad valley of the Belly River (now the Oldman) where the viaduct is located, with a route that had steep grades, sharp curves, and a number of timber trestles in need of rebuilding. Because the old route was expensive to operate and maintain, the CPR decided to invest in a new one and to bridge the Belly River Valley with

the viaduct at Lethbridge. It made twenty wooden trestles on the former route obsolete.

Once the concrete abutments and footings were in place and the initial steel sections erected, the bridge began to creep out over the valley under its own power—with the help of about a hundred workers. The viaduct was constructed using a 350-ton traveling crane that ran out on the completed portion of the bridge and picked up the steel for the bents and the deck from a loaded flatcar beneath it. The plate girder spans that form the deck rest on thirty-three towers. Over a mile (5,328 feet) long and 314 feet high, the viaduct, which cost $1.3 million, is the largest of its type ever built. It is still in use.

John Schwitzer (1870–1911) was born in Ottawa, Ontario, and started work for the CPR in 1899. While he was engaged with the Lethbridge Viaduct, he was also engineering the famous Spiral Tunnels on the CPR's main line in Kicking Horse Pass, British Columbia. This was a similar project designed to bypass a troublesome part of an original route, in this case 7.5 miles of mountain railroad with a 4.5 percent grade called the "big hill." Since its opening in 1886, it had proved to be an operational nightmare. After the first construction train to descend the "big hill" went off the tracks and into the Kicking Horse River, killing three crew members, the railroad built turnouts for runaway trains. Switzer's Spiral Tunnels, completed in 1909, reduced the grade to the standard 2.2 percent by tunneling 1.2 miles through the mountains, bypassing the "big hill." The Spiral Tunnels are also still in use, and the viewpoint location on Route 1 is the most popular in Yoho National Park. Based on his work on the Lethbridge Viaduct and the Spiral Tunnels, the CPR named Schwitzer its chief engineer in 1911, but he died of pneumonia three weeks later.

A venerable pair of steel railroad viaducts that have had quite dissimilar histories are the Erie Railroad's Kinzua Viaduct, near Mt. Jewett, Pennsylvania, and the Northern Pacific Railway's Marent Trestle, outside Missoula, Montana. The Kinzua Viaduct was built in 1882 with wrought-iron bents and replaced in 1900 with a structure using steel bents and plate girder spans. It was abandoned in 1957, half destroyed

Figure 12.10
Lethbrige Viaduct (circa 1909), Lethbridge, Alberta (courtesy of Library
and ArchivesCanada LAC Canadian Pacific Railway Pennsylvania-027637)

Figure 12.11
Lethbridge Viaduct,
Lethbridge, Alberta

in a hurricane in 2003, and rebuilt and opened in 2011 as the Kinzua Skywalk. The Marent Trestle was first erected as a timber span in 1883. Rebuilt in steel in 1885 and reinforced in 1945, it is still in railroad use.

The Tulip Trestle, near Solsberry, Indiana—erected for the Indianapolis Southern Railroad in 1906 with steel bents and plate girder spans—is one of the longer historic railroad trestles in the United States: it measures 2,300 feet in length. The Indiana Railroad still uses it. One of the newest structures of this type is the Latah Creek Bridge, outside Spokane, Washington. It was built by the Burlington Northern Railway in 1972. Its steel box girders rest on tall, slender piers of reinforced concrete; it is 3,950 feet long and 210 feet high.

COVERED RAILROAD BRIDGES
Boston and Maine Railroad
1889
Contoocook and Newport, NH

To walk into a covered railroad bridge on a hot summer day is to enter a cool, dim, aerated timber tunnel with slit windows. The thin vertical spaces between the board siding, too narrow to provide views of the muffled world outside, create Mondrian-like patterns of light and shadow. Crossing the Contoocook Bridge on a train would be similar to going through a very short tunnel. And you would miss the lone graffito: "Naked thoughts."

Just a handful of covered railroad bridges still exist, mostly in the timber country of the Northeast and the Pacific Northwest. In the Northeast, the majority of them are in New Hampshire. Three of these are on the same railroad, the Boston and Maine, which acquired the old Concord and Claremont Railroad in 1887 and rebuilt the bridges for heavier traffic on the sites of earlier ones. One is at Contoocook, west of Concord; the other two—both near Newport, thirty miles to the west—are the Pier Bridge (it has a central pier) and Wright's Bridge, which incorporates laminated arches (see below).

All three are double web Town lattice trusses. This kind of truss consists of a trellis-like pattern

Figure 12.12
Covered railroad bridge, Contoocook, New Hampshire

of intersecting diagonal timbers, "more suitable for a fence than a bridge truss," according to Robert Fletcher and J. P. Snow.[41] Snow, engineer for the Boston and Maine, designed the bridge at Contoocook, the oldest of the trio, which was built by David Hazelton (or Haselton).

The authors observed that in 1900 there were roughly a hundred such bridges on the Boston and Maine and enumerated their virtues: They were relatively cheap and suitable for train traffic, in spans up to two hundred feet long. They were quickly and easily built, using minimal hardware and three-by-ten-inch spruce planks (readily available from New England's sawmills), by the competent mechanics of the nineteenth century, carpenters who specialized in such work. When properly covered and maintained, such bridges would last for a hundred years.

Ithiel Town (1784–1844), the architect and bridge designer who developed the lattice truss, patented it in 1820 and wrote a pamphlet the following year promoting his idea (Town was a great promoter). According to him, what was needed in an extensive country with many rivers was a standard timber or iron bridge that would be simple, permanent, and economical to erect and repair—that is, a bridge that would require the least amount of materials and labor. The Town lattice truss was the answer, he claimed, and later events proved him right. Hundreds of highway and railroad bridges using his truss form were built throughout the United States, most of them timber but some iron. The railroads in Europe also built such bridges, mostly in iron.

The Town lattice truss was the first modern truss design that was not dependent on the arch. Earlier bridge builders—notably Timothy Palmer, Lewis Wernwag, and Theodore Burr—incorporated arches into their work (arches were recommended for Town lattice truss bridges that spanned more than eighty feet). Wooden pegs (also called tree nails or trunnels) fastened the timbers together at the intersections and stiffened the structure. The lattice formed the web of the truss, and horizontal string pieces at top and bottom were the chords.

The major fault of the Town lattice truss was that, lacking vertical members, it tended to warp and twist. Town received another patent in 1835 to double the web on each side of the bridge, thus making it suitable for heavy railroad traffic. The addition of vertical posts at the portals and over the piers and more lateral and transverse bracing further strengthened the bridge and helped keep it in alignment. The timber framework handily accommodated the deck, vertical siding, and roof. The last two protected the truss from the weather and rot—which, as its designer pointed out, was absolutely necessary to ensure its longevity.

Town was born in Connecticut. His father died when he was eight, and Town worked as a house carpenter, taught school for a time, and went on to become a highly sophisticated architect. He formed one of the nation's first professional architectural firms with Alexander Jackson Davis in 1829; designed three state capitols (in Connecticut, Indiana, and North Carolina—the last of which is extant); and heralded the arrival of eclecticism in nineteenth-century American architecture with a trilogy of early buildings on the New Haven Green. The first was the neoclassical Center Church (circa 1814). Town contributed to the design and was responsible for its construction, which included raising the spire to the top of the tower with his own equipment. He next designed the Gothic revival Trinity Church (1816) and added the Connecticut State Capitol, in the Greek revival style (circa 1831). Connecticut had two state capitals, New Haven and Hartford, until 1875—when Hartford won out.

About 1816, Town worked briefly in Boston with Asher Benjamin, an important Federal period architect who is best known for publishing the nation's first architectural handbooks, including *The American Builder's Companion* and *The Practical House Carpenter*, which were widely used. For the next ten years, Town concentrated on bridges, building several over the Connecticut River and more in North Carolina, where he developed his truss form. As noted above, he formed an architectural partnership with Davis in 1829; it lasted for six years. One of their most important works was Glen Ellen (later demolished), near Baltimore. The first Picturesque Gothic revival house in America, it was built for Robert Gilmor Jr., a merchant and art collector.

The rights payments of $1–$2 per foot from the use of his bridge design enabled Town to travel to Europe (with Samuel F. B. Morse) and begin his own career as a collector. He amassed the finest collection of books on engineering, architecture, and the fine arts in the United States at that time (larger than Thomas Jefferson's library, the collection consisted of 11,000 volumes and 25,000 prints) and housed it at his home in New Haven, which he designed. Thomas Cole borrowed some of these books and drawings for his monumental 1840 painting, *The Architect's Dream*, commissioned by Town. It depicts an architect (apparently Town), reclining atop a classical column with his arm draped over the books and a portfolio of drawings lying at his feet. He regards an array of classical monuments, including Greek and Roman temples and a Gothic church. It is an allegorical recapitulation of the sources of American architectural eclecticism—and of Town's own essay on the subject portrayed in his buildings on the New Haven Green. Town disliked the painting, refused to accept it (he thought the landscape should be dominant), and asked Cole to do another. The artist huffily refused and returned the books and drawings.

Figure 12.13

Thomas Cole, *"The Architect's Dream,"* 1840 (courtesy of the Toledo Museum of Art)

The Town lattice truss bridge at Contoocook is a survivor. A flood and a hurricane in the 1930s both knocked it off its foundations (the steel rails remained connected and kept it from washing downstream). After railroad service on the bridge ended around 1960, a local merchant used it as a warehouse until the state acquired it in 1990 and restored it with the help of private groups. Supported by stone abutments and a central pier, the bridge is 157 feet long and 19 feet high. The siding stops short of the roofline, forming a clerestory that vented the smoke from the steam locomotives. The Contoocook Riverway Association owns the nearby Concord and Claremont Railroad station (circa 1850) and has also restored that building.

The two other covered railroad bridges on the old Concord and Claremont line, near Newport, New Hampshire, are the Pier Bridge (1907), which is 217 feet long and also has a central pier; and Wright's Bridge (1906), which is 123 feet long and incorporates arches. Both bridges are on the eight-mile Claremont-Newport Sugar River Trail, which is popular with local riders of all-terrain vehicles.

Directions to the Pier Bridge and Wright's Bridge: take Chandler's Mill Road off Route 11–103, circa three miles west of Newport.

Three covered railroad bridges in the Pacific Northwest used the Howe truss: the Chicago, Milwaukee, St. Paul and Pacific Railroad's bridge (1914) at Port Angeles, Washington; the Harpole Bridge (1922), built by the Great Northern Railway near Colfax, Washington; and the Chambers Bridge (1925), built for a logging spur at Cottage Grove, Oregon. Combining timber and metal (it used wooden diagonals and metal verticals), the Howe truss was very popular with railroads in the nineteenth and twentieth centuries for bridges and the roofs of stations and train sheds.

Figure 12.14
Pier Bridge, Newport, New Hampshire

CAPE COD CANAL RAILROAD BRIDGE
1935, Parsons, Brinckerhoff, Klapp and Douglas, engineers; McKim, Mead and White, architects
Bourne, MA

Starkly functional, movable bridges are not renowned for their grace and beauty. The Cape Cod Canal Railroad Bridge, however, manages to be both utilitarian and esthetically pleasing; it is arguably the handsomest of its type in the United States. The simple steel X trusses of the towers and entrance spans give it a remarkably light appearance. The 544-foot lift span, which has a Warren truss with verticals and a curved top chord, is the country's second longest. The architects doubtless contributed the scrolls that decorate the portal frames and the latticed Christmas trees atop the towers, which also use X trusses. The latter were meant to symbolize lighthouses, since the

bridge marks the eastern gateway to the Cape Cod Canal (their tops are illuminated at night).

The bridge operates like a window sash, with weights. The 2,200-ton lift span is raised and lowered by two 1,100-ton steel and concrete counterweights on either side, which are connected to the span by steel cables running over massive sheaves—each sixteen feet in diameter and weighing 34 tons. The sheaves turn on roller bearings, an innovation at the time. Raising or lowering the bridge takes two and a half minutes. All of the machinery is contained within the towers, which contributes to the span's simplified profile. The bridge was rehabilitated in 2003 at a cost of $30 million and is in regular railroad use.

William Barclay Parsons (1859–1932), whose firm was responsible for the bridge, was the chief engineer of the Cape Cod Canal. He was also one of the most accomplished and productive of American civil engineers. The scion of a prominent family in New York City (his great-grandfather was rector of Trinity Church; his father was a businessman), Parsons had a privileged upbringing. Schooled in Europe, he entered Columba University at the age of sixteen, graduating in 1879 with a bachelor of arts degree. He was his class president and cofounder of the student newspaper, the *Columbia Daily Spectator* (which is still distributed in Manhattan's Morningside Heights). Parsons earned a civil engineering degree from the Columbia School of Mines in 1882. He worked for the Erie Railroad, where he became a district engineer, before founding his own engineering firm in 1885. It evolved into Parsons, Brinckerhoff, one of the largest and most successful engineering companies in the nation (now WSP/Parsons Brinckerhoff).

In the early 1600s, Miles Standish of the Plymouth Colony first had the idea of cutting a canal through the isthmus of Cape Cod. The New York financier August Belmont decided to build such a canal in 1904 and hired Parsons as the engineer. Construction began in 1909, and the seventeen-mile, sea-level canal was opened in 1914 as a privately operated toll facility. But problems of construction (huge glacial boulders had to be blasted out of the way with dynamite) had resulted in the canal's being shallower than originally planned, which limited its ability to accommodate large ships. There were also operational difficulties. Three bascule bridges—two highway and one railroad—had been constructed as part of the project. Their constant raising and lowering hindered vehicular as well as maritime traffic, and their narrow openings, together with tidal currents of five miles per hour, caused accidents that closed the canal for long periods.

The tolls fell short of projected amounts, and Belmont tried to sell the canal to the federal government. The government took the canal over near the close of World War I as a navigational safety measure and made some improvements, later returning it to Belmont. He resumed operations, as well as negotiations with the government—which finally bought the canal in 1928 for $11.5 million.

A $21-million improvement program was initiated to widen and deepen the waterway and construct new crossings: fixed high-level bridges for vehicular traffic at Sagamore and Bourne, and a vertical-lift bridge at Bourne that would provide 135 feet of clearance over the canal (a fixed high-level railroad bridge was not feasible). The New Deal project provided much-needed jobs for 700 workers during the Depression; it was completed in 1940.

In the meantime, Parsons had been engaged in a number of high-profile assignments, including the construction of New York City's first subway line. Belmont also built this, and Parsons was its engineer. He inaugurated the cut-and-cover method of

Figure 12.15
Cape Cod Canal Railroad Bridge, Bourne, Massachusetts

Figure 12.16
Penn Central Bridge No. 1, Cleveland, Ohio (courtesy of Scott Lothes)

construction for the tunnel, insisted on electric traction, and devised a four-track system for local and express trains. The nine-mile Interborough Rapid Transit (IRT) line opened in 1904 and is still in service. It was one of the few of Parsons' major projects (the canal was another) that he did not write a book about.

Parsons surveyed a thousand-mile long railroad in Hunan Province, China (he wrote about that in *An American Engineer in China*). During World War I, he commanded a regiment of engineers (*The American Engineer in France*). He was a public transportation consultant in the United States and Europe (*Rapid Transit in Foreign Cities*). His magnum opus was published posthumously: a supremely well researched, informative, and readable history of his profession by a master practitioner of it, titled *Engineers and Engineering in the Renaissance*. The research was based on original documents, many of which Parsons discovered in the Vatican Library in Rome. Typically, he recommended that the library reorganize its cataloging

system according to his plan. With the approval of Pope Pius XI and the assistance of the Carnegie Institution, the reorganization took place.

Directions to the Cape Cod Canal Railroad Bridge: from the traffic circle at the Bourne Bridge, take Trowbridge Road, Bell Road, and then the Canal Service Road to the parking lot at the foot of the bridge.

PENN CENTRAL BRIDGE NO. 1
1956, Howard, Needles, Tammen, Bergendoff, engineers
Main Ave., Cleveland, OH

The many movable bridges—lift, bascule, and swing, for both highway and railroad crossings—that line the banks of the Cuyahoga River as it winds its way, snakelike, through the industrial flatlands below downtown Cleveland constitute an outdoor museum on the subject. Some are in a permanently raised position, the roads or rail lines they served no longer active. Others are often in motion, as recreational crafts and large ships move up and down the river.

One of the latter bridges is the Penn Central Bridge No. 1 (known as the Iron Curtain) that marks the entrance into the Cuyahoga River from Lake Erie. It was built as part of a program overseen by the US Corps of Engineers after World War II to replace six of Cleveland's bridges. The 265-foot lift span rises to a height of 90 feet over the river—several times an hour, because the rail line is heavily used by the Norfolk Southern and Amtrak, and lake freighters are regular visitors to the city. The railroad photographer Scott Lothes caught one of the "lakers" inbound at dusk (the restaurant Shooters on the Water provides a prime viewing spot).

Figure 12.17
St. Charles Air Line Bridge, Chicago, Illinois

ST. CHARLES AIR LINE BRIDGE
1919, Strauss Bascule Bridge Company;
1930, rebuilt and relocated to Tom Ping Park, Chicago, IL

Bascule bridges operate quickly (taking only one and a half minutes) and require little energy, but certainly no one could love them for their looks—only for their efficiency. The span of the St. Charles Air Line Bridge, built for a consortium of railroads, was initially a record 260 feet long, but it was shortened to 220 feet when it was moved. The planned relocation was part of a project to straighten the south branch of the Chicago River. It coincided with the construction of Union Station and was one of the first of many attempts to rationalize the tangle of rail lines entering the city.

Joseph Strauss (1870–1938) did as much as anyone to perfect the design of the bascule bridge. He was small in stature (five feet tall) but more than made up for that in ambition and ego. Strauss was born in Cincinnati, Ohio. His parents were artistic: his father was a writer and painter; his mother, a pianist. As a young man, Strauss wrote poetry and considered a career in the arts, but he became fascinated with bridges while attending the University of Cincinnati, from which he received a civil engineering degree in 1892.

Strauss spent seven years as a draftsman for steel companies before landing a job in Chicago with Ralph Modjeski, the famous bridge designer. While there, Strauss developed his trademark bascule bridge (which he later patented; there are several other types of such bridges), but he left in a dispute over a design and formed his own company in 1904.

The hinged bascule bridge operates like a seesaw, with a counterweight to balance the weight of the span. When it is raised, it turns on a pivot called a trunnion. A major problem is where to position the counterweight when the bridge is in the upright position.

Strauss made his counterweights of concrete, which was much cheaper than steel, and divided them into two wings rather than having one massive central one. He also perfected a rocking truss that folded the counterweights compactly back into the structure when the bridge was raised. Strauss built hundreds of these bascule bridges, including several over the Chicago River that are still in operation.

He is mainly known as the chief engineer of San Francisco's Golden Gate Bridge (1937). Strauss had never built a suspension bridge before, and in an attempt to claim sole credit for it, he downplayed the contributions of the other engineers who were primarily responsible for its final configuration and minimalist profile. It was only a decade ago that one of them—Charles Ellis, the principal engineer—was recognized for his part in the design of the Golden Gate Bridge.

To the north of the St. Charles Air Line Bridge, the B&O Railroad Chicago Terminal bridge (1930) is also a Strauss bascule span. This particular rail line is no longer active, and the bridge is permanently locked in the upright position.

To the south is the Canal Street Railroad Bridge, a lift span designed by Waddell and Harrington, engineers; erected in 1915; and still in service. John Alexander Waddell (1854–1938), was born in Port Hope, Ontario, trained at the Rensselaer Polytechnic Institute, and wrote several books on bridge engineering. He was to vertical-lift spans what Strauss was to bascule bridges—that is, a major developer and practitioner. Waddell's firm designed over a hundred movable bridges.

All three Chicago bridges can be conveniently viewed from the 18th Street overpass or Ping Tom Memorial Park. The raised B&O Railroad Chicago Terminal bridge is a local landmark.

PETALUMA RIVER SWING BRIDGE
(also known as the Black Point Bridge)
1911
Northwestern Pacific Railroad, near Novato, CA

As opposed to moving up and down, swing bridges rotate horizontally on an axis—a central pier. They were the earliest kind of movable bridge used by railroads, but they fell out of favor due to the advantages of other types. Swing bridges take three to five times as long to open or close as vertical-lift and bascule bridges. And although the spans of swing bridges are normally left in the open position, the central piers pose a hazard to navigation. In fact, the Petaluma River Swing Bridge was hit by a tug towing a sand barge in 2008, but the structure was undamaged. It had been out of operation for a number of years when the accident happened, but it was reopened to rail service in 2011.

Figure 12.18

Petaluma River Swing Bridge, near Novato, California (photo by Marty Zwick)

Also known as the Black Point Bridge, it was built on a branch line—mainly a lumber route of the Northwestern Pacific Railway, which ran from San Rafael to Eureka. The 246-foot Warren truss swing span is approached by long trestles on either side. The 2007 photograph of Marty Zwick, an architect, catches it in a ghostly light, with the operator's shack atop the bridge.

Directions to the Petaluma River Swing Bridge:
take Route 37 off Highway 101 south of Novato; then take the Atherton Avenue. exit toward Black Point, and merge onto Harbor Drive.

People at the Vancouver, Washington, Amtrak station have a good view of the operation of the 1908 swing span designed by Modjeski at an important rail junction and crossing of the Columbia River.

STAPLE BEND TUNNEL
Allegheny Portage Railroad
1834, Sylvester Welch, chief engineer
near Johnstown, PA

A bicyclist approaching the western portal of the Staple Bend Tunnel in the hills five miles east of Johnstown, Pennsylvania, for the first time might feel a little like an explorer stumbling unexpectedly upon a vine-covered Mayan ruin in a Yucatan Peninsula jungle.

To impress travelers on the Allegheny Portage

Figure 12.19

Staple Bend Tunnel, near
Johnstown, Pennsylvania

Railroad—and to mark their own achievement in constructing it—the Irish
and Welsh masons who built America's first railroad tunnel decorated the
openings with classical façades. They chose the framed arch motif, seen
in the Coliseum and the triumphal arches of ancient Rome. Under a plain
frieze and cornice, Tuscan pilasters stood on either side of the voussoirs
outlining the elliptical arch. The matching façade at the eastern entrance
suffered a fate similar to that of many Roman monuments: parts of it were
stolen for use in other buildings.

The tunnel, 900 feet long and 20 feet in diameter, took two years to build
with hand drills and black power; the central section was blasted through
solid rock. Half of the $37,500 cost went to the classical tunnel faces.

The Staple Bend Tunnel was located near the western end of the thirty-
six-mile Allegheny Portage Railroad that extended from Hollidaysburg to
Johnstown. The railroad was a key piece of Pennsylvania's Main Line of
Internal Improvements, the state's entry in the race of the cities on the
Eastern seaboard to reach the inland waterways and capture the Western
trade. New York's Erie Canal and Maryland's B&O Railroad were its main
competitors. Pennsylvania's entry, running 395 miles between Philadelphia
and Pittsburgh, was a hybrid system: about two-thirds of it was made up
of canals, and one-third of railroads.

Since canals are unsuited to mountainous terrain, the Allegheny Portage
Railroad was constructed to link two canal segments of the route. Ten inclined planes powered by stationary steam engines lifted the freight and
passengers over the heights. The inclined planes were interspersed with
level sections. For example, the tunnel terminated in a long level stretch at
the eastern end.

Operating the Allegheny Portage Railroad required unloading the canal boats at one end, transferring the goods and people to railroad cars, and then reversing the process at the other end. Later, canal boats, built in two sections for easier handling, were floated onto railroad flatcars and pulled up on land in a procedure similar to that used in a marine railway. The boats were then attached to ropes and dragged up and down the hills by the stationary engines. Before locomotives were brought in, horsepower was used on the level sections between the planes.

Although it was regarded as an engineering marvel at the time, the Allegheny Portage Railroad was an operational nightmare. The frequent shifting of passengers and freight between the different modes of conveyance was troublesome, time-consuming, and labor-intensive. There was a great deal of putting on and taking off of ropes between the inclined planes and the level sections. In addition, the ropes—giant hawsers three and a half inches in diameter—failed frequently, partly because they were made of defective materials. Eventually they were replaced with the first wire rope manufactured by John Roebling at Johnstown, which was later used in the suspension cables supporting his Brooklyn Bridge. The entire Main Line of Internal Improvements shut down during the winter, when the canal sections froze.

Nevertheless, the Allegheny Portage Railroad did an acceptable job of moving the traffic over the mountain. In its first year of operation, it carried 40,000 tons of freight (roughly the payload weight of a single modern railroad boxcar). The shippers furnished their own horses.

The railroad lasted twenty years, until it was in 1854 replaced by the Pennsylvania Railroad. (The B&O Railroad found that locomotives could bypass the inclined planes on its route between Baltimore and the Potomac River in 1834, the same year that the Allegheny Portage Railroad opened.) The abandoned tunnel was used for water storage for a time in the twentieth century.

The Staple Bend Tunnel, restored by the National Park Service, is reached by a two-mile walk from the parking lot. It follows the former right-of-way of the Allegheny Portage Railroad and presents excellent examples of masonry such as culverts and the remaining single track of stone blocks to which the rails were attached. Nearby is the former Pennsylvania Railroad's main line, the all-rail route between Philadelphia and Pittsburgh and beyond that finally put the jury-rigged system of railroads and canals out of business. The line closely follows the Allegheny Portage's route in this area and carries frequent freight trains (now on the Norfolk Southern), a single one of which takes over the mountains what the Allegheny Portage would have needed many months to transport.

Directions to the Staple Bend Tunnel: take the Mundy's Corner/Nanty Glo exit from Route 22; go south on Route 271 for five miles to Mineral Point Road (PA 3030); take a left and go two miles to Beech Hill Road and through the railroad underpass to the parking lot on the right.

In the 1960s the National Park Service took over the Allegheny Portage Railroad and restored its other surviving facilities, in the 1990s adding a visitors' center at Gallitzin that has transportation exhibits. A short walk from the center takes visitors to the Cresson Summit, where there is a restored tavern that refreshed travelers at the top of the hill. A re-created stationary engine house, erected on the site of the original one, displays the complex machinery needed to operate the inclined plane—a good illustration of why stationary steam engines, which were once proposed as the motive power for railroads, were replaced by locomotives. In the immediate vicinity are the famed Horseshoe Curve and the Gallitzin Tunnels, built by the Pennsylvania Railroad around 1854.

BLUE RIDGE TUNNEL
1858, Claudius Crozet, engineer
near Waynesboro, VA

Like Pennsylvania, Virginia cobbled together a collection of canals and railroads to reach the West. Two integral components were the Blue Ridge Railroad and the James River and Kanawha Canal. It was not until

1873, that—under the direction of Collis P. Huntington (of Big Four fame; see chapter 11)—a complete railroad, the Chesapeake and Ohio Railway, ran the whole way from Richmond, the state's capital, to the Ohio River at Huntington, West Virginia. In 1881 the railroad was extended to the tidewater port of Newport News, Virginia.

In the mid-nineteenth century, the Virginia Central Railroad was laying track in the Waynesboro area, but it lacked the resources to build the four tunnels necessary to cross the Blue Ridge at Rockfish Gap. So in 1849 the State of Virginia formed the Blue Ridge Railroad and gave the job to its engineer, Claudius Crozet.

Figure 12.20
Blue Ridge Tunnel, near Waynesboro, Virginia

Born in France, Crozet (1790–1864) was a graduate of the prestigious Ecole Polytechnique and of military school; he served as a captain in the army under Napoleon. Crozet came to the United States in 1816 to become professor of engineering at the US Military Academy at West Point, New York—at that time the country's only source of trained engineers. He revised the curriculum, grounding it in French rationalism (France was then a world leader in civil engineering). Many of the West Point professors and engineering textbooks came from France, and the only foreign language taught at the academy was French (the language of science in the early nineteenth century).

In 1823, Crozet became the engineer for the State of Virginia and participated in the survey for the James River and Kanawha Canal. He was employed elsewhere after that, but he returned to Virginia about fifteen years later to take up his old job as state engineer just as Virginia's transportation priorities were shifting from canals to railroads. He surveyed the railroad route across the Blue Ridge in 1839. Work began on the tunnel, the longest of the four that were necessary, ten years later.

Its construction, with hand drills and black powder, by Irish laborers and black slaves under the direction of contractors John Kelly and John Larguey, was complicated by labor disputes, underground water, and a cholera epidemic that killed thirty-three Irish workers. When it was finished, it was the longest tunnel of its kind: four-fifths of a mile in length and about twenty feet high and sixteen feet wide. It was also the last major tunnel to be built without mechanical assistance. The first train passed through it in 1858. The final cost was $488,000.

The western entrance to the Blue Ridge Tunnel has a cut stone frieze and cornice, with voussoirs outlining the elliptical arch (the eastern entrance is just the bare rock opening). Crozet chose the unusual shape because he felt that it was the strongest arch form to use in an area where rock fissures had weakened the overlying greenstone—a volcanic rock common to the Shenandoah Valley.

In 1942 the C&O Railway built new tunnels in

the area to accommodate larger trains, and the Blue Ridge Tunnel was abandoned. A failed attempt in the following decade to use it to store natural gas left two reinforced concrete bulkheads, each about ten feet thick, inside the tunnel. In 2007, Nelson County acquired the property, and the Claudius Crozet Blue Ridge Tunnel Foundation was established to restore the tunnel and make the sections of the abandoned right-of-way on either side into a rail trail.

Directions to the Blue Ridge Tunnel: the western entrance with the finished tunnel face is accessible from Route 250, east of Waynesboro. Park opposite the Colony Hotel and follow the trail from an abandoned section of Route 250. The eastern entrance is also accessible from Route 250, east of the Blue Ridge Parkway. Take Route 6 south to Afton Depot Lane and turn right to the parking lot.

GREAT BEND TUNNEL
Chesapeake and Ohio Railway
1872
near Talcott, WV

As the C&O extended westward through the mountains, more tunnels were needed. With a length of one and a quarter miles, the Great Bend Tunnel was the longest in the entire C&O system. It was built to cut off a long meandering loop of the Greenbrier River located about ten miles east of its confluence with the New River, at Hinton, West Virginia.

Irish immigrant laborers and freed slaves— roughly eight hundred men altogether, made up the workforce, but this time they were probably aided by machinery. Construction started in 1870. Two vertical shafts were excavated from the ridgetop so that work could proceed at six tunnel faces simultaneously. The major problem was the material: the red shale crumbled when it was exposed to air, resulting in numerous collapses and landslides that killed several workers (as did silicosis, caused by inhaling the dust generated by the drilling and blasting).

Supposedly, one of the workers was the legendary John Henry—the African American steel-driving

Figure 12.21
Great Bend Tunnel, near Talcott, West Virginia

man who died with a hammer in his hand in a contest with a steam drill, according to the popular ballad (historical evidence suggests that there was a real John Henry who built railroads, but it is not clear exactly who he was or where he worked).

On the centennial of the tunnel's completion, the Hillsdale-Talcott Ruritan Club, dedicated to "community service in rural areas," unveiled Charles O. Cooper's bronze statue of John Henry. According to the plaque, "this statue was erected in 1972 by a group of people with the same determination as the one it honors."

The statue did not fare well on its ridgetop site over the tunnel. It was vandalized several times, pockmarked with bullet holes, and even knocked off its base and dragged down the highway behind a pickup truck. In 2012, the restored statue was moved to its present location in the twenty-six-acre John Henry Historical Park, near the mouth of the Great Bend Tunnel. The original tunnel was closed in 1974; CSX Transportation's freight trains pass regularly through the newer one next to it, built in 1932.

13

MOVING STRUCTURES
(Locomotives and Coaches)

Lucius Beebe, the grandiloquent chronicler of trains (he is the author of some forty books on the subject, including the first book of railroad photographs) regarded the luxurious Pullman passenger coaches and private railroad cars as "an extension of the deluxe hotels of the period in which railroading saw its golden era."[43] (Beebe's private railroad car, the Gold Coast, can be seen at the California State Railroad Museum, in Sacramento, California.)

Railroad coaches, in turn, influenced static architecture. The architectural historian Clay Lancaster likened Frank Lloyd Wright's famous Robie House in Chicago, Illinois, to an open-vestibule passenger coach. According to Lancaster, "the long, low lines of his characteristic 'prairie house,' with its horizontal strip windows, echo the forms of the trains that race across the flatlands."[44] Another architectural historian, Sigfried Giedion, has pointed out that the design of the domestic kitchen derives in part from the economical use of space in the railroad dining car.[45]

Prominent architects and leading industrial designers had a hand in creating railroad structures that moved: coaches; lounge, dining, and observation cars; locomotives; and entire streamlined trains. Most of this equipment ended up in the scrap yard, but there are some notable exceptions. Chief among them is the 1934 Pioneer Zephyr, the first successful high-speed diesel-electric train, which is exhibited at the Museum of Science and Industry in Chicago.

In the 1880s two well-known architects, Frank Furness and Bruce Price, designed entire passenger coaches (as opposed to only styling the interiors) that were built and run on the railroads. The Reading Railroad operated several passenger cars assembled according to Furness's plans. One, described as a Swiss cottage on wheels, had exposed wood and iron rafters and an interior of paneled oak. The architect also designed what were called two magnificent mahogany coaches for the Reading that were evidently as unique as his buildings. A reporter said they would be different, inside and outside, from any cars seen thus far on any railroad.

Trains were wonderfully powerful metaphors — of time and distance and journey, of setting out and return, of anticipation and adventure — and the architecture gloried in all that.

ROBERT IRWIN[42]

243

Besides his bay-window parlor car for the Pennsylvania Railroad (see chapter 2), Price also designed the interior of a drawing room car for the Boston and Albany Railroad. It offered passengers upholstered settees, armchairs, and footstools.

None of these architect-designed railroad cars seems to have survived. Plans and renderings of Price's passenger coaches appeared in railroad journals of the time, but no illustrations of Furness's cars have surfaced so far.

While Edward Colonna's name is less familiar than those of Furness and Price, he was a major figure in the art nouveau movement. He also designed railroad stations and passenger cars. Miraculously, his Milwaukee, Lakeshore and Western Railroad Coach No. 63, discovered in ignominious circumstances in a Chicago produce terminal, has been rescued and lovingly restored by the Mid-Continent Railway Museum, in North Freedom, Wisconsin—where it is on display. The coach is one of the very few remaining examples of Colonna's railroad designs.

PIONEER ZEPHYR
**Chicago, Burlington and Quincy Railroad
1934, Albert and Walter Dean, engineers;
 Paul Philippe Cret and John Harbeson, architects
Museum of Science and Industry, 5700 S. Lake Shore
 Drive, Chicago, IL**

The Pioneer Zephyr was in all ways revolutionary, from its articulated (see below), stainless steel body and its diesel power plant to its influence on subsequent developments in the railroad industry. The nation's first streamlined train with a diesel engine, it introduced high-speed rail travel to the United States. On its record-breaking May 26, 1934, run from Denver, Colorado, to the Century of Progress Exhibition in Chicago, the Pioneer Zephyr raced nonstop 1,015 miles in a little over thirteen hours, averaging 78 miles per hour and reaching speeds of 112 miles per hour. Two decades would pass before American railroads became fully convinced of the advantages of the diesel engine (which was four times more efficient than the steam engine), but the Pioneer Zephyr

signaled the demise of the steam locomotive as their prime mover.

Like most great inventions, the Pioneer Zephyr was the product of many minds and talents. The first mind belonged to Ralph Budd (1879–1962), who had become president of the Chicago, Burlington and Quincy Railroad in 1932. Like many a career railroad man, Budd started out as a surveyor. In the early 1900s, still in his twenties, he worked with the engineer John F. Stevens on the Panama Railway for the canal project. He followed Stevens to the Pacific Northwest, where the latter was serving as a consultant for his old boss, James J. Hill of the Great Northern Railway (see chapter 14). Stevens brought Budd to Hill's attention, and when Hill retired as president, he named Budd to replace him. In 1919, at the age of forty, Budd was the youngest head of a major railroad in the United States. He and Stevens continued their collaboration on the Great Northern's eight-mile Cascade Tunnel (1929) at Skykomish, Washington, which replaced an earlier tunnel in an area prone to heavy snows and avalanches.

At the Chicago, Burlington and Quincy, Budd was an innovator par excellence. During the height of the Depression, he approved an experimental high-speed train that he hoped would attract new riders—automobiles were serious competitors to the railroads, particularly over short distances—and reawaken a somnolent industry that had grown accustomed to doing things the old way.

Representatives of the Electro-Motive Division of the General Motors Corporation approached Budd in 1933 about a lightweight diesel engine they had been working on. Even though the engine was new and untried, Budd decided to use it for the new train, which he named the Zephyr. He chose the name after one of his officers suggested that since it was to be the last word in transportation, they should name the train after the last word in the dictionary. This proved unworkable, but Budd, recalling some lines from Chaucer's *Canterbury Tales* in which Zephyrus, god of the west wind, symbolizes rebirth, picked Zephyr.

Budd turned over the design of the train to Edward G. Budd (no relation), a metal fabricator and

Figure 13.1

Pioneer Zephyr, Museum of Science and Industry, Chicago, Illinois

machinist. In his Philadelphia plant in 1913, Edward Budd had made the first welded all-steel automobile bodies, which found ready buyers in Detroit and in Europe (one of his advertisements showed an elephant standing atop a Budd steel–frame automobile). The Edward G. Budd Manufacturing Company invented the "shotweld" technique for welding stainless steel without compromising its strength or corrosion resistance. Edward Budd used this new technology to produce the Pioneer Zephyr, whose welded, all-steel coach frames formed structural units (as opposed to being built up from individual wood and metal parts, as had previously been done).

Budd Company engineers Albert and Walter Dean, brothers and graduates of the Massachusetts Institute of Technology (MIT), worked on the train's power plant, running gear, and exterior appearance, including the sloping, shovel-nose engine front designed to facilitate air flow (tests at MIT showed that at high speeds the Zephyr had less than half the air resistance of a conventional train). The stainless steel sides of the cars were fluted. Power was transmitted to the wheels by electric traction motors. The train was articulated—that is, two cars were connected by and rode on a single truck, rather than having separate cars each riding on two trucks and linked by couplers (the standard arrangement). Its low center of gravity allowed it to take curves faster. The Zephyr was 196 feet long and weighed little more than a standard Pullman coach; it carried seventy passengers.

The architectural firm Cret and Harbeson designed the train's interior, which featured comfortable

Figure 13.2
Pioneer Zephyr, coach interior, Museum of
Science and Industry, Chicago, Illinois

upholstered seats, recessed fluorescent lighting, and large windows with curtains. Born in Lyon, France, Paul Philippe Cret (1876–1945) studied at the École des Beaux-Arts and came to the United States in 1903 to teach architecture at the University of Pennsylvania. He ended up heading the university's architecture department for thirty years. In 1907, Cret opened an architecture office in which John F. Harbeson (1888–1986), who also taught architecture at the University of Pennsylvania, was a partner. Cret was visiting France when World War I broke out. He joined the French Army and served for the duration of the war. He was awarded the Croix de Guerre.

Working in an abstract classical style, Cret designed a number of important buildings, bridges, and memorials. They include the Pan American Union Building (1910) and the Folger Shakespeare Library (1932), both in Washington, D.C.; the Detroit Institute of Arts (1921), in Michigan; and the Rodin Museum and Benjamin Franklin Bridge (both 1926), both in Philadelphia, Pennsylvania. Cret was a design consultant for Fellheimer and Wagner's Art Deco Cincinnati Union Terminal (1933), in Ohio.

Following its widely publicized debut, the Pioneer Zephyr was put into regular service between Kansas City, Missouri, and Lincoln, Nebraska. It attracted so much business that a car was added and five more trainsets, each consisting of the engine and three cars,

were ordered from the Budd Company. Even though the $250,000 Pioneer Zephyr was twice the price of a steam-powered train, it also produced twice the revenue and cut operating costs in half—and at the end of the year it showed a profit. The train starred in a 1934 Hollywood melodrama, *Silver Streak* (another movie by that name, also about a train and starring Gene Wilder and Richard Pryor, appeared in 1976).

Other railroads quickly got aboard. The Union Pacific's three-car, high-speed aluminum-covered train also appeared in 1934. More companies followed suit with their own streamliners. Many were redesigned steam trains with sleek, aerodynamic jackets for the locomotives and the latest in modern furnishings for the coaches. The industrial designer Henry Dreyfuss redesigned the New York Central's Twentieth Century Limited inside and out, and Raymond Loewy did the same for the Pennsylvania Railroad's Broadway Limited. The Santa Fe Railway's Super Chief was styled by the industrial designer Sterling McDonald and the artist Leland Knickerbocker (the latter came up with the famous warbonnet design that was painted on the engine. And there were later editions of the original, the Denver Zephyr and the California Zephyr.

Streamlined trains not only looked fast, they actually were faster than their predecessors. Schedules tightened, and running times between major terminals were reduced by about a third. By the end of the decade, "the ten fastest trains in the world were all U.S. streamliners."[46]

After his initial success with the Pioneer Zephyr, Cret continued to do a great deal of work for the railroads, including designs for the Denver Zephyr and the Seaboard Air Line Railway's Silver Meteor. A corner of his Philadelphia office was devoted to fabrics, color swatches, and paint samples.

The Edward G. Budd Manufacturing Company extended its success as a builder not only of automobile car bodies, but also of lightweight stainless steel railroad passenger and Vista Dome coaches and subway cars. In 1949, the company introduced the Rail Diesel Car, a stainless steel, self-propelled passenger coach. Also known as Budd cars, these were especially popular with commuter rail lines. In the 1960s, the Budd Company built the first Metroliner coaches for Amtrak.

Despite the initial resistance of conservative railroad executives to its innovative products; severe competition from the Pullman Company, builder of standard passenger coaches; and the vicissitudes of the economy, the Budd Company's designs and methods of fabrication became the railroad industry standard.

GG1 LOCOMOTIVE NO. 4935
Pennsylvania Railroad Juniata Shops
1943, Raymond Loewy, stylist
Railroad Museum of Pennsylvania,
    300 Gap Rd., Strasburg, PA

If you had taken the train between New York City and Washington, D.C., or from Philadelphia to Harrisburg, Pennsylvania, during the period 1935–80, chances are that you rode behind one of the classic GG1 locomotives. In 1934, the Pennsylvania Railroad, desiring an engine that could pull a dozen or more passenger coaches, ordered 139 of them. The overall design—contoured chassis and wheel arrangement—evolved gradually, after experimental testing with earlier electric locomotives.

The GG1 was double-ended, so it could travel in the opposite direction without having to be turned; the engineer's cabs were in the center for safety reasons; and the locomotive frame was articulated so it could negotiate tight curves. Loewy recommended that the engine shell be welded rather than riveted to produce a smooth finish and added the painted pinstripes. The result was a streamlined piece of functional railroad sculpture.

Eighty feet long, weighing 230 tons, and with 4,620 horsepower, the GG1 locomotive could cruise at a hundred miles per hour. Power was delivered to the traction motors via an overhead catenary wire (the routes were electrified in 1935).

Figure 13.3
GG1 Locomotive No. 4935, Railroad Museum of Pennsylvania, Strasburg, Pennsylvania

Of the 139 units built, 16 survive. When Engine 4935, in her original livery of Brunswick green with yellow pinstripes, pulled the Broadway Limited from New York City to Harrisburg in April 1980, it ended the GG1 era.

ENGINE NO. 490
Chesapeake and Ohio Railway,
    Huntington, West Virginia, shops
1947, Alexander C. Robinson III, stylist
B&O Railroad Museum
Pratt and Poppleton Sts., Baltimore, MD

Engine 490 is a good illustration of how the railroads streamlined their older steam engines. The Chesapeake and Ohio (C&O) Railway's Pacific type (4-6-2) passenger engine was built in 1926 by the American Locomotive Company (usually referred to as Alco), one of the two major builders of steam locomotives in America—the other being the Baldwin Locomotive Works. (Frederic M. Whyte of the New York Central Railroad devised a system for classifying steam locomotives according to the number of wheels, reading front to back—for example, a 4-6-2 engine has four leading wheels, six larger driving wheels, and two trailing wheels.) Engine 490 powered some of the railroad's premier passenger trains.

Following World War II, the C&O Railway wanted to upgrade its passenger service and improve its steam technology. Since it was cheaper to convert some of its older engines than to buy new ones, the company's shops rebuilt the Pacific type steam locomotives as Hudson (4-6-4) engines and modernized their equipment as well as their looks. New valves, drivers, and roller bearings were installed, and the locomotive and tender were clothed in a streamlined shroud. The latter had a bulbous nose and a curved monitor that started at the headlight and extended back over the top of the engine to the cab, giving it something of the appearance of a Roman helmet. The fluted side skirts were raised over the driving wheels.

The engine shroud was designed by Alexander Robinson (1892–1985), regarded as the dean of

Figure 13.4
Engine No. 490, B&O Railroad Museum, Baltimore, Maryland

architects in Cleveland, Ohio (the C&O, controlled by the Van Sweringen brothers [see chapter 3], was headquartered in Cleveland's Terminal Tower). Originally from Pennsylvania, Robinson was a graduate of Princeton University and had an architecture degree from Columbia University.

After practicing in Pittsburgh, Robinson moved to Cleveland in 1920 to work with Abram Garfield, the architect son of James A. Garfield, the former US president. The firm Garfield, Harris, Robinson and Schafer designed several landmark buildings in Cleveland and federal buildings elsewhere. Robinson, who served on planning commissions in Cleveland and Washington, D.C., was known to speak his mind. He said that Marcel Breuer's 1971 Cleveland Trust Tower reminded him of stacks of precast bathtubs. After he retired he said he became the father confessor to young architects.

Engine 490 continued to haul prestige passenger trains until its retirement in 1953, after which it was stored in the C&O Railway shops. The B&O Railroad Museum acquired it in 1968.

ENGINE NO. 611

**Norfolk and Western Railway,
Roanoke, Virginia, shops**

1950

**Virginia Museum of Transportation,
303 Norfolk Ave., SW, Roanoke, VA**

In late 1934, the New York Central Railroad shrouded one of its Hudson engines to create the first American streamlined steam locomotive. The final versions of these engines were built in the Norfolk and Western (N&W) Railway's legendary Roanoke shops (the N&W was the last railroad to abandon the use of steam as a driving force, enabling O. Winston Link to create his iconic photographs [see chapter 1]).

The N&W's streamlined Class J locomotive is unusual in that it was not styled by an architect or industrial designer, but rather by the talented mechanical engineers, locomotive designers, and shop craftsmen who built it. The design is simple and effective: a smooth, black, bullet-nosed jacket covers the boiler, leaving the wheels and running gear exposed.

Horizontal tubular chrome accents highlight the engine front, and a handrail of the same material stretches back to the cab. The only other decoration is a Tuscan Red stripe outlined in yellow that visually links the locomotive and tender and carries the messages "611" and "Norfolk and Western." The 4-8-4 Northern type steam locomotive could pull fifteen passenger coaches at 110 miles per hour.

No. 611 made its last scheduled run in 1959. The Norfolk Southern Railroad used the engine to haul excursion trains until 1994, when it was retired to the Virginia Museum of Transportation in Roanoke. Then in 2013, the decision was made to return No. 611 to steam excursion service. After a two-year, $4.5-million restoration at the North Carolina Transportation Museum (the former Southern Railway shop complex) at Spencer, North Carolina, No. 611 is once again back on the road. When it is not running, it can be seen at the Virginia Museum of Transportation.

Charles W. "Wick" Moorman—the former chairman of the Norfolk Southern Corporation and president of Amtrak (2016–17), who was instrumental in

Figure 13.5

Engine No. 611, Virginia Museum of Transportation, Roanoke, Virginia

Figure 13.6
Milwaukee, Lakeshore and Western Railway Coach No. 63, interior,
Mid-Continent Railway Museum, North Freedom, Wisconsin

sponsoring the railroad's steam excursion program and the restoration of No. 611—called the engine "an American classic, a reflection of a time and a people who put the country on their backs and carried it into the modern age of railroading."[47]

MILWAUKEE, LAKESHORE AND WESTERN RAILWAY COACH NO. 63
1888, Edward Colonna, interior designer
Mid-Continent Railway Museum,
E8948 Museum Rd., North Freedom, WI

The German-born Edward Colonna (1862–1948), an unsung pioneer of the art nouveau style, was also an architect and interior designer who did a good deal of work for the railroads. Colonna studied architecture in Brussels, Belgium, before emigrating to the United

States in 1882. In New York City, he was a member of Louis Comfort Tiffany's interior decorating firm for a few years and then was associated with the architect Bruce Price. Price had done some business with the Barney and Smith Manufacturing Company of Dayton, Ohio, major builders of railroad coaches. It was probably through Price that the company hired Colonna as a designer in 1885.

While he was in Dayton, Colonna published two small design books. The first, *Essay on Broom Corn* (1887) showed examples of his jewelry and other items whose sinuous, wavelike lines based on natural forms were prophetic of things to come. The second was *Materiae Signa, Alchemistic Signs of Various Materials in Common Usage* (1888), a book of architectural motifs.

Colonna left Barney and Smith in 1888 and went to

Figure 13.7

Milwaukee, Lakeshore and Western Railway Coach
No. 63, men's or women's room, Mid-Continent Railway
Museum, North Freedom, Wisconsin

Van Horne's Montreal mansion when it was altered in 1890 (it was later demolished). The rotunda and dining room of Toronto's King Edward Hotel (1903) were also designed by him.

In 1893 Colonna returned to Europe, joining Siegfried Bing's stable of artists in Paris. A German art dealer and entrepreneur, Bing had moved to France in the 1850s to manage his family's ceramics manufacturing business. He later operated an import-export firm, specializing in Oriental art. In 1895 Bing opened the Maison de l'Art Nouveau in Paris. A combined gallery and atelier, it promoted and provided the name for a modern art style that was new, not a recasting of historical styles (in Spain, art nouveau was called modernismo).

Henri van de Velde, a Belgian architect, painter, and writer, designed the galleries that displayed fabrics by William Morris, a leader of the British Arts and Crafts movement; Tiffany stained glass; and jewelry, paintings, ceramics, and furniture crafted by the artists who were members of Bing's atelier. They included the painter Georges de Fuere, the architect Eugene Gaillard, and Colonna.

The Paris Exposition Universelle of 1900 introduced the art nouveau style to the world. Bing's galleries were in the Blue Pavilion, whose art nouveau

Montreal, Quebec, where he opened an architectural office. At that time Price was working for the Canadian Pacific Railway (CPR) on Montreal's Windsor Station and the company's first hotels (see chapter 2). Price may have introduced Colonna to the CPR's president, William C. Van Horne. In any case, Colonna ended up designing car interiors for the CPR, which purchased passenger coaches from Barney and Smith.

He was also the architect for at least eight CPR train stations, stretching from Quebec to British Columbia, during the years 1889–93. His station for Windsor, Ontario, featured a distinctive medieval round tower with a flared conical roof. All have been demolished or substantially altered, with the possible exception of the station in Portage La Prairie, Minnesota (1893). That was badly damaged in a 2002 fire but restored in 2008. Colonna designed most of the interior of

Figure 13.8

Milwaukee, Lakeshore and Western Railway
Coach No. 63, Mid-Continent Railway Museum,
North Freedom, Wisconsin

façade stood out, like a building by Antonio Gaudí, from the surrounding landscape of overwrought classical architecture of the exposition. Colonna decorated a salon in the Blue Pavilion. He won a silver medal, and some of the furniture shown went into production. The previous year, at another Paris exposition, Bing exhibited the silver mounts that Colonna had designed for several Tiffany favrile glass vases.

Bing closed the Maison de l'Art Nouveau in 1903; he died two years later. Colonna returned to Canada —going to Toronto this time—where he continued his design work and became an antiques dealer. His declining years were spent in the south of France. He was buried in an unmarked pauper's grave in Nice.

The art nouveau movement had a profound influence on art and architecture—from the work of Charles Rennie Mackintosh in Scotland to that of Louis Sullivan in the United States—as well as on interior furnishings, jewelry, and even film. At the beginning of the twenty-first century, the Victoria and Albert Museum and the National Gallery of Art presented *Art Nouveau, 1890–1914*, the most comprehensive exhibit on the subject to date (the catalog shows examples of Colonna's textile designs and his salon for the Paris Exposition Universelle).

Subdued in comparison to the later developments in Paris, Colonna's 1888 interior design for the Milwaukee, Lakeshore and Western Railway coach is simple and tasteful. The interior—even the window blinds—is finished in cherry wood. Above the fluted pilasters that separate the windows are individual metal luggage racks, decorated with a floral motif. The coved ceiling is stenciled with patterns based on the anthemion and palmette, and the panels of the clerestory ceiling are likewise bordered by stenciled designs. The men's and women's rooms in diagonally opposite corners of the car have recessed panel doors and walls linked by a Corinthian column. The coach was heated by cast-iron coal stoves at the ends of the car. The seats—made of cast iron with wood frames—had upholstered backs and cushions covered in a maroon mohair fabric.

The Chicago and Northwestern Railway, which had taken over the original line, retired the coach in the 1920s and sent it to the company's Chicago produce terminal. With the wheels removed, it was set on a concrete foundation and used as an office. In 1970, no longer needing the office, the railroad donated the car body to the Mid-Continent Railway Museum. Enough was left of the original interior (after several coats of paint were removed) to enable craftsmen to replicate the stenciled panels and other details. The missing seats were replaced with new ones based on another Barney and Smith coach at the Nevada State Railway Museum that had been badly damaged in a fire that burned the top and sides of the car but left the seats. The cast-iron stoves are period reproductions created by Pennsylvania's Strasburg Railroad. The $350,000 restoration, which included remounting the car on wheels, was completed in 2003.

14

MONUMENTS

The railroads created monuments, including some designed by famous artists and architects, to commemorate their accomplishments and memorialize their officers and employees. The greatest is the Union Pacific Railway's Ames Monument, a six-story-tall granite pyramid at what was once Sherman, Wyoming. The oldest is a simple granite obelisk erected in 1835 to mark the building of the Baltimore and Ohio (B&O) Railroad's Thomas Viaduct at Relay, Maryland.

Railroad presidents were especially popular subjects for monuments. Ernst Plassmann's 1869 bronze statue of Cornelius Vanderbilt occupies a prominent spot in front of Grand Central Terminal in New York City. Gutzon Borglum, who sculpted the presidential faces on Mount Rushmore, executed the bronze statue of Collis P. Huntington that stands before the Huntington, West Virginia, station. Huntington was one of the founders of the Central Pacific Railway and later became president of the Chesapeake and Ohio Railway (see chapter 12).

Itinerant might be used to describe the statue of Samuel Spencer. Daniel Chester French's 1912 bronze likeness shows the Southern Railway president seated in his office chair. Its first home, atop a stone pedestal, was in Atlanta's magnificent Terminal Station, which was demolished by the city in 1970. The statue was then banished to the suburbs and placed on a brick base. In 1996, in time for the Summer Olympics, it returned to a downtown park and was reunited with its original pedestal. The statue's current location is on the grounds of the Norfolk Southern Building in Atlanta.

Engineers, mechanics, and laborers were likewise honored with statues and monuments. Finally, monumental sculptures were created to memorialize the thousands of railroad employees who gave their lives for their countries in the two world wars.

AMES MONUMENT

Union Pacific Railroad

1882, Henry Hobson Richardson, architect;
    Augustus Saint-Gaudens, sculptor

I-80, exit 329, between Cheyenne and Laramie, WY

In 1875, two years after the death of Congressman Oakes Ames from a massive stroke in the wake of the Credit Mobilier scandal (Ames had been censured by Congress for his role in the notorious affair; see chapter 4) the Union Pacific Railroad directors ordered that a monument be erected to honor him and his brother, Oliver, a former president of the Union Pacific. The railroad officers and Ames family members selected a location at Sherman, Wyoming, that marked the highest point (elevation 8,247 feet) on the Union Pacific's original transcontinental line.

Henry Hobson Richardson was a natural choice to design it, since he was the architect of the station and several other buildings in North Easton, Massachusetts, hometown of the Ames Shovel company (see chapter 4). Augustus Saint-Gaudens, the leading portrait sculptor of the time, was then painting the murals for Richardson's famous Trinity Church in Boston. The contractors were the Norcross Brothers of Boston, Richardson's builders of choice. Richardson consulted with Frederick Law Olmsted on the concept for the monument.

Sixty feet high, the massive pyramid was built of local pink granite laid up in broken range masonry. Below the top, which tapers to a sharp point, are Saint-Gaudens's nine-foot-high bas-relief medallions of the brothers, Oakes facing East and Oliver, West. The inscription on the north face reads "In memory of Oakes Ames and Oliver Ames."

Shortly after the beginning of the twentieth century, the Union Pacific rerouted its main line three miles to the south to take advantage of an easier

Figure 14.1
Ames Monument, between Cheyenne and Laramie, Wyoming

Figure 14.2
Thomas Viaduct Monument, Relay, Maryland
(courtesy of James Thomas)

grade. The frontier town of Sherman that had grown up around the railroad gradually disappeared, and the primal monument was stranded on the high plains.

THOMAS VIADUCT MONUMENT
Baltimore and Ohio Railroad
1835, Benjamin H. Latrobe, Jr., engineer;
John McCartney, builder
Relay, MD

Benjamin Latrobe, who designed the Thomas Viaduct, also designed the monument (see chapter 12). The granite obelisk, which sits on a base of the same material, lists the dates of the bridge's construction (July 1833–July 1835) and the names of the railroad's directors and engineers. John McCartney, the hard-driving Irish contractor who built the Thomas Viaduct and paid for the monument, is the only person whose name is listed twice: once for the bridge and once for the obelisk. Located in a neglected area, the oldest railroad monument in the United States is often the target of vandals, whose labors are then effaced by a coat of whitewash. The engraved names are now all but illegible.

THEODORE JUDAH MONUMENT
1931, John A. MacQurrie, sculptor
L and 2nd Sts., Sacramento, CA

Set into a carved granite boulder depicting a railroad bridge in the High Sierra is John MacQuarrie's bronze head of Theodore Judah (1826–63). An energetic promoter of a transmontane railroad that would link the growing settlements of the West with the interior of the United States, Judah got financing from the Big Four of Sacramento (Leland Stanford, Collis P. Huntington, Mark Hopkins, and Charles Crocker; see chapter 11) to build the Central Pacific Railroad. He became its chief engineer and located the route over the mountains. Ground was broken for the railroad on January 8, 1863, at the foot of K Street near the monument; Judah died November 2, 1863. The railroad was built past the site of the monument,

Figure 14.3
Theodore Judah Monument, Sacramento, California

over the lofty Sierra Mountains—along the line of Judah's survey—to a junction with the Union Pacific at Promontory, Utah. There, on May 10, 1869, the last spike was driven. The monument was erected by the men and women of the Southern Pacific Company, who in 1930 were carrying on the work that Judah began in 1860.

MacQuarrie (1871–1944), a San Francisco artist, was a graduate of the Mark Hopkins Institute of Art (now the San Francisco Art Institute). He painted a number of train station murals in the West and Southwest. The Sacramento Amtrak (formerly the Southern Pacific Railroad) station contains his mural of the ground breaking for the Central Pacific Railroad. Leland Stanford and the evolution of transportation in California are the subjects of his mural for the Southern Pacific Railroad station in Palo Alto.

The inscription on the Judah monument reads:

That the West may remember
Theodore Dehone Judah,
Pioneer, civil engineer, and tireless advocate
Of a great transcontinental railroad
—America's first—

ANDREW JACKSON STEVENS MONUMENT
1889, Albert Weinert, sculptor
Cesar Chavez Plaza, Sacramento, CA

His fellow workmen thought highly enough of Andrew Jackson Stevens, master mechanic of the vast Southern Pacific Railroad shops at Sacramento, that they contributed $5,000 to erect a statue of him in the plaza opposite City Hall.

The nine-foot-tall bronze figure is elevated on a high granite pedestal, whose four sides carry the following inscriptions:

Erected to a friend of labor by his co-workers
Think, look up and lift up
Labor is entitled to a just reward
Well directed genius elevates the people

Originally from Vermont, Stevens (1833–88) began working for the railroads as a teenager and trained to be a machinist. In the mid-1850s, he was foreman of the repair shops of the Chicago, Burlington and Quincy Railroad at Aurora, Illinois (see chapter 9). Stevens came to California in 1861, just as the Central Pacific Railroad was getting started, and by the end of the decade, he was master mechanic of the shops. He was also an inventor, making improvements to the radial valve gear of locomotives. Two thousand laborers participated in the parade at his funeral, marching behind large floral arrangements representing a boiler, a steam engine, and a sleeping car.

Albert Wienert (1863–1947), the sculptor, was born in Leipzig, Germany, studied art at several European institutions, and emigrated to San Francisco in 1886. He worked with Karl Bitter, another sculptor, at the 1893 Chicago World's Fair and later in Bitter's New York studio. In 1894, Wienert modeled some of the figures for the sculptural frieze at the Library of Congress in Washington, D.C., along with Augustus Saint-Gaudens and other noted sculptors.

Figure 14.4

A. J. Stevens Monument, Sacramento, California

Figure 14.5
John Frank Stevens Monument, Summit, Montana

JOHN FRANK STEVENS MONUMENT
1925, Gaetano Cecere
Route 2, Summit, MT

John Stevens, one of the most outstanding American civil engineers, is portrayed in a natural pose, dressed for winter exploration in the Rockies and wearing a characteristic look of strong determination. In his right hand, he carries a measuring tape, a symbol of his profession.

Stevens did not discover Marias Pass (it was known to Native Americans and some whites in the region), but he was the first to conduct a railroad engineering reconnaissance of it and to make his findings public. The area had actually been explored thirty-five years earlier as part of the federal surveys for a transcontinental railroad, but other routes had taken precedence. Gradually the pass receded from memory—local members of the Blackfeet Nation regarded it as the haunt of evil spirits—until the 1880s, when James J. Hill decided to extend his Great Northern Railway across western Montana to the Pacific.

Hill, known as the empire builder (see chapters 2 and 8), was a driven individual, and the engineer the company chose to explore the route was from the same mold. The two men knew of each other from their earlier work on the Canadian Pacific Railway, Canada's first transcontinental line. Hill was part of the syndicate that built it, and Stevens was a member of the survey team that discovered the route through the Canadian Rockies.

Two engineers were actually dispatched to seek the best alignment for the Great Northern in Montana, one heading east from Flathead Lake and the other (Stevens) in the opposite direction from Fort Assiniboine, near present-day Havre, Montana. Stevens set out in December 1889. It was not the ideal season for a hike in the high mountains (today's average annual snowfall in the Marias Pass area is twenty-three feet), but Hill and Stevens were, as usual, in a hurry.

Traveling with a Flathead Indian guide and a wagonload of supplies, including self-made snowshoes, Stevens was searching for the legendary and elusive Marias Pass. When they reached False Summit, several miles east of the true pass, the guide—a reluctant participant from the start—refused to go any further. Stevens left him by a fire and went on alone. Proceeding on snowshoes atop several feet of snow, he reached the pass, which he verified by locating a stream on the other side (Bear Creek) that flowed westward. He had crossed the continental divide. By this time it was dark. Unwilling to lie down in the sub-zero temperature, Stevens tramped back and forth all night to keep warm amid the tall pines, cedars, and Douglas firs. At daybreak, he retraced his steps, found the guide half-frozen, revived him, and returned with him to the settlement. The 5,214-foot Marias Pass is the lowest mainline railroad crossing of the Rocky Mountains in the United States or Canada.

Stevens (1853–1943) was born in West Gardiner, Maine. He graduated from the Western State Normal School and tried teaching, but he soon left it to pursue a career in engineering. He found work on a Maine field crew that was conducting surveys for mills and canals. Moving to Minneapolis, Stevens continued his field survey work and became assistant city engineer. He later worked for a series of railroads—the Denver and Rio Grande, where he learned about bridge construction; the Canadian Pacific; and several others—before arriving at the Great Northern and Marias Pass.

He became Hill's first-call engineer. Stevens's next assignment for the Great Northern was in the rugged Cascade Mountains of western Washington State. He again discovered the route for the railroad, through what is now Stevens Pass, and he supervised construction of the first 2.6-mile Cascade Tunnel (1900). By that time he had been named the railroad's chief engineer.

Stevens more than made up for his lack of formal engineering training by teaching himself mathematics, physics, and chemistry and through his strenuous expeditions in the field. Years of traversing difficult terrain regardless of weather with a pack on his back (he had survived Native American attacks and was once treed by wolves) hardened him physically and mentally. He developed the capacity to assess a difficult engineering problem, determine the means necessary to overcome it, and drive the work to completion.

In 1905, Hill convinced President Theodore Roosevelt to hire Stevens as chief engineer of the Panama Canal. After the French had started but failed to complete the job—in part because they underestimated the resources and equipment necessary for such a massive undertaking—the Americans had taken over but were not faring much better. Stevens arrived to find the whole project in disarray. At the construction site in Panama, he rebuilt the rudimentary rail system to haul away the excavated earth and bring in food, water, medicine, and supplies. He recruited a workforce of thousands of men and established housing and health programs for them. Stevens was

also instrumental in the decision to abandon the favored sea-level canal and build one with locks. Having successfully reorganized the entire operation, the restless engineer moved on after two years. He never explained why; possibly the reason was exhaustion.

More railroad work followed in New England, the Pacific Northwest, Spain, and Russia. Stevens was a consultant on the new eight-mile Cascade Tunnel, the longest in the United States, which opened in 1929 at the pass named for him in Washington State. He received numerous honors and medals in his lifetime. Railroad statuary was customarily devoted to company officials or laborers, and Stevens is one of the very few engineers accorded such an honor. The commemoration took place during his lifetime, and he was invited to participate in it.

The Great Northern Railway commissioned the sculpture, one of several to honor the great explorers of the West (including Meriwether Lewis), and organized the week-long Upper Missouri Historical Expedition to celebrate their achievements. In July 1925, a special train carrying a hundred passengers—state governors, historians, engineers, and other dignitaries—left St. Paul, Minnesota, and headed west. Marias Pass was the last stop. After the speeches, Stevens, hatless and wearing a suit for the occasion, told the crowd that Hill was one of the greatest men he had ever known and that his years with the Great Northern Railway were the best part of his active life.

The New York sculptor Gaetano Cecere (1894–1985) was under thirty when he was selected to produce the Stevens monument; it was his first commission and his first statue. His later works included statues of Lincoln for the City of Milwaukee and of a mail carrier for the US Postal Service headquarters in Washington, D.C. Cecere also taught sculpture for many years at Cooper Union, the National Academy in New York, and several other institutions.

The Stevens statue was subsequently moved from its original trackside location, where it stood on a tiered pedestal, to its present ground-level site near Route 2, next to a 1930 obelisk honoring Theodore Roosevelt. The highway, dating from the same year, traces the route of the railroad through the pass. The tracks on the opposite side of the road, which pass through several snow sheds to the west, are used by the many freight trains of the Burlington Northern Santa Fe Railroad and Amtrak's Empire Builder.

ANGEL OF RESURRECTION AND SPIRIT OF TRANSPORTATION
1952, Walker Hancock; 1895, Karl Bitter
30th Street Station, Market and 30th Sts., Philadelphia, PA

Philadelphia's vast 30th Street Station houses two monumental sculptures commissioned by the Pennsylvania Railroad. Walker Hancock's thirty-foot *Angel of Resurrection*, which dominates the waiting room,

Figure 14.6
Angel of Resurrection, Philadelphia, Pennsylvania

is a memorial to the 1,307 Pennsylvania Railroad employees who lost their lives in World War II; 150,000 of the railroad's workers served in the armed forces during the war. The bronze statue depicts the archangel Michael raising the body of a fallen soldier from the flames of war. The names of the employees who died in the conflict are inscribed on the black granite base. A similar monument to the 1,100 Canadian Pacific Railway employees who died in World War I stands in Montreal's Windsor Station (see chapter 2).

Walker Hancock (1901–98) was himself a World War II Army veteran and a member of the Monuments, Fine Arts, and Archives group (called the monuments men) established by President Franklin D. Roosevelt in 1943 to track down and recover artworks stolen by Adolf Hitler and the Nazis and hidden in mines and other places. Except for his time in the military, Hancock was the sculpture instructor at the Pennsylvania Academy of Fine Arts in Philadelphia from 1929 to 1967. His many sculptures include an altarpiece and a life-size statue of Abraham Lincoln for the National Cathedral in Washington, D.C., but *Angel of Resurrection* was his favorite.

Karl Bitter's *Spirit of Transportation*, a huge, panoramic wall sculpture situated in an anteroom of the station, is less conspicuous but equally impressive. The architectural sculptor created the piece for the waiting room of the railroad's Broad Street Station expansion in the 1890s. The plaster sculpture was removed and reinstalled in the new 30th Street Station when it opened in 1933. It shows the progress of American transportation, from the covered wagon to air travel.

Bitter (1867–1915) graduated from art school and was apprenticed to an architectural sculptor in his native Vienna. But he deserted from the Austrian Army because he objected to compulsory military service in peacetime, and he emigrated to New York in 1889. Bitter soon found work with an architectural decorating firm, where he came to the notice of architect Richard Morris Hunt. In the early 1890s, Bitter executed the bronze doors that Hunt had designed for New York's Trinity Church and did the sculptural decoration for Hunt's Administration Building at the

Figure 14.7
Spirit of Transportation, Philadelphia, Pennsylvania

Figure 14.8
Chinese Railroad Workers
Memorial, Toronto, Ontario

Chicago World's Fair. Bitter directed the sculpture programs for the Pan-American Exposition in Buffalo in 1901, the 1904 St. Louis World's Fair, and the Pan-Pacific Exposition in San Francisco in 1915. Bitter also created artworks for Biltmore, Hunt's mansion in Asheville, North Carolina, for George W. Vanderbilt. Bitter was struck by an automobile that jumped the curb as he and his wife were leaving New York's Metropolitan Opera House, at Broadway and 40th Street. The sculptor died as a result of the accident, at the age of forty-eight.

CHINESE RAILROAD WORKERS MEMORIAL
1989, Eldon Garnet and Francis LeBouthillier
Blue Jay Way and Navy Wharf Court, Toronto, ON

The Foundation to Commemorate the Chinese Railroad Workers of Canada commissioned one of the few monuments honoring the laborers who actually built the railroads. The large, realistic timber sculpture with bronze figures shows workmen using shears to hoist ties to the top of a timber trestle.

The plaque reads:

Dedicated to the Chinese railroad workers who helped construct the Canadian Pacific Railway through the Rocky Mountains of Alberta and British Columbia, thus uniting Canada geographically and politically.

From 1880 to 1885, seventeen thousand men from the province of Kwangtung [Guangdong], China, came to work on the western section of the railway through the treacherous terrain of the Canadian Rockies. Far from their families, amid hostile sentiments, these men labored long hours and made the completion of the railway physically and economically possible.

More than four thousand Chinese workers lost their lives during construction. With no means of going back to China when their labour was no longer needed, thousands drifted in near destitution along the completed track. All of them remained nameless in the history of Canada.

We erect this monument to remember them.

The monument was designed by Eldon Garnet, an artist and novelist who teaches at the Ontario College of Art and Design. The figures were executed by Francis LeBouthillier, head of the sculpture program at the same institution.

NOTES

1. Quoted in Calvin Tomkins, "The Piano Principle," *New Yorker*, August 22, 1994, 64.

2. John A. Droege, *Passenger Terminals and Trains* (New York: McGraw-Hill, 1916), 159.

3. Quoted in William D. Middleton, *Grand Central . . . the World's Greatest Railway Terminal* (San Marino, CA: Golden West Books, 1977), 58.

4. Rafael Guastavino—an architect and builder from Barcelona, Spain, who emigrated to New York City in 1881—patented a system of structural and decorative vault construction that used thin terra-cotta tiles built up in layers. Over a thousand buildings in North America made use of his system—immediately recognizable by its distinctive herringbone tile pattern—including the Boston Public Library and the Biltmore estate in Asheville, North Carolina.

5. Ada Louise Huxtable, "Grand Central at a Crossroads," *New York Times*, January 29, 1978.

6. Quoted in John Belle and Maxinne R. Leighton, *Grand Central: Gateway to a Million Lives* (New York: Norton, 2000), 95.

7. Quoted in "Bruce Price, 1845–1903," *Keystone*, summer 1998, 5.

8. Quoted in Harold D. Kalman, *The Railway Hotels and the Development of the Château Style in Canada* (Victoria, BC: University of Victoria, 1968), 14.

9. Pierre Berton, "'A Feeling, An Echo . . .' The Life of Union Station," in *The Open Gate: Toronto Union Station* (Toronto: Peter Martin, 1972), ed. Richard Bébout, 1.

10. Herbert H. Harwood Jr., *Invisible Giants: The Empire of Cleveland's Van Sweringen Brothers* (Bloomington: Indiana University Press, 2013), 239.

11. *The Cleveland Union Station: A Description of the New Passenger Facilities and Surrounding Improvements* (Cleveland, OH: Cleveland Union and Union Terminals Co., 1930), 5.

12. James D. Van Trump, *Pittsburgh's Neglected Gateway: The Rotunda of the Pennsylvania Railroad Station* (Pittsburgh, PA: Pittsburgh History and Landmarks Foundation, 1968), 8.

13. Michael J. Lewis, e-mail message to author, January 21, 2010.

14. Michael J. Lewis, *Frank Furness: Architecture and the Violent Mind* (New York: Norton, 2001), 146.

15. Carroll L. V. Meeks, *The Railroad Station: An Architectural History* (Mineola, NY: Dover, 1995), 62.

16. Quoted in Harold D. Kalman, *The Railway Hotels and the Development of the Château Style in Canada* (Victoria, BC: University of Victoria, 1968), 13.

17. Michael Billington, "Cause Celebre," *Guardian*, March 29, 2011.

18. For the role of the Northern Pacific Railway and other railroads in the creation of America's national parks, see Alfred Runte, *Trains of Discovery: Western Railroads and the National Parks* (Boulder, CO: Roberts, Rinehart, 1998).

19. Arnold Berke, *Mary Colter: Architect of the Southwest* (New York: Princeton Architectural Press, 2002), 13.

20. Allan Affeldt, "La Posada" (undated brochure), 2.

21. Bassett made this comment on a bus tour I took on June 6, 2014, with the Railroad and Locomotive Historical Society.

22. Nevada Northern Railway, "Nevada Northern Railway East Ely Complex, Locomotives, and Rolling Stock Recognized as National Historic Landmark," news release, September 28, 2006, accessed September 27, 2017, http://nnry.com/documents/pressroom /NationalHistoricLandmark.pdf.

23. Robert M. Vogel, ed., *Some Industrial Archeology of the*

Monumental City and Environs: The Physical Presence of Baltimore's Engineering and Industrial History (Washington: Society for Industrial Archeology, 1975), 8.

24. Quoted in Carl Abbott, "The Railroad Suburbs of Chicago, 1854–1875," *Journal of the Illinois State Historical Society* 73, no. 2 (1980): 121.

25. Quoted in Vonn Marie May, *Rancho Santa Fe* (Mount Pleasant, SC: Arcadia Publishing, 2010), 9.

26. One outcome of the Clark affair and the rampant bribery practices of the Anaconda Copper Company and other mining firms was the 1912 Montana Corrupt Practices Act that banned corporate contributions to political campaigns. It was struck down a century later by the US Supreme Court as a result of its 2010 ruling in *Citizens United v. Federal Election Commission*.

27. Mark Twain, *Mark Twain in Eruption: Hitherto Unpublished Pages about Men and Events*, edited and with an introduction by Bernard DeVoto. New York: Harper and Row, 1940.

28. Bill Dedman and Paul Clark Newell Jr., *Empty Mansions: The Mysterious Life of Huguette Clark and the Spending of a Great American Fortune*, trade paperback ed. (New York: Ballantine, 2014), 85–86.

29. John Summerson, *The Unromantic Castle and Other Essays* (London: Thames and Hudson, 1990), 14.

30. Montgomery Schuyler, "The House of Senator Clark," *Architectural Record*, January 1906, 29–30.

31. Franklin B. Gowen, president of the Philadelphia and Reading Railroad, hired the Pinkertons and McParlan. The railroad had a substantial investment in the Pennsylvania anthracite fields, and Gowen was determined to break the growing power of the miners' unions, which struck often and sometimes violently. A lawyer, he had been appointed special prosecutor for the Molly Maguire trials. A month after the hangings in Mauch Chunk, the Great Railroad Strike of 1877 began—the closest thing to a general strike in US history. The violence, which was precipitated by a wage cut on the Baltimore and Ohio Railroad, spread to several other lines, including the Philadelphia and Reading. There is no question that many murders, usually of mine foremen or other company officials, were committed in the coalfields; the Irish in America particularly have a long history of labor violence. But were the Molly Maguires (if they ever really existed as such) labor terrorists or long-suffering mineworkers striking for decent wages? Probably both. And was the carefully planned retaliation against them designed to rid the coalfields of violence, or to crush the growing power of the miners' unions? Probably both.

32. "Artists of the World Hardworked to Furnish Whitehall," *New York Herald*, March 30, 1902.

33. Quoted in Channing Blake, "The Early Interiors of Carrere and Hastings," *Antiques*, August 1976, 348.

34. Vladimir Mayakovsky, "Brooklyn Bridge," in *Vladimir Mayakovsky, Selected Poetry* (Moscow: Foreign Languages Publishing House, n.d.), 91.

35. William D. Middleton, "Hoosac Tunnel," *Trains*, November 2008, 67.

36. Carl W. Condit, *American Building: Materials and Techniques from the First Colonial Settlements to the Present* (Chicago: University of Chicago Press, 1968), 73.

37. Carl W. Condit, *American Building Art: The Nineteenth Century* (New York: Oxford University Press, 1960), 120–21.

38. Ben Keene, "Walkway Over the Hudson & Hudson Valley Rail Trail," *Rails to Trails*, fall 2011, 28.

39. Quoted in William D. Middleton, *The Bridge at Quebec* (Bloomington: Indiana University Press, 2001), 181.

40. Quoted in Ibid., 182.

41. Robert Fletcher and J. P. Snow, "A History of the Development of Wooden Bridges," ASCE *Transactions* 99 (1934): 332.

42. Quoted in Lawrence Wechsler, "In a Desert of Pure Feeling," *New Yorker*, June 7, 1993, 83.

43. Quoted in Kevin P. Keefe, "David and Lucius," *Trains*, February 2011, 55.

44. Clay Lancaster, "Transportation Design Elements in American Architecture," *American Quarterly*, fall 1956, 211.

45. Sigfried Giedion, *Space, Time and Architecture: The Growth of a New Tradition* (Cambridge, MA: Harvard University Press, 1956), 365.

46. Mark Reutter, "The Lost Promise of the American Railroad," *Wilson Quarterly* 18 (winter 1994): 20.

47. Quoted in John Gruber, "An Exciting Year for Railroad History," *Railway & Locomotive Historical Society Newsletter*, winter 2014, 8.

BIBLIOGRAPHY

Abbott, Carl. "The Railroad Suburbs of Chicago, 1854–1875." *Journal of the Illinois State Historical Society* 73, no. 2 (1980): 117–31.

"Artists of the World Hardworked to Furnish Whitehall." *New York Herald*, March 30, 1902.

Belle, John, and Maxinne R. Leighton. *Grand Central: Gateway to a Million Lives*. New York: Norton, 2000.

Berke, Arnold. *Mary Colter: Architect of the Southwest*. New York: Princeton Architectural Press, 2002.

Berton, Pierre. "'A Feeling, An Echo . . .' The Life of Union Station." In *The Open Gate: Toronto Union Station*, edited by Richard Bébout, 1–4. Toronto: Peter Martin, 1972.

Billington, Michael. "Cause Celebre." *Guardian*, March 29, 2011.

Blake, Channing. "The Early Interiors of Carrere and Hastings." *Antiques*, August 1976, 344–51.

"Bruce Price, 1845–1903." *Keystone*, summer 1998, 3–5.

The Cleveland Union Station: A Description of the New Passenger Facilities and Surrounding Improvements. Cleveland, OH: Cleveland Union and Union Terminals Co., 1930.

Condit, Carl W. *American Building: Materials and Techniques from the First Colonial Settlements to the Present*. Chicago: University of Chicago Press, 1968.

———. *American Building Art: The Nineteenth Century*. New York: Oxford University Press, 1960.

Dedman, Bill, and Paul Clark Newell Jr. *Empty Mansions: The Mysterious Life of Huguette Clark and the Spending of a Great American Fortune*. Trade paperback ed. New York: Ballantine, 2014.

Droege, John A. *Passenger Terminals and Trains*. New York: McGraw-Hill, 1916.

Fletcher, Robert, and J. P. Snow. "A History of the Development of Wooden Bridges." *ASCE Transactions* 99 (1934): 314–408.

Giedion, Sigfried. *Space, Time and Architecture: The Growth of a New Tradition*. Cambridge, MA; Harvard University Press, 1956.

Gruber, John. "An Exciting Year for Railroad History." *Railway & Locomotive Historical Society Newsletter*, winter 2014, 8–9.

Harwood, Herbert H., Jr. *Invisible Giants: The Empire of Cleveland's Van Sweringen Brothers*. Bloomington: Indiana University Press, 2013.

Huxtable, Ada Louise. "Grand Central at a Crossroads," *New York Times*, January 29, 1978.

Judt, Tony. "Bring Back the Rails!" *New York Review of Books*, January 13, 2011.

Kalman, Harold D. *The Railway Hotels and the Development of the Château Style in Canada*. Victoria, BC: University of Victoria, 1968.

Keefe, Kevin P. "David and Lucius." *Trains*, February 2011, 54–55.

Keene, Ben. "Walkway Over the Hudson & Hudson Valley Rail Trail." *Rails to Trails*, fall 2011, 27–29.

Lancaster, Clay. "Transportation Design Elements in American Architecture." *American Quarterly*, fall 1956, 199–215.

Lewis, Michael J. *Frank Furness: Architecture and the Violent Mind* (New York: Norton, 2001.

Little Richard. "When John Waters Met Little Richard." By John Waters, *Guardian*, November 27, 2010.

Loewy, Raymond. *The Locomotive: The New Vision*. 1937. Reprint, New York: Universe Books, 1987.

May, Vonn Marie. *Rancho Santa Fe*. Mount Pleasant, SC: Arcadia Publishing, 2010.

Mayakovsky, Vladimir. *Vladimir Mayakovsky, Selected Poetry*. Moscow: Foreign Languages Publishing House, n.d.

Meeks, Carroll L. V. *The Railroad Station: An Architectural History*. Mineola, NY: Dover, 1995.

Middleton, William D. *The Bridge at Quebec*. Bloomington: Indiana University Press, 2001.

————. *Grand Central . . . the World's Greatest Railway Terminal*. San Martino, CA: Golden West Books, 1977.

————. "Hoosac Tunnel." *Trains*, November 2008, 59–67.

Nevada Northern Railway. "Nevada Northern Railway East Ely Complex, Locomotives, and Rolling Stock Recognized as National Historic Landmark." News release, September 28, 2006. Accessed September 27, 2017. http://nnry.com/documents/pressroom /NationalHistoricLandmark.pdf.

Orrock, John W. *Railroad Structures and Estimates*. New York: Wiley, 1909.

Reutter, Mark. "The Lost Promise of the American Railroad." *Wilson Quarterly* 18 (winter 1994): 11–37.

Runte, Alfred. *Trains of Discovery: Western Railroads and the National Parks*. Boulder, CO: Roberts, Rinehart, 1998.

Schuyler, Montgomery. "The House of Senator Clark." *Architectural Record*, January 1906, 27–30.

Summerson, John. *The Unromantic Castle and Other Essays*. London: Thames and Hudson, 1990.

Tomkins, Calvin. "The Piano Principle." *New Yorker*, August 22, 1994, 52–65.

Twain, Mark. *Mark Twain in Eruption: Hitherto Unpublished Pages about Men and Events*. Edited and with an introduction by Bernard DeVoto. New York: Harper and Row, 1940.

Van Trump, James D. *Pittsburgh's Neglected Gateway: The Rotunda of the Pennsylvania Railroad Station*. Pittsburgh, PA: Pittsburgh History and Landmarks Foundation, 1968.

Vogel, Robert M., ed. *Some Industrial Archeology of the Monumental City and Environs: The Physical Presence of Baltimore's Engineering and Industrial History*. Washington: Society for Industrial Archeology, 1975.

Wechsler, Lawrence. "In a Desert of Pure Feeling." *New Yorker*, June 7, 1993, 81–90.

INDEX